MUFFLED DRUMS

THE NEWS MEDIA IN AFRICA

D1541566

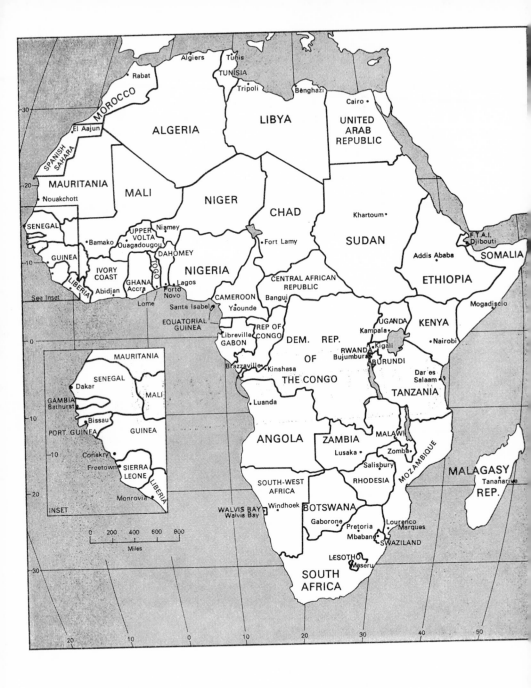

MUFFLED DRUMS
THE NEWS MEDIA IN AFRICA

WILLIAM A. HACHTEN
WITH THE EDITORIAL COLLABORATION OF **HARVA S. HACHTEN**

THE IOWA STATE UNIVERSITY PRESS

WILLIAM A. HACHTEN is Professor of Journalism, University of Wisconsin, where he has taught since 1959. He holds the B.A. degree from Stanford University, the M.S. degree from the University of California at Los Angeles, and the Ph.D. degree from the University of Minnesota. He has been a guest professor at the Berlin Institute for Mass Communication in Developing Nations (1964) and has done field research on mass media in tropical Africa (1965). In 1968 he was awarded a Fulbright-Hays fellowship for research on mass communication in Africa. His professional experience has included reporting and copy editing for California and Minnesota newspapers. Besides this book, he is author of *The Supreme Court on Freedom of the Press* and several journal articles allying the fields of journalism and political science.

© 1971 The Iowa State University Press
Ames, Iowa 50010. All rights reserved
Composed and printed by The Iowa State University Press
First edition, 1971
International Standard Book Number: 0-8138-1195-3
Library of Congress Catalog Card Number: 72-126165

TO AFRICA'S NEWSMEN

A SMALL, HARRIED, YET ADMIRABLE GROUP

CONTENTS

PREFACE

THIS BOOK both surveys generally and examines minutely the news media in contemporary Africa.

It is primarily focused on the news media as *institutions*. How were they established? How are they functioning in the contemporary African environment? And more especially, how do they interact with that age-old nemesis of the press, government? The emphasis is on news and public information rather than the cultural, educational, and social roles of mass communications.

Africa is an exceedingly complex continent, and the news media reflect much of what has been happening there. I have directed my attention to the journalistic aspects of the mass media as social and political institutions. The content of mass communications and their effects on audiences necessarily receive secondary consideration and could properly be the concern of another study.

It was impossible for me to observe the news media in every one of Africa's 43 nations. However, I visited most of the major regions: North Africa, anglophonic West Africa, francophonic West Africa, East Africa, and southern Africa. There cannot but be significant omissions; I did not go to Congo (Kinshasa), nor did I visit Liberia and Ethiopia, two important countries without colonial legacies. However, most new nations of Africa seem to share the mass communication characteristics of the nations I have studied closely.

The countries I visited were Kenya, Uganda, Tanzania, Zambia, South Africa, Nigeria, Ghana, Ivory Coast, Sierra Leone, Senegal, Morocco, and the United Arab Republic. Much of this book, especially the case studies, is based on data gathered in these countries.

My firsthand knowledge of these countries was acquired during two field trips. In the spring of 1965, with generous support from the University of Wisconsin, my wife and I visited Cairo, Nairobi, Dar es Salaam, Johannesburg, Lagos, Ibadan, Kaduna, Abidjan, Freetown, and Dakar.

To update the earlier material and gather new information,

we returned in 1968 on a Fulbright-Hays grant to interview journalists, broadcasters, and government information officials in Rabat, Accra, Lagos, Johannesburg, Cape Town, Lusaka, Nairobi, and Kampala.

Admittedly, the two itineraries were just a sampling of African nations. But they did include the major news communication centers for several regions: Nairobi for East Africa, Lagos and Accra for anglophonic West Africa, Abidjan and Dakar for *Afrique Noire* (the former French territories), Johannesburg for southern Africa, and Rabat for the Maghreb.

The collection of data would not have been possible without the help and cooperation of numerous persons we met on our travels. Almost without exception, we were received with the friendliness and hospitality common throughout Africa. It is impossible to list all who assisted us on both journeys but I would like to thank some individually.

Most of those listed are African journalists, a few are Americans, some are Britons or other Europeans; all are knowledgeable about mass communications in Africa and concerned about their problems. In random order they are John Dumoga, Adolphus Paterson, Irwin Teven, Tom Hopkinson, Kenneth Whiting, Lloyd Garrison, Angus McDermid, Peter Webb, Henry Reuter, Joel Mervis, Raymond Louw, Increase Coker, Kwame Kesse Adu, J. G. Amamoo, Henry Ofori, Laurent Dona-Fologa, Nerissa Williams, Kelvin Mlenga, Clyde Sanger, Frank Barton, William Dullforce, Derek Taylor, Daniel Nelson, Robert Hartland, Charles Harrison, Peter Gachathi, Dunston Kamana, Timothy Odubanjo, Herbert Unegbu, Alade Odunewu, Isaac Thomas, A. K. Disu, Roger Ross, John Hogan, John Twitty, Rajat Neogy, Hilary Ng'weno, Michael Curtis, Kenneth Bolton, Lee Fairley, Kenneth Snyder, Royal Bisbee, Gene Walton, Jerry Kallas, Jack Juergens, Will Petty, Francis Khamisi, Boaz Omori, George Githii, Laurence Dodge, John Adotevi, Georges Galipeau, Harry Land, David John, Bankole Timothy, John Akar, Kenneth Ridley, Paul Meredith, Alan Grossman, Ian Laval, Norman Hartley, Peter Gaskell, Stephen O. Hughes, Russell Warren Howe, Robert Conley, Hennie Kotze, Charles Still, P. Selwyn-Smith, S. Brooke-Norris, Nicholas Naudi, Eldred Green, John Stephens, Penuel Malafa, Cyprion Ekuenzi, Horatio Agedah, Alhagi Dodo Mustapha, A. Ojewumi, Peter Enahoro, Aissa Benchakroun, Sam Arthur, and Howard Lawrence.

In addition, I would like to acknowledge the research assistance provided by several former students, E. Lloyd Murphy, Mary Ellen Hughes, Daniel Ruskin, Lonnie Huff, and Posie Starkey.

I am especially indebted to Professors Ralph O. Nafziger and John T. McNelly for their comments on the manuscript.

The shortcomings of this book are, of course, the responsibility of the author.

The research for this work was supported in part by the Research Committee of the Graduate School of the University of Wisconsin from special funds voted by the Wisconsin State Legislature. Other major support came from the Department of Health, Education and Welfare which awarded me a Fulbright-Hays Center Faculty Fellowship for seven months field research in Africa in 1968. Additional financial help came from the Center for International Communications Studies at the University of Wisconsin.

However, the most important assistance came from my wife, Harva Sprager Hachten, who traveled with me the entire distance. She fully participated in the field work in Africa and was of special help with French-speaking informants. She helped revise and edit the manuscript and her insights are found on almost every page.

INTRODUCTION

MASS COMMUNICATION in Africa is so diverse as to be astonishing. It is a Sudanese camel driver jogging along listening to Radio Cairo on a small transistor radio; a Ghanaian civil servant reading the *Daily Graphic* while drinking a shandy at Accra's Ambassador Hotel; a Wolof man sitting with a group of his fellow Senegalese watching an experimental television program in Dakar.

Or it is a white South African reading the *Rand Daily Mail* on a bus carrying him to his office in bustling Johannesburg; a radio blaring out to the teeming Moroccan crowds in the labyrinth of the Fez medina; a band of tribal Africans intently watching a flickering motion picture projected from a mobile cinema van in a remote corner of Zambia.

It may be also a correspondent for *Time* magazine catching a jet plane at Nairobi airport to cover a reported coup in a minor central African nation, or a Hausa man in his mud hut in the feudal north of Nigeria listening to the news from Radio Nigeria in far-off Lagos.

The news in Hausa on Radio Nigeria is always preceded by a brief recording of a Hausa drummer. This is appropriate, for over much of Africa the drum has long been an important traditional means of communication and is still widely used today. In Africa's expanding modern sector, the news media— newspapers, radio, television, magazines—may be regarded as the new drums of Africa. But the news media are as yet "muffled drums"—they are too few and inadequate for the great tasks expected of them and they are often harassed and controlled by self-serving interests. The new drums reverberating printed and electronic messages are still too weak technologically, economically, or politically to carry very far. Their messages often are distorted, garbled, and muted. The new "talking drums" do not speak clearly and effectively to the millions of new Africans. Yet in both the colonial period and the years since independence, the press and broadcasting have played an increasingly significant role in the dissemination of news and public information.

If a particular culture can be viewed as a system of communication, as Edward T. Hall has suggested in *The Silent Language,* then Africa as one of the most culturally diverse regions of the world has such problems of cross-cultural communication as will challenge the new talking drums for many years to come.

Leaders of the more than forty, mostly fragile national structures of that vast continent have been struggling against painful odds during the 1960s to establish politically stable societies while dealing with the age-old problems of poverty, disease, ignorance, and ethnic rivalries. In the tortuous drama that President Julius Nyerere of Tanzania has called the "terrible ascent to modernization," the news media of communication have a part to play. As yet, however, this role is neither clearly defined nor adequately performed. The news media as social institutions have had a brief and tenuous existence and they are still very much at the mercy of harsh economic and political restrictions.

"Mass media of communication" is a somewhat misleading term when applied to the news media in Africa. In any country the pervasiveness of mass media is directly related to economic and educational levels and most African nations are, by Western standards, still poor and illiterate. The mass media as we know them in America and Europe are all present there in uneven patterns, but they (except for radio) do not reach any large numbers of people, much less the "masses." At best, they mostly reach the educated minorities in the cities.

Newspapers are read by those few interested and literate Africans who are able to buy or borrow a copy and who are fortunate enough to live in a place, usually the capital, where newspapers are available.

Broadcasting reaches more people, usually those in urban areas who own or have access to radio or television sets and are interested enough to use them. Radio has much the largest audience since it does extend into the hinterlands.

Clearly, in this least developed of all continents (Africa has been called "the continent that God kept in reserve") the mass media are the least developed of any comparable area of the world. This does not mean they are unimportant; while only a small fraction of today's Africans are consumers of mass communications, this is the fraction that is shaping Africa's destiny. Many of Africa's vexing problems are related to breakdowns in communication and tied to the fact that so many Africans are not in touch with their leaders nor with the cities whence come new ideas and the concepts of the modern world.

But though audiences are small, mass communications are important to Africans because they can help speed the processes of development and national integration and bring the continent into a fuller participation in the modern world.

A mass media system is also a kind of mirror image of a nation's political and economic structure. Each is sensitive to the other. Newspapers, radio, television, and other media do not operate in a vacuum; their content, their reach, their freedom, and their audiences are determined by the context of the nation in which they operate. For this reason I have devoted several chapters in Part 2 to case studies of news media in specific areas and these same chapters reflect the persistent groundswells evident beneath the stormy surface of African politics.

African peoples, in spite of their great linguistic and ethnic diversity, have been communicating among and between themselves in a wide variety of ways for a long time. In fact, the sheer range and variety of human or interpersonal communication on that immense continent offer a challenge to contemporary communications scholars.[1]

Mass communications, however, are not indigenous to Africa. A crucial element in the development of mass communications in Africa—both past and present—is the nature and extent of European influences. Differences in colonial experiences help explain differences in media systems.

The important component of any definition of mass communications is modern technology. To have *mass* communication, a message must be amplified or reproduced many thousands of times. This requires printing presses, newsprint, radio and television transmitters and receivers, and cinema projectors and theaters. These came from Europe with the Europeans. Initially, press and broadcasting facilities were largely established for the convenience and use of the colonizers and the few European settlers who followed. In most places Africans were excluded or were at best an eavesdropping audience. Only in a few areas have Africans historically produced their own newspapers and these were based on European models.

Colonial rule was, by and large, the source of each country's modern political institutions and the peculiar economic conditions still markedly inhibiting local media growth. What happened before independence profoundly affects the news media today even though new African governments have tried to shuck off all vestiges of colonialism. Since independence, the Africans have been converting these "foreign" communication instruments to their own uses and purposes.

Professional journalism—that is, a continuing and periodic effort to reach a public audience with news—was also a European importation. Apparently no precedents for it existed in the traditional societies of Africa or even in the Islamic civilization.

Part of today's communications crisis arises from attempts to expand and readapt the news media to the needs and purposes of independent Africa. Africans ask, should Europeans still own newspapers? Should most of the movies and television programs still come from Britain, France, and the United States? Should the world news agencies, headquartered in America and Europe, still dominate the flow of news in and out of Africa? Should not an African government control not only broadcasting but newspapers and news services as well?

In spite of the important outward trappings of self-rule—government by Africans, political parties, UN and OAU memberships, and even the nationalization of some foreign-controlled media—the basic mass communications situation has not significantly changed since independence. In the postindependence years, media institutions and practices, whether British, French, or Belgian, have had strong continuity. Apparently the new nations must go through a period of transition before indigenous thought, practice, and integrating influences produce news media content better adapted to the African milieu. (Historically, the United States, and more recently, India passed through such a period.)

However, the mass media in most of Africa cannot continue to expand or even hold their own today without continued financial and technical assistance from outside the continent, be it from the United States, Western Europe, or the Communist nations. Sensitive Africans call this assistance "neo-colonialism" and in a way they are right.

By entering onto the stage of modern world history, the African nations are increasingly involved in the worldwide system of international communications with all that it implies for the world flow of news, mass culture, exchange of technical information, and not least, political communication or propaganda.

As elsewhere, communications media in Africa are widely used for educational, cultural, and entertainment purposes. But in this study, as the title suggests, the main emphasis is on their role in the dissemination of news and public information. Hence, the main focus is on journalism and its implications for political communication and press-government relationships.

Primarily, this study is concerned with the news media—newspapers, news services, and the news-disseminating aspects of radio and television—as fragile but important institutions in Africa today. The case studies show the similarities of problems and demonstrate how the local political, social, and economic factors do shape the media system of an individual country.

In considering the problems of the mass communications in Africa, I have tried to be sympathetic to the views of Africans and to be aware of the enormous difficulties they face. In Africa as elsewhere, journalism and mass communication are highly subjective pursuits, relative to the place and circumstances of their production. The practices and techniques of Fleet Street or New York City should not and cannot be used as standards of performance in Lagos or Lusaka. It is not possible always to agree with African approaches to journalism and the handling of public information, but it is important that criticisms of these matters be presented with some understanding of the situations. Journalists—and students of journalism—should disagree at times with government officials and with other journalists. After all, the essence of journalism, whether in Nairobi or Washington, D.C., is diversity of ideas and the freedom to express them. The ultimate goal is always more freedom, but freedom is predicated on political order and economic opportunity.

PART ONE

OVERVIEW OF NEWS COMMUNICATION IN AFRICA

1

||||||||||||||||||||||||||||||||||||||||||||||||||||||||||||||||||||||||||

AFRICAN SETTING

ALMOST EXACTLY 100 YEARS AGO, James Gordon Bennett, editor of the New York *Herald,* instructed one of his reporters, Henry Morton Stanley: "I want you to attend the opening of the Suez Canal and then proceed up the Nile. Send us detailed descriptions of everything likely to interest the American tourists. Then go to Jerusalem, Constantinople, the Crimea, the Caspian Sea, through Persia as far as India. After that you can start looking around for Livingstone. If he is dead, bring back every possible proof of his death."[1]

Fourteen months later, on October 28, 1871, Stanley found the long-missing missionary at Ujiji on Lake Tanganyika, in what is now Tanzania. The meeting produced not only a famous greeting ("Dr. Livingstone, I presume") but the journalistic scoop of the century.

It may be that Stanley ignored the really important African story of the time—the news that Arab slavers had decimated the people of East and Central Africa.[2] But in any case, Americans and Europeans learned something about Africa from Stanley's reports, and they and the rest of the world have been finding out about the area from the press in rather a haphazard fashion ever since.

In the century since Stanley's journalistic feat, Africa has made news at an increasing rate. As nineteenth-century explorers who helped open up the "Dark Continent," Livingstone and Stanley were both participants and symbols of the tumultuous social and political events resulting from their meeting. The press's dramatization of Livingstone's work stirred the world's conscience, and finally the slave trade was ended. Stanley gave up journalism, explored much of Central Africa, and became personally involved with the Congo Free State and the colonial "scramble for Africa." The arbitrary and capricious borders drawn by the great powers at the Berlin Conference in 1885, which divided numerous ethnic groups, even now confound African political life.

The New York *Herald* itself is no more; it went under finally in 1966 with the demise of the New York *Herald-Tribune*. But its surviving European offspring, the *International Herald-Tribune*, published in Paris, can be purchased today on news-stands in Nairobi, Tunis, Dakar, or Lagos.

In Stanley's day the press was unknown in the great heartland of that enormous land mass. There were a few small papers on the continent's fringes—in Egypt, South Africa, and West Africa. But the colonizers—the British, the French, the Belgians, and the Portuguese—soon introduced newspapers into their colonies and protectorates just as they did railroads, telephones, mining techniques, cash crop agriculture, and other aspects of modern technology, and the "press"—newspapers, newssheets, government gazettes, and missionary publications—dates back to the early nineteenth century.

Egyptian historians date their earliest newspapers at the end of the eighteenth century. These were publications in French, appearing during the Napoleonic occupation of 1797, and by the middle of the nineteenth century, several regular newspapers circulated, most of them creatures of the Turkish regency.[3]

An alien institution, the newspaper grew slowly and haphazardly. More recent electronic media—radio, cinema, and news services—have been primarily phenomena of post-World War I. (Television took hold in the 1960s.)

At the other end of the continent, the *Cape Town Gazette* was published for the first time in 1800. This was just a year before the *Royal Gazette* in Sierra Leone became the first newspaper in tropical Africa. The latter paper was perhaps more significant because it was in British West Africa (Nigeria, Gold Coast [Ghana], Sierra Leone, and Gambia) that black Africans themselves first published their own newspapers for fellow Africans.

Basically there are two journalistic traditions in Africa: the European or "settler" tradition and the African nationalist tradition. Each is related to and directly influenced by the colonial incursion. In some areas, principally East, Central, and

South, the European influences predominated. French Africa was much the same story. An exception, and a bright exception at that, was British West Africa where a firm tradition of African-run, owned, and read newspapers preceded similar developments elsewhere on the continent by half a century or more. In North Africa, too, an indigenous nationalist press, usually in Arabic, grew up alongside the French newspapers.

Wherever Europeans settled in any numbers (Union of South Africa, the Rhodesias, Nyasaland, the Belgian Congo, Tanganyika, Kenya, and Uganda), there developed in differing degrees a European press and radio network, but an independent *African-owned* press was virtually absent. What newspapers and other literature were directed at Africans were owned by government or missionary societies or Europeans subservient to government policies. Only in Kenya and Uganda did the European-settler pattern vary at all; a number of ephemeral vernacular papers run by and for Africans appeared there.

Another variant of press development, this one characteristic of certain authoritarian polities, is present in two situations in Africa. One is that under tight, iron-fisted colonial control, such as in the Portuguese territories of Angola and Mozambique, which lack the liberalizing influences of the colonialism in British and even French territories; the other is the special case of Ethiopia and Liberia, the two long-independent nations of tropical Africa which received few of the positive benefits that accrued in colonial French and British Africa. The news media in Liberia and Ethiopia are characteristically instruments of government or are nonpolitical and highly deferential toward government.[4] Comparatively undeveloped, they barely extend beyond the capital and the dominant cultural minorities. In the relatively untouched hinterlands, tribally bound traditional communications predominate. Yet "in the absence of countervailing influences, an *assimilado* in Angola, or an educated Galla in Ethiopia, or a Mandingo in Liberia who is touched by these media, is likely to have his sense of identification with the dominant culture strengthened."[5]

European settlers became a crucial factor in newspaper evolution, for they soon had their own newspapers. These papers in varying degrees supported colonial rule and European economic interests and were unsympathetic, or sometimes hostile, to African nationalist and independence movements. One reason, perhaps, that press freedom is so little valued in postindependence Africa is that the dominant European papers did so little to encourage political rights for Africans.

The policies of colonial governments toward the local press—whether the authorities were generally permissive as in British West Africa or repressive as in French-controlled Africa—determined the degree of freedom that indigenous papers were to enjoy.

However, where the European contacts were the oldest and closest—British West Africa, South and North Africa—indigenous journalism took hold most effectively. For with journalism, as for much else, the colonial experience was a mixed blessing. Primary education, especially in European languages, the development of urban cultures, and modern elites with their increasing political awareness and organization were all by-products of colonialism that have contributed to the development of the media.

The cultural interaction of Europeans and Africans sparked political aspirations that fomented the development of indigenous African newspapers. During periods of the most intense political activities, after World War II and especially during the decade just before political independence, African newspapers were most numerous and most effective. African papers were invariably published by aspiring political leaders who used their ephemeral newssheets to build and cement a political organization. This indigenous press was essentially agitational and its activities were often circumscribed by restraints imposed by colonial authorities. But it prevailed. Further, by prevailing, the indigenous papers significantly aided the realization of preindependence goals.

WINDS OF CHANGE

Throughout most of Africa, decolonization has been rapid. Before 1950, only four African countries were independent. But the strong wave of nationalism that washed over the continent after World War II forced the European colonial powers to grant independence to most of their African possessions. Political freedom was carried on a north wind into Africa. In 1956 Tunisia, Morocco, and Sudan gained their independence. For the sub-Sahara, freedom dawned in 1957 when the British colony of the Gold Coast became the independent nation of Ghana under its charismatic leader, Kwame Nkrumah. In the years that followed—1960, 1962, 1964, 1965—the list of former colonies lengthened rapidly: Nigeria, Senegal, both Congos, Tanganyika (now Tanzania), Cameroon, Uganda, the Ivory Coast, Kenya, Zambia, Malawi, and even Gambia. Botswana and Lesotho, surrounded by white-dominated territories, won their independence in 1966. In all, 35 new nations emerged in the decade between 1956 and 1966. Of the 43 major national states (most of whose boundaries were inherited from Berlin's arbitrary mapmakers in 1885), the great majority today are ruled by African governments. The principal exceptions are in southern Africa—the Portuguese territories of Angola and Mozambique, South Africa, Rhodesia, and South West Africa—where white minorities impose their rule over African majorities. The big news story out of Africa during the late 1960s was the expanding guerrilla warfare backed by independent black nations against the white man's redoubt in southern Africa. With it was a growing fear of a racial war of ominous proportions. In the unstable Africa of today, mass communication systems are as shaky and volatile as the shifting political and social structures themselves. Since 1965, military coups d'état overturned thirteen African governments, including the militantly "African socialist" regime of Nkrumah in Ghana and the federal republic of giant Nigeria. Other African governments toppled by their own army or police forces were Congo (Kinshasa), Dahomey, Burundi, Central African Republic, Upper Volta, Congo (Brazzaville), Mali, Sudan, Sierra Leone, Libya, and Somalia. These coups were not isolated events; they were only the latest of an increasing number of political upheavals that have scarred the young lives of at least thirty of the thirty-nine independent African-governed states. At the decade's end, civil wars persisted in Sudan and Chad, as a devastating war ended in Nigeria.

Nevertheless, today every African nation has some kind of news media system. As a continent, however, Africa is more poorly endowed with newspapers, radio, cinema, television, books, and publications than any other comparable area in the world.

BARRIERS TO MEDIA DEVELOPMENT

This media poverty is not surprising; nowhere in the world are the barriers to the development of news media more formidable than in Africa as a whole.

SIZE

The great distances and geographical obstacles alone are awesome. With a land area of 11,673,000 square miles, Africa is four times the size of continental United States. From the Mediterranean to the Cape of Good Hope the distance is 5,000 miles and from Cape Verde in Senegal to the Horn of East Africa, 4,700 miles. Historically, the major avenue of "European" transportation has been the 22,921-mile-long seacoast. The few roads and railroads the colonizers built probed hesitatingly inland from the coast, usually staying within a single territory. Today all capitals are linked by airlines and this is a transportation boon; but roads and railroads are still markedly inadequate, partly due to the ease of developing air travel. Africa has only 39,000 miles of railroad, most of it in southern Africa. Many vast areas are not served by any highway, and most roads are gravel and impassable in wet seasons. Africa has about 2 million telephones (over half of them in South Africa), compared to more than 77 million in the United States. These distances, coupled with the lack of adequate transport and communications, have virtually cut off most countries from even their neighbors. This adds to the physical distances a profound feeling of psychological distance, which is beginning to be overcome in part by news communications.

To reach their potential audiences, therefore, the news media have greater distances to travel and receive meager assistance from roads, railroads, and telecommunications to facilitate the spread of news. They are also impeded by the problems of language.

LANGUAGE

The successful completion of most communication acts (i.e., transfer of a message from one person to another) is contingent on the understanding of a common language. But the variety of languages spoken in Africa is so bewildering that even authorities do not agree on how many there are. At a minimum there are more than 800 local languages and dialects. South of the Sahara, few of these are spoken by a clear *majority* in any country, except for Somalia, Swaziland, and Lesotho. In some countries, such as Central African Republic, Rwanda, Burundi, Mauritania, and Senegal, a single indigenous language dominates, but it is not usually widely spoken outside the borders of the country. Even languages that are, such as Swahili in East Africa and Hausa in West Africa (with eight to ten million speakers each), are not used by a majority of the peoples of their region. (Even so, Swahili, nearly a lingua franca in East Africa, has facilitated political activity of a range not possible in other parts of Africa.) Tiny Gabon, with only about 450,000 people, has ten languages while Nigeria, the most populous nation with about 55 million, has more than 250 languages, although large groups speak Hausa, English, Yoruba, or Ibo.

The Arabic widely used by the media across North Africa is essentially the written classical Arabic of the Koran, and is little used by the masses who speak dialects of street Arabic which vary from Morocco to Tunisia to the United Arab Republic.

Such linguistic diversity is a reminder that the new African nations are still badly split along tribal lines. Most Africans retain their loyalties to these subgroups, often creating an impasse between tribe and nation, between tradition and change. Tribalism not only inhibits progress toward modern nationhood and industrialization but also makes the task of mass communications much more difficult. Because language often means tribe, intertribal communication is difficult and many detribalized urban Africans rely, as do the mass media, on non-African languages. Most educated Africans communicate among themselves (and receive the bulk of mass media content) in the European languages of the colonizers—English, French, and Portuguese.

LITERACY

Coupled with the language diversity is the problem of literacy. Literacy levels for all languages are quite low. (See Table 1 in the Appendix.) Literacy is both an agent and an index of mass media development, as indeed it may be of national development itself. Certainly to produce and, to an extent, to consume mass communications requires literate people. Of Africa's over 300 million inhabitants, about 74 to 80 percent are functionally illiterate; this is the poorest rate of any major area of the world.

POVERTY

Poverty indices are equally discouraging. Most Africans support themselves by subsistence agriculture, which means they live outside a cash economy. In developing Africa as a whole, annual income is about $100 a person, and in recent years it has been increasing by a mere $1 per annum. Robert Gardiner, head of the Economic Commission for Africa, said: "The fact that from this level ($100 a person) and with this growth rate ($1 a year), it would take developing Africa some 270 years to attain the present income levels of a middle-range developed country may serve as a summary indication of just how difficult modern economic growth may prove to be."[6] Such poverty means that a man, if he can read, must go without a meal to buy a newspaper. It means there must be accumulated savings to buy an inexpensive transistor radio. This poverty, endemic throughout the continent, also bespeaks lack of industrialization and the lack of local entrepreneurial capital to invest in mass communications, as well as a shortage of technical skills to run the news media.

OTHER BARRIERS

These barriers—geography, language, illiteracy, and poverty—are the most obvious and formidable ones. Others are more subtle. One is the lack of urbanization. It has been estimated that less than 5 percent of sub-Saharan Africans live in cities.[7] The vast majority of Africans have their roots deep in villages and cattle camps or are migrant laborers on large farms or in mines. Part of the urban population remains only temporarily in the city before returning to their rural families. The typical African —if there can be such a person in such a diversity of humanity— lives in the bush, following traditional ways and supporting himself by subsistence agriculture.

Another obstacle is disease and malnutrition which shortens the average life-span to 32 years. Endemic diseases, such as malaria, bilharziasis, and trachoma, and malnutrition diseases, such as kwashiorkor, not only kill but also sharply restrict human efficiency.

All these factors contribute to a general lack of interest in or ability to cope with the aspects of modern life for which mass communications can be the connecting bridge.

COMMUNICATION CONTEXT

Yet, despite these barriers, communication—both interpersonal and mass—takes place in a context that is appropriately African. Africans were communicating with each other for thousands of years before Europeans introduced the printing press and radio broadcasting. Among these many diverse societies, usually rooted in an oral tradition, the language or dialect provided the boundary-setting function. People you could not talk to were aliens or foreigners. Language marked the boundary of the social system and when new dialects developed, new societies evolved. Historically, silent or nonoral interpersonal communication served well for intertribal dealings. The "silent barter" of the Middle Ages whereby the gold from the Guinea coast was exchanged wordlessly by forest dwellers for the much-desired salt brought by Arab caravans from the Sahara was a dramatic example of this.

Furthermore, lack of *mass* media, which implies technology, does not mean that no media have been used. The workings of the "bush telegraph"—usually associated with drums—have never been fully understood or explained by Europeans, said anthropologist Paul Bohannon, who considers African markets important facilitators of the "bush telegraph." "Africa is a country on the move, and it appears that it always has been," he wrote. "However, the peace of the colonial era and the improvement of roads that accompanied it meant that market places increased in number, that the amount of travel to and from marketing increased vastly, and therefore the 'bush telegraph' worked with better and better efficiency."[8] The "mammy wagons" of West Africa—the overloaded "tro-tro" buses or trucks carrying women traders to upcountry villages from the city—are still important channels for the flow of news.

The informal mechanisms of distributing information are often difficult to locate, not because they lack a structure, but because their very informality makes them less conspicuous and hence less amenable to research. "Among the Amhara of Ethiopia," Doob wrote, "communication 'by grapevine' is still the major method of dissemination of news, rumor, and entertainment."[9]

In studying communication patterns in Africa, it is necessary to understand the traditional and informal ways of exchanging information, if one is to understand the role of modern news media. For the news media are most effective when tied onto or coordinated with the older ways of communicating.

Ibrahim Abu-Lughod found that word-of-mouth communication explained why radio rather than the newspaper was the most effective means of reaching the fellahin of the Egyptian village with news of the outside world. How was radio used? In the small shops or bazaars, the traditional places of exchanging information, radios blared away all day. Thus, information from Cairo was passed on by the shopkeepers to the passing peasants and thereby fed into the traditional interpersonal channels.[10]

In many places the most important channel for the circulation of news and rumors is still word of mouth. Moroccans, for instance, have long been known for their intense interest in news. The phenomenon has been evident for centuries, yet it is a source of amazement to newcomers in Morocco to observe the speed with which news and rumors spread throughout the country. Within hours, news of the March 1965 Casablanca riots had reached the market places of every city and town in the country, despite the government's complete ban on the news in press and radio.[11] This high-speed informal communication network is popularly known as "radio medina."

In Africa the modern news media are concentrated in the cities. Daily newspapers (local and foreign), good reception of radio and television broadcasting, a variety of indoor movie houses, and magazines and books are readily available to literate Africans in government and commerce as well as foreigners in Lagos, Abidjan, Kinshasa, Accra, Cairo, Lusaka, Nairobi, Dakar, Rabat, and most other capitals. But these urban media users are but a small fraction of the total population in any African nation.

Mass communications are urban phenomena in part because in Africa the city is the center of life for the new social and political leadership.

"The city is the epitome of modernity, which is a synonym for development and freedom. It was the city which ruled and set the standards under colonialism and it continues to do so today. To the city, Africans come from the 'bush' for jobs and often for education."[12] In each new African nation, one city—usually the national capital (which often was the former colonial administrative center as well)—has dominated the political and economic life of the nation and it is here that the news media are concentrated. That city is "where the action is."

Most African capitals have had great population increases in postwar years. Leopoldville (now Kinshasa) went from 26,622 in 1935 to 340,000 in 1953 and today its population is over 1 million. Dakar grew from 24,915 in 1910 to over 576,000 in 1965; Bangui (Central African Republic) jumped from 25,000 in 1945 to about 100,000 in 1955, just ten years later.[13] Nairobi, with 100,000 in 1940, has burgeoned to over 400,000.

Cairo, now at 4.5 million people, has been absorbing but not providing gainful employment for the thousands of rural fellahin who come yearly. Booming Johannesburg, with over 1.5 million inhabitants, may be simultaneously the biggest "black African" city and biggest "European" city on the continent. In the world's developing areas, which until recently remained basically rural in character, urbanization is taking place three or four times as fast as in the United States. In Africa this is due partly to natural population increases and partly to great internal migrations to the cities. During the decade of the sixties in Asia, Africa, and Latin America, some 200 million people who dwelt in rural areas all their lives picked up and moved to cities. Most African cities are unable to absorb and provide employment for these new arrivals.[14]

Surveys of news media audiences in Africa indicate that the typical "heavy user" of mass communications lives in an urban center, usually the capital. Also, he is likely to be male, young (under 24), and is a student, a white-collar employee, or in a professional or managerial position. The clearest indicator of this heavy media consumer is education. In Nigeria it was found that virtually everyone with a secondary education listened to the radio. The Nigerian radio audience, with only primary school education, had almost as large a proportion of listeners, but listening dropped off sharply among adults with no formal education.[15]

The pull of the cities and the concentration of the media there means rural areas are ineffectively served. In rather over-simplified terms, the two basic kinds of communications systems in Africa are the modern mass media serving the capital and some other urban areas, and the various traditional or oral communications systems serving rural or "bush" areas. The characteristic urban-rural schism in Africa not only involves communications systems but cuts along linguistic, ethnic, economic, and social lines as well. It tends generally to partition the few urban detribalized and often educated Africans from the many illiterate Africans living in tribal societies on subsistence agriculture. "Modern" Africans are separated from "traditional" Africans. The schism is not complete, of course; many in the swelling urban slums are unassimilated into modern life and many frequently move back and forth between city and village.

A basic problem facing the news media in Africa is how to extend the modern city-concentrated media out to the hinterlands where traditional communications patterns still predominate. (Another basic problem is how to improve media content.) Nation building is largely a matter of developing patterns of communication which transcend rather than coincide with communal divisions. A marked characteristic of a highly developed industrial nation is the almost complete disappearance of the urban-rural schism in mass communications. A rural American, whether on a farm or in a small town, today has almost the same access to newspapers, radio, television, and movies as his urban counterpart. Such was not the case as recently as 40 years ago before the introduction of secondary roads, mass-produced automobiles, rural electrification, and rural mail delivery—all part of the infrastructure needed to support mass communications and still so badly lacking in Africa. Of course, there are in addition the many cultural and linguistic cleavages which exacerbate the urban-rural schism.

UNESCO and others have recognized the urgent need to develop rural media in Africa.[16]

Because of communication discontinuities, little news and information move back and forth between the bush and the capital.

The capital, as in former days of colonial rule, is still geared to news from the old metropolitan capital—London for anglophonic Africa, Paris for francophonic Africa. But there are neither adequate facilities nor enough news personnel in the African nations to report events in the new nations' own rural areas. While in Kenya in 1965, I was struck by how little news appeared in the Nairobi media about the conflict in the Northeast Province against the shifta (Somali insurgents) along the Somali Republic border. Later, on September 27, 1966, the Voice of Kenya in Nairobi summarized shifta losses: 198 killed in 1964, 335 killed in 1965, and 665 in the first ten months of 1966. Kenyan losses for the corresponding periods were 144, 320, and 244.[17] This was a rather hot war to be so inadequately reported. But it reflected a situation common throughout Africa: the facilities by which news can flow from bush areas into the capital are few.

During a 1968 visit to Uganda, I learned there had been numerous intermittent tribal clashes in the Fort Portal area which had never been reported in the Kampala press. In some cases, such news is blacked out not by lack of newsgathering facilities but by direct government censorship. Much happens in remote areas of Africa that is never adequately reported in the news media.

THE CONTINENT'S MEDIA FACILITIES

The news media, then, are sparsely scattered in irregular configurations as are the other underpinnings of modernity—railroads, paved highways, telephones, automobiles, industrial installations, shiny cities with jet airports, and Inter-Continental hotels. They tend to be concentrated in the larger capitals ringing the outer fringes of the continent: Dakar, Abidjan, Accra, Lagos, Cape Town, Johannesburg, Nairobi, Algiers, and Rabat.

In quick summary for the entire continent, excluding the United Arab Republic (which is usually considered in the Middle East), only about 175 daily newspapers circulated about 2.7 million copies daily; some 98 radio stations broadcast to 12.5 million radio receivers; 32 television stations transmitted to roughly 428,000 receiving sets; about 525 weeklies and fortnightlies had a combined circulation of more than 3.8 million; about 5,000 indoor motion picture theaters had about 1.3 million seats and an estimated weekly attendance of 3.7 million; and some 3,800 local libraries contained almost 14.8 million books.

Also, major world news services were available in most African countries and there were more than 27 local or national news services.[18]

These facilities are grossly insufficient to serve the almost 300 million people living in over 44 countries and islands, especially considering that two nations, South Africa and Nigeria, have a disproportionate share of media facilities. For example, just the 21 daily newspapers of South Africa account for 30 percent of all daily newspaper circulation in Africa.

(It must be noted that in developing nations, all social statistics are unreliable, and at best, approximate. This is especially true in mass communications. As in other parts of the *Tiers Monde,* the developed world's vast underbelly that cuts a wide swath through Asia, the Middle East, Africa, and Latin America, the mass media are growing unevenly and sporadically in Africa. Little wonder statistics and records are unreliable. New newspapers appear suddenly and established publications unexpectedly vanish. Determining the number of readers, or of radio and television sets in use, is almost guesswork in nations where reliable census data are nonexistent. Even data carefully assembled by UNESCO and other United Nations organizations are often inaccurate to begin with or become quickly outdated. Newspaper sales fluctuate greatly and broadcasters often have only a hazy notion of how many people are listening.)

In several places independence brought a dramatic and accelerating growth of some media, particularly radio and television, but in general, mass communications have continued to lag well behind other world areas, with the partial exception of the Middle East and South Asia.

Only radio increased significantly during the sixties. Daily newspaper circulation and cinema facilities (mostly indoor) did not keep pace with population increase even though Africa's population was not soaring as fast as in some areas of Latin America and Asia. Overpopulation is one problem that Africa does not as yet generally share with other regions of the Third

World. But its population is increasing faster than that of industrialized nations.

African media, with the exception of radio, are also well below the bare minimum standards set by UNESCO for "adequate communications." The UN organization has suggested as an immediate target that a country should aim to provide for every 100 of its inhabitants at least ten copies of daily newspapers, five radio receivers, two cinema seats, and two television receivers. (According to UNESCO, this arbitrary yardstick was established in order to measure the insufficiency of media *facilities* in developing nations. It tells us nothing about media *content* or *effects*.)

Most African nations, as well as many in Latin America and Asia (some 100 states and territories in all) fall below this very minimal "minimum" level in all four of the mass media. These countries have a combined population of 1,910 million or 66 percent of the world's total.[19] (See Table 2 in the Appendix.)

The number of radios in Africa is the bright exception (4.3 sets per 100 people) and is fast approaching the UNESCO minimum. Radio has an estimated audience of 50 million. Television, because it is still in its infancy, is the only other mass medium that has grown significantly over the past five years or more, and in 1965 had an estimated audience of 1.8 million.[20] More recently, however, television expansion has slowed.

There seems little doubt that daily newspapers and other publications have not been growing commensurate with broadcasting. This uneven growth of the news media in Africa can be explained in part by certain inherent characteristics of the news media themselves as they relate to the African setting.

2

NEWS MEDIA

FEW AFRICANS—whether they are Wolofs, Zulus, Somalis, Arabs, Bembas, Kikuyus, Hausas, Swahilis, or Baoules—ever read a daily newspaper, listen to a radio news program, or watch a cinema or television newsreel. On the other hand, though the media audience is small, it includes an important segment of African life. According to one U.S. Information Agency survey, "people most apt to devour mass media are exactly the people usually considered the most important in shaping the future of their countries."[1]

The pervasive dearth of modern mass communications adds to the burdens of those striving to modernize the continent, for printed pages, electronic broadcasting signals, and flickering film images are not merely divertisements or entertainment. Communication, whether mass or interpersonal, is intimately connected with the whole social fabric of a nation. As a nation moves from a traditional to a modern style of life, its means of news communication change accordingly, and often dramatically, from traditional or oral means to modern or media means. The need for news and public information increases as well. The news media perform an essential function in thus servicing a modernizing society, and each particular news medium has its own assets and limitations.

RADIO BROADCASTING

Radio demands first attention because of its wider acceptance in the African environment. Since it was first introduced in the years between the World Wars, mainly as a "news from home" service for the European populations, radio broadcasting has made far more progress than the press toward becoming a real *mass* medium in Africa.

The earliest radio broadcasting was in South Africa, which had the largest concentration of Europeans. The first radio station was opened at Johannesburg in 1920, followed by others in Cape Town and Durban. Kenya, in 1927, became the second country, and the first in tropical Africa, to initiate radio broadcasting. The earliest programs from Nairobi were designed for English settlers, but later broadcasts were transmitted in Kikuyu, Swahili, Arabic, and Hindustani.

On the west coast, radio on wired services began in Sierra Leone in 1934, on the Gold Coast (Ghana) in 1935, and Nigeria in 1936. In the latter year the British colonial government decided to develop radio in the British colonies as a public service. Because of this early emphasis, radio in the former British territories is still far ahead of that in other areas.[2] Radio in French Africa lagged behind and has never really caught up. While the British had a policy of establishing radio in each colony, the French, with their more centralized colonial administration, long relied on Dakar, Brazzaville, and Paris to provide radio signals for the far-flung regions of French West Africa and French Equatorial Africa. Broadcasting from Dakar began in 1939 but Radio Abidjan did not become an established satellite of Radio Dakar until 1951. Furthermore, radio under French colonial rule was always *French* radio; there was little effort to provide either broadcasting in vernaculars or any indigenous programming.

In most places, radio as a means of reaching the Africans was an afterthought. The government of Southern Rhodesia, for example, started a broadcast service from Salisbury in 1932 for European listeners in Southern Rhodesia, Northern Rhodesia, and Nyasaland. It was not until 1946 that facilities were established in Lusaka to broadcast to Africans of the three territories in Nyanja, Tonga, Lozi, Ndebele, Shona, and English.[3]

Before World War II, only seven tropical African territories possessed transmitting facilities. At war's end, fifteen had them. As new independent nations burgeoned, so did radio, for the new governments have fostered its development as their number one mass medium.

In 1955 Africa counted 151 transmitters; by early 1960 the same stations reported 252 transmitters (60 percent shortwave, the balance medium wave); by 1964 the number was up to 370 transmitters, with 43 African governments involved in broadcasting.[4] However, the number of programming services, a total of 98 in 1965, tended to be concentrated in a few nations: Angola, 16; Congo (Kinshasa), 8; Mozambique, 6; Nigeria, 7; and South Africa, 15.

The great increase in radio receivers—from 350,000 to almost 12 million in ten years—was due largely to the development of the low power drain radio receiver, popularly known as a transistor radio. Light and portable, radios were no longer dependent on an electricity power source and were comparatively inexpensive. Not surprisingly, in just the five-year period from the end of 1960 to the end of 1965, radio sets in use increased 140 percent. Even at that, Africa's 11,826,000 radios still represented only about 4 percent of all the radios outside the United States and Canada, and these were disproportionately located in Algeria, Morocco, Nigeria, and South Africa. (See Table 3 in the Appendix.)

Throughout Africa radio is recognized as the least expensive and most effective way of reaching people, particularly the illiterate tribalized African living in the bush. No wonder, then, radio in Africa is virtually always a function of government. At independence, the new African governments quickly brought radio fully under the official umbrella if it was not there already. In Kenya, for example, radio and television, both public corporations, were combined as the Voice of Kenya within the Ministry of Information. In the effort to Africanize programming, some stations discharged most European personnel and ended the long practice of relaying BBC news broadcasts.

Every government on the continent (including the remaining colonial regimes) gives radio a high priority in government information programs, is expanding technical facilities to reach the more remote areas, and is increasing internal coverage and programming to take advantage of radio's potential to mobilize public opinion.[5] Another marked trend is the increase of programming in the indigenous languages.

The advantages of radio in the African milieu are, perhaps, obvious: it easily overcomes great distance; it is, thanks to transistors, cheaply and easily received; listeners need not be literate; and, it is said, since Africans cling to their oral traditions, the spoken word offers the best results. Unquestionably, there is evidence of widespread use of radio in the rural and still-traditional areas.

Radio broadcasting, unlike the press, has surpassed markedly the position it held in colonial times. In fact, Africa, some feel, will not go through a newspaper age, as did Europe and America enroute to the electronic age of radio, television, and movies. Instead, it will proceed directly and fully into widespread adoption of the electronic media before newspapers and literacy are well established. Others reject such a McLuhanesque future for African media and argue that the printed word and literacy are essential to the modernization process and cannot be bypassed.

Tom Hopkinson, an authority on Africa and its press, wrote: "In the western world, the pattern has been newspapers, radio, television. In Africa and much of Asia, the first contact the ordinary man has with any means of mass communication is the radio. It is the transistor which is bringing the people of remote villages and lonely settlements into contact with the flow of modern life. For the tribesman entering the money economy, the transistor now ranks as his second most coveted possession, ousting the bicycle—a wrist watch still being the first priority."[6]

Impressive gains notwithstanding, radio is not without its problems. The pervasiveness of radio broadcasting varies from country to country rather markedly. It is furthest advanced in the south of the continent, in North Africa, and in English-speaking countries. Progress has been only fair in middle Africa, and despite transistors and universal government broadcasting, many gaps are still to be filled. Often the coastal city areas are blanketed by radio signals, but the hinterland is sparsely covered.[7] For economy reasons, shortwave broadcasting is widely used domestically, but shortwave transmissions in the tropics are severely affected by solar interference (sunspots) from October to April. The sunspot problem can be solved only by substituting frequency modulation (FM) broadcasting in combination with medium-wave booster services, an expensive changeover new governments cannot afford.

In spite of its potentialities, radio is not yet effectively reaching enough Africans in the bush. To do so requires broadcasting in a variety of languages which adds to the cost while reducing the efficiency. Radio may jump the literacy barrier, but the listener must understand the language coming out of his transistor set and at any given time a majority of listeners usually does not. Even now, much broadcasting is in English and French, and such programming is often European-slanted and irrelevant to the interests of many African listeners. In the Ivory Coast, for example, I observed that all but 6 of 175 hours of weekly radio broadcasting were in French.

Even though some nations claim both nationwide broadcasting capability and large numbers of rural listeners, African radio is still mainly an urban medium. USIA surveys often provide the best information available on local media habits. In a December 1960 survey in four West African cities, the USIA found that three out of four persons interviewed in Accra, Lagos, Abidjan, and Dakar listened to a radio and most of these had access to radio in their own homes.[8] These data analyzed against the low number of radio sets per 100 population for each country as a whole suggest that radio is mainly an urban phenomenon.

A later USIA survey in 1964 found that the total of regular radio listeners (at least several times a week) averaged about 60 to 65 percent in four of the five capitals surveyed (Abidjan, Accra, Lomé, and Douala) and ran up to 89 percent in Dakar. The report found "listening drops off in the hinterland cities and especially in the bush areas. The number of regular listeners is no more than 15 percent in the bush areas of the Ivory Coast, Togo, and Cameroon, within 30 miles of the capitals."[9]

Another problem is finding supporting revenue. The usual European device of raising it by license fees is subject to serious limitations. For one thing, in many countries the number of sets is small; for another, the administrative machinery required to collect fees is rarely available. This, coupled with the fact that transistors are frequently smuggled in and sold on the black market, has made it very difficult to collect either one-time or periodic fees. Commercial broadcasting is usually officially discouraged; most governments consider radio an educational and informational medium of too great a potential and too serious in purpose to be given over to commercial exploitation. However, some government-run radio stations have recently started to carry commercials to help defray expenses. Essentially, the usual financial support for radio comes from three sources: some license fees, a little commercial advertising, and large direct subsidies from the government.

The colonial experience has left its imprint on radio. The BBC influence pervades broadcasting in anglophonic Africa, most markedly in the presentation of news rendered in the curt, reserved style of the BBC. In the first years of Nigeria's highly professional Radio Nigeria, news shows not only sounded like the BBC, but approached that admirable British network in scope and reliability.

Unquestionably, radio has become the major channel by which news reaches the African public. All stations transmit regular news bulletins and a few provide bulletins every hour.

News on radio is almost always *official* news, not unexpected where radio is invariably government radio. Major sources for the news broadcasts are Reuters and Agence France Presse, as well as a local national news agency. Few stations have very extensive newsgathering staffs of their own. News is selective: comings and goings of government leaders receive a good deal of attention as do activities relating to national development. There is little negative news such as crime, strikes, unrest, or conflict of any kind. Government policy in several nations prohibits reporting any news that reflects badly on the nation. For example, Radio Maroc carries no news that might damage even slightly the image of King Hassan, the Kingdom of Morocco, or the Arab world.

The USIA survey in West Africa found

> radio to be not only the most widely used mass medium but also the one most frequently used to get the news. Radio is even more important than word-of-mouth communication as a source of news in the cities. However, radio news is still far less important than word-of-mouth in the bush areas, except in rural Senegal, where the government has made a special effort to spread radios. In addition, radio is also considered the most trustworthy by those who use more than one medium. . . . Newspapers generally run far behind radio and word-of-mouth as a source of news, although they are used by a significant proportion of the people in the bigger cities, especially in Ghana.[10]

Earlier field surveys tended to corroborate these findings on the central role of radio in African news communication.

Another USIA poll asked adult urban Africans in Abidjan and Lagos: "To know what is going on elsewhere in the world, how do you personally get your information?" Radio was named by 77 percent in Lagos and 68 percent in Abidjan; friends and relatives were cited by 56 percent and 50 percent. Newspapers were listed by 60 percent in Lagos and 52 percent in Abidjan.[11]

These results indicate not only the importance of radio but of interpersonal communication in West Africa. Across the continent on the other hand, a USIA survey in Kenya found that radio did not hold as much of an edge over the print media in East Africa.[12]

A cross section of 175 adult Africans in Nairobi was asked how they usually found out what was going on in the world and which medium—radio or newspapers—they considered most reliable.

Results showed that even though more people listened to radio at least once a week than read a newspaper regularly (70 percent to 54 percent), more said they got world news from news-papers (42 percent vs 34 percent via radio) as well as news in general (41 percent to 38 percent). However, 46 percent felt radio was the most reliable source for news as against 34 percent for newspapers. Only one in five in Nairobi owned his own radio; more than half listened in circumstances where programs were selected by others.

The importance of radio is underlined by the role it often plays in political crises. In almost all coups d'état—successful and unsuccessful—seizure of the radio transmitters is one of, if not the, primary goal. President Kasavubu of the Congo was able to win his struggle with Premier Patrice Lumumba because at a critical moment the United Nations forces denied Lumumba access to Radio Leopoldville. However Kasavubu's fellow Ba-kongo and personal friend, Abbé Youlou, then leader of Congo (Brazzaville), allowed Kasavubu to use the high-powered, French-built transmitter located in Brazzaville across the Congo River from Leopoldville.[13]

When rebellious army troops seized power in Dahomey in December 1969 (the fifth coup there in nine years of independ-ence) the insurgents captured the radio station *before* they stormed the presidential palace. An attempted coup in the Congo (Brazzaville) in March 1970 was crushed when loyalist troops and tanks surrounded the radio station held by a group of 30 rebel soldiers who had seized the transmitter and announced the ouster of President Marien Ngoubai.

In visits to Radio Ghana in Accra and Radio Nigeria in Lagos, I was struck by the fact that both broadcasting installa-tions, fenced with barbed wire, were heavily guarded by armed soldiers behind sandbagged barricades. This is indeed a tribute to the political importance of radio.

A number of conditions, then, have favored the development of radio as the leading mass medium. Indeed, it may be said that radio is the only news medium reaching a broad public. News-papers, television, cinema, magazines, and books do not reach large audiences and tend to be elite or specialized media. But under some circumstances, it may be more desirable to reach and influence the educated few rather than the illiterate many.

NEWSPAPERS

In various cities throughout the continent, there have been daily newspapers for all of the twentieth and part of the nineteenth century. Yet today the daily press is still pitifully small, weak, and inadequate. Of the 6,861 daily newspapers in the world in 1968–69, only 179 were in Africa.[14] None of the great newspapers of the world is there, although *Al Ahram* of Cairo has much influence in the Arab world and the *Rand Daily Mail* of Johannesburg has won a worldwide reputation for its opposition to South Africa's racial policies.

The circulation level of dailies in Africa (one copy per 100 population) was the lowest in the world. Total copies of *all* daily papers (2.7 million) was about half that of the tabloid *Daily Mirror* of London. Moreover, in the years since independence, the number of daily newspapers has not increased. (In absolute numbers there are certainly fewer dailies of any kind. Arno Huth in *Communications Media in Tropical Africa* said that Africa in 1960 had 220 to 250 daily newspapers. In late 1969, while compiling a table on world daily newspapers for the *Britannica Book of the Year 1970,* I found only 179 dailies.)

The variety and quality of the daily press reflect the diversity and inequities of Africa itself. Dailies are unequally concentrated in a few cities around the fringes of the continent. The largest and most modern newspapers, twenty-one dailies, are published in South Africa; Nigeria has had the liveliest and most diverse daily press in tropical Africa with about eighteen; and United Arab Republic has eight dailies. Two island nations off the East coast, the Malagasy Republic and Mauritius, had six and fourteen dailies, respectively. There are, however, vast expanses within the continental land mass where daily newspapers are never seen. Malawi, Botswana, Burundi, Rwanda, Lesotho, and Swaziland have no daily newspapers whatever. (See Table 4 in the Appendix.)

Since the press followed the Europeans into Africa, the earliest papers served the white settlers. By the 1880s South Africa had a variety of newspapers in English and Afrikaans. Salisbury, Rhodesia, has had a newspaper (the Rhodesia *Herald)* since 1891. Kampala, Uganda, and Mombasa, Kenya, had newspapers before World War I and Nairobi residents have been reading the *East African Standard* since 1914. *Paris-Dakar,* later *Dakar-Matin,* first appeared in Dakar, Senegal, the administrative center of French West Africa, in 1935.

Today European influences are immediately apparent in the format and style of African newspapers. In fact, one looks almost in vain for what might be an indigenous African influence.

The European-oriented *East African Standard* group, with papers in Kampala and Nairobi, and until recently, Mombasa and Dar es Salaam, has long dominated the journalism of East Africa. The press of Kenya is completely British in appearance and format because the editors and publishers have long been British journalists; only in the past several years have Africans been added to editorial staffs. The *East African Standard* in its typography, makeup, and writing style is similar to that of a conservative provincial paper in Britain. It is a newspaper with which the white settlers have long felt comfortable.

While East Africa reflects the stodgier side of British journalistic influences, West Africa's press is a direct descendent of Britain's lively tabloid tradition. The technically best newspapers of West Africa were financed by the London *Daily Mirror* group (but edited by Africans) and included Sierra Leone's *Daily Mail,* Ghana's *Daily Graphic,* and Nigeria's *Daily Times,* whose circulation of 120,000 was the largest in black Africa.

Not only the *Times* but most of the rest of Nigeria's lively and at times impudent press was still British influenced; however, much of the vigorous and colorful language of urban Nigerians showed in its writing. The *Daily Times* closely resembled its British cousin, the *Daily Mirror,* London's biggest daily. Unlike other African examples, the Nigerian press came close to being a popular press that looked beyond the Europeans and the African elites. But the journalism was unmistakably out of Fleet Street—breezy, light, heavy on crime and court news, plenty of tightly cropped pictures, bright and often irreverent headlines, and flamboyantly written.

The press in Senegal and Ivory Coast, both daily and periodical, is completely French in appearance, style, and makeup. The Ivoirien government daily, *Fraternité Matin,* could easily pass for a French provincial daily, so completely Gallicized is it, as could the weekly party newspaper, *Fraternité.* Comics, syndicated features, and "boilerplate" are straight from France.

Probably the three best newspapers on the continent are published in Johannesburg, South Africa, and their British roots are obvious. They are the vigorous and outspoken *Rand Daily Mail; Star,* the largest daily in both number of pages and circulation (179,000) in all of Africa; and the biggest weekly paper, the *Sunday Times* (circulation 400,000).

Such European-owned papers, edited for resident Europeans, have been better able to cope with the vexing obstacles that still inhibit the development of African daily journalism:

● High illiteracy and poverty which greatly restrict potential readership;

● Lack of local capital to support newspaper enterprises;

● High cost of printing and newsprint because the presses, typesetting equipment, and newsprint must be imported from abroad;

● Difficulties of distribution because of inadequate roads and lack of transport facilities;

● Continuing shortage of both technical staff and maintenance of equipment, to say nothing of trained journalists—a major problem in itself.

But despite the obstacles, newspapers have been published—and published by Africans—for a long time. British West Africa (Nigeria, Ghana, and Sierra Leone) has had a long and honorable newspaper tradition, extending back into the early years of the nineteenth century. In Nigeria alone, nearly 100 newspapers or periodicals have been published by Africans since the British intrusion and before independence. James S. Coleman said the *African-owned* nationalist press was the most potent instrument used in the propagation of nationalist ideas and racial consciousness.[15] In North Africa, an opposition press, often clandestine and in Arabic, played much the same role.

The whole nationalist political movement in tropical Africa, especially in West Africa but elsewhere as well, was ignited and nurtured by small political papers in English, French, and the vernaculars. Polemical, irresponsible, and lacking in hard news, these small sheets played a major role in wresting political control from the colonial governments.

Since independence, these partisan papers, often subsidized by political parties, have given way to government-owned newspapers as the nationalist leaders—the Nkrumahs, the Azikiwes, the Bourguibas, the Nyereres, the Kenyattas, and the Kaundas—moved into the government offices.

In addition to the European-owned papers, the remaining party-subsidized press, and the new government papers, there are some small independent or semi-independent journals which pursue a precarious and often ephemeral existence. In the provincial areas, government subsidies often help support monthlies and biweeklies in the vernaculars, but their technical quality is generally low. Mission and church-affiliated papers are found in most countries, ranging from the sophisticated and authoritative news weekly, *Afrique Nouvelle,* of Dakar, to small mimeographed sheets in the hinterlands.[16]

Regardless of the variety of papers, the striking fact remains that there were three times as many radio sets as copies of daily newspapers in Africa (12.5 million to 2.7 million, respectively). That statistic is vivid testimony to the fact that daily newspapers have been particularly vulnerable to the enormous barriers to media development—great distances, language diversity, poverty, illiteracy, etc.—and as a result are thin publications, lacking in most cases any firm economic base. (The 21 dailies of South Africa are a notable exception because they are essentially "European" publications, well-financed and directed at an affluent European public.)

The continent generally lacks adequate modern newspaper printing facilities—even Dr. Nnamdi Azikiwe's historically important and influential *West African Pilot* was published by handset type on a flatbed press. Printing machinery and newsprint must be imported and are costly.

Transport problems and slow mail delivery inhibit the circulation of daily newspapers in rural areas, although daily papers are often flown from one city to another. Newspaper sales tend to be confined to the city of publication, where street sales rather than home delivery is the rule.

The *Daily Times* of Lagos reached its comparatively high circulation not so much because it was undeniably a good newspaper but because it had dependable production facilities and a very efficient distribution system. The *Daily Times* was carried by plane, "mammy wagon" (the petty traders' buses), boat, and by the company's own trucks to all regions of Nigeria, usually arriving a day ahead of its competitors, who lacked the resources of this British-owned enterprise. As a result it has been one of the few national papers in Africa—"national" in that it could be purchased in most larger cities of Nigeria.

Many newspapers come and go; some quietly disappear and then without notice resume publishing. Press runs vary greatly and sales can be drastically affected by weather (a heavy rain may shrink sales sharply), political factors, and whether there is a good lead story with high reader interest. Abidjan in the Ivory Coast has had 40 papers in 25 years, but only one real daily during the 1960s.

The total circulation of daily newspapers for all of Africa in 1960 amounted to only 1 percent of the world's total, as compared to 4 percent for Latin America and 22 percent for Asia, and the African percentage has not improved significantly. However, newspapers reach more people than circulation figures indicate. Papers are passed from hand to hand or posted in public places.

Daily Times

THE INDEPENDENT NEWSPAPER
• 18,599 Friday, March 15, 1968 3d

◆ *FEDERAL troops examine rockets and rocket launchers captured from rebels fleeing near Abagana on the road to Onitsha. More pictures by Adeola Adelaja on page 3.*

University fees
re-echo in Ibadan

FATE OF 600 UNDERGRADUATES UNCERTAIN

AT least 600 students of the University of Ibadan including 300 final year students may be barred from taking their sessional examinations in May unless the Federal Government clarifies its stand on the aid plan for needy students.

In his fiscal policy statement, the Federal Commissioner for Finance, Chief Obafemi Awolowo, had said that Nigerian youths who have the innate talents but cannot obtain secondary or university education due to poverty will be assisted.

Consequently, defaulting students were allowed to attend lectures in all the four universities in the country without paying.

But last week, the University of Ibadan notified defaulting students to pay up immediately.

Defaulting students, relying on the Commissioner's statement, protested to their union against the decision of the university authority which they claimed meant that some of them will have to pay as much as £101 10s or they will not be allowed to sit for their examinations.

The Federal Commissioner for Education, Mr. Wenike Briggs, yesterday, confirmed that the student leaders of the University had met him on the problem. "We had a very cordial discussion," he said.

MR. WENIKE BRIGGS

Attitude

But in a special statement issued in Lagos last night to clarify government stand, Mr. Briggs condemned the attitude of the students for not paying their fees.

He said if secondary school pupils continue to pay their fees inspite of the statement, there was no moral justification in the action of the university students to misconstrue the statement to mean free university education for them.

He, however, repeated government's intention to give fullest possible financial assistance to indigenous students but warned that the good intention of the government should not be abused by "any dishonest practice."

20 REBEL AGENTS HELD

From SOLA ODUNFA,
Asaba Thursday.

SPECULATIONS are rife here that there are rebel agents in some banking houses in Lagos.

The speculations were aroused by the discovery of a big illegal currency traffic by which old Nigerian notes are still being changed to new ones in Lagos for rebel agents who pass them on to the secessionists.

Vigilant Federal troops in Asaba district have so far arrested about 20 collaborators in the area and confiscated more than £5,000 from them.

They were tried by a special Military tribunal in Asaba and given jail sentences ranging from five to 10 years.

During the trials, it was discovered that the collaborators received old notes from rebel agents who cross from the East Central State by some clandes-

Illegal traffic of old notes

tine routes and pass them on to other agents in some Lagos banking houses for exchange.

Thousands of pounds, it was learnt, have been so changed within the past few weeks.

On Monday, four more people were arrested near Ibusa, one of them was a woman who described herself as a herbalist when arrested. She was carrying £126 in coins.

One other man arrested on the same day was found with £258 10s in old 10s notes. He confessed later that he had

earlier that day sent £1,200 to Lagos for exchange. He, however, did not disclose the name of the person to whom he gave the money or the person who would effect the change in Lagos.

Earlier, one of the agents arrested had disclosed on interrogation that the traffic was "regular."

The old currency notes ceased to be legal tender since January 22. Rebel leader Ojukwu later issued a new set of notes for use in areas still under his control but these have been rejected in the international market.

But yesterday in Lagos, the Governor of the Central Bank, Dr. Clement Isong said:

"I do not know anything about this at all. It is not to my knowledge.

"The last date we changed the old notes for the new ones was the deadline of January 22," he said.

1re Année N° 109
MERCREDI
21 AVRIL
1965

Direction-Administration
Stade des 24? logements
Adidjan - B.P. 107
Tél. 294-52 et (in visib)
Publicité
Agence Havas - Abidjan
B.P. 4301 - Tél. 263-26

Le N° 20 F

Fraternité *matin*

le grand quotidien ivoirien d'information

Les missions du Conseil de l'Entente à travers l'Afrique

LES PRÉSIDENTS DIORI ET YAMÉOGO ARRIVERONT AUJOURD'HUI A LAGOS

tandis que M. Alliali et les ministres

des Affaires Étrangères du Niger et de Haute-Volta sont arrivés à Brazzaville

«...La subversion demeure organisée à partir du Ghana»

a répété le Président Diori au Cameroun

Lire nos informations en page 8

Venant de Lagos et partant vers Accra

Court séjour à Abidjan de la Mission de Bonne Volonté thaïlandaise

La mission thaïlandaise qui séjourne dans notre capitale depuis deux jours avant été accueillie par M. Dhoui, chargé du Protocole au Ministère des Affaires Étrangères que l'on reconnaît à gauche sur notre photo.

VIETNAM :

Explosion dans un bar

17 MORTS et 58 BLESSÉS

Intense activité vietcong remarquée depuis 48 heures

LIRE NOS INFORMATIONS U DERNIÈRE PAGE

Le 1er Séminaire International des directeurs de journaux africains ouvert hier à Abidjan par M. Mathieu Ékra Ministre de l'Information

En haut :
Voici M. Mathieu Ekra, ministre de l'Information pendant l'allocution d'ouverture du séminaire des directeurs et responsables de journaux africains organisé par l'I.I.P.

A droite : le ministre, MM. Dessinges et Anoma Kanie ; à la gauche MM. Van Gindertael et Perriard.

En bas :
Le ministre Ekra s'entretient avec M. Dessinges lors de la réception offerte par l'I.I.P.

LIRE NOS INFORMATIONS EN PAGE 4

Les Syndicalistes préparent le 1er Mai

Hier les syndicalistes ont tenu une importante séance de travail en vue du mardi, sur pied une bonne organisation des manifestations du 1er mai.
Nous reviendrons d'ailleurs très prochainement sur cette intéressante réunion.

Le ministre d'État malgache chargé de l'Intérieur :

PAS D'ÉLECTIONS LÉGISLATIVES A MADAGASCAR... AVANT LE 2 AOÛT

Pas de remaniement ministériel

LIRE NOS INFORMATIONS EN PAGE 8

D'après un récent sondage du «Gallup» français :

La popularité de de Gaulle reste stable

LIRE NOS INFORMATIONS EN DERNIÈRE PAGE

CYCLISME Ce matin à 7 h précises

départ d'Abidjan de la

« BOUCLE DU CAFÉ »

(Cinq étapes - 577 kms)

Défilé des coureurs à travers la ville jusqu'au départ réel donné au pont d'Agban

ARRIVÉE DIMANCHE AU PARC DES SPORTS

LIRE NOTRE ARTICLE EN PAGE 5

Daily Graphic

3np, THURSDAY, MAR. 7, 1968 No. 5422

3 Africans hanged

THE illegal Ian Smith regime defied the Queen of England, reprieve for three Africans by having them hanged in a Salisbury prison early yesterday.

The three had been sentenced to death by hanging for murder. An agency report said the execution took place at seven o'clock GMT after all legal measures to save them from the gallows had failed.

Their hanging was the strongest challenge yet to the British Government by the breakaway white-rule colony.

It plunged Britain and Rhodesia into their biggest head-on clash since the unilateral declaration of independence in November 1965.

The men were Victor Silarmi Mlambo and James Dhlamini, convicted of killing a white farmer with petrol bomb in 1964, and Daly Shadreck, condemned for the murder of a tribal chief.

Clemency

Their last-minute appeals for clemency were rejected after a meeting on Tuesday of the Executive Council of Prime Minister Ian Smith's Cabinet Ministers.

News of the execution came in brief typewritten notices posted outside the heavy grey gates of the prison two miles down the broad highway winding to Salisbury's rich northern suburbs.

Individual excerpt for the names and place of sentencing, they said: This is to certify that the sentence of death passed upon (and here each man's name was inserted) by the High Court at (and here) the place where the court sat was duly carried out, at Salisbury Prison this sixth day of March.

The three Africans were the first to be executed in

◆ Contd. on Page 3

◆ Mr B. A. Yakubu, Deputy Commissioner of Police and member of the National Liberation Council, delivering the council's message at a parade of schoolchildren and youth organisations in Accra yesterday.

Seated behind him are (from left), Nana Poku, Commissioner for Communications; Mr S. T. Netley, Commissioner for Labour and Social Welfare; Dr A. A. Y. Philips, Commissioner for Industries; Dr A. A. Y. Kyeremanten, Commissioner for Local Government; Mr Isifu Ali, Commissioner for Works and Housing; Mr P. D. Anin, Commissioner for External Affairs; Dr F. Akwei, Commissioner for Health, and Mr J. Ofori Torto, Commissioner for Forestry.

GHANA MARKS INDEPENDENCE ANNIVERSARY

By "Graphic" Reporters

THOUSANDS of schoolchildren and youth organisations all over the country turned out in the regional and district capitals for grand parades held to celebrate the celebration of Ghana's eleventh Independence anniversary.

IN ACCRA, the brightly coloured uniforms of the 49 schools which took part in the parade mixed up well with the attire of the other youth organisations at the parade ground. Their school teachers took part in the march-past.

All the four stands at the Black Star Square were filled with cheering school-

children who did not take part in the actual parade.

The square rocked with cheers from all the stands as Mr B. A. Yakubu, Deputy Commissioner of Police and member of the National Liberation Council, and his entourage arrived at exactly 2.30 p.m. to take the salute.

After the National Anthem was played the march-past commenced and Mr Yakubu in his police ceremonial uniform, took the salute. Nine Commissioners who accompanied him remained seated behind him.

Some of the youth organisations which took part in the parade were the Girl Guides, Boy Scouts, Sea Scouts, Boys Brigade, Red Cross, C.V.O, Y.M.C.A, and Y.W.C.A.

Ajax Bukana the popular comedian, stole the show at the parade when he and his partner, both on a motor-bicycle sent the Commissioners reeling with laughter when they rode past the saluting base.

The crowd, including diplomats, were held spellbound when Ajax, after passing the saluting base, suddenly fell off the bicycle headlong, somersaulted twice and walked in the opposite direction to take another salute.

This parade ended at nearly 3.25 a.m. after Mr Yakubu delivered a message from the N.L.C. to the children.

The message which was read, Chief the region called on parents, guardians and teachers to appreciate the important role that this brave section of the populace will in the course of events.

MORE GHANAIANS HONOURED

A NUMBER of Ghanaians and non-Ghanaians have been given awards according to an Independence Day Honours — Awards 1968 published in Accra yesterday.

The award of the Member of the Order of Volta (MOV), went to Mr John K. Hadley, Inspector-General of Police and Vice-Chairman of the N.L.C.; Mr Justice Edward Akufo-Addo, the Chief Justice; Nana Sir Chief Agyeman Prempeh II, Asantehene; and Nene Azu Mate-Kole, Konor of Manya Krobo.

The Distinguished Service Order (D.S.O) — police distinction award was given to Mr A. K. Deku, Commissioner of Police (C.I.D.), and Mr E. F. O. Nunoo, Acting Deputy of Police

bers of the N.L.C.

Sixty-eight people including two army and three police officers were awarded the Grand Medal. The army officers are Lt.-Col. Robert J. G. Doglah and Lt.-Col. Victor Coker Appiah.

The police officers are Mr B. A. Yakubu, Deputy Commissioner of Police and member of the N.L.C.; Mr John Henry Cobbina, Deputy Commissioner of Police, and Mr Charles Kwashie Mawuenyegah, director of the Special Branch. The others who were

included Dr E. N. Omaboe, Commissioner for Economic Affairs; Dr A. A. Y. Kyeremanten, Commissioner for Local Government; Dr K. A. Busia, chairman of the National Advisory Committee, Professor Joseph H. Nketia, director of the Institute of African Studies, University of Ghana; and Mr Justice Nii Amaa Ollenu, an Appeal Court judge.

Others are Major Seth Kobla Anthony, Ghana's High Commissioner in the United Kingdom; Mr A. A. Afful, Deputy Auditor-General

◆ Contd on Pages 6 & 7 ◆ Contd on Back Page

zambia mail

Price 3n   Vol. 2 No. 175   TUESDAY, MAY 21, 1968

WE BACK BIAFRA

LUSAKA, Monday. — Zambia today became the fourth independent African country to recognise Biafra as a sovereign and independent state. The other countries are Tanzania, Gabon and the Ivory Coast.

Announcing the recognition, the Minister of Foreign Affairs, Mr Reuben Kamanga, said Zambia was convinced that "the heritage of bitterness stemming from the horrifying war" between Federal Nigeria and Biafra would make it impossible to create any basis for political unity.

He continued: "We hope that the establishment of this republic will now allow Nigeria and the people of Biafra to work out a better framework for co-operation."

Said Mr Kamanga: "Whereas it is our ardent desire to foster African unity, it would be morally wrong to force anybody into unity founded on blood and bloodshed. For unity to be meaningful and beneficial it must be based on the consent of all the parties concerned, offering security and justice to all.

He said that in Zambia's opinion, war would not induce surrender, but would only, as had already been seen, continue to widen the gap between the two combatants and increase fear among those who were victims of war.

'Tragedy'

The Foreign Minister continued: "The tragedy which has befallen the Federation of Nigeria is a most unwelcome event in this phase of Africa's development. The current war and the atrocious excesses committed in waging the war, the loss of human life and property, have shaken this continent and there are no prospects yet that Biafra can yield to what has almost become a war of attrition."

Zambia had been concerned about the future of that "area of Africa" and was still most concerned about peace, stability and unity among the "peoples of that area", he said.

Late tonight, Nigeria announced that it had broken off diplomatic relations with Zambia. An announcement said the Nigerian High Commissioner would leave Zambia "on the first available plane".

80 DIE IN INDUSTRY

NDOLA, Monday. — About 80 workmen in industry lose their lives each year, and there are more than 10,000 claims from injured workmen presented to the Workmen's Compensation Board each year.

This was disclosed by the Minister of Labour, Mr Lewis Changufu, when he was opening the K200,000 building of the Board here today.

SIGN OF THE TIMES: Expatriates on the Copperbelt allegedly coined the slogan: LO ZAMBIA ENA KAWENA, LO MALI ENA KATINA (Zambia is yours, but the money is ours). Now, enterprising UNIP officials in Masala, Ndola, have changed the slogan to keep up with the changing times: ZAMBIA ENA KATINA, NALO MALI MANJE ENA KATINA (Zambia is ours, and now even the money is ours). This poster was displayed prominently at a party meeting last week. It refers to the Government's acquisition last month of 51 per cent controlling shares in 26 companies.

Botswana detains former P.I.

LUSAKA, Monday. — Botswana authorities have detained the chief representative in Zambia of the African National Congress of South Africa, Mr Tennyson Makiwane, the ANC office here confirmed today.

Mr Makiwane, who went to Botswana to attend the funeral of the late Botswana ambassador to the United States, Professor Z. K. Matthews, is believed to have been arrested on Thursday, May 16.

The Botswana High Commission in Lusaka confirmed the arrest and detention of Mr Makiwane, who was at one time a prohibited immigrant to that country and is a wanted man in South Africa.

A spokesman at the High Commission said a full report on the detention was being awaited from Gaberones, the Botswana capital. The spokesman said that Botswana had a policy under which "certain people are not allowed to re-enter the country".

Informed sources, however, said Mr Makiwane, who is one of the top executives of the ANC, had been granted permission to enter Botswana to attend Professor Matthews' funeral.

Meanwhile, President Kaunda, accompanied by two Zambian Ministers, will leave for Botswana tomorrow to begin a four-day State visit. The Ministers are Mr Reuben Kamanga (Foreign Affairs) and Mr Munukayumbwa Sipalo (Agriculture).

Botswana supplies Zambia with beef and Mr Sipalo is expected to hold talks with his Botswana counterpart on this vital subject during the visit. The two countries established diplomatic relations last year but the Zambian High Commissioner to Botswana, Mr Josphat Siyomunji, took up his post in Gaberones early this month.

Last year, President Seretse Khama of Botswana paid a state visit to Zambia.

[column]

KITWE, Monday. — Damage to council houses in the high density townships has this year increased at an alarming rate, Councillor Raphael Mwale, the deputy mayor told residents in Buchi Hall here on Sunday.

Mr Mwale and other councillors were addressing residents on the matter which resulted from political clashes.

The city council was now increasing the penalty for breaking a window pane from 25n to 50n as a further deterrent, Mr Mwale added.

Thirty-four houses had had window panes smashed during the UNIP-UP clashes in Chimwemwe township alone. More houses had been stoned in Kwacha, Kamitondo and Buchi townships.

Lashers strike ends

KITWE, Monday. — The strike by about 300 lashers at Rhokana Mine's South Ore Body and Central Shaft ended abruptly today. An Anglo-American Corporation spokesman said there had been a 100 per cent return to work this evening.

The strikers are believed to have returned on their own following the sudden disappearance of the pickets at the two shafts. Earlier, there had been persistent reports of lashers wanting to go back to work but fearing to do so because of the pickets.

Some observers who thought the "accumulated" appeals of their union leaders and the Minister of State for the Western Province, Mr Peter Chanda, had influenced the men to return to work without any preconditions.

The strike started last week over lashers' complaints that they were working at their jobs too long before being transferred to other better-paying departments. The Mineworkers' Union of Zambia did not support the strike.

Yesterday, MUZ president, Mr David Mwila held a meeting with the strikers after his return on Saturday from overseas. Mr Mwila also held talks with the general-secretary of the Zambia Congress of Trade Unions, Mr Wilson Chakulya, who had condemned the strike as illegal.

Kapwepwe visit

KITWE, Monday. — Vice-President Kapwepwe will tour Nkana and Nchanga Anglo-American mines on Thursday this week, a spokesman for Rhokana Corporation said.

On the same day, Mr John Mwanakatwe, Minister for Mines, will visit the welfare centres, hospital and Wusakili township here.

PAC OFFICE CLOSED

LUSAKA, Monday. — The office of the Pan Africanist Congress of South Africa at the Africa Liberation Centre here was closed down "indefinitely" today following an alleged attack on Mr Leslie Masimini, former chief representative in Zambia, by four other PAC men.

The closure was ordered by President Kaunda's personal representative at the centre, Mr Mukuka Nkoloso, who said the PAC had only themselves to blame for the action he had taken.

"Zambia," he told a Press conference at the centre, "should not be taken as being weak for according hospitality to foreign nationals' movements." He said he had warned the party on May 14 that "any further trouble of a factional nature would be uncalled for and unpatriotic".

Mr Nkoloso warned that he would take similar "stringent" measures against parties which are abusing Zambia's hospitality."

Mr Masimini, who represented his party in Zambia since 1964, was recently transferred to Algeria but remained in Zambia even after his replacement had arrived in Lusaka from Cairo.

The attack on him was alleged to have taken place at the centre. It was believed to be the second fight this year involving PAC members.

Often they are read aloud to illiterates on the streets or in public establishments.

It is difficult to determine how many persons read each copy of a newspaper. Readership varies, but is probably more than 2.5 persons estimated to read each copy of a daily newspaper in America. A study conducted by the Kenya Information Department in 1958 indicated that 5 to 6 persons read each copy of a vernacular newspaper.[17]

A market survey in French West Africa by Parisian advertisers found that a single copy of a newspaper was often read to a hundred illiterates and that the African public was regularly informed as to the news in the local press.[18] This estimate certainly seems high. Illiteracy, of course, restricts the potential number of readers for dailies, but according to one USIA study, this is not the whole story. It was found that those reached by newspapers, magazines, and books are most likely to be in positions of influence in their communities, and who thus can effectively channel the content and messages of the news media to the illiterates.[19] Much depends on how well newspaper readers are linked to interpersonal channels.

TELEVISION

Television, that newest and most versatile medium of mass communications (it has been called the "complete medium"), burst over postindependence Africa like a skyrocket, and like a skyrocket is already leveling off if not coming down. Unlike radio and press, television in Africa is almost entirely a product of the years since political independence; in some places television is regarded as a national status symbol comparable to an airline or a presidential palace.

A regular television service was established in Morocco in 1954 (for just two years), and in the Western Region of Nigeria in 1959, but the rest of the continent remained almost untouched until 1962. Then a number of new nations hurriedly established transmitting facilities, usually at great cost. Some 23 nations were soon transmitting to an estimated 428,000 receivers plus another 422,000 sets if the UAR was included. The biggest increases in the purchases of TV sets came in 1962–63 and the number of sets has not increased markedly since. Africa's total number of television sets accounted for less than half of 1 percent of all sets outside the United States and Canada. (See Table 5 in the Appendix.)

So far, television has proved to be an expensive and ineffective medium. The Sierra Leone Television Service, for example, was established in April 1963. Scottish Television was the original contractor but it was later operated by Thomson Television International. Cost of the studio and transmitter buildings, including equipment and staff expenses for the first year, came to about £150,000. Yet the transmitter at Aberdeen Hill covered only the city of Freetown (population 130,000) and an area with a radius of fifteen miles. The number of sets in use seven years later was optimistically estimated at only 1,500. Thus the *installation* of television broadcasting, not counting the cost of individual receivers, was about £1,000 or $2,800 for each television set.

Television in Africa was affected by a special set of circumstances, which the current slowdown in the medium's growth reflects. Foremost was the high initial price of receiving sets plus expensive maintenance costs and the necessity of electricity as a power source. (A low-cost, dependable transistor television receiver is not yet available.)

As recently as 1965 receivers in use were still quite low, particularly for the following countries: Congo (Kinshasa), 500; Gabon, 400; and Upper Volta, 100.[20] (How many are in working order at any given time is impossible to determine.) Among Kenya's 9,900 sets that year, less than 500 were reported to me as being in the hands of Africans; the others were all owned by Europeans and Asians.

The expense and complexity of producing programs further impede television growth. This is reflected in the hours-per-week of TV programming in 1965: Congo (Kinshasa) was on the air 10½ hours a week; Gabon, 10; Malagasy Republic, 15; Niger, 8.[21]

Television seems to be having a particularly difficult time getting underway in francophonic Africa. The experience of the Republic of the Congo (Brazzaville) has been typical. There, television was on the air 16 hours a week, but after a year of operation, only some 400 sets were in use, and the National Assembly recommended the abolition of television.[22]

Because of the desperate shortage of trained personnel to produce television programs, many African systems relied heavily on "canned" programming produced in the United States, France, and Britain.

Local television news programs, particularly, were few in number, unprofessionally produced, and lacking in substance. In African countries with both radio and television, the news was more effectively presented on radio. Foreign news film was often supplied by Visnews, an organization partly owned by BBC and Reuters. An African television station, typically on the air for four or five hours a night, included only about thirty minutes of news, with possibly some of it local news film. Unfortunately, most of the rest of the other time was filled with imported syndicated series such as "The Lucy Show," "Bewitched," "Perry Mason," "Bonanza," "The Nurses," "The Saint," etc., ad nauseum. At one time the most popular show on Nigerian television was "Wrestling from Chicago." Until Africans can produce the bulk of their own programming, including news and public affairs shows, the promise of television will remain unfulfilled.

In 1968, of the countries I visited, only South Africa and Senegal had yet no television. South Africa was moving into closed-circuit television for educational and special purposes and may soon have general television. Senegal has sensibly been conducting a five-year pilot television project to test its local feasibility.

In the countries where television has arrived, however, it has proved a costly and frustrating medium. African nations lack the economic base to support television as a *mass* medium. An overwhelming majority of Africans are not in any position to become television viewers, and broadcasters lack the capability and resources to provide meaningful and relevant programming. What development of television there has been has resulted from foreign technical assistance (BBC, NBC, Scottish television, France's OCORA, and others have set up the transmission systems) and from large injections of government funds which the African economies can ill afford. Consequently, television in Africa was just limping along and was viewed by a comparative handful of people, often mostly Europeans and Asians who lived within a few miles of the transmitter.

Although some argue that the money spent on television would have been better invested in extending radio broadcasting, few would deny the long-range potential of television in mass education, public information, entertainment, and as an aid to government efforts to speed national integration. Thus far, however, African television has taken only a few halting steps toward realizing its possibilities.

CINEMA

Movies are widely accepted in African urban life, and surveys by the U.S. Information Agency found that a majority in many African cities attended at least once a month, including a considerable number of persons who were illiterate.[23] Black Africa has no commercial production of feature-length films and remains dependent on imports from America, West Europe, UAR, India, and the Communist nations. The United Arab Republic produces about 60 to 70 films a year, mostly for Arabic-speaking countries.

As with television, the problem of developing the cinema as a mass medium is twofold: the need for local film production and for adequate viewing facilities. So far no nation has been able to overcome this double hurdle.

Newsreel and informational films, however, are produced by government agencies in Angola, Dahomey, Ghana, Mauritius, Morocco, Mozambique, Nigeria, Senegal, Sudan, Tunisia, Uganda, and South Africa, and in other countries on an irregular basis. But the main newsreel suppliers are France and the United Kingdom.[24]

The range of cinema-viewing facilities is wide but most of them are necessarily located in the cities. The increasing use of mobile cinema vans is bringing the motion picture to more and more Africans in the bush. But for the present, the cinema is far from achieving its potential in Africa, especially as a medium of news and public information. (See Table 6 in the Appendix.)

EXTERNAL MEDIA

Any overview of news media must note the importance of both foreign media and the media content produced abroad but carried in local media.

Every African nation has a modern sector, however small it may be, and those who operate in this sector use news and information in much the same way as do their opposite numbers in industrialized countries. Because their own communication network is less developed, however, they pay relatively more attention to communications originating abroad.[25] The extent to which urban, educated minorities in Africa attend to news and information from foreign sources is impressive indeed.

Some of this media fare is commercial in origin; some is from foreign government sources and hence is political communication, that is, propaganda.

As mentioned, most motion pictures and television programs viewed by Africans are produced in the United States or Western

Europe. In addition to hearing *locally* broadcast (or relayed) programs from abroad, many Africans listen to news and entertainment directly from the BBC from London, the Voice of America (relayed from Monrovia, Liberia), Radio Moscow, Radio Cairo, Radio South Africa, and other foreign senders.

Throughout francophonic Africa, newspapers and magazines of France are widely read by *évolués*. *Le Monde, France-Soir, Figaro,* and other Parisian dailies are on the newsstands of Rabat, Dakar, and Abidjan within twenty-four hours of publication. A broad range of British newspapers and magazines has an extensive readership in East and West Africa. *West Africa,* an informed and intelligent journal of news and opinion, is published weekly in London and is read by the African elites. The overwhelming majority of the books sold in African bookstores are published abroad. The *International Herald-Tribune,* printed in Paris, is widely available in Africa, as are *Time, Newsweek,* and *Life.*

Another genre of influential publications is the handful of intellectual magazines published both in Europe and Africa. The best examples are *Afrique Nouvelle* (Dakar), *Transition* (Kampala), *Jeune Afrique* (formerly published in Tunis but more recently in Paris), and the *Legon Observer* (Accra). Place of publication, however, is not especially important, for the bulk of readership is usually in other African countries or in Europe and the United States. Aimed directly at the intellectual elites, these publications have a disproportionately great influence because the intellectual class represents a large segment of the "effective" new Africans—those able to read, buy things, and in a position to influence events. The quality of writing, the seriousness and controversial nature of the content, and general overall editorial excellence of these magazines are well above that of the more provincial daily and weekly news publications.

This flood of foreign media fare is extremely significant. In one sense it denotes the new African nations' increasing enmeshment in the international network of mass communications, as part and parcel of their involvement in the modern world. In another sense it may be another indication of the lingering "neo-colonialist" relationship between African and Western nations as well as proof of the inadequacy of their own media.

Significantly, most of the content of radio, newspapers, television, and movies in Africa is disseminated in the languages of the colonizers—French, English, and Portuguese. (North Africa, where Arabic is most widely used, is a partial exception, but

French is still important there.) This is in part due to the be-wildering variety of African languages and the fact that in few nations below the Sahara is one African language spoken by a clear majority of the people. European influences are crucial; the media were originally in European languages and educated Africans usually have been taught in French or English. The broadcasting systems provide programs in the principal vernacu-lars (Swahili is widely broadcast in Kenya and Tanzania), but rely on French or English for the bulk of their programming. This is especially true in francophonic Africa.

Furthermore, the barrier between French and English speak-ers in tropical Africa is a much greater one than in Western Europe. Comparatively few Africans speak or read both lan-guages. After all, a European language is the second and often the third language an African learns. The French-English split among educated Africans also has become a formidable cultural barrier. Francophonic Africa looks to Paris or Brussels, anglo-phonic Africa to London or the United States, and from these places come much of the media fare—newspapers, international radio, movies, magazines, books, and television programs. Any European language provides a window to the outside world, but a particular language determines the direction that window faces and the nature of much of what is perceived.

There is, consequently, little contact between anglophonic and francophonic journalists. The International Press Institute made a pioneer effort to overcome this barrier by holding a bi-lingual regional meeting in Dakar, Senegal, in April 1968, for French- and English-speaking journalists to discuss common pro-fessional problems. Yet when the IPI held its first Assembly in Africa at Nairobi in June 1968, only one francophonic African editor was in attendance—Gabriel Makosso of *Le Courrier d'Afrique* of Kinshasa—and he was an invited participant.

The news media's reliance on non-African languages is not surprising since most of the modern sector of African life is con-ducted in European languages. This becomes readily apparent to the foreign correspondent. Russell Warren Howe, who has re-ported Africa for the Washington *Post* and the Baltimore *Sun,* wrote:

> Effective reporting in Africa requires knowledge of London and Paris—and naturally bilingualism—because most leading Af-ricans, especially in the mandarin class, are culturally provincial

Britons or provincial Frenchmen. Knowledge of Portuguese and even Afrikaans would be serviceable, but there is perhaps, after all, little point today in learning ki-Swahili, and even less in learning the less well-spoken indigenous tongues. It is rare indeed that a correspondent has to question someone who does not speak a European language.[26]

One indigenous language used officially in black Africa is Swahili, adopted by Tanzania where English is still widely used. The Swahili papers of East Africa are the most effective of any vernacular papers published in the sub-Sahara.

Hilary Ng'weno, former editor of Nairobi's *Daily Nation* and its Swahili counterpart, *Taifa Leo,* said that because of the prestige in knowing a European language, a Swahili reader will switch to the English-language press in East Africa as soon as he is able. The Swahili press, Ng'weno said, acts as a stepping stone for new literates.[27]

Future government policy on media language usage, and more important, languages used in education will determine whether this reliance on French and English will continue. This is an extremely important question because of its implications for the future cultural and social development of Africa. European languages *do* accentuate the cleavages between the elites and the masses as well as between the city and the rural areas.

The heavy reliance by educated Africans on mass communications content of the nation from which their education originated can, in some cases, mean a kind of psychological dependence on foreign news media.

Leonard Doob cited an example of the prestige importance of European media:

Africans struggling to learn European ways of behaving bestow upon Western media special symbolic value. The present writer once spent a week traveling with a bright, ambitious African university student in an adjacent country. Each evening, he would insist on hearing the BBC summary of the news rebroadcast by a station in his home capital. We would interrupt a leisurely stroll by the sea along a magnificent promenade or, once, a reasonably important interview with an African informant, in order to return to our hotel rooms to hear that particular broadcast. Often as the signal would fade away from the transistor set, he would place his ear close to the speaker in order, presumably, to miss not a phrase. Through subtle and unsubtle questions the writer sought again and again to discover whether he retained any of the news. Not a trace of it was evident. He had not forgotten what he had heard, rather he had not really paid attention in the first place. He may have been attempting to impress the writer, but this possibility is not likely. To be in the presence of the sounds from the BBC at 7 p.m. was important to him.[28]

One survey showed foreign radio listening in four West African capitals to be quite widespread. In Accra and Lagos, about one out of every two persons listened to a foreign radio station (usually the BBC) at least once a month; in francophonic Abidjan and Dakar it was about one out of every three persons and they preferred the RTF from France.[29]

When attending to their own news media, it is likely that the foreign news an African gets will come by way of one of the world news agencies from Britain or France or to a much lesser extent, the United States or the Soviet Union.

The reliance on foreign media and on foreign-produced content in African news media points up the fact that so little about African mass media is as yet indigenously African. This creates a quandary for African leaders who quite naturally wish to see their nations evolve an African style of life and culture and not be mere imitations of the departed colonial rulers. But much of this reliance on foreign media will undoubtedly continue; certain basic similarities in mass media persist all over the world.

On the other hand, those African nations with the most sophisticated *indigenous* media content are also the ones least dependent on European content. Nigeria and Ghana, two of the nations with the longest contact with Europe, have a style and verve in their newspapers, radio, and television that can only be described as West African. Such is not the case in francophonic Africa, where the French influence is much more pervasive, or in East and Central Africa, where European settlers have long set the style and tone of mass communications. The new African governments have been moving to alter this situation.

3

||||||||||||||||||||||||||||||||||||||||||||||||||||||||||||||||||||||||

GOVERNMENT INVOLVEMENT
IN NEWS MEDIA

WHEN KENYA'S PRESIDENT Jomo Kenyatta addressed the 17th
Assembly of the International Press Institute meeting at the
Nairobi City Hall in June 1968, he told the gathered editors and
publishers: "I hope you will take up the question of ownership
of the press. That is a very central problem here in Africa."

And so it is. The question of who will own and control
Africa's newspapers, magazines, radio and television stations, and
news agencies is still unresolved and most urgent, for control
of the news media determines the content of the news media.

Under colonial rule the media were either owned by European interests or subjected to harsh, arbitrary controls by colonial
administrators. Africans deeply resented the European or settler
newspapers' lack of enthusiasm or outright opposition to African
aspirations for independence. They were angered when indigenous vernacular papers were summarily suppressed as, for example, were some forty Kikuyu and Swahili newssheets in Kenya
during the Mau Mau Emergency.

Once independence was achieved during the early sixties,
pressure grew for Africanization of the news media. Questions
were quickly raised about ownership and control: Should new
African nations permit European ownership of their media to
continue after political independence? What should be the response of a new African government to a media system so thoroughly infused with "European" influences and content?

In the first decade after independence, the response was clear.
The new African governments themselves assumed a large degree

of ownership and control of all news media. Patterns of control then established will affect the African news media for many decades to come.

Government involvement was evident in several trends of the 1960s:

- Decline of independent newspapers and a sharp increase in government and official newspapers;
- Expansion of Ministries of Information;
- Nationalization of radio and television broadcasting;
- Establishment of national news agencies.

Whether European-owned or African-owned, whether espousing the views of white settlers or of African political parties, there are in 1970 fewer independent or nongovernmental papers in Africa than at the time of independence. The reasons are numerous: the consolidating tendencies of one-party political rule with its suspicion of dissent or even of divergent views; the the Africans' mistrust of foreign media ownership; and the lack of economic opportunity. All have contributed to the attrition of and to a marked instability in the newspaper press.

Scarcely any new independent daily newspapers have been successfully launched in black Africa since 1960, and there have been few efforts to do so.[1] (Two exceptions are *L'Étoile du Congo* and *Le Progrès,* both in Kinshasa.) Two of the London *Daily Mirror* group's three papers in West Africa, the *Daily Mail* of Freetown and the *Daily Graphic* of Accra, were sold to the governments of Sierra Leone and Ghana; only the *Daily Times* in Nigeria remained privately owned.

Lord Thomson of Fleet, the British press tycoon, closed down his lively *Daily* and *Sunday Express* in Nigeria in late 1965; it was gaining circulation while losing money at the rate of £50,000 a year.[2] At about the same time, the *East African Standard* group discontinued its 50-year-old *Mombasa Times* in Kenya.

Francophonic Africa never has had much of an independent press, and the influential de Breteuil family newspaper chain has dropped from the five dailies once produced in Senegal, Guinea, Morocco, the Ivory Coast, and Cameroon to just two: *Dakar-Matin* in Senegal and *La Presse du Cameroun. (Dakar-Matin* ceased publication in 1970 and was replaced by *Le Soleil du Sénégal,* a new national daily with the government as the principal shareholder.)

Particularly hard hit by the events since independence are the few independent newspapers, supported neither by foreign interests nor by African governments. Lacking both government subsidies and foreign capital, these papers cannot operate long while losing money, hence are weak and vulnerable. The most famous of this genre—the *West African Pilot* of Nigeria and the *Pioneer* of Ghana (the latter was revived in 1966 after being suppressed by Nkrumah in 1962)—are just barely hanging on. Both papers badly need generous infusions of capital for new printing equipment and to expand the staff.

Many small, irregular publications, once mouthpieces of political factions, have disappeared along with African political opposition.

The European-owned newspapers that remained in Africa tended to be newspapers without viewpoints and often without even editorials. These papers reflected a strong desire to get along with the government and to survive. Typical, in varying degrees, were *La Vigie* and *Le Petit Marocain* (two remnants of the once powerful Mas group) in Morocco, *Daily Times* of Nigeria, *East African Standard* of Kenya, the *Uganda Argus,* and the *Times of Zambia.*

GOVERNMENT NEWSPAPERS

As noted above, many new African governments became newspaper publishers. The proliferation of these government papers has been the most significant trend in African print journalism in the last ten years.

In Nigeria, the federal government established its own newspaper—*Morning Post* and *Sunday Post* in Lagos—and each of the regional governments did likewise: the *Daily Sketch* in the Western Region; the *New Nigerian* in the North; and in the East the *Nigerian Outlook,* which became the *Biafran Sun* during the secession and civil war. In Abidjan, the Ivoirien government's new paper, *Fraternité Matin,* replaced de Breteuil's ailing *Abidjan-Matin.* With technical help from the East Germans and a Ghanaian editor, the *Nationalist* was launched as a TANU party organ in Tanzania (in a one-party state, a party paper is in effect a government organ), and in February 1970, Tanzania nationalized the *Daily Standard* and *Sunday News.* The Zambian government took over the *Central African Mail* and made it the *Zambia Mail.* In Sierra Leone and Ghana the government purchased the most prosperous independent dailies. So far, Senegal and Kenya have resisted suggestions to start official papers, perhaps because they observed the difficulties that government newspapers have encountered.

Like newspapers anywhere, these government publications can lose money quickly; also they have shown they can embarrass their governments, as occasionally the *Nationalist* has done with its clumsy bogus stories charging foreign nations with intrigue in Tanzania.

An important question, of course, is whether government papers can provide the kind of objective information and comment that the African peoples and their governments need. When they do, they sometimes get into trouble with their employers as happened in Ghana in December 1967, when four editors on the three government dailies were summarily dismissed after criticizing a government contract with an American drug manufacturer. Although every newspaperman must deplore the silencing of criticism in such a manner, the Ghana example highlights a serious dilemma for the press in developing nations: At what point does honest, well-meaning press criticism become destructive of the processes of orderly national development?

But unquestionably, government papers are doing an important job of providing news and information of a sort unavailable before. They tell the government's story—explain government policies, publicize leaders, and contribute to the much-needed realization of "nation-ness."

This may very well be the most important role for journalism to play today in some of the developing countries—to use the printed and spoken word to espouse unity and national purpose. News broadcasts on Radio Zambia, for example, almost always start off with the words, "President Kaunda today . . . ," no matter what else is happening on the continent, in the world, or even in Zambia itself. Some may scoff at such an approach to news, but is it not extremely important for the diverse peoples of Zambia, who speak over thirty different languages, to know what *their* President and *their* government are doing?

The new African governments have generally recognized the need to use all the news media to reach their far-flung and disparate peoples and to speed national integration. The responsibility for implementing this process usually has been placed in the ministries of information, which have been greatly enlarged since independence.

Each new African government inherited from its colonial predecessors some kind of government department of information which published pamphlets, produced and exhibited films, and provided various kinds of information activities, including the collection and dissemination of news. The postindependence trend has been toward expansion and increasing bureaucratization of such activities under direct government control.

Practically all government newspapers are directly or indirectly responsible to a minister of information. The broadcast media are uniformly a function of the ministry of information. One survey found that forty-four broadcast transmitting systems in Africa are government operated, seven involve both government and commercial operation and only three such systems are predominantly commercial. Nineteen African countries have government-operated television systems, and two accept advertising and rely in part on such revenue. Two countries have government-operated television together with commercial operations, and one country (Mauritius) has a commercially operated system.[3]

Such government control assures an official stamp of approval on all news and public information carried on radio and television. In some places virtually all significant news communication is directly or indirectly controlled by the information ministry. Further, it means that in some countries, almost all journalists are government employees.

A minister of information in a contemporary African government is a person of influence and power. Not only are radio and television and the new government newspapers usually under his direction, but the new national news agency as well.

NATIONAL NEWS AGENCIES

Since independence the majority of African nations have started national news agencies to supplement and in part to counteract the influence of the world agencies. Government participation in such operations varied from outright control to government assistance to a commercially operated agency.[4]

Until the mid-1950s the only national agency in Africa was the nongovernmental South African Press Association (SAPA), originated in 1938 to supply domestic and foreign news to the press of South Africa, the Rhodesias, and the Portuguese territories.[5]

The first government-controlled or "official" African news service was the Middle East News Agency (MENA), started in Cairo in 1956, followed by the Ghana News Agency (GNA) in 1957, the year of Ghana's independence.

By 1969 there were more than twenty-seven official and semiofficial African news services in operation. In alphabetical order, they were Agence Camerounaise de Presse (ACAP) of Cameroon; Agence Congolaise d'Information (ACI) of Congo (Brazzaville); Agence Congolaise de Presse (ACP) of Congo (Kinshasa); Agence Dahoméene de Presse (ADP) of Dahomey; Agence Gabonaise d'Information (AGI) of Gabon; Agence Guinéene de Presse (AGP) of Guinea; Agence Ivoirenné de Presse (AIP) of Ivory Coast; Agence Malgache de Presse (AMP) of Malagasy Republic; Agence Nationale d'Information Malienne (ANIM) of Mali; Agence de Presse Sénégalaise (APS) of Senegal; Algérie Presse Service (APS) of Algeria; Agence de Presse Voltaique (APV) of Upper Volta; Agence Tchadienne de Presse (ATP) of Chad; Ethiopian National News Agency (ENNA) of Ethiopia; Ghana News Agency (GNA) of Ghana; Kenya News Agency (KNA) of Kenya; Liberian Information Service of Liberia; Libyan News Agency (LNA) of Libya; Maghreb Arabe Presse (MAP) of Morocco; Malawi Information Service of Malawi; Somali National News Agency of Somali Republic; Tunis-Afrique Presse (TAP) of Tunisia; and Zambia News Agency (ZANA) of Zambia. In addition, the U.S. Information Agency listed the following "independent" African news services: African News Service (ANS) of Sudan; East African News Agency (EANA) of Kenya; Kenya News Bureau of Kenya; South African Press Association (SAPA) of South Africa; Sudan News Agency (SNA) of Sudan; and the West African News Service (WANS) of Nigeria.[6]

About a dozen or more nations, including Nigeria and Tanzania, were without national news agencies, but most had blueprints for developing one.

In Nigeria before the Civil War, plans for a national news agency or at least a cooperative agency had been in the works since 1961. With its larger number of private media, a firmer tradition of free expression, and the (prewar) political balancing between regions, the Nigerian press had been leery of a national news agency. The stumbling-block question was, Who would control it? In 1968, however, the Nigerian government was moving toward establishment of a national news agency centrally controlled by the federal government in Lagos.[7]

The government or official agencies vary greatly in size, competence, and scope of operations. They range from the professional and effective Ghana News Agency to the inept and under-manned Agence de Presse Sénégalaise. The oldest African-controlled agency, Middle East News Agency, is also in many ways the most atypical. It was brought under government control in 1961, five years after it was established with headquarters in Cairo. Unlike the others, MENA maintained foreign bureaus or at least correspondents in all Arab nations. Although its main operations have been in the Middle East, it expanded into black Africa and has had correspondents or stringers in Accra, Dakar, Lagos, Addis Ababa, Nairobi, Khartoum, and Mogadiscio, as well as the Maghreb.[8]

However, most government news agencies were underfinanced and understaffed, with seldom more than six men.

Generally, their main contribution to the flow of news in and out of their country was to receive and to redistribute the news reports from the world news agencies, principally Agence France Presse and Reuters. In several nations a national news agency became a censor, a convenient mechanism for controlling all news coming in from abroad. The Kenya News Agency, while under the control of the now-deposed Achieng Oneko, effectively controlled and even censored news coming into Kenya. After his departure, the situation changed. Ideally, news services should be independent of government, as is the South African Press Association (SAPA), a cooperative agency owned by the English and Afrikaans newspapers. However, no other African nation has reached the economic level at which an agency such as SAPA is feasible.

In their formative years few national agencies had developed the facilities to gather much news within their own country (Ghana's GNA was a notable exception) and almost none had any correspondents of their own stationed abroad. For dissemination of their own news abroad, the majority depended on the world news agencies. A few, however, sent their news to other countries over shortwave transmitters. Among these were the Middle East News Agency, Algérie Presse Service, Tunis-Afrique Presse, Maghreb Arabe Presse, and Ghana News Agency.

Yet the national news agencies, when properly manned and equipped, are proving they can perform a useful news communication function, even if they remain under tight political control. They are significant, too, because they are indicative of the increased government involvement in news communication. Further, they represent the Africans' efforts to control and to influence the nature of the news flow within and without Africa and thus begin to end the dependence on foreign news media. They do help promote the diffusion of information and news in places where none existed before.

Unfortunately, so far the inevitable result is that each African government has become a gatekeeper and potential censor controlling the flow of news in and out of its territory.

It must be emphasized, too, that national news agencies are instruments for international political communication. A one-party African government regards it as one more means of consolidating its position at home and supporting its foreign policy abroad. European nations and their news agencies, in their efforts to maintain or win influence with the new African governments, compete with each other to help develop national news agencies. Such activities by AFP, Reuters, TASS, and CTK (the Czech agency) are one more manifestation of the East-West struggle in Africa.

Reuters helped to organize the Ghana News Agency in 1957 and trained Ghanaian journalists in wire-service operations. Reuters prepared national news agency blueprints for other countries, particularly Nigeria, Malawi, Libya, Uganda, Tanzania, and Ethiopia.

In francophonic Africa the national news agencies have been developed largely by Agence France Presse as an extension of its semiofficial position within the French colonial governments.

Of the eleven national news agencies in former French Africa, all but two, Guinea and Mali, were started by AFP. (Guinea's agency was assisted by TASS and Mali's by CTK.) AFP trained the African journalists, provided advisers, and sold the governments their own local offices and equipment. In effect, the local AFP bureau became the national news agency. AFP correspondents then moved into new quarters. In several places the AFP influence remained so pervasive that it was said the AFP was indeed the national news agency. The new agencies distributed the AFP reports and most had a contract with a clause binding the African agency "to distribute automatically and immediately, without omission or modification, the radio-teletype service received from AFP."[9]

Although most of the francophonic agencies also receive other wire services such as Reuters and UPI, the priority still seems to go to AFP.

Western news agency people have been rather dubious of the value and effectiveness of some national agencies. Stan Swinton, an executive of Associated Press, said: "The national agencies are just about useless for news-gathering. Eighty percent of them are just on paper and are actually part of the government's ministry of information. The African agencies will not take from other national agencies."[10]

But the shortcomings of most national news agencies reflect only one of the basic communication problems: little news or solid information flows from the capital to the rural areas and even less flows back to the capital. So far, national agencies have been unable to increase the flow to any significant extent. Most national news agencies, then, do serve an important function, but have not begun to live up to their potential usefulness as a part of a nation's news communications system. They just barely supplement the world agencies which still do the primary job of moving news in and out of the capitals.

THEORIES OF MEDIA CONTROL

During this period of increased government involvement there has been a search for a guiding ideological and theoretical framework to answer the needs of the African situation.

In postindependence Africa at least three kinds of ideological approaches—"revolutionary" or neo-communist, authoritarian, and libertarian—have been used to rationalize the role of mass communication.

Under the neo-communist ideology, all instruments of mass communications are brought under direct government control and ownership so they may best serve government policy in a "revolutionary" sense. Kwame Nkrumah, former president of Ghana, was an exponent of this approach, which he expounded to the Second Conference of African Journalists in Accra in November 1963:

> The truly African revolutionary Press does not exist merely for the purpose of enriching its proprietors or entertaining its readers. It is an integral part of our society, with which its purposes are in consonance. Just as in the capitalist countries, the Press represents and carries out the purposes of capitalism, so in revolutionary Africa our revolutionary African Press must present and carry forward our revolutionary purpose; this is to establish a progressive political and economic system upon our continent that will free men from want and every form of injustice, enable them to work out their social and cultural destinies in peace and ease.[11]

Most new African leaders prized newspapers, radio, cinema, and television for their "instrumental" value in furthering the aims of the nation-building and modernization as well as for supporting the government itself. News media were not perceived to be primarily independent sources of public information and objective critics of government activities. They were to be instruments of the government—or more to the point, of the political leadership.

However, only a few leaders, such as Nkrumah, have placed this approach to mass communication in an ideological context. Opening the new headquarters of the Ghana News Agency in the fall of 1965, Nkrumah reflected on the "role of the journalist in Ghana and Africa." The duties he laid down included helping to defeat imperialism and neo-colonialism and "hailing those who advance the revolution and exposing those who retard it." He went on, "We do not believe there are necessarily two sides to every question: we see right and wrong, just and unjust, progressive and reactionary, positive and negative, friend and foe. We are partisan."[12] Other African leaders, some of whom sharply disagreed with Nkrumah's political views, have followed his approach to communications in practice. Algeria, Guinea, Mali, and the UAR have all pursued much the same course, the same approach to mass media. The media must serve government, which is inseparable from the party and its leader. The press should inform and work for national integration and inspire the people, but not criticize the government or the leadership.

Although this rationale was known as a neo-communist approach, it would be a serious error to conclude that such media systems were controlled by Communists as such, which they were not; it was just that the purposes and uses of the news media were similar to those of Communist nations. (In Africa it was significant that there were no Communist governments.)

In practice, often little difference existed between the way ideologically different media systems did in fact operate. For example, about the only difference in the media in "radical" Ghana under Nkrumah and "conservative" Ivory Coast under Houphouët-Boigny was that the former had an ideology and the latter did not.

The libertarian approach argues that the press must be independent of government in order to be a critic and commentator on government, able to supply the people unbiased and objective information about their nation and the world. This "free press" approach has a very tenuous hold in Africa because freedom of the press needs a multiparty parliamentary government, protection of law, and a firm basis in private enterprise to flourish. When there is no legitimate opposition there is no free press. The best examples of a libertarian press in Africa have been the ebullient and iconoclastic newspapers of Nigeria before 1965 and the stubbornly critical English-language newspapers of South Africa. Tragically, press freedom has declined in both nations. Yet throughout Africa many leaders and journalists understand and value a free press. Kelvin Mlenga, former editor of the *Zambia Mail*, answered the Nkrumah argument when he said: "It is my view that a newspaper owned and run by the State for the sole purpose of spreading government propaganda is valueless. A newspaper must have freedom to disagree—sometimes quite violently—with government policy. . . . If a government wants to keep its finger on the pulse of public opinion, it is vital that there should be a free press in the country; for it is only in such a press that the true feelings of the public can be portrayed."[13]

A fine journalistic philosophy, but it has proved difficult to practice in Africa, for freedom of the press requires some privately owned or at least publicly owned media (the BBC is a good example) that are protected by law and independent of official coercion. Such news media are scarce today, but the ideals of a libertarian approach are kept alive by a few journalists, lawyers, and other public-spirited Africans imbued with the tenets of freedom and democracy.

For the present, authoritarian is a better term to describe the controls on most news media. These controls are often more implied than applied and are seldom if ever totalitarian. But they are real. The nongovernment newspapers are usually permitted wide latitude to report the news, provide entertainment, and pass along government information, as long as they do not directly challenge the government or its leadership. Some news media carry a good deal of news and even low-level criticism of public officials. Yet always lurking behind the newsman is the potential restraint of government; the newspapers usually know how far they can go.

Under this approach, of which the news media in Senegal, Kenya, Morocco, and Zambia are good examples, there was an effort to establish a modus vivendi with the European interests still heavily involved in mass communications. Editors may be warned and sometimes editions are suppressed, but seldom are newspapers closed down and journalists jailed. As the news media grow in both quality and self-sufficiency, the occasional imposition of authoritarian restraints will probably decrease in frequency.

What happens to news during a political crisis illustrates the disadvantages of authoritarian controls most clearly. When a government in Africa comes under great stress, it almost always cuts off and suppresses the flow of news, yet this is a time when the public is most in need of information. During the several crises preceding the Nigerian civil war, the admirable Radio Nigeria either went silent or ignored the news that people were discussing. During an attempted coup d'état, *Dakar-Matin,* Senegal's only daily newspaper, just ceased publication for several days until it saw which way events were moving. In Morocco during the Casablanca riots in 1965, the government forbade any news of the event to be carried in the country's news media; rumor and word-of-mouth communication took over. When a coup was attempted in the Ivory Coast in 1963, the foreign news service correspondents were prohibited from sending out any dispatches about the abortive plot even though the details were common knowledge around Abidjan. The news was, in fact, carried out to Dakar by air travelers.

FREEDOM OF THE PRESS

All over the world the press functions under some degree of government control. Politicians everywhere are too appreciative of the power and influence of mass communications to allow them to speak or print in complete freedom. If we define freedom of the press as the right to fully report and criticize the conduct of government without fear of official recriminations, then there is precious little of that kind of freedom anywhere in Africa.

The harsh conditions of life during the 1960s did not provide a favorable climate in which press freedom and independent journalism could flourish. There was little economic base for private ownership; political rights of free expression were not effectively protected by law; there was a general shortage of legitimate political oppositions. The right of free expression was not extended to many persons as in the pluralistic societies of Western Europe and the United States, but became of necessity a monopoly of governments which themselves were often inexperienced, insecure, and highly sensitive to criticism.

As Hilary Ng'weno, former editor of the *Nation* papers in Kenya, said:

> Under some of the conditions in which vast numbers of Africans, Asians, and Latin Americans live, it would be sacrilegious to talk about press freedom—for freedom loses meaning when human survival is the only operative principle on which a people lives. Such a state of affairs militates against the growth of newspapers. It militates against press freedom; it militates against the dignity of man and all the noble ideals for which the people living in ex-colonial countries fought so hard and for so long.[14]

Tom Hopkinson has described the situation well:

> Circumstances have involved the press of Africa in a conflict with the politicians at a time when the politicians themselves are facing a superhuman task. Criticism—in a large part of the continent—is equated with factious opposition: opposition with disloyalty: disloyalty, in some countries, with treason. . . . Over much of Africa today the freedom of the press is a highly unpopular cause and the press itself is regarded with suspicion. To the man in the African village, the abolition of press freedom—where it exists—would mean little or nothing.[15]

Government's sensitivity to criticism and the equating of criticism with subversion or even treason were the reasons for little real editorial comment in most African newspapers and periodicals. The problems for the press were further compounded because officials often failed to see the difference between criticism and legitimate news. Newspapers frequently generated official hostility merely by reporting something that had happened. Unsophisticated political leaders sometimes claimed that their government was being irresponsibly attacked or a problem created where none existed before if a newspaper reported, in a straightforward fashion, some news event such as a strike, a cabinet split, or even that on the opening day of school there were not enough places for all the new pupils. Politicians and government leaders need to be educated on the role of the press.

"TRANSITION" ON TRIAL

On the other hand freedom of the press was by no means a dying or dead concept. In fact, in 1969 two significant trials involved free-press issues. Both ended in partial—albeit Pyrrhic—

victories for the press: one involved editor Laurence Gandar and reporter Benjamin Pogrund of the *Rand Daily Mail* in South Africa (see Chapter 11 on South Africa for a review of this trial). In the other in Kampala, Uganda, the defendant was Rajat Neogy, the brilliant young editor of the widely acclaimed intellectual magazine, *Transition*.

On October 18, 1968, Neogy, a Uganda Asian, and Abu Mayanja, an opposition member of parliament, were arrested under emergency regulations. No reasons were given for the arrests; however the October issue of *Transition* had carried a letter from Mayanja commenting on the slow rate at which Ugandan judges were being appointed to the bench and implying that tribal considerations were the cause.

It was not until November 22 that Neogy and Mayanja were officially charged with publication with seditious intent. Both were released on bail by the magistrate and then both were immediately rearrested under emergency detention regulations. The trial itself opened on January 9, 1969.

On February 1, 1969, Neogy and Mayanja were both acquitted of the sedition charges. In a sweeping judgment the court upheld the independence of the judiciary as well as freedom of the press. The judge cited the defense of Tom Paine in 1792 that "every man . . . seeking to enlighten others with what his own conscience and reason, however erroneously have dictated to him as truth, may address himself to the universal reason of a whole nation." If criticism of the president or government were held to be seditious, this would contradict the constitutionally guaranteed freedom of expression, the Ugandan judge said.[16]

Despite their acquittal, the two prisoners were returned to Luzira prison under Uganda's detention laws. *Transition,* with a wide circulation and great influence, was without its editor and doomed, at least in Uganda. Neogy himself was released on March 27, 1969, and left Uganda. The court's decision may have a long-term effect on the uncertain new concept of press freedom in Africa. It was significant, certainly, that *Transition's* editor was tried in a court of law and not just arbitrarily jailed or deported as had happened with lesser known journalists all over the continent.

Perhaps it is irrelevant even to talk about freedom of the press in this context. The new African states have so little in common, economically and politically, with the handful of industrialized democracies of the West where press freedom does exist. Perhaps "freedom of the press" is a culture-bound concept of the West that does not travel very well—as yet—to Africa.

It is, in fact, surprising that as much diversity, freedom of expression, and criticism of government is permitted as there is. This is partly due to the influence and pervasiveness of foreign media—there are few "iron curtains" in Africa because no governments are really totalitarian. Widespread censorship and thought control require an efficiency still fortunately lacking in African governmental bureaucracies.

As Hopkinson wrote:

> Press freedom survives at all partly because, despite their quarrels with the press, many African leaders (Kenyatta and Kaunda are good examples) value the tradition of a free press, just as they value—often from personal experience—the independence of the law courts; having quite justifiably exploited press freedom on the way up, they have an honest hesitation about kicking the ladder away now that they are on top. Partly also because an independent press is known to be highly valued in the Western world, and it is to the Western world that the newly independent states look for most of the financial help and technical know-how they so desperately need.[17]

At the present state of development of many African nations, it is hard to argue against the thesis that the primary role of the news media is to act as an arm or instrument of official government policy. Freedom of expression and diversity of views may have to wait until there are adequate nongovernmental resources in the economy to support newspapers and outlets of expression as there are today in the industrialized nations of the North.

4

██

NEWS FLOW

THE BULK OF WORLD NEWS flows around the Northern Hemisphere on an East-West axis between the great news centers of New York, London, Paris, Moscow, and Tokyo. The nature and volume of world news is dominated by four great powers. It is no coincidence that the five world news agencies—Associated Press (AP), United Press International (UPI), Reuters, Agence France Presse (AFP), and TASS—have their home bases, respectively, in the United States (AP and UPI), Great Britain, France, and the Soviet Union. Most of their newspaper and broadcasting clients are in the United States or Europe and most of the news they transmit is of interest mainly to middle-class Americans or Europeans.

The developing nations of the Southern Hemisphere, especially those in Africa, are seriously disadvantaged by this prevailing pattern of world news flow. They want to participate fully in the modern world, and this requires an adequate exchange of news and information available at present only through a news-flow pattern that is essentially a legacy of colonialism.

Although they depend on the world agencies for news, many Africans feel those agencies do not effectively serve the needs or interests of the new nations. Many educated Africans fervently believe that the outside world, especially Europe and the United States, is receiving a distorted picture of events in Africa from the news reports sent out of Africa by the world news agencies and other foreign correspondents. Moreover, the Africans themselves receive this same biased (to them) version of the news when the European agencies send their reports back into Africa, thus compounding the distortion. The world agencies enjoy great advantages in the organization, experience, financial resources, and technology required to run a worldwide news communication network (indeed, that is why they are "world agencies"). In Africa neither the local media nor the governments have comparable facilities. African nations have had no choice but to use their services. The world agencies, especially Reuters and Agence France Presse, have been aggressively and successfully selling their services to the thirty-four new governments of Africa, and in many cases have helped to establish the national news agencies.

Although most of the new African nations have been independent for more than eight years, the news capitals of the continent today are not the bustling cities of Nairobi, Lagos, Kinshasa, Abidjan, Dakar, or even Cairo. They are London and Paris, the headquarters, respectively, of Reuters and AFP, the two agencies that dominate the flow of news to and from Africa. This is due in part to the organizational pattern of Reuters and AFP, and in part to the way telecommunications operate in Africa. Africa "hooks on" to the East-West flow of news at London and Paris.

On a diverse continent where over 800 languages are spoken, news flows mainly in French and English. Most news originating in any of the fourteen francophonic nations, for example, goes directly by way of AFP to Paris, from which it radiates back to other African capitals. Paris is the hub of an enormous communication wheel for Africa's French speakers.

It is the same in English-speaking Africa; the only difference is that Reuters usually carries the news and London is the hub.

In visits to Lagos and London, I found far more news information about the Nigerian civil war in the news media of Britain —newspapers, magazines, television, and radio, in addition to news services—than I found in Nigeria. And, of course, many of the British news media reach Nigeria as well. If a story breaks in Nairobi, Kenya, the media in neighboring Ethiopia learn about it only after Reuters flashes the story to London and then back to Addis Ababa. News continues to flow in patterns established under colonialism. The old empire cable rate of a penny a word still makes it cheaper to send news from former British colonies directly to London. In a way, news-flow patterns also reflect the economic situations of the new countries, which despite political independence are often still economically dependent on their former colonial masters.

Little news in Africa moves laterally by merely crossing the nearest border; usually lacking are the technical facilities—cables, telephone lines, telex or radio equipment, or even roads. A news dispatch, for example, has to pass through both London and

Paris to get from Dakar, Senegal, to Freetown in nearby Sierra Leone. In any African capital it is easier to obtain news of Europe than it is to find out what is happening in a neighboring country or even in that capital's own hinterlands.

In any given place in Africa, even a major city, it is difficult to learn directly what is happening elsewhere on the continent. Hence there is great reliance on information from Paris and London or the United States. The importance of Voice of America was cited by correspondent Russell Warren Howe:

> The main encyclopedia of what took place during the day in Africa, for specialist correspondents, is the two-hour broadcast of news and news commentary of the Voice of America which begins every night at 1800 GMT. . . . The radio network treats each part of Africa as equally important. If one was in, say, Addis Ababa, it would probably be the only way of knowing of a cabinet reshuffle in Fort Lamy, the death of a minister in Mali or the appearance of an important new Nigerian novel.[1]

Although imported daily papers, magazines, shortwave broadcasts, television news film, and motion pictures are all part of the international news flow, the world news agencies play the crucial role, for Reuters, AFP, AP, UPI, and to a lesser extent, TASS, are the prime suppliers of both overseas and African news to African newspapers and broadcast stations. Equally important, these world agencies are the major conduits to the outside world for news *from* Africa.

MOST POORLY REPORTED CONTINENT

Partly because it is on the lower fringe of the great East-West news-flow patterns, the African continent today is the most poorly "covered" or reported of any major region in the world.

This is particularly true of the American news media that assign a small fraction of their correspondents to Africa. In a 1969 survey Ralph E. Kliesch found that the American news media employed 1,462 newsmen overseas. Over half of them, 793, were stationed in Europe, mostly in London, Paris, Rome, Bonn, Berlin, and Frankfurt; 332 were in Asia and Australia; 169 in Latin America and Canada; and 76 in the Middle East.[2]

Only 92 (or about 5 to 6 percent) were in all of Africa. But of these 92, only 24 were staff or full-time correspondents; the others were 2 full-time stringers and 66 part-time employees. The

TABLE 4.1: Geographical Distribution of U.S. Network Television Foreign Correspondents

	NBC	CBS	ABC	Totals
Europe	23	25	19	67
Asia	24	14	16	54
Africa	2	1	1	4
Middle East	4	2	2	8
The Americas	10	8	4	22
Totals	63	50	42	155

Source: John Wilhelm, "The Overseas Correspondents: 1,376 People in 93 Lands," in *1966 Directory Overseas Press Club of America* (New York: Overseas Press Club, 1966).

great majority were non-Americans; only 11 of the 92 were U.S. citizens and of the 11 Americans, only 7 were full-time correspondents and 6 of them were stationed in Nairobi (4) and Lagos (2). (There were 5 other American newsmen in Cairo, which is usually counted in the Middle East.)

Most Americans today get their news first through television. The 3 major U.S. television networks maintained 155 correspondents abroad in 1965 and only 4 of these were in Africa. The American Broadcasting Corporation's correspondent also had responsibilities in the Middle East and was based in Beirut; the CBS man operated out of London. (See Table 4.1.)

The Associated Press, the U.S. news media's major source for both foreign and domestic news, had 6 U.S. nationals in Africa in 1968 with 1 each in Cairo, Johannesburg, Salisbury, Nairobi, Kinshasa, and Lagos.[3] United Press International had no U.S. nationals covering Africa, relying instead on Europeans and Africans.

Few U.S. newspapers have maintained resident correspondents on the African continent. The exception, as always, was the New York *Times,* which has had staff correspondents there since the end of World War II and stringers since 1950. In the mid-1960s there were *Times* staff correspondents in Nairobi, Lagos, Johannesburg, and Cairo, plus 9 stringers (5 British, 2 American, 1 Egyptian, and 1 Nigerian) located in Algiers, Nairobi, Leopoldville, Johannesburg, Rabat, Cairo, Salisbury, and Lagos.[4] The Cairo and Johannesburg bureaus were later forced to close.

Other U.S. papers which have had resident American correspondents in Africa include the Washington *Post, Christian Science Monitor,* Los Angeles *Times,* and Chicago *Daily News.* In 1965 the only resident correspondent for a British newspaper was

Clyde Sanger of the *Guardian*. The great *Times* of London maintained its extensive African coverage entirely through stringers and news services. The London *Daily Telegraph* often sent in reporters for short periods to cover specific stories such as the Nigerian civil war or the rebellion in Rhodesia.

Time magazine had staff correspondents in Nairobi and Lagos, while *Newsweek* had 2 men in Nairobi.

The lack of U.S. journalists in Africa meant the U.S. news media carry relatively little news about Africa. This was shown in a survey by William Payne of press coverage of Africa in 11 major U.S. newspapers (the so-called "prestige papers") for the month of June 1965. As would be expected, the New York *Times* led the field. It carried an average of 5.64 African news items per day which came to 66.3 column inches in mean daily coverage. More typical of the 11 papers, however, was the Washington *Star*, which carried an average of 1.80 items daily that averaged 23.8 inches in daily coverage.[5] The coverage of African news for the other 1,750 or so U.S. daily newspapers is, of course, far below what it is for these few metropolitan dailies.

Payne found that the 4 newspapers then maintaining correspondents in Africa—the New York *Times*, Los Angeles *Times*, *Christian Science Monitor*, and Washington *Post*—carried significantly more news on Africa than did papers without correspondents in Africa. The late New York *Herald-Tribune*, which surpassed the Washington *Post* in total inches, did not claim a reporter assigned to Africa, but the paper did have an extensive foreign staff at the time. A summary of Payne's report[6] is given in Table 4.2.

Yet news of Africa in U.S. news media greatly increased from what it was before the mid-1950s. Then, with most of the con-

TABLE 4.2: News on Africa in Eleven U.S. Papers for June 1965

Paper	No. African Items	Items (avg.)	Total African Inches	Avg. Inches per Day
New York *Times*	164	5.64	1,922	66.3
Los Angeles *Times*	66	2.34	1,246	44.5
Christian Science *Monitor* ..	64	2.37	1,095	40.5
New York *Herald-Tribune* ..	51	1.96	1,164	43.2
Washington *Post*	102	3.40	1,052	35.0
Washington *Star*	54	1.80	715	23.8
Baltimore *Sun*	52	1.74	552	18.4
St. Louis *Post-Dispatch*	49	1.81	495	18.3
Chicago *Daily News*	30	1.20	403	15.5
San Francisco *Chronicle* ...	50	1.71	408	13.4
Atlanta *Constitution*	26	1.04	242	9.68

tinent still under colonial rule, Africa was "covered," as to a certain extent it still is, by U.S. journalists stationed in London, Paris, Brussels, and Lisbon to which the news flowed from territories and colonies. Airline connections today make it possible for a newsman in London or Paris to fly to a trouble spot in Africa as easily as from any place in Africa itself.

Few would contend that the quality and quantity of news carried by the U.S. mass media is sufficient for an accurate picture of Africa. The situation is compounded by the general reluctance of U.S. editors to use what news is available. In a 1963 study of United Press International's African news as carried in Michigan's largest daily newspaper, the Detroit *News,* researcher James Wallington of Michigan State University found that UPI transmitted fifty-five stories concerning Africa during the two-week period of the study. The *News* used only three stories, totaling seventeen and one-fourth inches.[7]

William Attwood, former executive editor of Cowles Communications, who served as U.S. Ambassador to Guinea and later to Kenya during 1961 to 1966, has criticized U.S. reporting in Africa:

> American reporting from Africa, for example, frequently seems designed to perpetuate Soviet myths: Africans are more often than not portrayed as racist, anti-Western and susceptible to Communist blandishments. Month after month, hope fades, violence flares, whites flee and targets ripen for Communist take-overs. I have a collection of clippings that don't make me proud of the profession I have returned to.
>
> So far as Africa is concerned, the problem is essentially that most editors, like most senior Foreign Service officers, are Europe-oriented. Newspapers, wire services, and networks bunch their correspondents in Europe (and now Vietnam) and generally cover Africa and even South America with stringers and an occasional roving reporter looking for the kind of story ("Race War Looms") that will make page one and justify his expense account. The result is that a good deal of the history now being made abroad never gets reported at home, while relatively insignificant political developments in Europe get more attention than they deserve. During the Kenyatta-Odinga showdown in 1966, when eleven Communist intelligence agents were expelled from Kenya, I found no Nairobi dateline in either the New York *Times* international edition or the New York *Herald-Tribune* European edition; but the Belgian cabinet crisis was reported in detail and the *Tribune* even had a half-column on the reduction in Luxembourg's armed forces.[8]

COMMUNICATIONS NETWORK UNDER COLONIALISM

Today's news-flow patterns are rooted in the earlier need of European governments for effective communications between their own capitals and the administrative centers of their colonial territories. Hence excellent communications facilities were developed between London and such African cities as Nairobi, Salisbury, Johannesburg, Cape Town, Lagos, Accra, Freetown, Cairo, and Khartoum. Similarly, there were good communications between Paris and Dakar, Abidjan, Brazzaville, and Tananarive; and from Brussels to Leopoldville (now Kinshasa).

In 1879 a submarine cable was laid along the east coast of Africa via Aden to Durban and then by landline to Cape Town. In 1885 a direct link was established between England and West Africa via a cable from England to Bathurst, in Gambia, through Cape Verde in Senegal. Domestic overland telegraphic systems were established afterwards, and much later telephones, and eventually international links by radio-telegraph and radio-telephone circuits.[9] The great limitation of such a system was that the lines of communication all went toward Europe.

The first direct radio, telephone, and teletype circuits between Abidjan, Ivory Coast, and Accra in neighboring Ghana, two major cities in West Africa, were not opened until September 26, 1966. Abidjan has had good communications to Paris, and Accra to London for quite a while.

Ainslie points out that at the time of independence Africa's internal communications network consisted of the following:

> one telegraphic undersea cable (part of the Commonwealth Common User system that skimmed the coast off the continent from Ascension Island off the West Coast around the Cape to Port Sudan and Aden); no telephone cable at all; overland, and often inadequate, telegraphic and telephonic systems that crossed national boundaries only in exceptional cases (such as between South Africa and Rhodesia; between Kenya, Uganda and Tanganyika and between some countries of French West and Equatorial Africa); and most important, radio circuits that look on the map rather like two great fans, their bases in London and Paris.[10]

By late 1969 a new cable was laid from London, via Lisbon, to Cape Town. This will improve the service to southern Africa. The colonial systems of communications—highly discriminatory with special cable rates, radio telephonic rates, airline routes, and mail delivery patterns, all based on French, British, or Belgian colonial interests—have greatly inhibited inter-African communications. Abidjan cannot communicate with Lusaka, Nairobi is out of touch with Dakar, and Lagos cannot communicate with Addis Ababa—not without an expensive and inconvenient detour through Europe. Such a communication pattern has obvious political implications at a time when African leaders are trying to establish regional and continental political and economic ties through such groups as the Organization of African Unity and the Economic Commission for Africa.

Because they could get their African news in European capitals and because they had few customers in Africa (the few white-owned newspapers in South Africa were an exception), the world news agencies were late in arriving in Africa. However, two of them, Reuters and Agence France Presse, were there before the others and have been working hard to expand their positions of dominance.

REUTERS IN AFRICA

Reuters has been in Africa longer than any of the other world agencies and claimed to be in every African country except Burundi and Rwanda. In 1912 it started the Reuters South African News Agency, a news service in South Africa in association with local newspapers. By 1938 the news service had been taken over by South African newspapers and became the South African Press Agency (SAPA). In combination with SAPA which covered southern Africa, Reuters supplied international news for the white settler dailies of South Africa and Rhodesia and the *Standard* papers of East Africa.

The *West African Pilot,* Nnamdi Azikiwe's famous nationalist paper in Nigeria, became Reuter's first West African client in 1945, but the report amounted to only 800 words a day, received by radio in Morse code. Azikiwe himself was a Reuters stringer in those days.

Unlike Agence France Presse, Reuters was not in colonial Africa in any extensive way before 1960; in part, because Africa could be covered from Europe and because British colonial officials did not particularly welcome foreign correspondents. The colonies relied mainly on the British Information Service (BIS) and the BBC for their news.

As independence neared, Reuters sent Patrick Cross to make a continental survey, and as a result Reuters has greatly expanded its African service in recent years.

News from Africa flows into the London headquarters of Reuters at an average rate of 20,000 words a day—about 120 stories bearing a variety of datelines. The agency claims to have 22 staff correspondents out of a network of 106 on the continent. However, one Reuters correspondent told me that *London-appointed staffers* were located only at Algiers, Accra, Lagos, Kinshasa, Lusaka, Dar es Salaam, Addis Ababa, Cairo, Nairobi, Johannesburg, and Salisbury. (*All* news services appear to exaggerate their manpower figures.) The output of these correspondents is returned to Africa in several "services" delivered by radioteletype or direct circuit to all African states except Rwanda and Burundi.[11] Reuters provides five services in Africa, which reflect the differing political and linguistic conditions a news agency encounters there. They include (1) a South African service for South Africa, Rhodesia, Angola, and Mozambique; (2) a West African service in English; (3) an East African service in English; (4) a West African service in French, and (5) a twenty-four-hour service to North Africa in English and Arabic.

The three services to tropical Africa are all about 15,000 words in length. They are beamed from London by radio teletype for about sixteen hours a day—seven hours in French and nine hours in English. Basically the same report is sent to all three regions.

The 15,000-word "Africa Report" is considerably shorter than Reuters's 60,000-word "World Service." The shorter version is closely edited and is heavy on short African news items collected by Reuters staffers, plus more than 500 stringers. One U.S. newsman calls this practice (which is followed by AFP as well) "journalistic colonialism" because the agencies are selecting news for the Africans rather than letting them do it for themselves. Reuters answers that the small African media cannot make effective use of a full budget and are mainly interested in African news anyway.

Another controversial aspect of Reuters service is that it is often sold exclusively to an African government news agency which in turn can redistribute it to its own media and resell it at a profit to any private media. In Kenya, for example, Reuters's only client is the Kenya News Agency, which redistributes it. This makes it very difficult for competing news agencies to sell their reports.

By selling its services exclusively to the African government, Reuters places that government as a gatekeeper (and potential censor) on incoming foreign news. During the Belgian paratroop drop on Stanleyville in the Congo in November 1964, the Kenya News Agency in Nairobi withheld the Reuters report for twelve hours. This was vigorously protested by the Kenya Union of Journalists, which called it a "flagrant contravention by the Kenya government of the Bill of Rights and its provisions of freedom of expression." It was the Reuters contract which made this possible.[12]

Reuters argues that in many new countries the government is the only one in a position to afford the service anyway.

There is also the feeling among some newsmen that a wire service cannot maintain its objectivity and independence when its principal (and sometimes only) client in the country is the government itself.

Credibility of outgoing wire service stories is potentially compromised because the resident wire service correspondent thinks twice before sending out news embarrassing to the local regime, the sole client in the country for his own news service. Also, in too many cases the prestigious world services are represented by stringers who work for an African government. In Abidjan in 1965, I was told that the Reuters stringer in Niger was the Minister of Information of Niger! It is unlikely that such a stringer would file many stories critical of or unflattering to the Niger government.

Reuters's Africa service is expensive to maintain, and Reuters claims that it breaks even, but this is doubtful. It is a way, an important way, of maintaining British influence in Africa, but there is no evidence that the British government subsidizes Reuters.

In recent years Reuters has been seeking clients in francophonic nations just as Agence France Presse has been among anglophonic nations. But the Reuters correspondents often find it difficult to gain access to francophonic government officials, many of them Frenchmen, who have long been in the habit of dealing with AFP. And most newsmen in French Africa once worked for or were trained by AFP.

The Reuters bureau chief in Abidjan, Ivory Coast, was Manasse Jiminiga, a competent Togolese journalist who had been press secretary to the late President Sylvanus Olympio of Togo. His predecessor was an Englishman who found it difficult to compete with AFP which usually received news tips first from the government. Jiminiga had stringers in Upper Volta, Mali, Sierra Leone, Niger, and Liberia who usually filed their stories by telex. However he oversaw their coverage and occasionally visited them. The differential telex rate to Paris made it much cheaper to file stories there and then reroute them to London. From Abidjan the telex rate for a minimum of three minutes to Paris was 1,215 CFA (Central African Francs) (250 CFA = U.S. $1) as compared with 2,232 CFA for three minutes to London. To New York it was 2,976 CFA for three minutes.

But despite these handicaps, the Reuters service now goes to all French-speaking countries in Africa, which means it has contracts with all these governments. Some francophonic countries take Reuters in part to show their independence of France and AFP.

Some Americans in Africa, both newsmen and government officials, feel the Reuters Africa Report is often unduly anti-American in tone. An Associated Press man told U.S. newsman John Strohmeyer: "Reuters interprets America as a sea of race riots while rarely is one in Britain ever reported. . . . In fact, the day-to-day image of America reported by Reuters is far more devastating than the net propaganda impact of TASS." When arriving in Lagos, Strohmeyer was greeted by a banner headline in the *Nigerian Sunday Express* which read "1,000 NEGROES KILLED," a report on a 1964 race riot in Rochester, New York. The Reuters story was garbled and the word "rioted" was missing so the editor inserted "killed" instead. Despite U.S. protests and a modest correction ("1,000 Negroes not killed"), the damage had been done.[13]

The news agency business is extremely competitive in Africa, and Reuters's fiercest rival is France's AFP.

AGENCE FRANCE PRESSE

As the only other world agency with a full African service, Agence France Presse is in direct competition with Reuters, and the two have no agreements to exchange news.

Building from its strong base in preindependence French Africa, Agence France Presse now has permanent French correspondents in the following African capitals: Algiers, Rabat, Tunis, Addis Ababa, Nouakchott, Ouagadougou, Abidjan, Lomé, Cotonou, Lagos, Dakar, Nairobi, Kinshasa, Cairo, Brazzaville, Bangui, Fort Lamy, Monrovia, Niamey, Johannesburg, Tananarive, Bamako, Libreville, and Yaoundé. Locally recruited full-time staffers and stringers contribute news from twenty-four other African cities.

AFP's principal bureaus are Johannesburg for southern Africa and Algiers for the Maghreb. All news comes to Paris by three main routes: (1) direct permanent radio teletype links to Algiers and Johannesburg; (2) telex through post offices, and (3) normal cables. Each correspondent has a telex capability for contributing to the flow of news that comes into AFP in Paris at the average rate of 18,426 words a day. There, at AFP's Place de la Bourse headquarters, the news is centralized, edited, rewritten, and broadcast back to Africa in four transmissions in French and one in English, each at the rate of 25,000 words daily. The English service goes to both the independent black countries such as Nigeria, Ghana, Sierra Leone, Kenya, and Tanzania, as well as the white-controlled nations of southern Africa. There is a problem of writing the news in a manner acceptable to both areas.

Important differences are found in the content of the two language services of which about 40 percent is African news. The English wire has more spot news while the French wire is more concerned with area problems, reports, texts of presidents' speeches, etc.

The AFP reports are broadcast from transmitters at Paris and Toulouse and beamed to various parts of Africa where they are monitored by AFP customers, usually the African governments. Guinea, which has long been at odds with the French government, has bootlegged the service for years. At the same time Guinea did not permit Western correspondents to be in residence at Conakry, although TASS, NCNA, and other Communist agencies were represented. AFP, Reuters, and UPI kept up with news in Guinea by monitoring daily the radio broadcasts from the government station at Conakry.

AFP appears to be the only world agency, besides TASS, clearly subsidized by its government. According to both AP and UPI sources, Agence France Presse annually receives about $7.8 million in government subsidy for making the wire service available to various embassies and ministries. There are about 350 such subscriptions. Most of the francophonic African governments that receive AFP pay for it with funds provided by France. One AP source in Africa told me that AFP's African service costs three times what it earns in sales to Africans and that the French government's annual subsidy there amounted to $12 million.

AFP, however, claims that since the new statutes of April

1957, it no longer has government ties and is now an independent commercial agency. The agency can trace its ancestry back to 1835 when it was established as Agence Havas in Paris by Charles Havas. Two members of Havas's staff were Julius Reuter and Bernard Wolff, who later departed to form the famous English and German agencies bearing their names. Following the Armistice in 1940, Agence Havas was dissolved in France. It resumed service in London under the Free French as Agence Française Independente in 1944, when France itself was still under Nazi occupation.

After the war, AFP took over AFI bureaus in Rabat, Algiers, Tunis, and Cairo and placed correspondents in Dakar and Tananarive. Its then semiofficial status with the French government enabled it to become well established in *Afrique Noire* in the years before African independence. AFP was so well entrenched in French West Africa that it was actively competing with what commercial press there was. Private publishers complained that the news bulletin AFP sold to subscribers cut badly into their already small circulations.[14]

Currently Agence France Presse has the following services for Africa:

1. *Afrique du Nord*—a 35,000-word daily report in French to Algiers, Rabat, and Tunis, averaging 240 items of which 30 percent are African news.

2. *Afrique Noire*—a 23,000-word daily French service with 150 items of which 60 percent are African news.

3. *Africabeams*—a 23,000-word daily service in English with about 150 news items of which 40 percent are African news.

4. *Moyen Orient*—a 35,000-word French service that is picked up in Cairo. Twenty percent of 280 items are African; the others Middle Eastern.

5. *Ocean Indien*—a 21,000-word French service that is picked up by the Malagasy Republic.

6. A daily publication called "Bulletin Quotidien d'Outre-Mer."

7. A semiweekly English bulletin called "Africa South of the Sahara."

8. A semiweekly French bulletin called "L'Afrique au Sud du Sahara."

9. A semimonthly bulletin called "Sahara."

10. A semiweekly bulletin called "Les Cahiers de l'Afrique Occidentale et Equatoriale."[15]

Because of its long involvement in French Africa and France's close ties and substantial aid to most of its former African colonies, AFP has made the transition to independence smoothly and remained in a strong position.

ASSOCIATED PRESS AND UNITED PRESS INTERNATIONAL

The two American news services, the Associated Press and United Press International, lag well behind Reuters and Agence France Presse in Africa. According to U.S. Information Agency statistics, Reuters was received in thirty-nine African countries, while AFP had clients in thirty-three countries. AP was received in only fourteen countries and UPI in nineteen. TASS, which is not sold but given away free, was received in nineteen countries also.

Unlike the two European agencies, AP and UPI have not made a concerted effort to expand their African operations, in part because the American services were not involved in Africa before independence.

AP finds it difficult to compete because it does not offer a special African service. It sells only its world service, which is beamed into Africa by radio teletype by way of New York and London. This longer report, about 120,000 words, taking seventeen and one-half hours to deliver, includes much information, such as U.S. baseball and basketball scores, which is of little interest to African clients.

AP's six staff writers in 1968 (numbers will fluctuate) were all correspondents with considerable experience in Africa. AP was also represented by forty-four stringers in all capitals except Brazzaville and Conakry (which would not let Western correspondents in), Bamako, Djibouti, and Nouakchott.

AP staff correspondents file an average total of 5,172 words of spot news copy daily, including 4,840 words via telex and cable. Seventeen stringer correspondents in francophonic Africa file to the agency's Paris bureau, but a stringer in Somalia files to the Rome bureau. The six full-time staffers and the other twenty-six file to London.

The American services find it difficult to obtain good stringers and so often operate on a task force basis. When a big story breaks, an AP staff man will fly in to cover the story with the help of local stringers. At other times, a regional staff correspondent, such as in Lagos, will make a tour of about ten countries doing "backgrounders" on each one in cooperation with the local stringer. Since there are so many countries and so little saleable news (because AP lacks African clients), AP concentrates on a roundup story every six weeks or so. In fact, the Maghreb is covered by the AP man at Geneva who occasionally travels to Tunisia, Morocco, and Algeria. AP recently went into Ethiopia and into Liberia again and hopes to go into Mali and Zambia as well, according to Stan Swinton, an AP executive. AP in London has recently started to beam some special area news into Africa and the Middle East.

Because Reuters and AFP are so firmly entrenched, AP has little incentive to expand its operations since it receives no government subsidies and must pay its own way. AP does, however, sell its service to some U.S. embassies in Africa.

UPI has a slight advantage over AP (and a few more clients) because it operates two separate radio beams sending news into Africa: one service in French, edited in Paris, is transmitted six hours a day, and an English service, transmitted from Kootwijk in Holland, is edited in London. UPI's total cable and telex coverage from Africa is about 10,000 words filed daily.

In 1968 UPI had five staff correspondents (none were Americans), twenty-three stringers, and three major bureaus in English-speaking Africa at Nairobi, Salisbury, and Johannesburg. Bureaus in francophonic Africa were in Abidjan, Rabat, Algiers, and Tunis. UPI said its stringer correspondents were usually top editors on leading local newspapers. The agency had what it called "firemen" correspondents in London ready to fly out, especially to West Africa, whenever a big story broke. The range and quality of UPI reportage in Africa were well below that of the other three major services, in part because it had less manpower covering larger areas. Most UPI men have heavy filing requirements; at ten points on the continent they must file daily.

The West German agency, Deutsche Presse Agentur, is not quite a world agency, but is increasing its involvement in Africa as is the West German government itself. DPA maintained four offices with the same number of staffers in Africa and was planning a fifth desk to be based in West Africa. In addition, it had seventeen local correspondents. The agency received about twenty stories a day, averaging about 2,000 words, from its African correspondents.[16]

TASS IN AFRICA

TASS, and to a lesser extent the other major news services from the Communist commonwealth, are represented in some twenty-two African nations and thus contribute to the flow of news in and out of Africa.

TASS, the fifth of the world news agencies, is becoming increasingly like a Western news agency. It now pays more attention to news coverage and less to propaganda and intelligence activities, and is trying to compete with Western services. But because of its close identification with the Soviet government, TASS maintains bureaus and is received only in those countries where the USSR is represented diplomatically or has ongoing aid programs: Algeria, Cameroon, Central African Republic, Congo (Brazzaville), Dahomey, Ethiopia, Ghana, Guinea, Kenya, Liberia, Libya, Mali, Morocco, Nigeria, Senegal, Somali Republic, Sudan, Tanzania, Tunisia, Uganda, United Arab Republic, and Zanzibar.[17]

The other Communist news agencies received in Africa are Novosti, the Soviet feature agency; CTK, the Czech agency; ADN, the East German agency; TANYUG, the Yugoslav agency; NCNA, the New China News Agency from Peking; and Prensa Latina, the Cuban agency. These agencies transmit to just a few African nations, principally Algeria, Ethiopia, Ghana, Guinea, Mali, Morocco, Sudan, Tanzania, and Tunisia.[18]

But because Communist agency reports are slower and less complete than AFP and Reuters in reporting African news, their influence is more in the area of international political communication than in day-to-day news coverage.

CRITICISMS OF COMMERCIAL WORLD AGENCIES

The commercial world agencies—AFP, Reuters, AP, and UPI—operate in Africa with great advantages over the local national news agencies. Each has a worldwide network of correspondents and each can provide a full coverage of international news. But their operations in Africa can be criticized from both Western and African points of view.

The Western agencies are sorely undermanned and inadequate to cover African news with speed, accuracy, and comprehensiveness. Professionally trained correspondents are too few, and there is too much reliance on stringers, most of whom are either professionally incompetent or too involved with local governments to report news objectively.

Colin Legum, the London *Observer*'s Commonwealth correspondent and one journalist who is a real authority on Africa, said that it is impossible to rely on stringers and the practice is an indictment of the wealthier sections of the press who are inadequately represented. He urged far more resident correspondents. "The American press tend to do rather better than either the French or British press in this regard and the British press tend to do considerably worse than the French press," Legum told the International Press Institute.[19]

It can be said, at least from an American viewpoint, that Reuters and AFP, in an effort to maintain their influence, are so deeply involved with African governments, who are their major clients and sources of revenue, that they cannot report the news with real independence. The relatively rich American agencies, it can be argued, are much too parsimonious in Africa; they need more and better reporters there.

In response to such criticism, the news agencies say they must sell to governments since they are the major clients in a region so lacking in private media. The lack of clients, both to buy news services and to help report the news, is a major reason that AP and UPI do not expand their operations. Moreover, they argue that their American clients, the main basis of their support, would not use more news of Africa even if more were available.

The AP's Stan Swinton said that U.S. members of the cooperative AP are not interested in broader coverage, but at that, they are more interested in Africa than are AP clients on any other continent. Latin America and Asia will not print African news, and Europe does not use as much as the United States, he said. There is evidence, too, that since decolonization, the reading publics of Britain, France, and Belgium are much less interested in Africa and are more concerned with their own domestic problems.[20]

The newly independent African states have directed a number of criticisms at the world news agencies; how valid they are often depends upon one's political orientation. Much of this criticism arises because the flow of news via world agencies seems to go against African interests.

Although there have been a number of studies on news flow, little research has been done on the relation of news flow to national development problems such as Africa faces. Wilbur

Schramm wrote that "the currents of information in the world today are nearly as predictable as the currents of air that we call the winds. Frequently, an event or series of events disrupts the information flow as a storm disrupts the meteorological chart. But underneath these disruptions are repetitive patterns as regular as trade winds."[21] He said the heaviness of news from a *few* countries is less disturbing than the thinness of news from *many* countries. "We must conclude," he wrote, "that the flow of news among nations is thin, that it is unbalanced, with heavy coverage of a few highly developed countries and light coverage of many less-developed ones, and that, in some cases at least, it tends to ignore important events and to distort the reality it presents."[22]

AFP and Reuters, and to a less degree AP and UPI, are viewed by some Africans as neo-colonialist institutions that determine the kind of news Africans shall read or hear. They see AFP and Reuters as just two more examples of French and British efforts to maintain influence in their former African territories. Some Americans, in and out of government, agree. It is certainly true that the English-language African services of Reuters carry a disproportionate amount of news about Great Britain and other Commonwealth nations.

I found in a study of African news flow that for English-language African papers in Nigeria, Kenya, and South Africa, some 67 percent of foreign news items were from English-speaking or Commonwealth nations. Since Reuters was the prime news source for these papers as well as for the British Commonwealth, perhaps it is Reuters which overselects this kind of news.[23]

If the nations studied had been from francophonic Africa (e.g., Senegal, Ivory Coast, and Congo [Brazzaville]), the large amount of news about France by way of Agence France Presse would have been readily apparent.

Indeed there seem to be wire service "spheres of influences": Reuters in English-speaking African and Commonwealth nations; AFP in francophonic Africa (although AFP and Reuters now overlap greatly in Africa); AP and especially UPI in Latin America; TASS for Communist nations, minus Red China. Each of these spheres is dominated by news from the respective news capital: London, Paris, New York, and Moscow. Significantly, despite considerable efforts to do so, AP, UPI, and TASS have not yet gained a real foothold in the African spheres of AFP and Reuters.

Africans resent, too, that London and Paris continue as Africa's major news centers. Furthermore, Africans are dismayed that the world news agencies are mostly manned by Europeans who are reporting the news as Europeans for European audiences. (This is a particularly valid criticism of Reuters and AFP, whose African services send their correspondents' news right back to Africa.)

The flow of news in and out of a developing African nation is very different from that of an industrialized European nation. It is a difference not only of quantity but of quality or kind. Different *kinds* of news pass between the more and less developed nations.

Africans think that the news wires of the West are too full of news about the Cold War and of happenings concerning the great rich powers. Developing nations, it is argued, need news of their neighbors who face similar problems and with whom they seek political and economic ties. They require news of what is happening in other parts of the vast developing world where two-thirds of the world's burgeoning population lives. But little of that news comes into Africa. The news-flow study previously quoted found a general lack of news flow *between* the developing nations. At a time when there was much talk of Afro-Asian political solidarity, only 6.5 percent of the foreign news in the African papers came from the five great nations with over half of the world's population (China, India, Indonesia, Japan, and Pakistan). Only 2 percent of the foreign news in African papers came from another great area of developing nations, Latin America.[24]

Some African leaders and journalists feel that these prevailing patterns of world news flow, so much dominated by the world's five great agencies, do not now effectively supply the kinds of news and information they feel suit Africa's needs.

Instead, the developing nations of Africa get the hard news of the Cold War (in which most would like to avoid involvement) and various kinds of trivial "soft news" from the industrialized North. This soft news flow, greatly supplemented by what they see in movies and on television (mostly produced in the United States and Western Europe), probably only adds to the "revolution of rising frustrations" that Daniel Lerner has depicted.[25]

The melancholy fact seems to be that the struggling new African nations that most need an effective exchange of news and information from other similar nations are getting little help from the prevailing news dissemination patterns. News flow and national development seem to be working at cross-purposes. Mere increased communication between nations is not necessarily an unmixed blessing any more than is increased literacy.

On the other hand, the news from Africa that finds its way into the great world news flow is a small trickle indeed. The picture that the European and American publics often get of the developing world is painted in vivid strokes of violence, political upheaval, military coups, and conflict of one kind or another. The conflicts and coups are often important news stories and must be reported, but they are not the whole story. Background and interpretive news, and the day-to-day accounts of slow, tortuous, economic and social progress against great odds, are not being effectively told. All of this, perceptive Africans feel, is directly related to the ways that the world news services tell the news.

To an African nation eager for economic independence or self-sufficiency (which may be illusory in an interdependent world) to match its political independence, a pattern of news flow that reiterates and emphasizes past colonial relationships and reflects a European bias in a news service only adds some credence to the vague but politically potent charges of "neo-colonialism" and "imperialism."

AN AFRICAN RESPONSE: A CONTINENTAL AFRICAN NEWS SERVICE

Along with the development of individual national news agencies, there also came quite naturally a desire among the new African governments for some kind of Pan-African news agency that would obviate or at least minimize their dependence on the European agencies.

The first step in this logical extension of national news agencies came as an aftermath of a UNESCO-sponsored gathering called "A Meeting of Experts on the Development of News Agencies in Africa."[26] News agency directors and other press experts from some twenty-five African countries attended the 1963 Tunis meeting. The meeting not only considered ways to establish more national agencies (there were twenty) but also ways to promote the wider exchange of news services within Africa and with other regions of the world. At the Tunis meeting the Union of African News Agencies was formed, with an Algerian, Muhammad Ben Mehal, elected as first president.

As a professional association the Union was intended to link the existing twenty agencies and any new ones that would come along. The first General Assembly was to be held six months later.

The Union's General Assembly met in Algiers in December 1963 and at that time Ghana proposed a Pan-African News Agency (PANAF). Statutes for such an agency were adopted at a later meeting of the General Assembly of the Union of African News Agencies in December 1964 at Yaoundé, Cameroon.

A report of the Yaoundé meeting stated the duty of the agency would be to project the "true image of each African country and promote better understanding between African states. It would then be possible for countries outside to view events in the continent through African minds."[27] At that time, a broadcasting organization, Union of National Radio and Television Organizations of Africa (URTNA) was brought in as well. By then the difficulties inherent in such a plan became more apparent.

For one thing, the impetus for an all-African news system was mostly generated by the more radical nations.

One Algerian delegate declared that the projected agency "should become an instrument of combat for the liberation of Africa and all the world." Such dramatic rhetoric emphasized the political cleavages: the more radical nations such as Algeria and Ghana (before Ben Bella and Nkrumah were deposed), Mali, Congo (Brazzaville), and the UAR envisioned the organization as a propaganda and agitational tool of a militant and politically united Africa. In fact the Ghana news agency, GNA, had suggested that "such a continental news agency can be most effective when it is under the *political* direction of a continental union government."[28]

Typical was the viewpoint of Radio Brazzaville to the December 1964 meeting: "The imperialist and neo-colonialist press is a giant mechanic of African brains which unrivets and adjusts to make them receptive to certain distorted images of the world. . . . The only way we can resist the imperialist press is to supply Africa with the means of producing African news written by Africans."[29]

Such views probably had the effect of alienating the more conservative African states from such a militant news organization. African governments such as Nigeria, Senegal, and Ivory Coast had political differences with the more radical nations and suspected the motives of those pushing the Pan-African News Agency.

An obvious obstacle was that the news for a Pan-African exchange must perforce come from each nation's official news agency, which was usually under the political control of each government. So the possibility of very much reliable and objective news passing back and forth and being accepted by mutually hostile or at least suspicious neighbors was small indeed.

Another problem was that most African nations lacked the financial resources and skilled personnel to establish the technical facilities needed for a true Pan-African agency.

The project to establish a Pan-African News Agency was indefinitely postponed by the Political Commission of the Organization of African Unity meeting in Addis Ababa in the fall of 1966. Financial reasons were said to lie behind the decision: costs of setting up the agency and running it for one year had been estimated at more than $2 million.[30]

However, during December 7–9, 1967, the executive committee of the Union of African News Agencies held its tenth meeting in Addis Ababa and was attended by Nigeria, Cameroon, Congo (Kinshasa), Ethiopia, Ghana, Guinea, Ivory Coast, Morocco, Senegal, Tunisia, and the UAR. The committee issued a statement calling for (1) creation of national news agencies in countries lacking them, (2) establishment of a Pan-African News Agency which the committee said was still "technically possible," and (3) expansion of training programs for African journalists by national news agencies.[31] The Union's secretary-general, Ferid Soudani of Tunis Afrique Presse, said the executive committee had called on all agencies to install receivers for the services of sister agencies for "it is in their interest to give more credit to items coming from African agencies than to information on the same subjects from foreign agencies."[32]

There was also a move underway to establish an inter-African agency among the francophonic nations. In April 1967, OCAM (Organization Commune Africaine et Malagache) drew up plans for an Inter-Africa Press (IAP) agency at a meeting of the organization's Ministers of Information held in Abidjan. Ministers from eleven countries agreed on establishment as soon as possible of the press agency and a commission was elected to study the project. On January 16, 1968, Ministers of Foreign Affairs of OCAM met at Niamey and approved the establishment of the Inter-Africa Press. Capital of 300 million CFA was to be provided, with 55 percent from member states and 45 percent from other international agencies.[33]

A Pan-African news agency in which governments are directly

involved is dependent on considerably more Pan-African political harmony than exists on the continent today.

For the foreseeable future, African news media will continue to be largely dependent on the world news agencies—which now means mainly Reuters and AFP—for news of the world and even about themselves. Even European-owned commercial agencies offer far more promise of providing reliable and objective news than do agencies under African political control, no matter how idealistic the motives may be for such a Pan-African agency.

In the long run, commercial agencies, owned and run by Africans and free from political and government interference, offer the best hope of providing Africans the kinds of news exchanges they require. In the meantime, other Western agencies such as Associated Press, United Press International, and Deutsche Presse Agentur could help the situation by improving and expanding their newsgathering and disseminating operations on the continent. Diversity of views would help neutralize the "wire-service nationalism." Unquestionably, Africans would get a fairer and more complete picture of America if the AP and UPI were more widely used. It has been suggested that the U.S. government subsidize the AP and UPI so they can expand their African operations.[34] Such an idea has merit, perhaps, and would help break the near monopoly of Reuters and AFP. But in the long run, such government subsidization of the independent U.S. wire services would be self-defeating and would raise cries of "neo-colonialism," for the only foundation on which a free press can ever hope to build in Africa must be that of independent units of news communications with no government connections, whether domestic or foreign.

Such a free press is unfortunately a long way off for most of Africa, but American news media representatives can provide a model of the way a free press does indeed operate. For in Africa there is too little understanding of the role and problems of the foreign correspondent.

5

FOREIGN CORRESPONDENTS

ON SEPTEMBER 10, 1967, the American Broadcasting Company broadcast a 4-hour television program devoted exclusively to Africa. The $2 million documentary, the longest to date in the history of U.S. television, was based on some 2 million feet of film shot by teams of writers and cameramen who had traveled thousands of miles over the continent for about 250 days.

The lengthy documentary not only drew critical praise but held its own in the ratings that Sunday evening. Surveys showed 31.3 percent of the total U.S. television audience saw the marathon program. *Africa Report* reviewed the program and found it generally good.[1] And without doubt, many millions of Americans learned more about Africa in less time and effort than on any previous occasion.

This journalistic feat for the new and lively news medium occurred almost a century—98 years, in fact—after James Gordon Bennett of the New York *Herald* commissioned Henry Morton Stanley to go into the heart of Africa in search of Dr. David Livingstone.

In the century between these two events, foreign correspondents have been traveling through Africa and reporting the Dark Continent to an ever-growing number of readers, and now viewers, in Europe and America. Sometimes readers have been informed and enlightened; at other times, misled and confused by what correspondents have reported. Today's foreign correspondents, especially those from America, are still controversial figures in Africa.

One of the best of the current generation of foreign correspondents in Africa, Clyde Sanger, of the *Guardian,* had some thoughts about African reporting:

> Would Africa have been better off if no foreign correspondents had ever gone there? Would there be less misunderstanding, and more brotherly peace, if Stanley had never set out to find Dr. Livingstone, if Negley Farson had never gone Behind God's Back, if John Gunther had never got Inside Africa, and if a host of us smaller fry had not swum along behind? . . . I believe on the contrary that foreign correspondents have a crucial role to play in Africa, now more than ever.[2]

The foreign correspondent's role in Africa's modern history and its relations with the outside world is pivotal because, more so than in other places, the *report* of the event can be as important as the event itself. The attitudes and understanding of Westerners about Africa have been shaped to a great extent by what the press has told them about Africa.

One African journalist, Peter Enahoro of Nigeria, said of his predecessors, "Beginning from the days of early contact with Europeans, journalists have been responsible for influencing some of the valuable achievements of Africa. One may say that without the role of watch-dog which journalists played, the iniquities of slavery and the indignities of imperialism would not have ceased at the time they did."[3]

On the other hand, many journalists and travel writers managed to convey misleading and confusing pictures of life there. Such stereotypes, conditioned by Tarzan movies and similar adventure movies and stories, still inhibit clear understanding of events in Africa today.

Blaine Littell, an American journalist who has covered Africa for CBS News, has written candidly about the shortcomings and difficulties of reportage:

> I had been a reporter among other reporters in Africa and I had failed. I think we all failed in one way or another not through any fault of our own, but because Africa today is at best an elusive target and we were shooting at it with weapons designed for more conventional coverage. The fact of the matter is that much of what is going on in Africa defies description. The novelists and the poets have tried, and some have succeeded, but what is a newspaper editor or a headline writer to make of a war in which no one is killed; of a power struggle in which the participants remain the best of friends, and of a coup d'état which takes place without the knowledge of its architect? The result was that we journalists tended to leave out the little things that might

confuse or bewilder. Occasionally we tried to explain what we thought had really happened, but all too often we found that these were stories which weren't used.

This is not to say that the reporting out of Africa was stereotyped. On the contrary, it was—especially during the journalistic heyday of the Congo immediately after independence—incredibly varied. We brought to Leopoldville and Katanga our passions and our prejudices (some preconceived and some conceived on the spot), and who, even now, is to say who was right? There were those who viewed the whole business as a colossal joke. The liberals among us insisted that there *was* hope and spent their time seeking events that would buttress their contention. The racists saw the Congo as still another example of the black man's incompetence and inability to progress, and there were those who felt that the preservation of the United Nations was more important than what happened to the Congo itself. And vice versa. As a consequence, the diligent reader could pay his money and take his choice. But I am afraid that most readers decided fairly early in the game that it wasn't worth the effort and determined then and there to ignore the Congo—and Africa.

I am not sure whose fault it was—the readers', the Africans', or our own—but I am quite certain that the journalists must share in the blame.[4]

As pointed out, Africa has fewer resident foreign correspondents than any other major region of the world. The Kliesch survey found only twenty-four full-time resident American correspondents representing all the American mass media.[5]

Yet the American media have more journalists there than the European nations which have long and close ties to Africa.

Some think that the best coverage is provided by the *Times* of London and *Le Monde* of Paris, yet neither paper has had a full-time resident correspondent in Africa.

From no one central place can a correspondent cover Africa with a minimum of travel and communications difficulties. John Wilhelm wrote:

The problem of covering Africa is frightening. There is no hub of the wheel such as Paris or Geneva might be for Europe. If you take a spot with the most datelines during the past year (1962), probably Leopoldville (now Kinshasa), and decide to put a permanent staffer there, you commit a man (and probably his family) to a difficult life in a tropically hot city with innumerable hardships with every chance that he may go months without another breaking news story.[6]

Wilhelm's two surveys show how correspondents are shifted. In his 1963 survey there were fifteen correspondents of U.S. news media in Leopoldville; in his 1966 tally there was only one U.S. correspondent, Don Shannon of the Los Angeles *Times*.

Wilhelm said, "An ingenious answer has been conceived by CBS, which stations its African bureau chief in London. He can get to any spot in Africa quicker than anyone sitting down on the continent (barring the latter's immediate area). And his family can live a fairly normal life with good schools for the children."[7] But such a fly-in journalist is often considered an uninformed intruder by both resident correspondents and African officials.

Yet a good deal of reportage on Africa in American news media is done by the jet correspondent passing through on a quick trip. Although often shallow, such reporting need not be if the reporter is a good one, is knowledgeable about Africa, and makes proper use of local sources of information. Many fine newspapers —Milwaukee *Journal,* Kansas City *Star,* and Toronto *Globe* are examples—feel it is not worthwhile to maintain a full-time correspondent on the continent, but will occasionally send a staff reporter on a swing through the continent to do a series of stories.

The resident foreign press in Africa, however, tend to congregate in a few "news capitals." The requirements for a news capital are several: there must be good communications to Europe and excellent air connections to other African capitals; the city should be an important news center in a fairly stable country which is tolerant of foreign correspondents and not given to summarily deporting them; and the capital should, it is hoped, be an attractive and modern city with a salubrious climate.

The cities that most closely fit these requirements are, of course, Paris and London—still the great news centers of Africa— followed by Nairobi, Dakar, and Lagos. Local political upheavals can make or break a news capital. Other important news capitals have been, in earlier years, Leopoldville, Tunis, Salisbury, Addis Ababa, Abidjan, Cairo, and Algiers.

Russell Warren Howe, using a scale based on local government pressures, news availability, telecommunications, air communications, and climate/city, rated in order the following cities as desirable locales for continental correspondents: London, Paris, Dakar, Leopoldville, Tunis, Nairobi, Lagos, Salisbury, and Addis Ababa.[8]

Nairobi, now the favorite base for the foreign press, did not develop as a news capital until after independence in 1963 because foreign reporters, especially from Communist countries, were not welcomed by the British administrators.

The number of foreign correspondents, especially Americans,

has increased greatly in the years since independence. John Hughes, a British-born journalist who covered Africa for the *Christian Science Monitor,* told what it was like when he first went to Africa in 1955: "When I arrived . . . there were only two other American foreign correspondents stationed in my territory. For some while thereafter, three of us, from the New York *Times, Time-Life,* and the *Christian Science Monitor,* were the sole full-time resident correspondents of the American press covering Africa south of the Sahara."[9]

Peter Webb, *Newsweek's* senior African correspondent, was probably typical of the handful of first-rate journalists. Based in Nairobi, Webb was responsible for all of Africa and traveled a great deal. *Newsweek* had stringers in almost all countries, but Webb became personally involved in all the major stories. The only real pressure was the threat of expulsion:

> One has to weigh one's words very carefully to think of the possible repercussions before committing them to print. As a result, I think that most foreign correspondents on this continent exercise a form of self-censorship which may, in some ways, be no bad thing. To paraphrase Sam Johnson, the thought of having to pack up one's whole household within twenty-four hours concentrates the mind wonderfully.
> Should he or should he not file a certain story, knowing that it may get him in trouble? Every correspondent has to overcome this problem in his own way. My own rough rule of thumb is that if the story is sufficiently important then publish and be damned, but if it's something that is essentially trivial, and will be forgotten by tomorrow then perhaps it is better to pass it by. . . . Reporting Africa is like walking through a minefield; you have to be very careful where you put your feet.[10]

Webb found the African leaders difficult to see and sensitive to criticism. "Though they have achieved political independence, they realize they still don't have economic independence. They see economic control still in the hands of the whites and there are not enough educated Africans yet to take over. This frustrates them and they consider Western press criticism as the last straw. I just go ahead and do my job and write things as I see them. If they expel me, they'll expel me," he said.[11]

Webb felt that in the mid-sixties the New York *Times,* the Associated Press, and Richard Beeston of the London *Daily Telegraph* did the best job of reporting Africa. Webb believed that too many African officials live with myths:

They see Western press criticism as a wicked plot. They can't believe that Western correspondents don't get daily briefings from the U.S. embassy on the line to follow. Then there is the myth of the neo-colonists who are out to steal the riches of Africa. What riches? Or the myth that the United States is in the Congo to protect its uranium supply. If they knew what was happening, they'd know the mines have been closed for two years and that we have a stockpile to last out the century.[12]

Webb has found in some, but not all, African countries a rooted belief in the conspiracy theory of history:

In this theory words like "imperialist," "neo-colonialist," and "plot" are used to describe practically anything that goes wrong in the country, and this is extended to cover critical reporting. According to this theory, foreign reporters are "lackeys" or "puppets" of their capitalist masters and, therefore, anything they write about the country which can be construed as derogatory is part of a plot to undermine the country concerned. Frankly, there is nothing to be done about this attitude of mind, except to shake one's head sadly and hope that time will cure the malady.[13]

CRITICISMS OF FOREIGN JOURNALISTS

Africans tend to lump together all European newsmen when they criticize the "foreign press." Representatives of the New York *Times,* TASS, *Time* magazine, New China News Agency, or a racist paper in Rhodesia are all considered to come out of the same mold. And African leaders, the best as well as the worst, have not been sparing in the criticisms of the foreign press.

The African's suspicions of foreign correspondents were well expressed by the late Tom Mboya:

It is therefore important that the press should concern itself with finding out what goes on in the African mind. In the majority of cases the world's press is served by foreign correspondents who pay short visits to the various parts of Africa and on whom the world's verdict over Africa may rest. The news agencies are often relying on such journalists or reporters who may not themselves know enough or physically be able to cover the area assigned to them, to be able to interpret the African scene.

The result is that the news coming out of Africa is often, if not always, related to the already biased and prejudiced mind that keeps asking such questions as "Is this pro-East or pro-West?" Very few, if any, of the world's press ask such logical, in our view, and simple questions, as: "Is this pro-African?"[14]

Mboya, an intelligent and able man, who was considered a pro-U.S. moderate, also said, "The American press is America's worst enemy in Africa."[15] Ambassador George Padmore of Liberia, a conservative African state with a long tradition of friendship with the United States, said, "The American press, more than any other foreign news [medium] castigates the efforts of Africa's pioneers." The damage it does to the influence of the United States abroad "cannot be undone by foreign aid or by sending emissaries of the same racial or religious background to these foreign lands."[16]

African leaders are perhaps overly sensitive to what the foreign press says about them. President Kenneth Kaunda of Zambia told a group of foreign journalists: "We are conscious that Africa for a long time has been judged by the negative events which have been taking place. What has been emphasized are those events which portend trouble for us. Our achievements have always been played down. This may not be deliberate. However, the effect is that certain sections of the sensational press have led world opinion to disregard the startling advancements in the fields of economic development and social improvement."[17]

Kaunda himself was reported to receive daily a summary of everything said in the British press about Zambia.

African leaders are particularly critical of the two American news-magazines, *Time* and *Newsweek,* which are widely read throughout Africa. At times their coverage of African news events can be trivial, anecdotal, and even cynical. The correspondent in the field, who may have filed a complete and accurate story, is often blamed (and sometimes deported) when an editor in New York rewrites his material, changing the emphasis completely. For example, *Time*'s coverage of the historic founding conference of the Organization of African Unity in Addis Ababa in May 1963 consisted mostly of a few paragraphs about dancing girls in Ethiopian night clubs. Payne wrote: "At the above-mentioned OAU conference, I watched two *Time* correspondents with typewriters balanced on their knees conscientiously spin out sheet after sheet of copy until there was a mound of paper on the floor. The few racy paragraphs distilled from this caused the subsequent issue to be banned in Ethiopia."[18]

American and West European correspondents suffer from the fact that African officials are often unaware of how a free press and its representatives operate. This is complicated by the increasing number of "journalists" from Communist countries.

A few are journalists genuinely interested in African problems, but others are concerned only with the propagation of international Communism and some are even political and espionage agents for their governments. Hence it is often difficult for an official in an African ministry of information to believe that the New York *Times* man does not really work for the U.S. government.

Sanger found African officials make three main complaints against Western correspondents: (1) "Too much directly hostile comment." Too many Africans believe that the press should only praise or at least not criticize any actions of an African government. (2) "Too much writing about personalities, especially to illustrate divisions within an African country." If a newsman writes a story about one African politician, his political rivals usually conclude it is an effort to build him up, to enhance his political stature. They often fail to understand that to Western media, people make news and often indeed are news. (3) "Too much 'speculation' in news stories." Communist bloc newsmen avoid this and tend to rely on handouts which they file with little comment. African critics fail to see that "speculation" can often be the necessary interpretation needed to make a story or situation understandable to readers thousands of miles away.[19]

Much of the misunderstanding is caused not by the resident correspondents but by the nonspecialist or the junketing correspondent who flies in, does a hasty and frequently unbalanced reporting job, and then flies off again. There has been undoubtedly a good deal of sensationalized reporting, especially in regard to such stories as the upheavals in the Congo and the Nigerian civil war.

It is also regrettably true that some resident correspondents have written sensational and inaccurate stories that appeared abroad under pseudonyms.

Certainly there is much truth in many African criticisms of U.S. reporting in Africa. Many of these criticisms are shared by American experts on Africa.

Many reporters (and editors) tend to relate news of Africa to the Cold War. Events in Africa are presented not in African terms, but according to how they affect East-West tensions, and as the Cold War has retreated from Africa, so has news coverage. Misleading reportage not only angers Africans but does a disservice to American audiences. Some foreign correspondents use a double standard in evaluating African states, which they tend to divide into "good" and "bad." Much has been written about the authoritarian tendencies in the "bad" Casablanca group (Ghana, Algeria, Mali, etc.), while the same shortcomings in one-party states in Liberia, Ivory Coast, Kenya, and other conservative nations that may be more "pro-Western" are glossed over or ignored.[20]

American reporters may show their cultural arrogance and inadvertently reveal old stereotypes and prejudices about Negoes. Such lack of knowledge of African culture and politics often results in oversimplified and misleading reporting, according to Philip Curtin, an eminent Africanist.

The war, for instance, between the long-oppressed Bahutu majority in Rwanda against the traditional Batutsi aristocracy in 1959 was labeled by the press as "tribal warfare" instead of a peasants' revolt for which there is ample historical precedent in Europe. Such wars are called "irrational" or "primitive" when there may be quite rational reasons for what has occurred, reasons at least as rational as those used to justify wars in Europe. All too often Western reporters are guilty of characterizing Africans as "primitive," "cannibalistic," and quick to slaughter their fellow-man.

The American press, too, is guilty of not making proper distinctions. Nkrumah's Ghana was indeed a dictatorship, but not as completely pro-Communist and anti-American as the press made it out to be.

Admittedly it is much more difficult for Americans to understand events in Africa than those of Europe because Americans share cultural similarities with Europeans and have a greater knowledge of European history.

In reporting Africa the Western press tends to stress differences where there are similarities with Americans' experiences and similarities where there are differences.

One of the basic causes of misunderstanding is that the American reporter, whether working for the Associated Press, *Time,* or the New York *Times,* is writing primarily for American readers and not for an African audience. To an editor in New York City, a particular story coming out of Africa may not be news for his readers unless there is an angle of interest to American readers, whether it be something relating to the Cold War or to what is happening to a handful of American missionaries stranded in the Congo.

To the sensitive African, this is often just the kind of news that he feels distorts or misrepresents events in Africa. But as one correspondent said, "Do you want to be reading about the Sudan when there is nothing happening there?" Or another comment, "Why the hell should anyone but a specialist be interested in the Congo when there is not a crisis there?"[21]

Laurence Fellows, East African correspondent of the New York *Times*, agrees:

> The greatest problem in presenting news of Africa to American readers is, to my mind, the lack of interest American readers have in the ordinary run of news out of Africa. Lately, American interest has been absorbed by problems which touch closer to home. One is the war in Vietnam. The other is the violence and social dislocation that have attended our racial problems. . . . For the ordinary, mildly exciting story we file out of Africa we have to slog constantly uphill in the battle to find space in the paper.[22]

INTERVENTION AT STANLEYVILLE

The frequent "double misunderstanding" over African news events was well illustrated by the events of November 1964 when Belgian paratroops, transported in U.S. planes, rescued Americans and Europeans held as hostages by Congolese rebels in Stanleyville in the Eastern Congo.

The press reaction to these events, which was markedly different in the U.S. and European papers from those of Africa, showed how the modern African sees or perceives a certain news event in quite a different way from a European. Each reacted reflexively according to his own stereotypes.

The Western press stressed the humanitarian aspects of the paratroop drop, but not the fact that it was (at least in African eyes) a swift military intervention by a former colonial ruler, Belgium, in an African civil war. *Time*'s cover story of December 4, 1964, featured Dr. Paul Carlson, the American medical missionary who was killed, along with several white hostages, just before he could be rescued in Stanleyville.

Stories in the Western press stressed the plight of the stranded whites and the savagery and primitiveness of the Congo rebels who slaughtered and mutilated many of their hostages.

From an African point of view, the Western press gave too little or no attention to the brutal tactics of the hated white mercenaries who worked for Congo Premier Moise Tshombe or the fact that during the prolonged revolt in the Eastern Congo, thousands of Congolese civilians, including mostly teachers and civil servants, had been systematically killed off by the rebels.

So under the circumstances it was easy for the Westerner to approve of the paradrop because it meant the saving of noncombatant white lives in a turbulent conflict. Accordingly, Westerners were somewhat shocked to see such respected and moderate African leaders as President Jomo Kenyatta of Kenya and President Julius Nyerere of Tanzania (who called it "another Pearl Harbor") publicly and vehemently disapprove of the paradrop.

The Africans looked past the humanitarian aspects, possibly because the humanitarian concern seemed to be only for whites, and instead saw the paradrop as an imperialist military intervention in a civil war directed against Tshombe, who was widely regarded throughout black Africa as a tool of neo-colonists trying to reassert their authority in independent black Africa.

The New York *Times* felt that there was too much publicity surrounding the rescue efforts. Shortly after the drop, the *Times* editorialized:

> The dramatic U.S.-Belgian airborne operation in the Congo was fully justified and effectively carried out but—in retrospect—it should have been done sooner and it should have been kept secret until after the event. The political and psychological disadvantages of the operation, illustrated by the expected Soviet and African protests, were an inherent part of it no matter when it was done: the objective—the saving of lives—far outweighed these disadvantages. Prior permission of the Tshombe government was of course necessary, but the last-minute nature of the air drop and publicity concerning it probably helped to cause loss of life.[23]

The New York *Herald-Tribune* editorialized on November 26, 1964:

> The massacre of hostages in Lumumba Square proved what already had become apparent—the Congolese rebels of Stanleyville were savages. . . . The intervention was purely and strictly a humanitarian one to save innocent men, women, and children, including Congolese and citizens of at least 18 foreign countries, after the Tshombe government refused to submit to blackmail.

The *Spark,* Nkrumah's partisan paper in Ghana, editorialized on the incident the next day:

How long is the world prepared to tolerate the naked open aggression of American, Belgian, and British imperialism in the heart of the African continent? How long will the world stand by while Congolese women are shot (by Tshombe's white mercenaries) before the eyes of their little children? How long do we contemplate, passive and inactive, while Congolese patriots are tortured and murdered by hired assassins of imperialism? . . . Why does not the conscience of the world shriek aloud at such horrors being perpetrated?[24]

It is difficult to believe that both editorials were commenting on the same news event, yet the *Spark*'s view was one generally accepted by African nationalists.

An important African journalist, Hilary Ng'weno, then editor of the *Nation* in Nairobi, wrote:

As if the intervention had not hurt the West's image in Africa badly enough, the Western Press added insult to injury by painting a picture of the Stanleyville affair which was anything but true to the facts. For the brutal death of about a hundred hostages and white civilians, the Western Press, particularly American, accused the Congolese of primitive savagery and revelled in lewd description of events and scenes more suited for a surgeon's handbook. But of the death of thousands of Congolese at the hands, not of nationalists, but reprisal-hungry mercenary and Tshombe troops, little was said. The Western press's reporting of the Stanleyville affair was a clear indication of the urgent need for Africa to develop an efficient system of news agencies, which besides striving to report the truth as they see it, would endeavour to check the very obvious, however unofficial, propaganda which the Western press is capable of unleashing. If such agencies were in existence at the time of the Stanleyville affair, Africa would most certainly have heard more about Congolese orphans and widows whose parents and husbands died at the hands of Tshombe troops and very much less of the smaller number of European women and children who anxiously waited to be reunited with their families newly rescued from Stanleyville and to hear their long litany of miraculous escapes, real and imagined, from the "Simbas."[25]

William Attwood, U.S. ambassador to Kenya who was handling negotiations with the Congo rebels for release of the hostages, has well expressed the double misunderstanding aspects of the situation:

We saw the Stanleyville rescue operation as a dramatic effort to save hundreds of helpless, innocent people. It was humanitarian, and it was necessary, since all other attempts to release them had failed. . . . But if you could put yourself in the shoes of an average educated African, you got quite a different picture. When he looked at the Congo, he saw a black government in Stanleyville being attacked by a gang of hired South African thugs, and black people being killed by rockets from American planes. He did not know about the thousands of blacks who were tortured and murdered by the Simbas, but he did know that the mercenaries and their Katangan auxiliaries left a trail of African corpses in their wake. . . . Even more galling to the educated African was the shattering of so many of his illusions—that Africans were now masters of their own continent, that OAU was a force to be reckoned with, that a black man with a gun was the equal of a white man with a gun. For in a matter of weeks, two hundred swaggering white mercenaries had driven through an area the size of France, scattered the Simbas, and captured their capital; and in a matter of hours, 545 Belgians in American planes had defied the OAU, jumped into the heart of Africa and taken out nearly 2,000 people—with the loss of one trooper.

The weakness and impotence of newly independent Africa had been harshly and dramatically revealed to the whole world, and the educated African felt deeply humiliated; the white man with a gun, the old plunderer who had enslaved his ancestors, was back again, doing what he pleased, when he pleased, where he pleased. And there wasn't a damn thing Africa could do about it, except yell rape.[26]

WIRE SERVICE NATIONALISM

Unquestionably, most Americans know little about Africa, and unfortunately, what little they know is often culled from misleading sources—that is, Tarzan movies and "Daktari"-type television shows, exaggerated travel accounts, etc.

Despite the high professional competence of many foreign correspondents, it must be recognized that there is something operating here which has been called "wire service nationalism." That is, a well-trained and experienced correspondent, his claims of objectivity notwithstanding, still must report the news from the point of view of his own readers' interests, as well as the national interests and foreign policy considerations of his own government. Much of the kind of "wire service nationalism" so obvious in the Stanleyville story is inextricably tied up with definitions of what is *news*, whether in London or Accra.

This kind of bias (often intentional and with good reason) can result in Reuters carrying a great deal of racial strife stories from the United States but seldom any from Britain. It can cause

AFP to carry a disproportionate amount of news about France in its African services. And African news services, whether national or Pan-African, are subject to the same kind of bias, perhaps even more so. News is relative. The professional journalist understands this and tries to be as fair and objective as possible.

IN DEFENSE OF THE AMERICAN CORRESPONDENT

The foreign correspondent is often criticized—and should be—because no aspect of journalism should be exempt from critical appraisal. But much of the criticism should be directed at his editors back home, for the foreign correspondent in Africa must work under difficult and trying conditions—conditions often not understood.

Howe, who covered Africa for the Washington *Post* and Baltimore *Sun,* wrote:

> On the whole, I think the U.S. press has done a remarkably good job of adapting to this new field and interpreting this bewildering new political complex with its motivations and political cultures so different from the motivations and political cultures to which correspondents are accustomed. Given the paucity and frequent ineffectiveness of information services and the uncooperative attitude of many African leaders—there are, of course, some shining exceptions—given the problems of travel and communications, I do not think there is cause for serious complaint about American coverage of Africa in general.[27]

Howe makes a telling point often overlooked by African critics:

> It should be remembered that our basic task is not to promote African interests. We often do, of course, by bringing to the attention of our readers important public and private African projects that need financing, by stressing the plight of certain African populations, by introducing African leaders to the American public, and in many other ways. But promoting African interests is not our role or duty. Our task is to interpret.

Howe has his criticisms too of the critics:

> On the news coverage front, the self-centeredness of African leaders, the parochial view which African governments have of world problems, and consequently toward the world press, leads to African leaders expecting us to praise without blaming, to bleed

for African predicaments but not to bleed for the predicaments Africa causes.[28]

Due to inside leaks and trial balloons, many news rumors circulate in African capitals, but correspondents find it impossible to check them out because officials are "not in" or are difficult to see. Correspondents often find it difficult to get much news out of African government leaders when they do get in. Not only are interviews hard to get, but leaders are often reluctant to speak candidly to the press. And the correspondent who does report candidly can get into trouble.

Almost everywhere in Africa the foreign correspondent must work with the threat of expulsion hanging over his head if his story, or the publication he works for, displeases someone in the government. In the years since independence, a large number of foreign journalists have been deported, often on very short notice, and some even jailed.

Reporters from both Western and Communist nations have been deported. However, there is a difference: the Communist reporters have usually been ousted, not for overzealous reporting, but for involvement or suspected involvement in political intrigue and espionage.

Some Western correspondents who have run afoul of African governments have indeed been guilty of sensationalized and irresponsible reporting. But most of those ousted had merely been doing the kind of thorough and objective reporting they had been trained to do.

Western correspondents have been faced with a variety of difficulties. Correspondents have run into trouble in both black- and white-controlled countries. Here are some typical examples:

In mid-1967 Lt. Colonel Gowon, military ruler of Nigeria, issued a decree prohibiting foreign correspondents from publishing or relaying anything detrimental to the federal government. Lloyd Garrison, senior African correspondent of the New York *Times*, was expelled.[29]

Jean Burfin, correspondent of AFP, was expelled from Chad the same year because of his reports of a clash between government forces and bandits.[30]

In Rhodesia, also in 1967, the Ian Smith government acted against several British correspondents: John Osman, BBC Commonwealth correspondent, and his two-man television camera team were put on board a plane for Johannesburg after spending seventeen hours in custody on arrival in Salisbury. John de St. Jorre, the *Observer's* Central African correspondent, and Colin Legum, the *Observer's* Commonwealth correspondent, were notified that they were prohibited immigrants.[31]

Robert Dewez, director of the printing press of *Presse Congolaise* and correspondent for Reuters and AP, was arrested in Kinshasa, Congo. No reason was given.[32]

Edward Jones, a British journalist representing several British newspapers and American news services, was expelled by the Uganda government on six hours notice in April 1966. No reason was given.[33]

In Algeria, a Swiss journalist, Pierre Moser, correspondent of *Le Monde,* AP, and Radio Lausanne, was expelled in March 1966 for "interfering in the internal affairs of the country." In Guinea, Harold Sieve, *Daily Telegraph* (of London) correspondent, was expelled at the same time.[34]

The threat of expulsion is certainly a tangible impediment to a correspondent. So is the vast geographical area of his responsibility. Not only are there fewer correspondents in Africa than elsewhere but they must travel more. A survey of foreign correspondents found that in an average month a correspondent in Africa traveled 4,044 miles compared with 1,523 miles for Western Europe, and 2,362 miles for Asia, and 3,133 miles for Latin America.[35]

"Communications"—getting the story out—can often be a bigger problem than transportation or censorship by unfriendly government officials.

Newsmen almost unanimously rank the lack of good, inexpensive communications facilities as *the* major obstacle to covering Africa. Indifference of communications officials to newsmen's requirements can cause long delays in transmitting stories. Some countries do not yet have public telex systems, and even where telex does exist, the number of transmitting machines is so small that newsmen often wait in line for hours for a turn at the teleprinters. In West Africa there is growing use of telex, but the rates remain high, often one pound sterling ($2.40) or more per minute to Europe. In francophonic Africa, the rates are even higher. Press cable rates out of most French-speaking African countries are about nine U.S. cents per word. Telecommunications often close down at night and telephone links are tenuous and expensive.[36]

Fellows placed high priority on effective communications.

"The correspondent must know how to operate a telex machine, in spite of all the advice he might get to the contrary before he comes. He must learn the telegraph and telephone routes that are open to him, for when the censor and atmospherics are combining to spoil one circuit, there is always another."[37]

Garrison, another *Times* man, recalled some of his communications problems:

> Getting a story to New York can involve almost every device but the proverbial cleft stick, and once included smuggling copy out of Katanga in an empty Vat 69 bottle. Missionary ham radios are good emergency outlets. One night in the Congo we roused an elderly ham in Nova Scotia. "You really with the *Times?*" he queried. It scarcely surprised him: he'd performed a similar service relaying copy for a *Times* reporter covering an ill-fated German trans-Atlantic seaplane race back in 1919.
>
> During the first Nigerian coup (in January 1966) all normal communications were cut. Several alternative routes were tried: putting copy on a plane to Nairobi, broadcasting a pooled report by ham to the BBC in London and chugging in an open 30-h.p. outboard across the Lagos bar and three miles out to sea to a Norwegian ship. For $10 and a bottle of Scotch the captain was persuaded to radio the story to his company office in Oslo; the copy was in the London bureau a scant five hours later.
>
> Tramp steamers plying Africa's west coast call at almost every port, and crewmen, one noticed, could go ashore at will—without passports or visas. This stood the *Times* in good stead recently when I tried to get into Conakry, Guinea, without a visa. No American newsman had been allowed in for over a year. But as an "assistant purser" aboard a freighter, getting past immigration proved a piece of cake.[38]

Sometimes correspondents have to use ingenuity to avoid physical danger. Weldon Wallace, Baltimore *Sun* reporter, was beaten and threatened by drunken soldiers after he tried to get into Katanga January 2, 1963, with Arthur Bonner of CBS and Lionel Fleming, a British newsman. Drunken soldiers halted the trio on learning that two had U.S. passports and Fleming an Irish passport. They once got as far as their car but again were halted by drunken soldiers, while the crowds that gathered shouted: "Shoot them, kill them, they are Americans, they are filthy pigs, they are United Nations spies."

They were taken to a mud hut where they were slapped and threatened with loaded guns, Eventually, they caught sight of Peter Younghusband of the London *Daily Mail*, who quickly sized up the situation but dared not reply to their waving. Then the three were whisked to a quiet glade where they were ordered from the Katangan car and made to strip. Suddenly a major ran up and ordered the reporters released. Wallace said he learned later that Younghusband had notified authorities.[39]

An outstanding journalist, George Clay of NBC News, was killed by a sniper's bullet while riding with mercenaries toward Stanleyville in November 1964.

Civil wars and coups d'état are extraordinary situations, of course, and the foreign correspondent must somehow transport himself there, obtain the story, and then get the story out of Africa.

Andrew Borowiec, who covered the Algerian war for Associated Press from 1958 onward, considers unpredictability to be the most important of a dozen obstacles hampering efforts to cover Africa: "Any day may bring a revolution, the downfall of a dictator believed secure, a savage tribal onslaught or a riot pitting one ethnic group against another. Months can go by on the huge continent without a major news story. Then, as if by a magic chain reaction, events may follow one another with staggering speed, again proving nothing beyond the fact that Africa is unpredictable." Other obstacles that Borowiec cited are bad communications, whimsical officials, visa problems, tropical ailments, and frequent threat of death or mutilation.

"Most reporters covering the continent have become stoics," Borowiec said, "perhaps to a greater degree than those working elsewhere. You have to be that to sit through a news conference at which a Congolese official accuses Americans of cannibalism."[40]

The present logistics of foreign reportage in Africa require that correspondents keep hopping from one country to another. This so-called "crisis reporting" has been much criticized as emphasizing only the violence and upheavals of Africa, not the steady day-to-day events, many of them constructive and progressive. But few African capitals produce daily stories—at least, according to the definitions of news accepted by the world's news media. Since it costs an estimated $40,000 to $60,000 a year—including salary, housing, travel, and message-sending expenses—to maintain an American resident correspondent abroad, few of the news media, whether newspaper, news service, or broadcasting network, are willing to maintain more than several correspondents in Africa.

Sometimes covering a planned event like a conference of

African leaders can involve problems not encountered by journalists operating in areas where government/press relations are more highly developed.

The 400 newsmen who gathered at Accra, Ghana, for the Organization of African Unity summit meeting in October 1965 were told there would be space for only 35 inside the hall. "Your complaint will be taken under advisement," said the briefing officer. Lynn Heinzerling, a veteran AP newsman, who did get inside, found that the formidable Ghanaian matrons serving as ushers had filled the aisles and many seats with their friends. Another AP correspondent, Kenneth Whiting, managed to find a secluded veranda on which he wrote one story, away from security guards seeking to confiscate the speaker's advance text. Another newsman lost his copy in a grabbing match with the guards.[41]

HOW TO IMPROVE THE SITUATION

Despite the difficulties, about a dozen or more American correspondents have been outstanding reporters of Africa during the turbulent 1960s. Regrettably, some of the best have been transferred to other assignments and replaced by newcomers without the background and experience that comes only from years of residence.

Thus U.S. press coverage is far from what it should be. An outstanding U.S. Africanist, Professor Vernon McKay, feels it hurts U.S. interests in Africa. He wrote:

> The oversimplified treatment of African issues in the press leads to unsophisticated public reactions which can be harmful to our foreign policy when they inspire such heated and ill-informed controversies as the debate over American policy toward Katanga. While it would be unfair to focus blame on hardworking and conscientious journalists for this situation, the American press must nonetheless improve its Africa reporting if American policy in Africa is to be effective. Heaven forbid that professors take over the duties of journalists, but it would be helpful if more journalists could obtain special training in African studies. The kind of reporting usually found in the *Times* of London, the *Economist,* and the weekly *West Africa* shows that relatively impartial analysis rather than one-sided opinion is both feasible and desirable.[42]

McKay's suggestion of reporters better trained in African area studies is being slowly implemented. A good example is

Kenneth Whiting who covered West Africa for AP after he had been in the Peace Corps in Africa and after he had been to Columbia University's gradute program in international reporting. He later headed AP's bureau in Johannesburg.

Better trained reporters, well versed in African history, politics, languages, and problems, is only the beginning for improving the coverage of Africa in American news media. But it may help to break the "vicious circle" of U.S. reporting about Africa which goes something like this:

● News services maintain few correspondents in Africa because U.S. newspapers and broadcasting stations carry little news on Africa.

● U.S. press and broadcasting outlets carry little African news because they say the wire services supply little and also that readers and listeners are not interested in Africa anyway. (With the de-emphasis of the Cold War in Africa in the late 1960s and Western nations' increasing concern with their own domestic problems, there probably was even less interest in Africa than in early years of the decade.)

● The average person is not interested in African news, it is said, mainly because he is uninformed about that part of the world and the reason he is uninformed is that the mass media have not told him much about it.

Several other factors may help break the cycle.

First, prospects for improving foreign reportage are tied up with the prospects for the local news media in Africa. As the local press grows and improves, there will be more clients for the world news agencies who will improve the coverage also because the local press will help gather the news that news agencies carry—as they now do in Europe and other industrialized nations.

Second, as the local press grows and matures, the caliber of African journalists will improve accordingly. And the foreign media, particularly the world news agencies, will come to rely more and more on African nationals to represent them in African nations instead of relying on Europeans.

Third, African coverage (and the American public's knowledge about African affairs) will improve when the U.S. mass media begin to take Africa a lot more seriously. This means primarily investing much more money in covering this significant portion of the world. It means better trained reporters, more knowledgeable editors and desk men, and a more mature and responsible approach to news about Africa. It is no longer enough to write features about witch doctors and "restless natives" and safaris to see wild animals.

But the more immediate problem is how to expand and sustain the interest of the outside world in Africa. Philip W. Quigg, managing editor of *Foreign Affairs,* wrote: "More disturbing than the distortions or sensation-seeking of some correspondents is the fact that, as the high drama of newly won independence recedes, substantive (as contrasted to crisis) reporting from Africa appears to be declining."[43] If this is true of U.S. news media, in part because of our growing domestic crises and disillusionment over Vietnam, then all who care about Africa will be much the poorer.

6

INTERNATIONAL POLITICAL COMMUNICATION

INDEPENDENCE in the new nations of Africa has meant national sovereignty, government by Africans, membership in the United Nations, diplomatic recognition, and the exchange of ambassadors with foreign nations. It has meant, too, involvement in the Cold War.

Both East and West have been vying for influence with the new nations. Foreign powers of all sizes and political persuasions are involved: the former colonial rulers—France, Britain, and Belgium; the great powers—the United States, Soviet Union, and Red China; as well as the smaller European nations. All have adjusted their foreign policies to seek influence and friends among the thirty-seven new national states established from Cape Verde to the Horn of East Africa and from Tunis to Tananarive.

Whether they have wanted to or not (and most have not), the new African states have been caught up in the crosscurrents of great power politics. Developing nations are by definition at a distinct disadvantage economically and politically with the great industrialized states of the Northern Hemisphere. They are also at an international communication disadvantage—they receive a lot more than they can send out.

African independence has not upset the balance of power in the world, but it has added some new elements: a new voting bloc in the United Nations; a far-flung strategic area of diverse peoples; and great resources of raw materials and minerals, the riches of which are just beginning to be revealed.

African international relations with the rest of the world is a complex subject belonging properly to political scientists. However the role that news communications play in Africa's international relations is relevant here.

Not unexpectedly, the United States, the Soviet Union, and Red China have been most significantly involved, so will be given the most attention.

Much of the international news communications flow into Africa has direct political implications. The Cold War has been fought with many weapons—espionage, bribery, subversion, technical aid, development programs, cultural exchanges, diplomatic maneuvers, and not the least, the news media.

Foreign governments have used mass communications in attempts to influence directly the uncommitted African peoples—news broadcasts by Radio Moscow or Voice of America are good examples. But also, foreign diplomatic personnel—press attachés and "information officers"—have made intensive efforts to directly influence the Africans' own news media and the journalists who run them. In the industrialized nations, journalists were under nothing like the pressures that African news "gatekeepers" were subjected to. The African journalist or mass communicator was among that tiny elite of "influentials" that foreign governments cultivated intensively in the new nations.

The undeclared and often rather polite news media war in Africa during the 1960s was essentially a three-way struggle: the United States and Western Europe versus the Soviet Union and Eastern European nations versus Communist China.

The great schism in the Communist world had an impact on Africa as elsewhere, and the resulting competition between Russia and the Communist Chinese was often more intense and bitter than that with Western nations.

But it would oversimplify a complex situation to describe international political communication in Africa as merely a three-way competition. The Eastern European nations—Hungary, Rumania, Czechoslovakia, East Germany, etc.—have been active in Africa and often seem to act on their own volition.

West Germany and East Germany have been carrying on their own rivalry, with recognition by the Africans of either Bonn or East Berlin as the prize. Israel has intensively curried favor with non-Arab nations.

The political communication activities of the three great Western powers—France, Britain, and the United States—at times operated at cross-purposes, since the former colonial powers were eager to maintain their influence in their former possessions. Through its subsidies to AFP, its training of broadcasters and journalists in Paris, and its financial support of local government newspapers and national news agencies, the French government greatly influenced news communications in francophonic Africa. One media venture was the Nouvelle Agence de Presse (NAP), an ostensibly private news feature agency which provided stories for both the French- and English-language press in Africa. Although most of the feature material was useful and nonpolitical, some of it was frankly pro-French in bias. Ainslie quoted an item in the bulletin of February 23, 1965, on "re-establishing Peace in South East Asia," which was not so much factual as an explanation and apology for French policy in South East Asia: "General De Gaulle's aim is in fact the true independence of Viet Nam, Laos and Cambodia. Africans and Malagasies should not wonder at this. Since his return to power in Paris, the President of the French Republic has based his whole policy on respect for the independence of every country."[1]

There was good reason to believe that the NAP was covertly financed by the French government and was an instrument of French policy in Africa.

The African situation reflected two important developments in world politics: (1) the weakening of both the Western alliance (France leaving NATO, for example) and the Communist bloc, which is no longer a "bloc" but more of a commonwealth; and (2) the gradual withdrawal of the old Cold War from Africa during the late 1960s. Theodore Draper pointed out that during the Congo crisis of 1960, Africa "suddenly and improbably became the neuralgic point of world politics. Since then, all sorts of things have happened in Africa, some not too dissimilar to the 1960 struggle, and no world crisis has ensued. The reason is simply that the United States and Russia have decided not to fight over Africa and not again to make an African civil war into an international issue."[2] If the great powers had really embroiled themselves in Nigeria in 1967–70, that civil war would have become a world crisis comparable to the Congo hostilities in 1960; instead it was a very tragic West African civil war, notable for the nonintervention of the great powers.

The Cold War, or any of its various mutations, can return quickly to Africa at any time, of course.

AFRICA'S OWN COLD WAR

Significantly, a few of the African nations themselves—most notably the United Arab Republic, Ghana under Nkrumah, and

South Africa—have intensively used mass communications for political advantage in Africa and elsewhere. As the old Cold War lessens, the smaller intra-African cold war (which has often turned hot) between the independent black nations and white-dominated southern African countries has increased.

News itself, much less political communication, is handled very differently on both sides of Africa's "thorntree curtain."

Black "terrorists" in the Rhodesian press are "freedom fighters" in papers throughout middle Africa. The rhetoric and hyperbole of the struggle permeates the news media on both sides. In the sub-Sahara, more and more African news centers around the southern African problem. And in South Africa even liberal antigovernment newspapers, such as the *Rand Daily Mail*, move closer to the Nationalist position as the external threat of "terrorists" (or "freedom fighters") crossing the Zambezi becomes more imminent.

This struggle along the "southern African battleline" is increasingly dominating international political communication in Africa. And this battle to rid Africa "of the last vestiges of colonialism" (or to "defend Western civilization on the continent") threatens to precipitate a head-on collision of the great powers in Africa. By supporting the African Nationalist cause, the Communist powers have an opportunity to win a real foothold in black Africa. The pressures on Britain and the United States, each with large economic investments in South Africa but each supporting majority rule and black self-determination, are great and will probably increase.

The term "international political communication" is clumsy and somewhat vague, but probably the best available. Other terms apply to only part of the process or are emotionally charged. As Davison wrote, "news," "information," "education," "entertainment," "culture," and "propaganda" are all involved in international political communication, but none is broad enough to include the others.[3]

Much of what has been communicated into Africa by outside nations can properly be defined as propaganda—that is, the attempt to influence the attitudes or behavior of others through the systematic use of words or other symbols. Propaganda is not inherently disreputable, but it is a loaded term, a pejorative epithet that is subjectively defined as a "persuasive statement I don't like." No one—whether a foreign correspondent, an artist, an educator, or a government information specialist—likes to be called a propagandist.

Nevertheless the term "international political communication" is still useful to distinguish between communications primarily intended to have a political effect and those that are not. Also a distinction should be made between government and nongovernment *sources* of international information.[4]

In any case, the lines are often fuzzy because government involvement itself is not always clear. Sometimes organizations such as Agence France Presse are indirectly subsidized by government because of the contribution they make to foreign policy objectives. American paperback books are sold in African bookstores far below the U.S. selling price because they are covertly subsidized by the U.S. Information Agency. And many a newsreel or movie "short" shown in an African commercial cinema is produced by a European government, but not so identified to the audience.

Often the best library in an African capital and its most important cultural center is maintained and run by a foreign nation. United States Information Service (USIS) reading room and offices in Sierra Leone occupy one of the best buildings and sites in downtown Freetown. The finest theatrical productions there have been produced by the British Council.

Such activities enable the United States, Britain, and France to enjoy a certain advantage in the East-West political communication tug-of-war. The flood of private or commercial communication content flowing to Africa from London, Paris, and New York does much to orient the cosmopolitan African toward those world capitals. And the effects of this exposure can have indirect political implications. However, some of the cheaper and more tawdry popular music, motion pictures, and television shows give a distorted picture of America.

Some news reports and pictures emanating from the United States give Africans an uncomplimentary and critical view of American life. This is unfortunate, but it is the necessary byproduct of an open and free society. It is impossible to estimate, for example, the damage done to American foreign policy objectives in Africa by the news stories and pictures of civil strife and urban ghetto riots originating in American news media and exploited by Communist propagandists. Such news cannot be hidden from the Africans and, of course, should not be.

COMMUNICATION ACTIVITIES OF COMMUNIST NATIONS

On the whole, the preponderant communication flow to Africa from Western sources probably gives the West an edge in the political propaganda competition with Communist nations.

The Communist nations enjoy certain advantages, however. The Soviet Union has had long experience in exporting vigorous international propaganda. Communist leaders have always taken an active part in foreign information policy and cultural affairs. This top-level attention to propaganda, combined with a totalitarian form of government of which the Soviet media system is an integral part, has made it easy for the Communists to adjust communication activities and messages to foreign policy objectives. Moreover, a Communist party in an African nation is organized so that central direction of international political communication is readily provided.

DIRECT COMMUNIST POLITICAL COMMUNICATION

In addition to covert subversion, the Communists employ pretty much the same wide range of activities used by the West: radio broadcasts, distribution of printed materials, training of journalists, diplomatic missions, recruitment of students and delegation exchanges, film showings, cultural performances, and selective use of wire services.

Communist nations' communication objectives have been twofold: to communicate directly to African leaders and peoples, and to influence directly the African news media and the people who run them.

Communist influence on mass communications varied considerably from one country to another and naturally was most pronounced in nations politically sympathetic to the Soviet Union or Red China. During the early 1960s, which may have been the high water mark of Communist influence on African media, the nations most affected were Ghana, Mali, Guinea, Congo (Brazzaville), Algeria, Tanzania, and the United Arab Republic. In some of the more conservative countries, such as the Ivory Coast, there was neither Communist diplomatic representation nor correspondents for TASS or other East European news agencies.

Publications. Large quantities of Soviet-printed materials were distributed throughout Africa, principally through two Communist-controlled publishing houses in London and Paris. Publications were also distributed through local contacts arranged by Communist embassies and by direct mail to individuals and organizations. Considerable amounts were distributed on newsstands, in bookstores, and by street hawkers. In addition, large numbers of books, principally in English and French, were sent to Africa.[5]

East Germany published two periodicals written exclusively for Africa: the *News,* a monthly magazine in English and French, and *Voix de l'Amitie* in French.[6]

A Russian periodical, *Soviet Weekly,* was published in London by the Soviet Embassy and sent in plain postal wrappers to British colonial and ex-colonial territories, particularly in Africa. The *African Communist,* a quarterly, was printed by the Farleigh Press in England for the South African Communist party and was outlawed in South Africa.[7]

John Cooley, a *Christian Science Monitor* correspondent who studied Chinese activities, wrote that Red China had a well-coordinated publication program aimed at Africa. Its mainstay was the ubiquitous *Peking Review,* published also in French as *Pekin Informations,* and mailed around the world by Chifa, the China Publications Center. Many copies were found in Stanley-ville amid litter the Congolese rebels left behind in late 1964. *Peking Review* reached individual subscribers and distribution centers in Africa (in English, French, Spanish, and Portuguese editions) by airmail, direct from Peking. Local Chinese emis-saries regularly compiled address lists of key persons, who then received free introductory copies.[8]

Chinese embassies in Africa distributed many press releases (distinct from those of the NCNA) and special studies on such subjects as light industry, agriculture, and petroleum in China. From Switzerland came briefly the slick-paper *Revolution,* edited by French Communist Jacques Verges and American Richard Gibson, pushing the Chinese line; this was suspended in 1965.[9] Peking sent a wide variety of brochures, pamphlets, and books in the major European and African languages. These included Chinese folk tales for children and adults, books on Chinese art, art reproductions of Chinese paintings, and some purely political pamphlets with such ponderous titles as "Statement Calling on the Peoples of the World to Unite to Oppose Racial Discrimina-tion by U.S. Imperialism and Support the American Negroes in Their Struggle against Racial Discrimination."[10]

The Communist Chinese embassy in the Central African Re-public, closed after a coup in early 1966, was considered the main distribution center for Central Africa.[11]

Broadcasting. The Communist nations give major emphasis to direct broadcasting into Africa.

Communist bloc broadcasting increased from 298 to 333½ hours per week (an 11 percent increase) from the end of 1962 to the end of 1963 and was characterized by a greater use of African languages. Communist international stations were using thirteen African languages (not counting Arabic). More than half the broadcasts were in the major vernaculars: Amharic, Bambara, Hausa, Swahili, Lingala, Malagasy, and Zulu.

A limited amount of television material was placed with African stations. It amounted to a yearly payload of less than 250 hours, most of it broadcast in Algeria. The content was mainly newsreels, light cultural material, and entertainment shows.[12]

Radio Peking is the best known and most effective propaganda channel of Red China in Africa. It began its African service in November 1956, fully two years ahead of the Soviet Union, but early broadcasts had very limited reception. The first two-hour program in English was beamed from Peking in September 1959. Two years later Peking was already well ahead of Moscow in total air time: African listening posts were logging thirty-five hours weekly in English, seven in Cantonese, seven in Portuguese, seven in Swahili, four in French, and another three hours in English not beamed exclusively to Africa.[13]

By July 1962, *Communist Affairs* reported, East European radio stations in Warsaw, Prague, East Berlin, Bucharest, and Sofia were all beaming programs to Africa.[14]

Communists have made special efforts to increase and hold their audiences. African listeners were encouraged to organize Listener's Clubs, and such groups have been reported in Nigeria, Ghana, Sierra Leone, Tanzania, and Kenya. Radio Prague has offered free transistor radios to Africans who can answer questions asked on its programs. Radio Sofia offered free trips to Sofia for Arab listeners.

Radio Peking has even tried to trick Africans into listening to its programs. Cooley said he monitored Peking broadcasts in both American-accented and British-accented English beamed to Africa. In the latter case, frequencies were often right next to the BBC frequency, and chimes that sound startlingly like BBC chimes were sometimes used.[15]

Imitation must indeed be the sincerest form of flattery in international political communication. The external news broadcasts of "Voice of South Africa" also followed closely the format of the famous BBC news bulletins which enjoy a high credibility in Africa.

U.S. Information Agency statistics show that by the end of 1963 Red China was broadcasting 63 hours a week to Africa,

Russia was broadcasting 126 hours a week, and the nations of East Europe were broadcasting a combined total of 140 hours a week.[16]

The level has remained fairly constant. By 1967 the USSR was broadcasting 147 hours a week directly to the sub-Sahara, while Red China was broadcasting 77 hours. (The United Arab Republic was broadcasting 161 hours weekly.)[17]

According to a 1964 BBC report, the ranking nations in foreign broadcast radio time in Africa were Red China, Russia, the United States, Britain, and the United Arab Republic, in that order.[18]

Cinema. Africans must import their films, and a number of film exchange agreements have been signed between Communist and African nations. Motion pictures are admittedly a difficult medium to break into if only because of the dominance of the commercial films from the United States, Britain, France, and India. However, more than 200 Soviet documentary films were sent to Africa in 1965. The most popular subject was space exploration, and for the first time, many sound tracks were dubbed in Swahili.

Chinese Communists have been increasing their use of film as a propaganda weapon. They have shot documentaries on African locations, processed them in China, and shipped them back for showing. These include the color film "Resolute Algeria" and black-and-white films entitled "Cities of Morocco," "An Ode to the Nile," "Independent Mali," "Chinese People Condemn the Murder of Patrice Lumumba," and others on Ghana, Guinea, and Tanzania.[19] "Chinese Film Weeks" have been held frequently in African capitals.

The Soviet Union and Eastern Europe, as well as Red China, have increased their film production. However, their efforts to penetrate the commercial film markets have met with little success. In view of their lack of cultural centers and access to commercial outlets, film showings were largely restricted to partisan groups, especially in nations where Communists were not particularly welcomed.[20]

COMMUNIST EFFORTS TO INFLUENCE AFRICAN NEWS MEDIA

Examining the Communist nations of East Europe, Robert and Elizabeth Bass wrote:

> The current aim of the "People's Democracies" seems to be not so much to increase the flow of material from Eastern Europe

> as to generate essentially pro-Communist sources of news and comment in the independent African states. . . . Very clearly, their hope is to wean the small number of practicing African journalists and broadcasters from reliance on Western press agencies and to train a new generation of writers and commentators who will be not only anti-Western by inclination but propagandists by training.[21]

This strategy has been implemented in a variety of ways and certainly shows the importance that Communists place on news communications. Since they originate abroad, the direct political communication by foreign broadcasting, Communist-produced films, and Communist-printed publications would seem to have smaller impact and credibility than political communication disseminated by African news media themselves. Communist news agencies provide one important channel for working through the local media.

News Services. As mentioned earlier, TASS and the other principal news agencies of the Communist world—Novosti, CTK, ADN, NCNA, TANYUG, and Prensa Latina—were received in about twenty-one African nations. Usually their reports went directly to the national news agency and then were disseminated to various publications, broadcasting stations, government offices, and embassies.

A daily English news service, relayed in Morse code at dictation speed, was started by Radio Peking in 1956 as a service for African editors. New China News Agency (NCNA) opened its first African office at Cairo in 1958 and soon had branches in several other capitals—Accra, Conakry, and Rabat—as soon as Chinese diplomats were accredited there.[22]

In 1964 and 1965 NCNA transmitted by radio to a number of regional bureaus in London, Berne, Algiers, Cairo, Conakry, Brazzaville, and Dar es Salaam a long daily news file in high-speed Morse code. Adapted to each region, this was transcribed, mimeographed in French and English, and either mailed free or sold for a nominal fee to newspapers, periodicals, and radio and television stations all over Africa. The Cairo branch of NCNA had thirty correspondents, three of whom were assigned to travel full-time in Syria and North Africa. In addition, the Cairo bureau had more than 100 "electricians." It was obvious that an agency branch with so large an organization was more than merely a news agency.[23]

Correspondents of NCNA obviously did a lot more than

merely gather and disseminate news. Their role was defined for them by a party journal in China in 1957 as "acting as the ears and mouth of the Party, the government and the people."[24] Such quasi-diplomatic or intelligence functions have caused a number of their representatives to be deported from African countries. Wang Te-ming, Nairobi correspondent for NCNA, for instance, was expelled in July 1965 because he was considered the paymaster for groups seeking to overthrow the moderate regime of Jomo Kenyatta.[25]

The following March, in 1966, the Kenya government ordered the expulsion of twelve Communist diplomatic officials, including two Soviet news service correspondents and a film representative, and one Czech news service man. The *Daily Nation* of Nairobi on March 11, 1966, commented on the deportations:

> Here is a method of spying, subversion and espionage which has now become fashionable in Africa. People from various countries come under the banner of "journalists," "employees of news agencies," or just "clerks" in the embassies without diplomatic protection. While in Africa these people deny any association with their own governments. Yet it is known that these newspapers and agencies are owned and run by governments. It is no secret that some of these men who pose as newspapermen are high officials in the intelligence network of their governments. . . . Some are known to be traveling throughout the country, in their plausible and seemingly harmless capacities as "newsmen," "cameramen," "news agents," or simply as "tourists." Those who were deported yesterday were not only doing these things but actually were engaging in political organization on behalf of some misguided groups in the country. What nation can tolerate this kind of thing?

Unfortunately, bona fide Western newsmen are often unfairly suspected of similar activities. In any case, the lines between legitimate newsgathering, political communication, espionage, and even subversion become blurred because of the activities of "journalists" from Communist nations.

In their political communication activities, as distinct from either newsgathering or intelligence work, TASS, NCNA, and other Communist agencies should be compared with the U.S. Information Agency and the British Information Service (BIS) rather than the Associated Press or Reuters. The expenditures of the NCNA, for example, are part of the Chinese national budget, and its content is controlled by the Chinese Communist Party's propaganda department.[26]

The organization of TASS is similar. It is an official agency of the Soviet government directly attached to the Council of Ministers. "TASS in essence is the creature of the top Soviet leadership. . . . When this role of government functionary is combined with that of foreign correspondent, there is a blurring of the lines of demarcation between the journalist, the propagandist, and the spy."[27]

In 1961 a new Soviet press service, Novosti, was launched. In contrast to TASS, which is overtly attached to the government, Novosti has been described as "unofficial." Its aims were defined as the "wide dissemination abroad of truthful information about the Soviet Union and informing the Soviet public of life of the peoples of other countries." Besides providing background and feature material to the news media, it published some thirty magazines abroad. Novosti's daily information bulletin, *News from the Soviet Union,* was transmitted by wire to forty nations.[28] Novosti, with thirteen bureaus in Africa, may be "unofficial," but it is still controlled by the Soviet government.

As government-subsidized press services, the Communist agencies can undercut the prices of Western services; as noted, the services are often offered free or at very minimal costs. Perhaps they have no choice, since the news offered is usually selective, incomplete, often biased, and frequently twenty-four hours or so behind the commercial agencies.

Technical and Economic Assistance to Media. Possibly the most valuable help to African media, certainly from the Africans' point of view, has been the direct Communist aid to build and expand media facilities. Politics aside, African news media do need such help.

Guinea, for example, received $110 million in credits and grants in 1961 from Communist nations. This assistance included a radio station from the USSR, a printing plant supplied by East Germany, and Polish and Czech journalism teachers for the National School of Journalism. In 1962 Czechoslovakia built a 150-kilowatt shortwave radio transmitter in Guinea.

Ghana received $182 million in credits and grants during 1961, including an East German printing plant and Czech film technicians.

The printing plant in Dar es Salaam, Tanzania, used to publish the party newspaper, the *Nationalist,* was furnished by East Germany and supervised by East German technicians. On December 10, 1966, a new radio station built by Communist

China opened in Dar es Salaam. The 100-kilowatt facility cost $560,000. President Julius Nyerere said the station would carry messages of encouragement and support "to oppressed people throughout the world."[29]

Russia provided a Soviet-built press and a radio station for the Somali Republic, and Mali received six Czechoslovakian-built radio transmitters for Radio Mali.

Journalists' Organizations. Much Communist assistance to African news media has been funneled through international "front organizations" for which there are no exact counterpart organizations in the West.

For the Soviet Union and the Eastern European countries, the key body has been the International Organization of Journalists, which is Soviet-backed and Czech-sponsored. The group held its first African conference at Bamako, Mali, in May 1961. About thirty journalists and official government representatives from nine African nations faced a group of IOJ representatives almost as numerous as themselves, culled from the various national organizations affiliated with the IOJ and from Communist journalist organizations of the Soviet bloc.[30] One stated purpose of the meeting was to establish a Pan-African Union of Journalists with emphasis not on the professional role of journalists but on the political role "in the struggle against colonialism, imperialism, and neo-colonialism and in favor of peace."[31] The journalists attending agreed to play up African news in their own countries and to watch carefully news from "imperialist news agencies" which operate as "tools of colonialism." Resolutions called for a Pan-African news agency and a Voice of Africa radio station.[32] The IOJ has remained active in Africa, particularly in training journalists.

The Chinese Communists established a rival journalist front group in 1963—the Afro-Asian Journalists Organization (AAJO)—and from the beginning it has competed with the IOJ. The AAJO was planning a news center, a periodical for the association, and an "Afro-Asian Academy of Journalism."[33] As far as is known, these plans have not been carried out.

Indigenous Communist Newspapers. Outside Communist groups have given direct financial support to and supplied materials for various indigenous Communist newspapers scattered about the continent. But how many are there and how do you identify them? This is admittedly a difficult and highly subjective task for an outsider. To be identified absolutely as a Communist paper, it should be labeled as such by its editor or publisher. A few have done so, but more have been called Communist by others because their contents follow Communist propaganda themes and/or are run by people believed to be Communists or Communist sympathizers. Many papers in this category are merely Communist oriented and on occasion will depart from the Communist line. (There is a saying in Africa that "Communists can rent an African, but they can't buy him!") And some African papers will carry Communist handouts and propaganda merely because a Communist official asked them to print it and perhaps gave the editor a pound note or a few hundred francs for the favor. (Such practices are not unheard of in Western countries as well!)

Not many out-and-out Communist newspapers have appeared in Africa. The U.S. Information Agency estimated there were twenty such papers in 1962, with a combined circulation of 64,-000. A year before, there were supposedly nineteen Communist papers, with 53,000 circulation.[34]

It should be noted that most "Communist papers," even in African nations hospitable to them, were modest publications of limited circulation that appeared irregularly.

Undoubtedly the Communist bloc could take credit for such papers as *Dipanda,* in Congo (Brazzaville), edited by two Congolese students trained in Moscow. They were actively advised by members of the New China News Agency staff.[35]

The *Alger-Républicain,* over thirty years old, does not fit into the usual pattern of African Communist papers. It was founded in 1938 under the influence of the Communist-encouraged French coalition of leftist political parties, the Popular Front. It was owned by a cooperative company whose shareholders were mostly officials, workers, or small farmers whose opinions ranged from Socialism to Communism.[36] Wartime censorship and financial difficulties forced the newspaper, then edited by Albert Camus (quite a distinction for *any* newspaper), to stop publishing in 1940. It reappeared in 1943 and continued until 1955, when it was banned, along with the Communist party in Algeria. The newspaper's editor, Henri Alleg, remained in prison until 1962 when the *Alger-Républicain* reappeared again. The newspaper was put under the control of the National Liberation Front (FLN) in 1964 and became the "organ of the Marxist tendency" within the party.[37] It became a fervent supporter of Ben Bella's policies when the government "embarked on the road to total socialization." It was again discontinued and its editors were arrested when Ben Bella was deposed in 1965.

Alger-Républicain, like the Madagascar paper, *Fraternité* (banned in the late 1940s), and some of those in South Africa, were products of Western European Communist parties rather than of Russian or Chinese Communism. This points up the difficulties of classifying papers as "Communist" when Communist influences vary so much from one country to another.

Suffice it to say that some indigenous African publications, sympathetic in varying degrees to Communist ideology, have been a significant outlet for Communist political communication in Africa during the 1960s.

THE U.S. INFORMATION AGENCY IN AFRICA

As it did for the Communist nations, the appearance of so many new independent African nations presented an opportunity and challenge to the architects of U.S. foreign policy. The principal American agency assigned the task of implementing by international political communication the foreign policy objectives of the United States was the United States Information Agency (USIA).

The U.S. Information Service (USIS) (the overseas name for USIA activities) was not a complete stranger to Africa. Prior to 1960 it had sixteen posts and ten subposts in sixteen African countries or territories. The first U.S. information post on the continent was in the Belgian Congo in June 1942.

The number of USIS staff positions in Africa, both Americans and "locals," increased from 312 in 1959 to 724 in 1966 in order to man the additional USIS posts, which expanded from twenty-four to fifty-six.[38]

INFORMATION CENTERS

The U.S. Information Agency places a much higher priority on information centers and reading rooms than do other foreign powers, especially the Communists, as Table 6.1 indicates.

The lack of competition here from the Communist nations was primarily due to their heavy reliance on indigenous Communist parties or front organizations as well as direct mail to disseminate information and their strong emphasis on trade fairs,

TABLE 6.1: Information Center Activities in Africa, 1965

Countries	Centers	No. of Countries
United States	51 info. centers & 10 reading rooms	34
Britain	43	21
France	36	25
West Germany	16	16
India	8	8
UAR	12	11
USSR	5	5
Red China	2	2
Czechoslovakia	2	2
East Germany	1	1
Bulgaria	1	1

Source: USIA, *Communications Data Book for Africa*, pp. 84–89.

cultural tours, and student exchanges to carry their messages.

The USIS Information Center is the institutional core of the agency's African program. It is the base of operations from which personal and multimedia contacts can be extended in all directions. USIS libraries are widely used in African capitals and are highly regarded by students because they help fill an acute need. Table 6.2 illustrates the growth of this activity.

The information center is also used for cultural programs, including music, exhibits, presentations, movies, and English classes.

PRESS AND PUBLICATIONS

Most USIS publications in Africa were at first intended for the secondary school audience and lower echelon civil servants. In 1965 the agency changed its objectives and aimed higher on the educational continuum: the university student, faculty, and graduates—the new elites.

In the mid-1960s nine basic periodicals were printed by

TABLE 6.2: USIS-Africa Library Book Circulation and Attendance Growth

Fiscal Year	Book Circulation	Attendance
1960	391,335	1,756,848
1966	501,497	6,345,174
Increase	110,162	4,588,326

Source: Records maintained at the office of the Chief, African Libraries and Centers Branch, USIA, in January 1967.

either USIS-African posts or the Regional Service Center at Beirut:

American Outlook was a sixteen-page monthly produced at Accra, with a circulation of 106,000, and distributed in Ghana, Nigeria, Liberia, Sierra Leone, and Gambia. A French edition of 25,000 circulation went to Senegal, Cameroon, Tunisia, Ivory Coast, and Congo (Brazzaville). The English edition was later distributed in East Africa.

Perspectives Americaines was a four-page French monthly produced in Kinshasa, with a circulation of 60,000 throughout francophonic Africa. As did *American Outlook,* it featured articles on African accomplishments, Africans in the United States, U.S. foreign policy toward Africa, and some Americana.[39]

West African University News was produced by USIS-Lagos. This quarterly "intellectual journal" had a circulation of 3,000 and was primarily aimed at Nigerians who had studied in the United States. A French edition extended its circulation to 6,000.

USIS-Addis-Ababa published two periodicals: *Cooperation,* an Amharic-English bimonthly with 12,000 circulation, and *Pictorial Review,* a biweekly Amharic-English "wall newspaper" slanted for semiliterates. Its circulation was 9,000 in Amharic and 2,000 in English.

The Beirut USIS center published and distributed four magazines: *Al Ma'arifa* (Knowledge), a biweekly Arabic language magazine of 15,000; *Al Akhbar* (News Review), a weekly Arabic and English magazine widely distributed through Arabic-speaking Africa; *Al Hayat fi America* (Life in America), a slick *Life*-style, bimonthly magazine designed for commercial release throughout the Arab world, with a circulation of 52,466; and *Topic,* a monthly, slick-paper "prestige" magazine, which was offset printed in two editions—French, with 20,500 circulation; and English, with 31,000. *Topic* was first distributed throughout the sub-Sahara in July 1965, the year the first substantial numbers of university students in Communist countries began returning to Africa. Edited in Washington, it was aimed at the new intellectual elites—present and potential African leaders from universities in Africa, United States, Europe, and Communist countries. Its content treated the broad spectrum of Afro-American life. and its emphasis was on youth.

USIS-Africa also produced news bulletins and newsletters at some local posts. By 1963 the agency was producing them in nine countries and distributing throughout the continent. In addition, special articles, features, reprints, cartoons, and plastic plates were placed with local publications and broadcasting stations.

PRESS SERVICE

The African press is considered a high priority target for USIS information efforts. Before World War II, no American embassies had press officers. Today the press officers constitute the most extensive noncommercial press service in the world.[40] This news service consists in part of direct-mail feature stories, photos, and mats—and a daily wireless file prepared at USIA headquarters in Washington in six separate editions: Latin American, Far Eastern, Near Eastern, West European, East European, and African. The special African file was started in 1960 in English; a French edition was added the following year. The wireless file was received in ten African countries in 1959 and by thirty-eight posts in thirty-three countries in 1966.[41]

About half the file consists of commentaries, background stories, roundups, and sidebars of the major stories of interest to embassy officials, African editors, government officials, and other influentials. USIA says it tries not to compete with the AP and UPI, although the wire services do not necessarily agree. Its purpose is to place world news in context, particularly stories coming from foreign sources which USIA feels are distorted, incomplete, or biased. Former USIA Director Carl T. Rowan said, "One of our big jobs is to wipe out distortions created abroad by commercial media."[42]

MOTION PICTURES

USIS films are produced for selected key audiences but are intended to be understood by a mass audience as well. Thus, a slower narrative and visual pace is used in films for Africa. Subject matter falls into three main categories: Africans in the United States, African development through self-help and U.S. aid, and Americans in Africa. USIS-Africa produces and distributes "Today," a twenty-five minute newsreel devoted exclusively to African affairs. Eighty percent of the film is shot on location in Africa and edited and printed in the United States. The films are produced in English, French, and Swahili versions and have won wide acceptance in Africa, USIA believes. In 1959 "Today" was shown regularly in 180 commercial theaters in six African countries. By 1963 it was appearing regularly in over 700 commercial theaters in thirty-one countries to an annual audience of about 34 million. USIA also produced a number of documentary films annually, and the agency claimed that a total African audience of almost 80 million saw USIS films during 1965.[43]

TELEVISION

Television made its sub-Sahara debut in 1959 and spread quickly. By 1963 USIS placed 800 hours of agency-produced programs in six African countries; local productions were placed in only Nigeria and Morocco.

By 1965 USIS television programs were shown in eleven African countries, with local production in five.[44]

RADIO

In 1959 the Voice of America ranked fourth behind Moscow, Cairo, and Peking in hours of direct African broadcasting. VOA's principal handicap was the weak signal it generated over its antiquated and low-powered 100-kilowatt facilities in New York and New Jersey. This signal was received by VOA's Tangier transmitters and relayed. While it could be heard all over Africa, it was usually drowned out during the peak evening listening hours by its competitors. Two major improvements were needed: a powerful transmitting station in continental United States and a relay station close to the African heartland.

Toward this end, the $23 million transmitter at Greenville, North Carolina, became operational in December 1962, and in the following month the African Program and Relay Center was established at Monrovia, Liberia. The center was formed to produce and transmit specially tailored African broadcast material in English, French, Arabic, Swahili, Hausa, and Amharic.

Regional Service Centers were established in Addis Ababa, Nairobi, Rabat, Lagos, Kinshasa (Leopoldville), and Dakar to assist in the production of sectional program materials for broadcast by either VOA-Monrovia or VOA-Washington.

Table 6.3 charts the growth of VOA broadcasting on the continent. As the African radio broadcasting systems grow, the category of "radio placement" becomes increasingly important.

TABLE 6.3:   Voice of America Activity in Africa (hours per week)

Types of Broadcasts	1960	1961	1962	1963	1964	1965
Direct Broadcasts:						
Regional English[a] ...	...	7:00	7:00	17:30	24:30	24:30
Worldwide English[b] ..	27:45	70:00	78:45	64:45	75:15	75:15
French	:30	7:00	10:30	10:30	14:00	17:30
Hindi	...	3:00	3:30	3:30	3:30	...
Swahili	...	...	3:30	7:00	7:00	7:30
Arabic	...	...	...	7:00	7:00	7:00
Subtotal	28:15	87:00	103:15	110:15	131:15	131:15
Radio Placements						
Tapes and scripts	na[c]	14:16	46:53	42:00	70:41	78:50
Delays & feeds	na	1:48	10:09	14:00	3:05	10:25
USIS local production	na	8:28	31:09	25:00	27:59	16:06
Subtotal	na	24:32	88:11	81:00	101:45	105:21
Grand Total	28:15	112:02	184:26	191:15	233:00	236:36

Sources: Compiled from USIA, 14th through 25th Review of Operations; and statistical data from files of Director of VOA in Washington, D.C.
   [a] Programs specially tailored for Africa.
   [b] General English program audible in Africa.
   [c] Figures not available.

Among foreign broadcasters, VOA has been the chief user of the local placement technique. Communist nations still stress direct broadcasting even without benefit of radio relay.

Yet the international competition was still very keen indeed. In 1964 Russia broadcast to Africa a total of 126 hours a week in eight African languages, including 28 hours in Swahili. East European countries were also active. Communist direct broadcasting far outdistanced the BBC (61:45 hours per week) and VOA's *direct* African broadcasts (56 hours per week) which continued to rely heavily on English. The West was bolstered, however, by the growing West German involvement which included broadcasts in Kinyarwanda, Hausa, and Amharic.[45] VOA uses mainly English, French, Arabic, and Swahili for its programs to Africa.

Statistics on foreign Swahili broadcasts to East Africa in 1964 are an indicator of the increasing international emphasis on vernacular broadcasting. (They are also an indication of how the Swahili speakers of East Africa are caught in the cross-fire of the Cold War.) (Table 6.4.)

Because of the growth of English as a world language or a second language for many millions, VOA is broadcasting more and more in English, especially in "special English" which uses a vocabulary of about 1,200 words delivered slowly. Thus, listening to a VOA broadcast becomes an opportunity to practice Eng-

TABLE 6.4: Principal Foreign Broadcasting in Swahili to East Africa, 1964

Country or Group	Hours per Week
USSR	28:00
Ghana	15:00
BBC	14:00
East Germany	10:30
Communist China	10:30
UAR	10:30
West Germany	10:00
Lutheran World Federation	7:00
VOA	7:00
Totals:	
Communist Nations	49:00
Other Nations	72:35

Source: New York *Times*, November 24, 1965, 77:4.

lish, and in the case of Africa, most of the elites that VOA wants to reach usually know either English or French.

The USIA's direct communication efforts to Africa and its indirect use of local African media carried political communication themes designed to support and explain U.S. foreign policy and to present a sympathetic and believable image of the United States and its people to Africans.

How well the USIA has performed its mission in Africa cannot be empirically demonstrated; the effects of international political communication are extremely difficult to evaluate. In many situations, the "propaganda of events" overtakes and neutralizes the "propaganda of words." For instance, USIA's efforts to explain U.S. Negroes' civil rights progress were to a great extent nullified by the Negro riots in U.S. cities and the assassination of Martin Luther King.

But in any case, the USIS came to the new nations of Africa, firmly established itself during the early 1960s, and is still there telling America's version of ideas and events. That, certainly, is one indication of its effectiveness. Another was that there was no Communist government in Africa.

BRITISH ACTIVITIES

Unlike the United States program which is almost entirely under the USIA, the British political communication effort is divided among three different bodies. The British Council, financed by a grant from the government and semiautonomous in operation, takes care of the cultural and educational exchange program. The Overseas Information Program, operated by the Central Office of Information in London, had a 1968 budget of £11 million and provided an overseas press service as well as television and feature material. More and more of its output is directed to areas, especially in Africa, where Britain has economic interests.

The third arm is the External Services of the British Broadcasting Corporation. On a worldwide basis, BBC External Services broadcast radio programs, mostly news and music, in thirty-nine languages, totaling about 400 hours a week. The External Services are subsidized by the British government but run by BBC personnel. Once it gets its assignment from the Foreign Office as to how many hours it should broadcast to what countries on what budget, etc., BBC then operates independently of Whitehall or at least so it claims. The BBC beams about 100 hours weekly specifically for East, West, and South Africa, but its World Service in English, direct from London, is widely heard there also. Most of the External Services programming, however, was originally prepared for the BBC's domestic service.

The BBC's long tradition of objectivity and fairness in reporting the news has won it high credibility in Africa as elsewhere. The BBC influence on anglophonic radio in Africa has been tremendous, largely because many of the broadcasting personnel in former British territories were trained by the BBC, which also often helped to establish broadcast facilities in the African countries.

The BBC continues as a strong influence in the Commonwealth nations—Nigeria, Ghana, Sierra Leone, Botswana, Gambia, Kenya, Lesotho, Malawi, Swaziland, Tanzania, Uganda, and Zambia. Its listenership is high, in large part because the BBC reports their news, and in some cases, BBC programs, such as "Radio Newsreel," are rebroadcast on local African stations.

BBC maintains two resident correspondents in middle Africa —one in West Africa (Lagos) and the other in East Africa (Nairobi). Stringers are located in Johannesburg, Lusaka, Dar es Salaam, and elsewhere.

For both Englishmen and Africans, the BBC is a major source of news and information about Africa; as such BBC ably serves Britain's foreign policy and economic interests there.

INTERNATIONAL POLITICAL COMMUNICATION BY AFRICAN STATES

Several African nations have been active in international political communication, although on a much smaller scale than the great powers. South Africa, Ghana, and the UAR have made the greatest efforts to influence their neighbors.

Other African governments that have engaged in external broadcasting are Nigeria, Tunisia, Tanzania, Congo (Kinshasa), Congo (Brazzaville), Algeria, Angola, Ethiopia, Ivory Coast, Liberia, Malagasy Republic, Morocco, and Mozambique.

To aid the late Gamal Abdul Nasser's ambitions to be the leader of black Africa as well as the Arab world, the United Arab Republic had done a good deal of external broadcasting. For example, in 1964 it was broadcasting ten and one-half hours a week in Swahili into East Africa. The UAR has literally saturated the Maghreb with its strident international broadcasting. In 1964 Egypt ranked fourth in the world in international broadcasting directed to Africa. And the activities of its Middle East News Agency (MENA) were probably more concerned with political communication and political intrigue than with news dissemination.

This evaluation had a good deal of truth in it: "Nasser is virtually a creature of radio, having used it within Egypt and internationally ever since he came to power. His Radio Cairo reaches out to all the Arab world and far beyond. With the spread of the transistor, this reach became longer and deeper. It took only one broadcast over Radio Cairo during the Middle East war to convince most of the Arab world that the United States and Britain were giving Israel air cover and many still believe it."[46] Since the 1967 war with Israel, the UAR has been less concerned with black Africa.

Among the new nations of black Africa, Ghana under Kwame Nkrumah was by far the most active in international political communication. Ghanaian propaganda activities abroad were conducted mainly by the embassies, the Bureau of African Affairs, and most important, by the International Service of the Ghana Broadcasting System.

The International Service was launched in mid-1961 on one 100-kilowatt shortwave transmitter. The programming included news bulletins (twenty-one a day), commentaries, and music and feature programs, and was hailed as a "true expression of the African personality." Late in October 1961, after the Teme transmitting station was inaugurated, four 100-kilowatt shortwave transmitters were operating, beaming programs eight hours a day to all of Africa in English, French, Hausa, Arabic, and Spanish.

By 1965 Ghana was putting out an ambitious schedule of international broadcasting: 161 hours weekly in English, 15 hours weekly in Arabic, 15 in Bambara, 21 in Hausa, 19 in Swahili, 26 in Portuguese, and 68 in French.[47]

Nkrumah hoped the programs would be a powerful tool for the liberation and unity of the entire continent—under his leadership, of course. The new "Voice of Africa," as it was called, claimed to be truly African in content, outlook, and imagination, and neither anti-East nor anti-West. On the whole, however, the programs were anti-Western, although sudden changes in tone and line occurred.

The Bureau of African Affairs (a department of the President's Office) published two periodicals for external distribution. The shrill *Voice of Africa,* a four-page, 7-by-10-inch newssheet, was distributed in various African nations as a propaganda outlet for the Nkrumah brand of Pan-African nationalism.[48]

Another paper, *Spark,* was started in December 1962 as a weekly "serious Marxist analytical journal on African questions" and had a French counterpart, *l'Etincelle,* which carried some but not all material in *Spark.* The animus for *Spark* was explained by Nkrumah in a message on the anniversary of its 100th issue in 1964: "The new African needs an ideology, socialist in content and continental in outlook. The propagation of such an ideology demands an ideological journal or journals serving all Africa."[49]

Since the overthrow of Nkrumah in 1966, international political communication emanating from Ghana has been severely curtailed—for both financial (Nkrumah left Ghana almost bankrupt) and ideological reasons (the current rulers have no apparent ambitions to lead the continent).

EFFORTS BY SOUTH AFRICA

To carry out a sustained campaign of international political communication requires money, capability, and motivation, which most new African nations have lacked. The Republic of South Africa, however, has all three in abundance and over the years has waged the subtlest and most ambitious campaign of propaganda abroad of any nation on the continent.

Long the target of worldwide criticism for its apartheid policies, South Africa has greatly stepped up its counterattack and has aimed its principal efforts at the United States. South Africa has spent millions of dollars on films, periodicals, and booklets produced by its South African Information Service (SAIS), employed U.S. public relations firms, provided free junkets for U.S. journalists and others, and widely publicized the views of certain Americans who expressed strong sympathy for white South Africa and who extolled opportunities there for American investors.

Vernon McKay perceptively analyzed the methods used; he wrote:

> This revitalized propaganda offensive merits attention because of its effect on the much larger problem of the images that Africans and Americans are developing of each other. The Cabinet Ministers who portray South Africa as a stable, prosperous Western ally in contrast to a chaotic and savage black Africa infected with Communism are striking a responsive chord, particularly among American conservatives, who are beginning to organize themselves to fight what they term the "fallacious liberal" approach to African issues. The ultimate objective is to change U.S. Government policy toward Africa.[50]

In the United States, South Africa's official spokesmen have been wooing the American public with these five propaganda themes, each at least debatable, if not actually untrue:

● South Africa is a bulwark against Communism;

● South Africa has a stable government and a lucrative, fully protected investment climate;

● South Africa is Western civilization's staunchest defender on the continent;

● The great Bantu migrations into its territory occurred only *after* the whites settled South Africa;

● The whites are properly providing for the well-being of the blacks through the policy of separate development (apartheid).[51]

Using free trips for American journalists to promote these themes has been only partially successful. Fifteen journalists took an expenses-paid tour of South Africa in 1965; fourteen more made the trip in 1966 at a reported cost to the South African government of $35,000. There have been other journalist tours since.

The idea was that the journalists would write glowing accounts of South Africa. Ed Fitzhugh of the Phoenix (Arizona)

Gazette wrote at least fourteen articles and the headline of one read: "Bantus, Whites Both Sold on Race Policy." He quoted one African who, he wrote, "is typical of many blacks." The African said, "I think I am better off here than I would be if the government were all black, as in the north. I do not want to change."[52]

However, Joseph Lelyveld, a New York *Times* correspondent who was later forced to leave South Africa, wrote: "Most ordinary American journalists it brings out 'double-cross' it by writing nasty things. So it concentrates now on right wingers. Recently it toured a bunch of journalists from what was described here as a 'cross section of right-wing American newspapers.' At the moment, William A. Simpson, head of the Citizens Council of America, of Jackson, Mississippi, is getting the tour."[53]

On the other hand, South African officials do not put out the welcome mat for American newsmen and scholars they feel will not present their case favorably to the American public. Lelyveld's experience was an example; he was told in April 1966 that his visa would not be renewed when it expired. Visas have been denied to such reputable American Africanists as Professor Gwendolen M. Carter, director of the African Studies Program at Northwestern University, and Waldemar A. Nielsen, president of the African-American Institute. Both have written critically about South Africa.

Journalist William R. Frye wrote a series of articles on South Africa for his syndicated column after a visit there in March and April 1964. His erstwhile hosts considered them offensive, and South African officials wrote letters of protest to the editors of many of the seventy-eight papers carrying his syndicated column. Some editors subsequently cancelled Frye's column.[54]

The South African government has the most elaborate information program of any nation on the continent. The SAIS turns out hundreds of pamphlets and booklets, press releases, informative periodicals, and films for showing in cinemas or on television. Six periodicals regularly reach American readers: three are produced in South Africa and three in New York. By December 1965, according to information filed with the U.S. Justice Department, circulation of *Scope,* an elaborately illustrated monthly on current affairs, had risen 14,000 in the United States; that of *South African Summary,* a weekly news release, to 4,800; and *South African Business Report,* which stresses economic and business information, was at 3,100.

The television section of SAIS produced several hundred

films for television, even though the South African government has so far blocked general television for South Africa itself. (In Chapter 11, South Africa's news media are fully discussed.)

According to SAIS's 1968 report, its television films were reaching millions of people on overseas television networks. In the United States, for instance, 450 transmissions over different television stations and networks in 1966 were seen by 15,300,000 people. In 1967, 198 prints of ten films were made available to television stations, and a survey found that these films were seen by 24 million people.

Immediately after the closing of the Suez Canal in 1967, three short films were made to place the Cape sea route in its "proper perspective." These and similar films were viewed by 30 million people in the United States, Europe, Rhodesia, Australia, New Zealand, and Canada, according to SAIS.[55]

South Africa started broadcasting externally on a modest scale in 1950. Then, on April 1, 1964, the service was greatly expanded with the creation of an External Services Department within the South African Broadcasting Corporation. On October 27, 1965, Prime Minister Henrik Verwoerd officially opened the new Bloemendal international shortwave radio center near Meyerton. On that day the first of four powerful 250-kilowatt transmitters was put into operation.

The new RSA, the Voice of South Africa, kept expanding both its programming and reach until by 1967 it was broadcasting twenty-four hours a day in Afrikaans, English, French, Portuguese, Dutch, German, Swahili, Zulu, and Tshonga. The highly sophisticated transmitting facilities specifically targeted special programs for all the African continent, the Middle East, United States, Europe, and Canada. Forty-six news bulletins and news surveys were broadcast daily in the same languages. The External Services also had an Overseas Transcription Services Department which distributed radio programs in eight languages to 500 radio stations in eighty different countries "to give a sound picture of the South Africa of today."[56]

The United States has been a prime target of the Voice of South Africa, and its signal is picked up easily all across America. South Africa has also used other methods to soften and change U.S. attitudes toward apartheid.

In 1960 the South African government hired Hamilton Wright, a New York public relations firm, to help sell South Africa to the American public mainly through films. The Wright organization received $274,500 between January 1961 and January 1963 (according to U.S. Justice Department records), but insisted that it was not producing "political propaganda." However, the U.S. Senate Committee on Foreign Relations, headed by Senator J. William Fulbright, felt otherwise during its investigation of the activities of nondiplomatic representatives of foreign governments in the United States. The Fulbright committee did not question the right of Hamilton Wright to do business with foreign governments; the only issue was whether the material the American public was being fed was properly labeled foreign propaganda as required by the Foreign Agents Registration Act. In the investigation, Fulbright produced a letter from Wright to an official of the South African government dated November 22, 1961, describing the firm's activities of the previous seven months. Wright wrote:

> What much of this work proves—beyond doubt—is the value of nonpolitical propaganda to create an effect essentially political. Political propaganda as such would have been largely ineffective. But institutional publicity—touching on South Africa's general life, economic, social, and cultural accomplishments, tourist attractions, sports, festivals, etc.—can tend to soften hard political attitudes, make for good feeling, and tend to correct misinformation about the country.[57]

In addition to the PR expenditures, the South African government paid over $141,000 during the first six months of 1965 for the tourist publicity of the New York office of the South African Tourist Corporation.

By 1965–66 the information budget in South Africa had risen to $4,459,000 under a separate Department of Information created in 1962 with its own minister in the cabinet. No other African government could begin to match such an effort in international political communication.

How effective is South Africa's political information in the United States? It is difficult to assess, but certainly the whole outlay is on a much larger scale than that of other African countries, most of whom are strongly opposed to South African policies. In 1964 the Department of Information was able to report, according to McKay, that while many Americans remained "cynical" about South Africa's racial experiment, "there was an appreciable decline in the eagerness of journalists to forecast nothing but darkness for South Africa."[58]

The political utilization of mass communications by both African and overseas governments is another reminder of the danger of underestimating the influence of the printed and electronic word in that turbulent continent.

7

‖‖

NEED FOR TECHNOLOGY
AND TRAINING

WESTERN AND COMMUNIST NATIONS, seeking to curry political favor with the new African governments, have given considerable direct assistance to African news media by providing technical facilities and by training journalists. Such aid may be just one more facet of the Cold War, but the help itself was much needed.

The technical inadequacies of Africa's news media are many; printing presses, paper production, distribution facilities, broadcasting transmitters and receivers, and telecommunications infrastructure are all in short supply. And yet the lack of trained personnel to man the news media may be the most critical shortage of all, because only journalists themselves can improve the content of news communication.

The need for technology and training is essentially part of a general economic situation. Mass communications are very much limited and circumscribed by the economic context in which they operate, and the level of economic development in a country determines whether the mass media spread. The general rule is that mass media spread in a direct relationship with the rising level of industrial capacity.

News is after all a commodity that must be produced, distributed, and consumed like other commodities. There must be "the capacity to produce" the physical plants, the equipment (presses, transmitters, amplifiers, TV and radio sets, etc.), and the trained personnel. There must be the "capacity to consume," which in simple terms can mean individuals must have the cash, literacy, and motivation necessary to be media users.

Because they lack industrial capacity, local entrepreneurial capital, and "cash customers" (much less a middle class), most African nations are seriously handicapped in efforts to develop their own mass media.

Per capita income must rise to the point where the average person can afford the news media. Either the individual African or his government must be able to pay the "price of admission." In addition, enough local savings must accumulate so that private African businessmen or investors (including governments) can afford to invest in newspapers, magazines, radio stations, etc., as profit-making ventures. Such local investment capital is generally unavailable today; hence the continued need for foreign investment and government involvement in mass communications.

Foreign ownership of newspapers remains unpopular in many places, especially in more socialistically oriented African states. Yet the record of foreign ownership in West Africa by the London *Daily Mirror* group, for example, has proved that foreign proprietorship need not prevent African newspapers being run by Africans and edited for an African public. Even newspapers subsidized by foreign Communist funds (another form of "neo-colonialism"—or foreign investment certainly) have served the useful purpose of providing more publications, viewpoints, and not least, more reading matter.

But since local capital is lacking, much more foreign investment in Africa's news media is needed from both private and governmental sources. The American newspaper industry, with over 1,750 daily newspapers enjoying unprecedented prosperity, has been notably remiss in not supporting the struggling press of Africa. I know of no direct effort by any American newspaper or newspaper group either as a gesture of unselfish help or as a business investment.

Any sort of hard-headed attempt by an American publisher to establish and run a paper in Africa to make money could have all kinds of beneficial side effects on the journalism and public communication in that locality.

Foreign newspaper investments in independent Africa today are invariably made in cooperation with the local government. One advantage is that the stigma of neo-colonialism is thereby eased; government control and ownership is considered clearly preferable to full foreign ownership.

Three major official newspapers—*Fraternité Matin* of the Ivory Coast, the *Nationalist* of Tanzania, and the *New Nigerian* of northern Nigeria—have all been substantially aided by French, East German, and British publishing groups, respectively.

Reuters and Agence France Presse helped set up most of the new national news agencies, and the BBC, France's OCORA, Thomson Television, America's NBC and AID, and other foreign interests have helped expand radio and television broadcasting facilities. Europeans, too, have trained journalists and technicians. Foreign media interests have not all departed with the colonial rulers; some have joined forces with the new governments as the latter have increased their involvement in mass communications. Such foreign aid and assistance will have to increase if news media growth is to continue.

To many Africans such help is "neo-colonialism," which in a way it is. Even partial foreign ownership or involvement in the media understandably arouses suspicions and resentment among nationalistic Africans. But for the present there are few alternatives.

In the long run, the fragile young nations must nationalize their media systems in two important ways. First, the newspapers and broadcasting must be effectively extended and dispersed from the capital and urban areas out to the rural areas where the great majority of Africans still live tribalized lives dependent on subsistence agriculture.

Second, the news media should become nationalized in another sense—that is, become indigenously African, drawing on the talents and experiences of Africans and on the historical and cultural traditions of African society. It means developing new standards and reference points, not merely imitating British or French models. It means Africans producing the content of mass communications and not relying on imported news, television, and movies.

To help accomplish these goals, there is a need for foreign journalists to encourage and increase their professional ties with African journalists. This is done now in a limited way, but should be expanded.

The African newsman, underpaid and lacking in social status, must be made to understand that he belongs to a worldwide fraternity, based on an ethic of public service.

Professional organizations of journalists have been started in Nigeria, Ghana, Kenya, South Africa, and a few other countries. On occasion they have protested government intrusions into press activities. Self organization by journalists is an important step toward an independent press. In time such groups can band together on a continental basis and form an organization comparable to the Inter-American Press Association of the Western Hemisphere.

NEED FOR INFRASTRUCTURE: HOPE FROM SATELLITES

The African continent urgently requires expanded infrastructure to support a modern system of news communications. Africa lacks sufficient roads and railroads, telephone lines, and telegraph and teletype facilities that provide essential underpinning of both print and electronic communications. The post-independence telecommunications system is still oriented toward Europe.

Until recently the prospects of providing a really *African* system of telecommunications with adequate intracontinental communications were not promising because of the great expense involved.

Now the development of communications satellites has made the outlook much brighter. They offer the very real prospect of a continental communications system which will leapfrog a century of slow, costly telecommunications development. In Europe and America, the advent of communications satellites is basically an evolutionary development building onto and extending the present system. In Africa, however, communications satellites may well revolutionize communications, making possible a continental system where none existed before.

On March 22, 1967, the third Intelsat II communications satellite was successfully launched from Cape Kennedy into a synchronous equatorial orbit over the Gulf of Guinea. From this position, the new satellite provided communications capabilities between Africa and the capitals of Europe, North America, Latin America, and possibly most important, between African nations themselves. The new satellite's position covered all the African continent and served as a space relay station for telephone, telegraph, television, data, and facsimile communications between earth stations all the way from Karachi, Pakistan, to Lima, Peru.[1] By 1969 five synchronous Intelsat (International Telecommunications Consortium) satellites were completely girdling the earth: two over the Atlantic, two over the Pacific and a fifth launched into orbit over the Indian Ocean. (Three satellites, positioned at 22,300 miles above the equator and adequately spaced, cover by line of sight most of the world's land mass.)

Satellites have importance for much more than mass media, but for the news media they mean that news service reports, news photos, television programs (including live color telecasts from all over the globe), radio news programs, and even facsimile newspapers can easily be communicated to nearly inaccessible places all over the continent.

The March 1967 launch was also significant because nine African nations had a direct investment as members of Intelsat. They were Algeria, Ethiopia, Libya, Morocco, Nigeria, South Africa, Sudan, Tunisia, and the United Arab Republic, and each contributed more than $1.1 million toward the establishment of the global communications satellite system of which Intelsat II was a significant part.

In addition to the nine, Tanzania, Kenya, and Uganda later announced that they would join as a group.

The system naturally cannot function without earth stations; the building of stations on the African continent, therefore, will determine the pace at which Africa benefits from satellite communications. The three East African nations have agreed to start construction of one. It was to be built near Nairobi by the Marconi company of Britain, at a cost of £1.5 million and was scheduled to start operations in 1970.

But actual construction of the first satellite communications ground station in Africa began near Rabat, Morocco, on October 24, 1968. The system began operating with eight channels in December 1969 and was to expand to 41 channels in 1978.[2]

Other nations have announced plans for building earth stations: Ivory Coast, Nigeria, and Senegal in 1969–70; Cameroon, Ethiopia, and Sudan in 1970; and Zambia and the UAR in 1971.

Why is Africa moving so fast to take advantage of satellites? First, the existing high frequency radio circuits between Africa and Europe have become overloaded with the worldwide boom in telecommunications. Second, the new African nations feel a strong need to increase their internation communication as a result of their increasing regional ties. The continent seeks not only expansion of its present links to the outside world, but establishment of entirely new intra-African circuits. Satellites offer the cheapest and fastest way of accomplishing this. As OAU Secretary General Diallo Telli said to the January 1967 meeting of the ITU Plan Committee, "Africa is looking for the decolonization of its entire communications system, whose anachronistic and irrational structure is one of the most serious obstacles to our economic and social development and the attainment of African unity."[3]

Initially the global satellite system will be employed mostly on the established communications routes between Africa and

Europe. The traffic of any country using the system between Africa and Europe was expected to double during the first year of satellite system operations because of the improved quality. This has happened elsewhere in the world. Once earth stations are installed and financially justified by traffic with Europe, they will be available for communication among African countries at a small additional cost. In this way, satellites can eventually link all parts of Africa, economically and efficiently, over difficult terrain which in many places discourages the installation of conventional systems. Unavoidably, even this radical new system is a reminder to Africans of their dependence on Europe in expanding their own communications. But all communication, by definition, implies some interdependence.

SOVIET PROPOSAL

The Soviet Union and the Communist commonwealth have not accepted repeated invitations to cooperate with the United States-sponsored Intelsat. On August 14, 1968, Soviet Premier Alexei Kosygin announced that the Soviet Union and "other Socialist countries" will establish their own satellite communications network to compete with Intelsat. Kosygin appealed to the developing nations of Africa to join "Intersputnik," as the new satellite system will be known.[4] The Soviet action indicated that satellite communications may yet become another arena of East-West competition, rather than cooperation. However, there was still hope that the Communist nations would in time participate in Intelsat.

The full implications of communications satellites are difficult to foresee, but the prospects for widened and more effective *intra*-African news communication are indeed impressive.

NEED FOR CHEAPER AND MORE EFFICIENT FACILITIES

Though not as dramatic as communications satellites, other innovations in media technology promise to speed news communications development in Africa.

The transistor radio already has had a great impact on radio broadcasting.

> In terms of human lives, one of the most revolutionary inventions in the age of communications is the transistor radio.

. . . In much the same way as the printing press opened up vast new possibilities to 15th century Europe, the transistor is letting in the world to hundreds of millions still isolated from the 20th century by geography, poverty, and exploitation. On the grassy Tanzanian plain a stately Masai herdsman strides behind his scrawny cattle, a lion-killing spear in one hand and a country-music blaring Japanese transistor in the other.[5]

The introduction into Africa of a cheap, transistorized television receiver will probably have a similarly dramatic impact on television broadcasting. But so far, one is not generally available. Radio broadcasting will be strengthened, too, as more AM and FM transmitting facilities are operating. Frequency modulation (FM) broadcasting, which for 60 miles or so is free of interference and excellent in receiving quality, is especially useful in the tropics, and Nigeria, for one, has been installing an FM system to supplement its shortwave and AM transmitting facilities. Such improved AM and FM reception will make the Africans much less dependent on foreign broadcasting which must use shortwave because of the great distances involved.

Videotape recordings of television programs make it possible to record and exchange programs more easily among African stations not yet capable of producing much of their own programming.

New technology in printing promises to ease the production difficulties, since all publishing equipment must be imported and has proved to be costly, cumbersome, and difficult to maintain.

The new offset presses with cold type or phototypesetting not only greatly improve the quality of printing, especially photo reproduction, but also cut the cost and maintenance requirements.

One new government newspaper, *Fraternité Matin* of Abidjan, is a model of an offset-printed cold-type newspaper. It is set by Monophoto and printed on a Goss offset rotary press capable of producing a 16-page paper at a speed of 18,000 copies per hour. Cost of construction of the printing plant was $800,000, but the plant also prints other publications and some books.

In Africa, where trained staff is scarce and other resources limited, cold-type and offset printing provide better quality printing, increased speed and ease of typesetting, and better illustrations.

Newsprint is scarce and costly and must be imported. (Only South Africa and Rhodesia manufacture newsprint in Africa in any quantity.) There is hope that improved methods will make it possible to produce paper pulp from a variety of fast-growing trees found in tropical Africa instead of relying on coniferous pulpwood, so abundant in Canada and Scandinavia.

Lloyd Sommerlad, formerly with UNESCO, has suggested that paper should be included in bilateral aid arrangements:

> Because of the key role mass media play in development, and because paper shortage is such a bottleneck in press development, gifts of newsprint could contribute materially to national progress. Although newsprint may not actually be in oversupply, surplus capacity exists in Canada, the United States, Britain, Scandinavia, Japan, and USSR, and they could step up production to provide paper for their foreign aid programs. This could well be good business for the future, because once paper consumption is established at a certain level, it is extremely difficult to reduce it.[6]

NEED FOR RURAL MIMEO NEWSPAPERS

The printed word has some essential tasks to perform in the new nations. Two of the most important certainly are to provide reading material for new literates and to bridge the wide chasm between the urban and bush sectors with news.

One media development that may help is the rural mimeo newspaper. Much of the optimism for these modest papers, which often resemble the student paper of a small American high school, was generated during a 1963 experiment in Liberia. A series of small local newssheets was established throughout the underdeveloped interior, enabling people in the hinterland villages to read news of their countrymen from other villages and from the capital at Monrovia for the first time. The papers also made available some world news and, important too, people of the capital were provided with regular news of the interior. The papers also helped maintain literacy at the levels developed at the local schools.[7]

Some students of African press problems see great potential in such rural papers. Professor M. Neff Smart of the University of Utah, who has been a Fulbright lecturer in Ethiopia, wrote: "The establishment of a system of community newspapers—nonpolitical and government subsidized—is a surer key and faster route to the emergence of the developing countries of Africa than the establishment of schools."[8]

Elsewhere Smart added:

> Because the typical African villager has no newspaper, no books, no bulletins or pamphlets that are easy enough or vital enough

to interest him, he has no felt need to become literate. His oral communication with friends and neighbors is adequate for his success in subsistence agriculture, in community politics and in his religious worship. But as national politics intrudes, as high birth rates demand better agricultural methods, and as the need arises for him to increase his productivity in order to compete and survive, his illiteracy becomes a deadly handicap. Thus the African needs an introduction to the value of the printed word as the key to increased productivity and he needs to be induced to acquire that skill. I am convinced that there is no more effective tool for getting this job done than the community newspaper.[9]

"When the first issue of the *Gbarnga Gbele News* was published on April 29, 1963, it marked the beginning of a rural newspaper revolution in the interior of Liberia. Before the end of the year there were 30 of these two-columned, brightly titled, neatly mimeographed newspapers, covering the entire country, where none had existed before."[10]

So wrote Robert de T. Lawrence, a former newspaperman on the staff of the U.S. Agency for International Development, who was an adviser to the Liberian project undertaken by the Liberian Information Service. UNESCO became interested in the Liberian project and Lawrence wrote for them a detailed case history of the project, including specific advice on launching and producing such papers.

The mimeograph method of printing was chosen for its simplicity of operation and inexpensive equipment. (Reproduction methods such as xerography also may have great significance for small, local papers in the future.)

The UNESCO report claimed that attractive mimeo papers—one-man businesses or small concerns employing several people part time—could be produced with an investment of little more than $100 and could be self-supporting from the outset. Basic equipment was a standard typewriter; a crank mimeograph machine; a battery-powered, shortwave radio receiver; and a stapling machine.

The original plan called for the bulk of the news to be gathered from a thirty-minute radio newscast each morning at dictation speed from Monrovia. Local news could be gathered the day before—one or two stories or more—and typed on the first page of the stencil. The editor would then type the news from the radio directly onto the stencil as received over the air.

Although such projects seem exceedingly modest, they can help meet basic needs. They provide relevant and current reading material and establish small business enterprises years before they would be economically possible with conventional printing techniques. The little mimeographed papers enjoy the advantages of being simple, inexpensive, personal, and local. Whether they can sustain themselves over an extended period of time is quite another matter—perhaps the biggest question of all.

A follow-up study of the 1963 Liberian project found that six years later only five of the original thirty papers were still publishing and none of these was self-supporting.[11] For rural papers to persist in the Liberian hinterland, they apparently must be subsidized either by government or by interested private organizations such as mining corporations.

The U.S. Agency for International Development, the Peace Corps, and UNESCO have all continued their interest in the development of rural mimeo newspapers.

TRAINING OF JOURNALISTS

Any effort to improve facilities must also be concerned with personnel. In point of fact, the training of journalists and mass communicators has been given the highest priority in the years since independence.

A 1962 UNESCO meeting of African information specialists in Paris called training the "indispensable first step in establishing new information media and services and developing existing media."[12]

E. J. B. Rose surveyed African news media for the International Press Institute:

> One of the greatest shortcomings in the African press today is the lack of skill in the lower ranks of the profession. There are a number of good editors but there is an almost Himalayan gap between the editor and his staff, between the editor and his reporters and subeditors. Radio stations and news agencies suffer equally from the shortage of competent reliable reporters and subeditors. Governments also lack information officers who are trained in the techniques of good journalism.[13]

The need for able African journalists is indeed great if not critical. Of the many new nations between the Sahara and the Kalahari, Nigeria—and to a lesser extent, Ghana—are the only ones with anything like a cadre of trained and experienced *African* newsmen—and they do not have enough.

Since independence the Europeans who dominated Africa's journalism for so long have been withdrawing—and with reason. The new political leaders of Africa are sensitive to criticism from expatriate journalists on foreign-owned papers. There is an understandable desire to have a nation's own nationals run its media. The push for Africanization thus only increases the urgency of training Africans. Yet for a variety of reasons, Europeans still hold key positions in many of Africa's news media.

For example, Kenya, where media were earlier mostly operated by Europeans, has been under strong pressure to Africanize all media positions, and yet finds itself desperately short of adequately prepared Africans to fill the jobs. Michael Curtis, publisher of the *Nation* papers in Nairobi, said in 1965 he expected that within a few years Africans would hold all positions in the news media in Kenya.[14]

Yet revisiting Nairobi three years later, I found that the editorial staffs of the *Daily Nation* and *East African Standard* were still dominated by Europeans. The editor of the *Daily Nation,* George Githii, had only recently been to Britain to recruit five more European journalists for the *Daily Nation*'s staff.

There has been a firm response to the training need—both from within and outside the African continent. In addition to the activities of various African governments, such organizations as UNESCO, the International Press Institute (IPI), International Organization of Journalists (IOJ), International Federation of Journalists (IFJ), African-American Institute (AAI), Ford Foundation, American Press Institute, and the Thomson Foundation have initiated and supported various journalism-training activities.

Some of what has been done by both East and West to train African journalists falls clearly within the category of international political communication—that is, efforts to gain political influence—and some training courses have stressed ideology rather than journalism techniques. But the general result has been to provide much-needed training.[15]

SHORT-TERM TRAINING PROGRAMS IN AFRICA

Perhaps the most effective program has been the Africa Training Scheme of the International Press Institute. From early 1963, a series of six-month courses was given in Nairobi for journalists from East and Central Africa and from 1964 to 1966 in Lagos for journalists from anglophonic West Africa. The program was financed by the Ford Foundation and directed by noted journalist Tom Hopkinson and other British newspapermen with considerable experience in Africa. The twenty students in each course were given some academic training (African history, African geography, current affairs, newspaper law, and English) by university lecturers. The course also emphasized professional training, reporting, editing, layout, photography, and shorthand. Part of the time, students were attached to newspapers or radio stations for practical experience. The nine 6-month courses were well conceived for the critical short-term need for beginning African journalists.

By mid-1968, when their third Ford grant had expired, the IPI had trained more than 300 African journalists from eighteen different countries.

Unfortunately, there have been no comparable programs in francophonic Africa where until recently there was little interest in journalism training. There were few permanent journalism schools in former French Africa; most of its African journalists and broadcasters were trained in France.

Francophonic Africa has received help in journalism training from UNESCO. Through its various conferences, seminars, surveys, and publications, UNESCO has brought together in Africa and elsewhere representatives of the new nations, helped them examine their mass communications needs, and aided them in initiating training programs. Dakar has been the site of several short training courses and of a permanent journalism program at the University of Dakar, under the direction of a UNESCO expert, M. Georges Galipeau, a French Canadian. UNESCO's great value is as a catalyst; it helps the new governments help themselves. It enjoys the advantage of being politically neutral, so its activities are not identified with either East or West. (Fairly or unfairly, some short-term training programs both in and out of Africa have become identified with efforts to influence African journalists toward either East or West in the Cold War. Even the scrupulously nonpolitical and professionally oriented IPI courses have not escaped such criticism.)

The International Federation of Journalists, a West European press group based in Brussels, has supported an African Journalism Institute which has conducted short-term training sessions for French- and English-speaking journalists during a two-year period. A team of 3 journalists (2 Swiss and 1 Nigerian) conducted the three-week sessions in various places. The Institute grew out of an IFJ seminar in Ibadan in September 1964 for 28 journalists under the joint sponsorship of the IFJ and the Nigerian Union of Journalists. Its alumni total 166 men and women from sixteen French- and English-speaking countries.[16]

The International Organization of Journalists, an East European newsmen's group, held journalism courses of several months duration in four African capitals: Conakry, Guinea, in 1961; Bamako, Mali, in 1962; Algiers, Algeria, in 1964; and Accra, Ghana, in 1965. These courses had the full cooperation of the host governments, but were not established on a continuing basis.[17]

PERMANENT TRAINING PROGRAMS IN AFRICA

Several journalism education programs affiliated with African universities or schools have been established in recent years. Although slower in getting started than the short-term "crash" courses, they may prove more important in the long run.

One of the first was the Ghana Institute of Journalism, started by Nkrumah in 1959, and which from the beginning included students from outside Ghana. Since Nkrumah, the government-sponsored program has been cut back and now teaches only Ghanaians. Recently there was talk of starting a journalism training program at the University of Ghana at Legon.

The Department of Journalism at the University of Nigeria at Nsukka was established in 1961 and patterned after an American university journalism school. Courses were offered in newspaper, magazine, and broadcast journalism as well as public relations. The first B.A. degrees in journalism were offered to five graduates in 1964. However, the University of Nigeria closed down completely in 1967, a casualty of the Nigerian civil war, and this very promising course was interrupted.

Partly in response to this situation, an Institute of Mass Communications was started at the University of Lagos in 1966. The first students were six 4th-year Nigerians who had transferred from Nsukka because of the crisis. The university now offers a one-year diploma course which includes public relations, journalism, radio, television, advertising, etc. The one-year course is tailored to meet the needs of practicing journalists with no university background. A three-year undergraduate course leading to an honors degree was also planned at Lagos.

The training needs have been so great in Zambia that most of the education has been at the secondary school level, principally at the excellent College of Further Education. Under various sponsorships (U.S. AID, UNESCO, and the Zambia Information Service), it has been training young Zambians for careers in mass communications since several years before independence.

Another beginners course is that conducted by the Institute of Publicity Media at Mwanza on Lake Victoria in northern Tanzania. About twenty-two students each year start the eighteen-month program run by the Catholic White Fathers under Tanzanian government auspices. Besides journalism, students study English, typing, shorthand, and the use of the telephone. Students are drawn from all parts of eastern and southern Africa. The Institute is part of the large Social Training Center at Mwanza.

In Congo (Kinshasa) and the Malagasy Republic, there have been recent efforts to establish permanent training programs in journalism. "Permanent" may be an inaccurate term to apply to specific educational endeavors in tropical Africa, as the experience at Nsukka indicates. But if these various programs take hold, they may in the future play a significant part in supplying competent journalists for the news media.

South Africa, the one nation in Africa with a university system sufficient to train numerous journalists academically, has so far paid little heed to journalism education. Potchefstroom University, a small Afrikaans university, was the only institution of higher education offering a degree course in journalism, but this was not concerned with professional training.

A new school of journalism was inaugurated at the University of Nairobi in 1970. This was an outgrowth of the IPI program.

JOURNALISM TRAINING OUTSIDE AFRICA

Africans have been receiving journalism training in Europe and the United States for some time. Many young Africans have come to American universities over the years and some have studied journalism. The most famous was undoubtedly Nnamdi Azikiwe, the Nigerian journalist and political leader, who was active in college journalism at Lincoln University and studied journalism at Columbia University. More recently the African Scholarship Program of American Universities (ASPAU) and the

African-American Institute have helped direct Africans to journalism schools and departments in U.S. universities. Others have come to the United States under sponsorship of the State Department and the Agency for International Development.

In the last ten years, several hundred French-speaking Africans have been receiving journalism training at three institutions in France: École Supérieure de Journalisme de Lille; the Centre de Formation des Journalistes in Paris, where students take some professional courses while attending the Sorbonne; and at the French government's agency for broadcasting training, Studio-Écho de L'Office de Coopération Radiophonique (OCORA) at the Maisons-Lafitte near Paris, which prepares both technicians and broadcast journalists. To maintain standards, a common competitive examination is given in each of twelve francophonic capitals from Nouakchott to Tananarive to screen the students. Most study for two or three years in France.

In England, would-be African journalists long have worked as apprentices on British newspapers or participated in correspondence courses. The Commonwealth Press Union in London arranges for refresher courses for journalists on leave from African papers. Over a number of years, the National Union of Journalists in Great Britain has organized short courses for cadet African journalists in cooperation with the National Council for the Training of Journalists. The Regent Street Polytechnic, a London vocational school, trained hundreds of West African journalists before it closed. The lack of formalized journalism education in England has been met to some extent by the Thomson Foundation, which provides newspaper training in a three-month course at Cardiff, Wales, and television training at Glasgow, Scotland. Aspiring communicators from Africa, as well as other developing areas, have attended the Thomson Foundation courses.

The Berlin Institute for Mass Communication in Developing Countries has conducted a number of three-month programs for journalists from Africa.

The International Organization of Journalists (IOJ) has helped launch similar programs in East Germany at the "School of Friendship" in Buckow, East Berlin, and at the International Training Center for Journalists from Developing Countries at Budapest, Hungary.

First among the permanent IOJ journalism schools was the International School for News Agency Editors founded in 1961 and located in a castle of the Union of Czechoslovak Journalists near Kutna Hora, Czechoslovakia. The school was designed to train journalists and technicians for the new national news agencies in Africa. By 1968 the school had been attended by 135 students; of these, 74 were journalists, 56 technicians, and 5 press photographers.[18]

PROS AND CONS OF JOURNALISM TRAINING

The various programs and approaches to training African journalists have raised a number of questions.

First, are crash courses such as the IPI Training Scheme more valuable than permanent university programs? Certainly at present both kinds of training are badly needed. A three- or six-month course is probably too brief to impart thorough grounding in journalistic techniques, especially if the student lacks writing skills and background knowledge in the social sciences. But many young African journalists on the job today, although woefully lacking in journalistic skills and experience, do benefit from even brief contacts with the various short courses.

At the same time, it is essential that journalism instruction be incorporated into the curricula of the new African universities. In this way, the continent's long-term need for broadly educated journalists can begin to be met, especially if such courses are designed to attract bright beginners into journalism careers.

The seminars and short courses, whether in Africa or abroad, are useful, but are, by definition, stop-gap and temporary expedients. It is hoped that in time they will no longer be needed.

Another question is where the journalism training should be done—in Africa or abroad?

Training in the United States or Europe has the obvious advantage of providing the models of highly developed media systems. A variety of experts is readily available for instruction or consultation. Established schools and curricula can be utilized and newspapers and broadcasting stations are available for internships. For the African journalist himself, just the travel alone —the experience of living and working abroad and what he learns about the problems of the greater world—provides a useful background for a career in journalism.

But it is also argued the journalism he sees and learns in London, Paris, or New York is so unlike that he will practice at home, that it is of little help. The African journalist, it is said, needs to know the politics, history, social problems, and economics of his own region of Africa, not of Europe or America. Some argue that extended stays abroad make students unhappy with things at home and hence unable to work effectively.

Since independence there have been so many opportunities to attend courses abroad and there is such a shortage of qualified journalists that some African journalists go again and again, spending little time putting into practice what they have learned. The proliferation of training courses partly resulted from the Cold War competition. A typical experience was that of a promising young broadcasting journalist who finished the six-month IPI training course in Nairobi. He was eager to apply what he had learned in his job with the Voice of Kenya where his services were badly needed. But before he could, the Kenyan government received an invitation to send journalists to a two-year training program in Yugoslavia. Since the government wished to maintain its nonalignment policy, the same young man was tapped to go.

Among those agencies training African journalists, there is a growing consensus that the best place to train beginning journalists is in Africa where they will work. Often, local political conditions, lack of educational facilities, and the dearth of qualified teachers make this difficult, if not impossible. But when it can be done, conditions then are more realistic; the trainee learns and practices what he needs to know on the job, and he is more likely to stay in his job afterward. Also, it is highly desirable, where possible, that Africans train other Africans. It is argued that many Africans receiving extended academic journalism education abroad go into other fields, usually government, after returning. And some, of course, never come back at all.

It may be more desirable for beginning journalists to receive their initial training in Africa, preferably in permanent schools or courses. Regional courses, such as at UNESCO centers, are well suited for intermediate training. Foreign travel or short-term courses abroad should be reserved for the senior and experienced journalists most likely to benefit from the experience. Extended education abroad should be provided only for the unusual and talented student who cannot obtain needed knowledge or skills at home. But the advanced student should have a specific position waiting for him when he returns home—a job he has been trained abroad to fill.

It should be emphasized that training is just one aspect of the problem of developing professional journalists in Africa.

Journalists are usually poorly paid and do not enjoy high social status in Africa. Driving a taxi is often a more lucrative occupation. The field has had little attraction so far for Africans with university educations. Journalists fare a little better on the government newspapers, broadcasting facilities, and information ministries, but such experience is not usually conducive to developing a professional outlook.

The lot of the African journalist, in the long run, will improve as the news media themselves develop and offer better working conditions and career opportunities for the talented and ambitious young African.

PART TWO

CASE STUDIES
OF NEWS MEDIA SYSTEMS

THE NEWS MEDIA of the seven countries examined here in detail are representative of various types of communications systems that have evolved in the years since independence. In addition, the countries are representative of several major geographic regions of Africa.

The news media of Nigeria and Ghana were both products of British colonialism, and perhaps there more than anywhere else, the news is reported by Africans for other Africans. The lingering influences of France characterize the media of the Ivory Coast and Senegal. In Kenya and Zambia the once dominant settler press has given way to an increasingly government-controlled, one-party media system. South Africa, the white man's bastion, is the special case of an entrenched and pervasive European media system.

The historical background, which determined the path the press of each region followed, sets the scene for the primary concern with the news media's activities in the first decade of African independence. The emphasis again is on the journalistic aspects of mass communications and the involvement of the press with government.

These analyses illustrate the similarities as well as the differences in the press and broadcasting facilities concentrated in Lagos, Accra, Abidjan, Dakar, Nairobi, Lusaka, and Johannesburg. Admittedly, this is but a selected sampling of a great and heterogeneous continent, but these are important cities whose news media make up in significance what they may lack in representativeness.

8

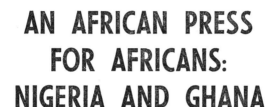

AN AFRICAN PRESS
FOR AFRICANS:
NIGERIA AND GHANA

"THE SPEARHEAD OF NATIONALISM"

AFRICAN JOURNALISM really began in British West Africa. The first newspapers published by Africans for other Africans were in the British colonies of Sierra Leone, Gold Coast (Ghana), and later Nigeria. The motivation was quite simply politics—the strategy of gaining power.

The press everywhere—Africa included—is intimately involved with politics, government, and efforts to attain political power. But the greater opportunities for journalists to use the printed word to gain political leverage directly affected the growth of the West African press.

An *indigenous* English-language press developed in British West Africa first to publicize grievances and criticize the British rulers. Later, it became a political weapon in the struggle for nationalism, to facilitate organization of political parties, and finally to win independence itself.

Nationalism, in a variety of evolving forms, provided the impetus for West African journalism, and the many small newspapers produced in Freetown, Accra, Lagos, and elsewhere were a principal weapon Africans wielded to gain their eventual independence.

Several noted Africanist scholars bear this out:

James S. Coleman wrote, "African-owned newspapers and

presses were the media through which the nationalist ideas of educated Africans found an outlet; they were responsible partly for the ever-growing number of Nigerians predisposed to a nationalist ideology. There can be little doubt that nationalist newspapers and pamphlets have been among the main influences in the awakening of racial and political consciousness."[1]

St. Clair Drake: "More than anything else, perhaps, it was the constant plugging by the little African-run papers of the case for self-government that hastened the end of colonialism in Commonwealth West Africa."[2]

F. A. O. Schwarz: "There was a tradition of hard-hitting fearless and independent journalism (in Nigeria) in the colonial days when the press was the spearhead of nationalism."[3]

One writer called these newspapers "mouthpieces of politicians in search of a party." Earlier perhaps they might have been described as mouthpieces of nationalists in search of an issue.[4]

That search was not limited by areas; there was a marked mobility of nationalist leaders and ideology across British colonial borders. Several major nationalists were active in two or more colonies and one even edited papers in the three larger ones. Distinct ties among most of the leading nationalists-journalists can be traced for three or four generations. This mobility or "commerce of ideas" was aided by the common English language and the relatively free expression permitted by British authorities.

To study either nationalism or the press in British West Africa is to study the other. The press gave to nationalism its prime means of diffusion, the medium through which the *idea* could be disseminated. Nationalism gave to the press its principal message, its *raison d'être*, in extending its circulation. But the separation of the two is not feasible because they were wedded by a common heart and mind—that of the editor-nationalist. There have been important editor-nationalists elsewhere in Africa—Habib Bourguiba in Tunisia, Jomo Kenyatta in Kenya, Kenneth Kaunda in Zambia—but the pattern was much more frequently repeated in British West Africa.

Sierra Leone established the model; newspaper development then traveled eastward to the Gold Coast and then to Nigeria.

EARLIEST NEWSPAPERS

The colony at Freetown in Sierra Leone was founded in 1792 by freed slaves from Nova Scotia, and they became the first permanent outside settlers in West Africa. The first printing press arrived in July 1794, but was destroyed two months later by the French in a raid. It was replaced or repaired and used for official printing after 1796.[5] That press produced the *Royal Gazette and Sierra Leone Advertiser,* believed to be the first newspaper in tropical Africa, which appeared in February 1801 at Fort Thornton, near Freetown. It lasted about a year, probably until the printers left the colony to trade in slaves.[6]

In 1822 the *Royal Gold Coast Gazette and Commercial Intelligencer* was launched as a handwritten gazette in Accra. It continued until 1825 as a semiofficial organ, the first newspaper in the Gold Coast.[7]

The first private paper in the Gold Coast was started some 30 years after the demise of the *Royal Gold Coast Gazette* and was also transcribed by hand at least during the early years. Edited by Charles Bannerman, it started as the *Accra Herald* in 1857 but after two years was moved to Cape Coast and renamed the *West Africa Herald.* In 1859 Bannerman claimed to have 310 subscribers, two-thirds of them natives. The paper continued intermittently until 1873, although for two to four years after 1868 it was published in Freetown.[8]

Even before the British acquired control over the Lagos area, the first newspaper in Nigeria had been printed by missionaries. The first known newspaper in Nigeria was the *Iwe Irohin fun awon ara Egba Yorubas* ("the newspaper for the Egba people and the Yorubas"), *Iwe Irohin* for short, and first appeared in 1859.[9]

The *Iwe Irohin* was primarily a news bulletin for the Christian Missionary Society (CMS) and was edited by Rev. Henry Townsend, who had established the mission north of Lagos at Abeokuta in 1842. By 1848 Townsend was putting the Yoruba language into written form. In 1854 the first printing press arrived, and five years later he started the *Iwe Irohin* as a fortnightly in the Yoruba language and later partly in Yoruba and partly in English. An estimated 3,000 Yorubas had learned to read their language by 1859, when the paper first appeared. Three years later the first Bible in Yoruba came off the same press. In addition to being the first paper in Nigeria, *Iwe Irohin* was probably the first vernacular paper in British West Africa.

By 1900 thirty-four newspapers had appeared in Sierra Leone, nineteen in the Gold Coast, nine in Nigeria, and one in Gambia, for a total of sixty-three. Only a dozen had lasted ten years or more. Elsewhere in black Africa, an *African* press was virtually nonexistent at that time except in South Africa.

By the twentieth century, British West Africa had assumed its present political boundaries. At the same time there was a continuous series of newspaper-supported anti-colonial protests, particularly in Lagos. The growth of nationalism, though, was most evident in the Gold Coast during the first two decades, reaching its apogee in the activities in 1920 of the National Congress of British West Africa, a high point in the Pan-West Africanism movement. Casely Hayford, a Gold Coast editor, was the prime organizer, and journalists in all four colonies were active leaders in the National Congress.

A slack period in journalism followed until the return from America of Nnamdi Azikiwe to West Africa in the mid-1930s. Outstanding both as a nationalist leader and as a journalist, his activities in the next three years in the Gold Coast and then, after 1937 in Nigeria, sparked a revival of both nationalism and journalism which was delayed only by World War II.

In early 1948 political attention shifted to the Gold Coast with the Accra "disturbances" and their political consequences. Kwame Nkrumah founded his *Evening News* in 1948 and it served as a rallying point around which the Convention People's Party was eventually constructed.[10] Dennis Austin wrote: "The CPP warned its readers to read the *Evening News* daily to enable the national headquarters to guide the country to victory. . . ." (i.e., independence).[11] From then on, Gold Coast nationalists, led by Nkrumah, were in the forefront in West Africa and by 1951 had won national elections. Independence came in 1957.

In Nigeria, temporary unity on major issues among the three main regional-tribal-political factions (the Hausa-Fulani North, the Yoruba West, and the Ibo East) led that nation to independence in 1960. Sierra Leone followed in 1961.

In the early 1950s, once independence was assured, a subtle shift began from militant nationalism to internal political struggle among rival regional groups. Owning a newspaper was a *sine qua non* for a successful politician. In Nigeria, Azikiwe and his NCNC party controlled ten newspapers by 1959, and in the same year Obafemi Awolowo and his Action Group in the Western Region controlled fourteen papers. In the Gold Coast, Nkrumah and his Convention People's Party had seven papers at one time or another. Milton A. S. Margai and his Sierra Leone People's Party controlled two newspapers. A dozen lesser parties and politicians were supported by their own newspapers.

By independence nearly all African-owned newspapers were either controlled by or in full support of political parties and nearly all leading newspapermen continued their involvement in politics.

A major development of the 1940s was the entry of foreign newspaper capital into West African journalism. The London *Daily Mirror* group, then headed by Cecil H. King, used its financial and technical resources to establish three West Coast dailies—the *Daily Times* in Nigeria, the *Daily Graphic* in Ghana, and the *Daily Mail* in Sierra Leone. From the beginning the policy of these papers was vigorous neutrality between the competing parties, objective reporting of news by African reporters and editors, constructive criticism, volume production, and territory-wide distribution, using air transport for remoter areas. Such papers were instrumental in establishing a more professional basis for the press and tended to link literate Africans with their new nationalist leaders.[12] The papers were staffed editorially by Africans and were never identified with the colonial governments.

The number and range of newspapers in preindependence British West Africa were, in contrast to the dormant state of *African* journalism elsewhere on the continent, an impressive accomplishment. Lloyd Murphy's study found a total of 227 newspapers in British West Africa during the colonial period. This included 52 in Sierra Leone, 70 in the Gold Coast, 100 in Nigeria, and 5 in Gambia. And this total does not include the strictly religious, commercial, or educational publications, nor does it include any government-operated gazette, except the initial ones in each colony. Leading journalists were nearly always the leading nationalists or political leaders.

GOVERNMENT ACTIVITIES

In addition to the foreign-owned press, news communications in British West Africa were affected by the expansion of public relations activities of the colonial governments. At the height of agitational politics when colonial governments were subjected to unrelenting invective by the nationalist press, the British government gave high priority to the development of public relations departments specifically to counter nationalist propaganda and explain government policies and programs to the public.[13]

This led to fierce competition between the nationalist press and colonial governments. As the nationalists approached political power they vowed to end all government information programs. However, once in control, they saw the utility of this official apparatus of mass communications that had been developed during terminal colonialism. The result was that public information programs received a new lease on life and their programs were expanded after independence. In fact the government information apparatus (in Nigeria at the regional as well as federal level) provided an important new dimension to news communications—not only government-run radio and television but also government-run newspapers evolved in all of the former British West African territories.

Why was the African or non-European press so dynamic and influential in the political struggles of British West Africa?

The use of English as a *lingua franca* among educated Africans contributed greatly to the proliferation of nationalist ideology. The press in all four colonies was predominantly in English; this provided a common meeting ground for the educated Africans from each colony and facilitated the crossing of colonial boundaries.

Few newspapers were in the vernaculars. One exception was the government-sponsored Gaskiya Corporation of Northern Nigeria which published several papers and other publications in vernaculars, beginning in the mid-1940s. A Hausa weekly, *Gaskiya Tafi Kwabo* ("truth is worth more than a penny"—a name borrowed from an early missionary paper), was started in 1939, and periodicals in Fulani, Tiv, and Kanuri languages were published as well. However education and literacy development motivated these publications, not agitational politics as in southern Nigeria.

FREE EXPRESSION PERMITTED

The British tradition of press freedom was generally sustained in colonial West Africa. Occasionally there were examples of suppression, particularly when the colonial government was under pressure. But the colonial authorities showed remarkable tolerance for the African-run papers, which indeed were often shrilly and libelously hypercritical of British policy. There were some suppressions of papers, and several well-known nationalists-journalists, including J. Bright Davies, I.T.A. Wallace-Johnson, and Azikiwe, ran afoul of the law on occasion.

In general, however, the British authorities exercised restraint and usually acted within British common law. No other area of Africa enjoyed as much comparative press freedom, and the West African journalists, many of whom had spent years in

Britain or America, seemed to have internalized British press traditions. This greater tolerance of political activity and expression was due in part to the absence of large numbers of British settlers on the land. Consequently, a European-oriented settler press did not develop as in East and South Africa.

This more fluid and unstructured political climate, Murphy's study suggested, is the reason so many newspapers appeared in West Africa. When the political control of a country was "up for grabs," such as in a colony at its immediate preindependence stage, a wide-open opportunity for political alternatives resulted in the arrival of new newspapers to present those ideas. The most open political situation in Ghana was in 1950 before the first national elections. During that year a total of twenty dailies appeared. But soon, Nkrumah and the CPP began gaining control, and with their consolidation of political power, the number of newspapers began decreasing until by the time nationhood was attained in 1957 there were only four daily newspapers extant. After independence there, opposition papers disappeared altogether.

The relationship between political fluidity and numbers of newspapers was evident also in Nigeria where each succeeding election brought more papers, since none of the three major parties could gain dominance over the other two. In this instance, as independence neared, most new papers were tied to one of the three major parties, not to other political minorities.

Undoubtedly newspapers played a major role in formulating an effective public opinion on political matters in British West Africa. But public opinion was not mass opinion. The only public influenced by the press until the 1940s was the educated, English-speaking African elites, living mostly in urban areas of each colony. Newspapers were written largely "of, by, and for" these few. They had only one other important audience—the colonial administrators and Whitehall. But the size of the readership was not as important as who the readers were.

Actually Azikiwe's entry into journalism marked the first attempts to reach the larger public. Jones-Quartey credits "Zik's combative and provocative journalism" as the "most crucial single precipitant of Nigerian awakening."[14] The press undoubtedly reached the "influentials" among the African elites who in turn influenced the masses. But large audiences were not really reached directly by the press until the high-circulation British-owned papers arrived in the 1947–52 period.

As in Britain and America, increased newspaper circulation

came with the development of primary education. The number of children attending primary schools in Ghana rose from about 15,000 in 1902 to about 50,000 in 1924, to 65,000 in 1935; then, more steeply, to 185,000 in 1945, 301,000 in 1951, and 456,000 in 1957. In Nigeria students in primary schools increased from about 150,000 in the mid-1920s to about 1,100,000 in the early 1950s.

By the mid-1930s the literate population of Ghana and southern Nigeria had increased to a point at which the new techniques of popular journalism that Zik introduced from the United States and perfected in West Africa could be successful. From 1935 to 1937, when he was convicted of sedition for an article appearing in his paper, Zik edited the Accra *African Morning Post.* Thereafter, he returned to Nigeria to start the famous *West African Pilot* and built up around it a chain of provincial daily papers based in Ibadan, Onitsha, Port Harcourt, and Kano.[15]

The press in British West Africa played a more dynamic and active role than the press has played there in the turbulent and often discouraging days since independence.

It may be that the agitational journalism of British West Africa, with its notable involvement in the long struggle for nationalism and independence, was ill suited to the postindependence needs of the new fragile nations.

In any case, the small nationalist newspapers of Nigeria, the Gold Coast, and Sierra Leone have earned a place in history.

It is curious that Nigeria and Ghana, who share so much in their colonial history, should have followed such divergent paths in the first rocky decade of political independence. Yet in each new nation, Ghanaians and Nigerians, not Europeans, were grappling with their problems and political frictions. And this is what makes the news media systems of anglophonic West Africa significant: they are run by and intended for other Africans.

INDEPENDENT NIGERIA: DIVERSITY AND DISCORD

The Federal Republic of Nigeria, located in West Africa on the north side of the Gulf of Guinea, began independence on October 1, 1960, with the most promising prospects of any new nation in Africa. The former colony of Britain was called the "giant of Africa" for more reason than its 356,669-square-mile size. It has a dynamic and heterogeneous population of 58.6 millions (1966 estimate), abundant resources, and real prospects for modernization and economic viability.

It also has the most extensive system of mass communications of any nation in black Africa, backed by a long tradition of indigenous journalism.

During the colonial period, indirect rule and a regional pattern of government had resulted in the Northern, Eastern, and Western Regions. Regional legislatures and regional self-government preceded the federal government. This governmental structure was unique in Africa; consequently, Nigeria did not produce one nationalist movement as in Ghana, but three, based on the country's major tribal and linguistic groupings—principally the Yorubas in the West, the Ibos in the East, and (to a lesser extent) the Hausa and Fulanis in the Moslem North.

The major political parties and their newspaper spokesmen evolved from these regional movements, and the political in-fighting and strife that have rent Nigeria in recent years stem essentially from the unresolved regional, as well as tribal, rivalries. Nigeria has never been a true nation.

Nigeria's system of mass communications accurately reflected these political conditions. At independence in 1960, Nigeria had four systems of government-controlled mass communications, not just one: a national system based in the teeming federal capital of Lagos; a Western Region system in Ibadan, the metropolis of the Yorubas; a nearly self-contained system controlled by the Moslem Emirs of the North; and another in the Ibo-dominated Eastern Region. (A Midwest Region was created in 1963 and initiated some communication activities.)

When the first military coup of January 15, 1966, ended civilian parliamentary rule, or the First Nigerian Federation, each system had its own ministry of information, radio broadcasting facility, television broadcasting facility, and official or government newspaper.

Within the regions these official communications systems were manipulated by the regional governments to their own political advantage against both their local rivals and their political counterparts nationally.

But at the federal level, because of the uneasy balance between the three regions, the political atmosphere permitted a degree of press freedom and diversity of expression that was unusual in postindependence Africa.

In other parts of Africa, one of the factors that nudged African leaders toward greater authoritarianism was the constant threat that dissident tribal, ethnic, or regional groups posed to the integrity of the new states. This was particularly true of Sudan,

Guinea, and Ghana. James S. Coleman wrote, before the 1966 coup: "In Nigeria, however, it could be argued that the tensions between the three regions, each the political core area of a major cultural group, and each unable either to dominate or to separate from the others, has created a structured, multi-party system that is largely responsible for the fact that, at the federal level, Nigeria is unquestionably the most free and open polity in independent Africa."[16]

And while this uneasy balance lasted, Nigeria enjoyed the reputation of having the freest and most outspoken press in Africa. This enabled the politically oriented agitational press to continue to operate after independence much as it had before the British relinquished control. It was unprecedented in independent black Africa for newspapers so vehemently to espouse differing political causes and so recklessly to castigate politicians. French-speaking Africans were reportedly shocked when coming to Nigeria and reading what the local press wrote about public officials. But this freedom existed primarily in Lagos, not out in the regions where a much different relationship between press and government prevailed.

MEDIA FACILITIES

Besides possessing black Africa's most extensive system of mass communications, Nigeria had as well the largest and most receptive audience. According to U.S. Information Agency data, Nigeria in 1967 had:

Radio: 17 working transmitters that broadcast to 690,625 sets, reaching 8 to 10 million people.

Press: 18 daily newspapers, 15 weeklies, and 22 periodicals, with a total circulation of over 2 million and a readership of about 4 million.

Television: 5 programming stations and 4 relay stations broadcasting 180 hours weekly to 35,000 licensed sets and an estimated 2,800 unlicensed sets, with a total audience estimated at 400,000.

Motion pictures: 83 roofed theaters, drawing weekly audiences of 500,000. The outdoor weekly audience for films was estimated to be 875,000.[17]

No other black African nation came close to Nigeria in media facilities and audiences.

The mass media of Nigeria were directly involved in and se-riously affected by the tumultuous events beginning in late 1965. One of the many casualties of the time of troubles was Nigeria's reputation as locale of the freest and most outspoken newspapers in tropical Africa. That freedom had contributed to the growth of the press.

The daily newspapers published in Lagos have long enjoyed a certain amount of nationwide circulation, especially in Ibadan, Enugu, Kaduna, and other cities; hence they were national news-papers. (Unlike most African nations, Nigeria had had a number of provincial dailies, as well.) But vast areas of bush and many small towns and villages are not reached by any dailies.

The most successful of these nationals has been the combina-tion *Daily Times* and *Sunday Times,* owned by the Overseas News-papers, Ltd. (publishers of London's *Daily Mirror*) since 1947. With a modern and well-equipped printing plant on Kakawa Street in downtown Lagos, the *Times*'s facilities were the finest and most extensive in West Africa and its staff perhaps the most professional. In addition to the newspapers, the *Times* also pub-lished *Spear* (a *Drum*-like magazine), *Woman's World, Home Studies, Lagos Weekend,* and printed a large share of the press run for *West Africa,* the London weekly of news and comment also published by Overseas Newspapers.

During 1966, the *Daily Times* circulation climbed to 136,937 and the *Sunday Times* to 218,537, the largest for tropical Africa. These were average figures and on at least one occasion daily sales went over half a million. The *Daily Times* was a rare phe-nomenon in black Africa—a successful and profitable daily news-paper. Although the paper always was edited by and for Africans (but with British management), the *Times* was sensitive about foreign ownership. Therefore stock was offered to Nigerians, and in 1967, 26.8 percent of the ordinary stock was owned by Nige-rians or Nigerian pension funds and companies. This, too, was unusual for an African paper.

Although not "above politics," the *Times* tended to be nomi-nally independent of political factions and in fact carried few editorials. But this did not stop it from getting into bitter has-sles with its daily rivals in Lagos. Some of the best African jour-nalists have worked on the *Times,* including Peter Enahoro, the former editor whose "Peter Pan" column was a delight to read, and Alhaji Babatunde Jose, its former managing director. These editors directed an editorial staff of over forty-five, including reporters in all the regional capitals who sent in stories by telex.

Although the *Times*, like its rivals, had a distinctively Nigerian flavor, the imprint of the London *Mirror* showed in the bright features, closely cropped pictures, and catchy headlines.

The civil war cut off all *Times* circulation (estimated at 50,000) to the Eastern Region. That, coupled with the fact that many of the *Times*'s readers in the North were Ibos who fled to their Eastern Region homeland after the racial disorders of 1966, caused the *Daily Times* circulation to drop to 100,000.

But, although its news content and editorials were blander and mostly apolitical, and there was even less hard news whether domestic or foreign, the *Times* maintained its position as Nigeria's leading newspaper.

In fact its rival national papers slipped far more. The *Times*'s principal competitor, the *Daily Express* and *Sunday Express*, folded completely in December 1965, soon after the election troubles in the Western Region. Death of the *Express* was a real loss to Nigerian journalism. Often superior to the *Times* in news coverage, it was less politically flamboyant than the *West African Pilot*. The *Express*'s able editor, Timothy Ulo Adebanjo, did some excellent investigative reporting of political skulduggery under the byline of "Mickey Mouse."

The *Express* was started in late 1960 as a replacement for the old *Daily Service*, the long-time spokesman of the Action Group, the Yoruba political party. After losing the 1959 election, the Action Group went into partnership with Lord Thomson of Fleet, the British publisher, to put out a daily edited with a more national approach and less tied to Action Group politics. Although the *Daily Express* reached a daily circulation of 55,000 to 60,000 and the *Sunday Express* went to 70,000 to 80,000, the paper persistently lost money, and even Thomson could not keep pouring money into such a losing enterprise. The *Express* operated in the manner of the *Daily Times:* the all-African editorial staff ran the paper, although there was a British expatriate who supervised the business side. (The Thomson organization's media investments in Africa were more recently confined to one biweekly, the *Malawi Times*, and to television enterprises in Sierra Leone, the Ivory Coast, and Ethiopia.)[18]

The *Daily Express* reappeared in Lagos four years later in August 1969. The Thomson group had no connection with the new *Daily Express* which was owned entirely by Nigerians.

DECLINE OF THE "PILOT"

The proud old *West African Pilot,* the tarnished jewel in the crown of Dr. Nnamdi Azikiwe's once extensive newspaper chain, has managed to hang on—but just barely—during the turbulent sixties. In 1960 when he joined the federal government as Gover-nor-General and later as President, "Zik" sold the paper's title and goodwill but retained ownership of the building, press, and equipment at the Yaba plant. Actually the paper was still in effect owned by Zik and continued to support the National Coun-cil of Nigerian Citizens (NCNC), the East's political party.

Always more of an agitational and political polemicist than a newspaper, the *Pilot* involved itself in most of the political in-fighting. Often wildly irresponsible and reckless in its name-call-ing, it also took a decidedly leftist line at times, either by print-ing Communist handouts or by supporting anti-Western causes. This was not because the *Pilot* was a Communist paper, but prob-ably because an editor received "dash" or a bribe to print a hand-out from Communist sources.

Lacking the modern printing equipment of the *Times* and *Post,* the *Pilot* was poorly produced with hand-set type on an old flatbed press. Appealing mostly to Easterners and NCNC party faithful, the *Pilot* managed to reach a circulation of about 50,000 during its heyday.

However, Biafra's secession and civil war sent the old fire-brand into a tailspin. With the NCNC dissolved and Zik's funds cut off (he returned to Biafra and then later came back), the *Pilot* decided to give nominal support to the military regime and to try to hold on until the postwar reconstruction. The editorial staffers —most were Ibos, many of whom returned to the East—dropped from forty-seven to seven, and those remaining went unpaid for months at a time. Circulation in 1968 was down to a bare 5,000, if that much, and Reuters had finally discontinued its service for nonpayment of its long overdue bill. The war-time *Pilot* was a bad joke: pictures upside down, its usual four pages filled mostly with irrelevant handouts from foreign embassies, and pictures without either captions or point.[19]

The sad state of this historic paper which played such a sig-nificant role in the Nigerian nationalist movement illustrates the plight of African papers without financial support from either government or overseas newspaper interests. Given the economic conditions of tropical Africa today, theirs is a difficult situation, especially when subsidies from a political party dry up.

But strong financial backing does not automatically assure success either. Another ailing paper was the federal government's *Morning Post* and *Sunday Post,* the combination started in October 1961 to give the government a voice against the foreign-owned *Times* and the *Express.* Despite first-rate printing facilities and an excellent editorial staff, including Abiodun Aloba and Increase Coker, the paper never did well.

The reasons were several. The *Post* was unable to maintain transport facilities to compete with the efficient *Times* and had to cope with numerous printing breakdowns as well. By always supporting government positions, even on the unpopular Newspaper Law Amendment of 1964, it gained little public acceptance and was roundly disliked by other papers, which accused the *Post* of using taxpayers' money to compete with the independent press.

Circulation until late 1963 was 65,000 daily and 75,000 Sunday, but had dropped to 45,000 and 50,000, respectively, by March 1965.[20] By 1968 the *Morning Post* had plummeted to about 25,000 and the *Sunday Post* to 32,000, and rumors were abroad in Lagos that the federal military government planned to discontinue it. The military regime was also unhappy with the *Post* because it had been embroiled in politics, voicing the viewpoints of remnants of the old Nigerian National Democratic Party (NNDP), the late S. L. Akintola's Western Region party, in verbal jousts with the *Daily Sketch* and *Nigerian Tribune.*

So only the *Daily Times,* of Nigeria's once-flourishing national press, was managing at the decade's end to maintain itself fairly effectively. As for the regions, their papers were hard hit too by the events of the late 1960s.

In March 1964 the Western Region government, then headed by Chief Akintola, started its own paper in Ibadan, the *Daily Sketch,* as the voice of the NNDP in its bitter political wrangles with the Action Group, the "other" Yoruba party then out of office and its leader Chief Obafemi Awolowo in jail. The *Sketch,* well-printed in a new plant on a two-unit rotary press from West Germany, was until Akintola's assassination under his personal control and used to reinforce his political position. Little effort was made to provide comprehensive and objective news coverage.[21]

The *Sketch*'s main adversary in the Western Region was the Action Group's *Nigerian Daily Tribune* and *Sunday Tribune,* also published in Ibadan. The *Nigerian Tribune* was started in 1947 by Awolowo, who owned it until 1951 when a private corporation (i.e., Action Group) took it over, although Mrs. Awolowo was reported in 1968 to be a major stockholder.

Limping along with about 5,000 circulation in 1965, the *Tribune*, as the opposition paper in the Western Region, was subjected to considerable harassment from the regional government. When I interviewed the *Tribune*'s editor, Ayo Ojewumi, in 1965, he had just finished a six-month jail term for sedition after the *Tribune* commented on possible irregularities in the regional government's budget. Moreover, Ojewumi was due in court the following week to answer charges concerning another story in the *Tribune*. The political persecution of the *Tribune* in Ibadan underlined the fact that there was much more freedom to publish in Lagos than in the regional capitals.

Political harassment was not the *Tribune*'s only handicap. When visiting its Ibadan offices, I found the paper was being published daily without the benefit of any wire service or even a telephone.

Yet in 1968 the *Tribune* was still in business and Ojewumi was still its editor, although he had been in and out of jail several times, including several months detention without charges by the military government. Although still a scraggly-looking paper of only four to six pages, its stock (and security) increased after Awolowo was released from jail and became the leading civilian in the federal military government. The *Tribune*, with only a dilapidated flatbed press, also continued to publish its Yoruba language weekly, *Irohin Yoruba*. That vernacular paper once reached 70,000 circulation in the heyday of the Action Group before the split between Akintola and Awolowo, both of whom had early journalism careers in preindependence politics.

Numerous daily papers have been published by the energetic Ibos in the East: *Eastern Observer,* a daily in English and Ibo in Onitsha; *Nigerian Spokesman,* another English daily in Onitsha; the *Eastern Sentinel,* a Zik-owned daily in Enugu; and the *Midwest Echo* in Benin. The government paper of the Eastern Region was the *Nigerian Outlook,* an English daily published in Enugu. Almost all the provincial papers in the Eastern Region became casualties of the civil war. The *Outlook* became the *Biafran Sun,* a lively but irregularly produced paper of the Ojukwu government. (The new East Central state announced in mid-1970 that it would launch a new daily, *Renaissance,* to replace the defunct *Outlook.*) The strife also forced the demise of three dailies in the Northern Region, all catering basically to Southerners (mostly Ibos) living in the north—the *Daily Comet* of Kano, the *Northern Star* of Kano, and the *Middle Belt Herald* of Jos had all ceased publication by early 1968.[22]

The *Nigerian Citizen,* a biweekly subsidized by the Northern government, was the principal spokesman for the Moslem leadership of the Northern Peoples' Congress. It was published by the Gaskiya Corporation at Zaria, which also put out a number of vernacular papers, including *Gaskiya Ta Fi Kwabo,* a Hausa language weekly of 23,000 circulation, carrying substantially the same editorial content as the *Nigerian Citizen.*

The one bright spot in the Nigerian newspaper scene during the civil upheavals was the launching of the *New Nigerian* in Kaduna in 1966 by the Northern Region government in collaboration with British newspaper interests headed by Charles Sharp. A very smart and attractive daily printed on a web offset press, it carried a good deal of news and useful information, and was quite possibly the best newspaper in Nigeria. In its own fleet of trucks, it was widely distributed throughout the enormous North.

But the *New Nigerian* was an expensive government operation and was reportedly losing £300,000 a year in 1968.[23]

THE PRESS'S TIME OF TROUBLES: 1965–66

The violence that swept western Nigeria following the disputed elections there in October 1965 illustrated the vulnerability of Nigeria's highly politicized press to political passions. Until then, there had been more freedom for the press in Nigeria than almost anywhere. Despite some harassment, opposition papers circulated—if not actually flourished—in the various regions, and the Federation's uneasy balance owed much to the vigor of the press (although it may also be charged that irresponsible press performance contributed to the eventual political disintegration).

All that changed when the 1965 election results, which favored Akintola's NNDP party, were disputed by the opposition (an alliance of the Action Group and the NCNC), and outbreaks of violence followed. All kinds of papers—government, party-supported, and foreign-owned—were swept up in the violence.

The Ibadan printing workshop of the *Nigerian Tribune* was attacked and set on fire. About twenty people injured three employees and destroyed printing machinery and eight cars belonging to the company.

Along with the *West African Pilot,* the *Nigerian Outlook,* and four other papers, the *Tribune* was banned by the Ibadan City Council. Anyone caught reading the papers was liable to a £100 fine or six months in jail, and anyone caught listening to the Eastern Nigeria Broadcasting Service was liable to a £25 fine or two months in jail.[24]

Western Region police in Ibadan declared the premises of the Nigerian Press (publishers of the *Tribune* and *Irohin*) a prohibited area and detained, without charges, twenty-five press personnel.

In retaliation, a number of eastern Nigerian local councils supporting the opposition in western Nigeria banned from their bailiwicks the *Daily Times, Daily Express, Sunday Times, Sunday Express, Morning Post,* and *Daily Sketch.*[25]

Angry partisans of the Action Group-NCNC coalition protested the police seizure of the *Tribune* by raiding the Ibadan offices of the *Daily Sketch* and the *Morning Post,* burning several thousand copies of the papers and attacking news vendors.

Two editors, Stephen Iweakya of the *West African Pilot* and Smart Ebby of the *Daily Telegraph,* were arrested on charges of sedition and false publication.

The first military coup soon followed in January 1966 and the first military government instructed authorities to lift all locally imposed bans on Nigerian newspapers.

Despite declarations by the new military rulers that freedom of the press was to be restored, Nigeria's press has been in eclipse ever since.

RADIO AND TELEVISION

Most African nations have only one government broadcasting system but Nigeria's federal arrangement spawned four: the Nigerian Broadcasting Corporation (NBC) or "Radio Nigeria," based in Lagos; Eastern Nigeria Broadcasting Service (ENBS) in Enugu; Western Nigeria Broadcasting Service (WNBS) in Ibadan; and the Broadcasting Company of Northern Nigeria (BCNN) in Kaduna. This resulted in unnecessary duplication of facilities and overlapping of programs, but each regional government was eager to control its own radio outlet for political reasons.

Nigerian broadcasting must be praised for its effort to deal with the country's linguistic diversity. Although large numbers speak the principal languages of Hausa, Yoruba, Ibo, and English, an estimated 250 languages and dialects are used in Nigeria, and radio, both at the federal and regional levels, has provided a wide range of programming in vernaculars to reach many traditional Africans heretofore untouched by mass communications. (By contrast, it should be noted that the Nigerian press has long been mostly an English-language news medium with the few vernacular papers playing a limited role.)

The most extensive system was the federal government's Radio Nigeria, which employed more than 3,000 people and could lay claim to being the most professional broadcasting system in black Africa.

Radio Nigeria transmitted a national service from Lagos and three regional programs from facilities at Kaduna, Enugu, and Ibadan, plus local programs from thirteen provincial broadcasting houses scattered over the Federation.

The professionally handled news broadcasts on Radio Nigeria showed a balance and objectivity rare in African radio. They were, at least until 1965, generally free of the heavy-handed government propaganda and general dullness so often found in news bulletins on most government radio stations. While Nigeria was still at war, Radio Nigeria had lost much of its disinterested objectivity, especially when reporting news of the war itself and political developments.[26]

With newscasts almost every hour, NBC regularly gave the news—not only in English but in Hausa, Yoruba, and Ibo. At its regional stations, news was given in five other vernaculars of the North, at Ibadan in three other vernaculars, in the East in four other vernaculars, and at its Midwest regional station at Benin in three other vernaculars. The regional NBC stations, which originated much of their own programming, were required to take certain programs from Lagos, including news shows. For instance, at NBC's regional station at Kaduna the full NBC national news bulletins from Lagos at 7 a.m., 1 p.m., 9 p.m., and 10 p.m. were carried. In addition, regional news bulletins were read in English and Hausa at 12 noon and 8 p.m.; then at 3 p.m. news was broadcast in Kanuri, Fulani, Yoruba, and Tiv. In the North, the NBC had relay stations (middle wave) at Kano, Kaduna, Zaria, Sokoto, Katsina, Maiduguri, Ilorin, and Jos to carry its signal over that far-ranging region.

Radio Nigeria had a staff of thirty-two in Lagos preparing news programs. For foreign news they relied on Reuters, Associated Press, and Agence France Presse—a wider range of news sources than most African stations had. For Nigerian news, they used staffers and stringers who sent in stories by telephone or telegraph to the regional stations that relayed them by teleprinter to Lagos for final processing before being aired.

The NBC's External Service, the "Voice of Nigeria," was inaugurated on January 1, 1962, and was on the air from 1 p.m. to 9 p.m. daily, broadcasting principally in four languages: English, French, Hausa, and Arabic.

The civil war provided a certain urgency to foreign broadcasting; it was one obvious way to sell the federal case abroad.

In 1968 the NBC was carrying a good many commercials which were aired between 7 to 9 a.m., noon to 2 p.m., and 5 to 8 p.m. The only other noticeable change in the three years between my visits was the previously noted loss of objectivity, especially in reporting the civil war, and a slightly more strident tone.

The NBC also has administrative control of the federal government's television service—NBC-TV, which was organized in Lagos in April 1962 but did not start broadcasting until 1963. It was initially set up and managed by the National Broadcasting Company (International) of America, which contracted to train Nigerians to take over the service by March 31, 1967.

Like Radio Nigeria, NBC-TV also carried commercials, but was on the air only from 6 p.m. to 11 or 11:30 p.m., whereas Radio Nigeria broadcast from 5:30 a.m. to 12 midnight daily.

There were four news shows daily on television: two five-minute reports at 6 and 7 p.m., a fifteen-minute show at 9 p.m., and then a brief bulletin at closing.[27]

The NBC, both radio and television, was subsidized by the federal government at a reported £1 million a year. The remainder of operating expenses came from advertising revenue and license fees. Television sets cost their owners an annual license fee of £3 a year; owners of radio receivers paid ten shillings. Collection of radio license fees was difficult; keeping track of the country's many small transistor sets was a nearly impossible task.

Since Lagos itself is in western Nigeria, NBC's radio and television services directly competed with those of the Western Region government, which had long experience in both media.

WNTV was the first television service in black Africa, having started broadcasting on October 31, 1959.

News programs for both television and radio were prepared by the same staff, who, unlike the NBC, exerted more direct political control of the news. The news director of WNBS and WNTV told me in 1965 that news was played the way Chief Akintola, then regional prime minister, wanted it. The news tended to be biased, propagandistic, and full of government pronouncements. The news director admitted he was often pressured by party officials to broadcast scurrilous attacks on Akintola's political opponents.[28]

The Northern Region, proud, feudal, and traditional, was fully in broadcasting too, although it got a later start. Radio Kaduna began in 1961 and a television service was started on March 15, 1962. Both were controlled and operated by the Broadcasting Company of Northern Nigeria (BCNN), whose ownership was divided between government and two British firms, Granada and Electrical and Musical Industries, Ltd.[29]

The North's broadcasting operations were much more modest than those elsewhere in Nigeria in part because the audiences were much smaller. Television officials "hoped" there were 3,000 sets in the North (there were probably fewer) and it was claimed radio was picked up by 20,000 receivers. Television was on the air from 6:30 to 10:30 p.m., only six days a week. On the seventh day, Saturday night, the transmitter was shut down and engineers performed necessary maintenance. As elsewhere, television programming was modest: two brief news reports and syndicated entertainment shows from the United States and Britain.

On Radio Kaduna, news bulletins were broadcast several times daily in English and also in Hausa, Tiv, Fulani, Nupe, Yoruba, and Kanuri. The broadcasting day opened and closed with readings from the Koran.

The Eastern Region, before the secession and civil war, had radio and television services similar to those of the North and the West. In Enugu, locally prepared news shows were given periodically in Ibo, Ijaw, Efik, and Yoruba, as well as English. The Eastern Nigeria Television Service had the same limited evening pattern of two brief news shows and foreign programs.

ENTV expired with the fall of Enugu and ENBS became "Radio Biafra," the elusive "rebel" radio station which was picked up clearly in Lagos and was conceded to be an effective propaganda arm of Biafra.

Generally, radio and television broadcasting in federal Nigeria, with the four systems (plus a limited Midwest Region radio service added in 1965), was the most comprehensive in tropical

Africa. On radio, the variety of programs and the widespread use of vernaculars to reach the diverse population made Nigeria's radio systems probably the most effective in black Africa. Variety and quality, for both the modern and the traditional sectors, were available to Nigeria's estimated eight to nine million listeners. However, it should be remembered that the ultimate effect of the regional broadcast systems, both in news and general programming, was to reinforce tribal and regional loyalties to the detriment of national and "Nigerian" tendencies. Moreover, regional broadcasting was the captive of the regional political factions. The insularity of the North and the disdain of the Moslem Emirs for the South (which many of them considered to be a foreign land of infidels) were accurately reflected in the provincial outlook of Northern broadcasting. Often, major news stories emanating from the federal capital in Lagos were not reported on Radio Kaduna because they were considered of no concern to the North.

None of the four television services, each independent of the other, was able to make more than a modest beginning; each offered only limited programming to a handful of listeners situated near the transmitters.

GOVERNMENT-PRESS RELATIONSHIPS

During the free-swinging libertarian era of the 1950s and early 1960s, the relations between the Nigerian newspapers and government officials were often abrasive and tense. Yet despite the often reckless and irresponsible exchanges between press and government, the restrictions and restraints on the Nigerian press have generally been within the framework of law—British common law. Intensely partisan and political, newspapers have long been subject to a certain amount of political harassment. Fairly frequently, police would search a newspaper office looking for evidence, but the papers rarely were intimidated by such tactics, usually considering such a search a badge of honor.[30]

Newspapers were also subjected to prosecutions under the "Seditious Offenses Ordinance" of 1909, revised in 1924, 1942, and 1949.

The volatile *West African Pilot* was often the subject of official attention. In 1963 the *Pilot* offices were searched by a CID squad. On December 1, 1964, the *Pilot* published a poem, contributed by a reader, urging the election of UPGA candidates, and for this the editor, Herbert Unegbu, was charged with sedition. The offending passages of the poem, "Vote for UGPA and Free Awo," were:

> Since that day hope vanished
> That AWO to prison returned
> Do I weep every morning.
> Since AWO's departure to Calabar
> Do I sincerely keeping mourning—
> 'Cause Law has taken its course
> Truth silenced! and Liberty chained
> Freedom Lovers vote for UPGA.

Unegbu was later acquitted.

In 1963 the Official Secrets Act was tightened.

In the fall of 1964 the Nigerian government introduced an amendment to the newspaper law designed "to curb recklessness and irresponsibility of certain sections of the Press." The amendment imposed a £200 fine or one year in prison for publishing unconfirmed rumors and stories that later proved to be false. Newspapers were also required to publish the names of publishers and editors. Newspapers vehemently opposed it, but the law went through anyway.

Such a law was (and still is) a potent weapon for governmental retaliation against press criticism.

Actually the regions passed similar "false news" laws earlier: the East in 1955, the West in 1957, and the North in 1958. And newspapers were subject to laws at both federal and regional levels.

This double jeopardy situation pointed up the need to nationalize Nigeria's press laws so that newspapers would be protected anywhere in the nation. As noted earlier, the provincial or regional press, if in opposition, had nothing like the freedom of the Lagos newspapers.

With the abolition of political parties and of civilian rule in 1966, the press-government relationships changed drastically. The press, without its political bases of support, was clearly muffled, as was most political opposition. The bland, apolitical, and noncritical "look" of the once outspoken Nigerian papers was in some respects due to the exigencies of the civil war and its aftermath. The papers were strictly forbidden to publish *any* material *considered* helpful to Biafra. And since the federal military government itself provided little solid war news, the press was often reduced to reporting propaganda features that lacked even surface credibility. There was no overt government control of newspapers, but all knew how far they could go under the federal military government.

When civilian rule is restored, there are still prospects for a fair amount of press freedom under law. The legal precedents are there, and press freedom as a political ideal or value is still widely held among educated Nigerians—in much the same way that the concept of press freedom did not disappear in Ghana during the rule of Nkrumah.

COMPARATIVE ROLES OF PRESS AND BROADCASTING

In the last decade the newspapers and the broadcasting systems played quite different sorts of roles in Nigeria. The press, in the main, was highly politicized, polemical but informative, and—most important—an authentically indigenous press that grew out of the Nigerian nationalist movement and that was an integral part of Nigerian urban life. It was often corrupt, irresponsible, and venal; but it gave representation to and was an outlet for the views and feelings of important elements of Nigerian society. The give and take of editorial discussion and public affairs reporting certainly helped the cause of political socialization and the fostering of democratic institutions. It was an important outlet for many concerned and articulate Nigerians. But it may also be argued that the press—like the regional broadcasting systems—contributed to and exacerbated the divisive, tribal rivalries that destroyed the first federation and eclipsed democratic institutions.

In any case, the Nigerian press of 1960 to 1965 was in many ways a unique phenomenon for black Africa: diverse, outspoken, competitive, and irreverent. While opposition papers were silenced and one-party conformity imposed elsewhere, the Nigerian press was mostly unfettered. But in the latter half of the decade freedom of expression was curtailed.

Broadcasting of news was always under the control of government in Nigeria. At the federal level, the news and information were comparatively unbiased and objective—except in crisis situations such as the General Strike of 1964, when Radio Nigeria lost its nerve and kept silent, and in the process lost much of its credibility. The regional broadcasting systems, while providing rather extensive programming in vernaculars, were under the political control of the regional governments and contributed little to national unity. Radio reached a much larger audience in Nigeria than the printed word, but each played very different and complementary roles.

With Nigeria still unsettled, it is difficult (and hazardous) to predict the news media's future. However, it would not be surprising if one or all of the following came about:

● Centralization of news communications in the sense that the national government at Lagos will exert greater control.

● Official regional media systems largely to fade away; information services and broadcasting to become almost entirely the province of the national government. However, there may still be some independent provincial papers.

● A national news service, if one were established, would increase the centralized control and diminish the influence of foreign news agencies, especially Reuters, in Nigeria. This would impede the flow of international news.

● The four television services to be combined some way into a national service, with continued slow growth.

● Fewer but better newspapers. Well-run and financially sound papers like the *Daily Times* to continue prospering, with the small polemical newssheets, unfortunately, disappearing. Some diversity would be lost.

● Because the economic potential is still there, Nigeria will probably remain in the vanguard of the few African nations able to support successful newspapers locally financed and owned.

But because of the tragic events of recent years, the news media of Nigeria may never be quite what they were during the first heady years of independence.

Nearby Ghana, also greatly influenced by British colonial rule, followed a very different path, undergoing nine years of one-man autocratic rule before *its* military leaders took over the government and the news media.

GHANA: NKRUMAH AND AFTER

In the first decade of its independence, the West African nation of Ghana acquired several important dates to celebrate. On March 6, 1957, the former Gold Coast under the leadership of Kwame Nkrumah became Ghana, the first British colony in black Africa to gain independence. On February 24, 1966, the by-then-despotic regime of Nkrumah was overthrown in a coup d'état led by military officers who ruled as the National Liberation Council until a civilian democratic government was restored by elections on August 30, 1969.

The dates were important for Ghana's news media as well, for they meant that the press and broadcasting have functioned under two divergent approaches: a well-articulated neo-communist theory under Nkrumah and a paternalistic libertarian theory under his successors. The facilities of press and broadcasting continued to operate in much the same fashion, but with significant differences in the methods of control and the purposes to which the media were put. Yet the news media were always in the hands of Ghanaians who were communicating to Ghanaian audiences.

By African standards Ghana is small in area—92,100 square miles or about the size of Oregon. It is about 350 miles wide and 400 miles in length, lying just north of the equator and bounded by three new francophonic nations: Togo, Upper Volta, and the Ivory Coast. English is the official language for its 8,376,000 inhabitants, but some fifty vernaculars are spoken as well.

Although small, Ghana has influenced the new Africa far out of proportion to its size. As tropical Africa's first state to be free from colonial rule, Ghana under Nkrumah considered itself the catalyst for African liberation and political unification. Economically and culturally, Ghana at independence in 1957 was one of the continent's most richly endowed nations, with one of the highest per capita incomes in Africa (about $175 per year), one of the better educational systems, and considerable economic potential in timber, minerals, and especially cocoa, which accounted for more than 60 percent of the nation's foreign exchange earnings.

Ghana under Nkrumah became a leader among the more radical of the new states—Guinea, Mali, Algeria, Congo (Brazzaville), and the U.A.R.—most of which tried to apply socialistic approaches to economic development. Among these nations the view developed that mass media should be completely under government control to assure full utilization and commitment to the urgent aims of national integration and modernization. All through Africa the news media are to a greater or lesser extent controlled by government, but Nkrumah carried the concept further than most and provided an ideological rationale as well.

Nkrumah espoused a neo-communist theory of the press under which the mass media are an integral part of the state—an instrument to further the purposes of the party and the state.

Mass media were to have no utility or purpose other than serving the state.

He rejected private ownership of the press. Opening the Pan-African Union of Journalists Conference in 1963, Nkrumah said: "It is part of our revolutionary credo that within the competitive system of capitalism the press cannot function in accordance with a strict regard for the sacredness of facts and that it therefore should not remain in private hands."[31] Whether or not Nkrumah was a Communist is immaterial here, but his *approach* to mass communications closely followed that of Lenin, and as in Communist nations, he gave a high priority to mass communications and brought Ghana's media more and more under direct government ownership and control.

DAILY NEWSPAPERS

At independence Ghana had four daily newspapers: The *Daily Graphic, Evening News, Ghanaian Times,* and the *Ashanti Pioneer,* and in time Nkrumah dominated them all.

The most widely read papers were (and still are) the *Daily Graphic* (morning) and the *Sunday Mirror,* founded in 1950 by the Overseas Newspapers, Inc. The *Graphic* originally supported Nkrumah but soon became disenchanted and by mid-1961 had given up even running editorials. As a privately owned paper, its success in both circulation and advertising was an embarrassment to the government's *News* and *Times.* Seeing the handwriting on the wall, Cecil King in 1963 sold the paper to the Nkrumah government, which placed it under a government trust and appointed a new board of directors favorable to the government.

The government- and party-controlled Guinea Press, Ltd., at that time published two daily newspapers, one free weekly paper, and several publications for specialized audiences.

One daily was the *Evening News,* both a party paper and a scandal sheet, which lived up to its promise to "titivate, scintillate, and scandalize." It was edited by Eric Heymann, a political intimate of Nkrumah. As the organ of the Convention People's Party (CPP), it acted as the official sounding board of the CPP and the government. Its masthead carried a silhouette of Nkrumah and the slogan, "The Party is Supreme." A kind of *Pravda* of the CPP, its usual eight pages carried details about CPP meetings and members but less hard news than the other papers. In 1959 there were editions in Akan, Ga, Ewe, Hausa, and French, as well as in English.

The front page often carried some of the Leader's famous quotations like "Seek ye first the political kingdom and all other things shall be added unto it." On its second page, the *Evening News* printed open letters addressed to "His Messianic Dedication Osagyefo [Redeemer] Dr. Kwame Nkrumah." One typical letter said, "History continues to record your political and national exploits. . . . Gone are the days when any two-by-four nation [probably meaning Britain] could splash nonsensical effusions on the integrity of Ghana and her leadership."[32]

The Guinea Press's second daily was the *Ghanaian Times*, the first product of the Guinea Press and established with public funds in 1956. It was another party mouthpiece, but published more news and was less sensational than its sister paper. Its circulation in 1964 was about 12,000 compared to 17,000 to 20,000 for the *News* and 106,000 for the more successful *Graphic*.

The fourth daily and the only one to oppose Nkrumah was the *Ashanti Pioneer*. Founded in 1939, this independent paper was published in Kumasi, Ashanti, by John and Nancy Tsiboe. The *Pioneer* vigorously opposed Nkrumah and the CPP from its rise to power in 1951. Off and on since 1960, it was subjected to government censorship until finally on October 19, 1962, it was announced in the official *Gazette* that the government was taking it over. Both the paper's editor, A. D. Appea, and its city editor, Kwame Kesse-Adu, were arrested earlier. Kesse-Adu spent $4\frac{1}{2}$ years in detention in the notorious Fort Ussher prison for "destructive criticism of the government." Appea was detained 7 months. This drastic action by the government against an independent newspaper was unprecedented even during the 113 years of British colonial rule on the Gold Coast.[33]

About the same time, the Nkrumah government began to show less and less patience with foreign journalists. Deportations were frequent and reasons given ranged from incorrect and unfavorable reporting and engaging in other than professional activities to refusing to stand up when the national anthem was played.[34]

Nkrumah was very critical of what the Western press was saying about him. He saw the potentialities of a national news agency both to monopolize information at home and to extend Ghana's influence abroad—and, incidentally, to improve his own image. Hence the Ghana News Agency was developed, with considerable assistance from Reuters, into the most extensive and effective agency of its kind in black Africa. Beginning in 1957 with four teleprinters in Accra, the GNA by 1960 had expanded to twenty-four teleprinters in Accra, three in Kumasi, two in Cape Coast, and one each in Takoradi, Koforidua, and Tamale. It carried some 12,000 words daily and another 7,000 for Reuters. Early in 1961 the agency was Africanized and Goodwin T. Anim was appointed director, replacing a Reuters man. GNA received various Communist bloc news services such as TASS, ADN, NCNA, and TANYUG, but relied mostly on Reuters.

The transformation of the GNA into the much-publicized All-Africa News Agency was to take place in October 1961 and the GNA received a grant of $130,553 from Nkrumah's government for that purpose. The proposed new agency, with offices throughout Africa, was to provide better coverage of African news, as well as set up an information center in Accra, a newsroom, and a hostel for journalists—all fully air-conditioned. This was another aspect of Nkrumah's program of tying inter-African activities to Accra, but like most of his grandiose ideas, it never came to fruition.[35]

However, as a one-time journalist himself, Nkrumah believed strongly in mass communications, and despite Ghana's increasing financial difficulties, the government media were, by African standards, well financed. This was especially true of broadcasting.

RADIO AND TELEVISION

The British established a broadcasting service in the Gold Coast in 1935, but it was not until the 1950s that it was expanded into a national system. Radio Ghana was on the air for seventeen and a half hours daily, broadcasting in English and six local languages (Akan [Twi and Fanti], Nzima, Ewe, Ga, Dagbani, and Hausa), as well as in French, Portuguese, Arabic, and Swahili on Radio Ghana's External Service.

News commentaries were usually written at President Nkrumah's office, and there was little doubt of Radio Ghana's assignment as an instrument of Nkrumah's political purposes.

There was some evidence of deliberate falsification in broadcasting. In 1961 people who witnessed Nkrumah's return from his visit to Communist countries, for instance, said that his reception was quiet and unenthusiastic. Radio Ghana rebroadcast the event with much applause and cheering, presumably dubbed in from an earlier homecoming.[36]

Television was not established in Ghana until August 1965. It was set up by the government in partnership with the Sanyo electrical company of Japan, which had built a television set assembly plant at Tema to produce cheap receiver sets. Nkrumah said of television: "Its paramount objective will be for education. It will not cater to cheap entertainment or commercialism. Television must assist in the social transformation of Ghana." He added that it would also be a weapon against imperialism and neo-colonialism.[37]

Because of high illiteracy, the relative underdevelopment of press and broadcasting, and the oral tradition, the informal channels of communication have continued to be important in Ghana. And Nkrumah's Ghana deserves credit for utilizing these informal channels more effectively than have most African nations.

Information is still spread quickly by word of mouth, especially by bus ("mammy lorry" or "tro-tro") drivers and in eating and drinking places in the towns. The bus drivers, who carry passengers back and forth across the country, pick up and pass along a good deal of news and were used by Nkrumah from his earliest political days as one of the best and quickest means to get word of political events and ideas out to the bush.

In 1961 the government devised an organized version of this technique, paying small additional sums to literate government employees whose work took them to the bush regularly. These "messenger-interpreters"—health officers, veterinarians, agricultural experts—distributed government bulletins and visual material and explained the subject in the local languages to small groups at each stop.[38] Also, in the rural areas the traditional "town criers" were paid nominal sums by the government to spread news and opinion orally to interested villages.[39]

Rallies, loudspeaker trucks, and mobile cinema vans were used by the government and CPP to spread propaganda and inform the populace about new government moves.

Songs have long been a vehicle of social and political comment, and the government used them too. But the oral tradition can also be a medium for criticism. In September 1961, seven people were arrested for singing at a funeral a song which allegedly ran: "The President of Ghana has deducted six shillings from the price of cocoa; shame on him."[40]

ASSESSMENT OF NKRUMAH

How effective were Nkrumah's efforts at mass communication? At relatively great expense (certainly more than the Ghanaian economy could afford), he did build one of the most comprehensive national media systems in black Africa. Radio Ghana, the Ghana News Agency, and his Ministry of Information in particular were quite outstanding, from a technical viewpoint, and are still models of their type. But as news media they were deficient; they carried little reliable, objective news.

Dissenting views, both domestic and foreign, were systematically silenced, and unquestionably the regime suffered from a lack of credibility. Nkrumah was often faced with rumor problems. For example, in early 1964 the U.S. embassy was accused of "rumor mongering." Why? Lloyd Garrison of the New York *Times* explained:

> The answer has its roots in the fact that Ghana's press and radio are entirely government-controlled. The accent is on propaganda with very little news—and that only news that reflects favorably on the Nkrumah government. The result is that rumors about "what's going on" fan through Accra like brush fires. They are never quite stamped out and the size of each little fire tends to expand with each retelling.
> Before finishing breakfast one morning this week, a reporter picked up the following without even trying: "Nkrumah shot one of his soldiers in the castle last night," said the waiter serving coffee. A Ghanaian contact called to say a friend of a friend reported that "the army may mutiny at any time" . . . and so on.[41]

Nkrumah had a control over the news media that was unusually tight for a one-party African government. One student of the Nkrumah regime, Henry Bretton, wrote:

> The principal editors were owned by Nkrumah, who had trapped them into accepting government housing for which they paid, at most, only a nominal sum. The press was owned by the state as personified by the President's office in the person of the publicity secretary, who supervised, among other things related to communications media, the organization set up specifically to control the press. The editors were free to discuss all internal and external affairs that did not reflect adversely upon the person and acts of the President. Since all matters of substance in Ghana were in one way or another traceable to the President, very little of substance was left for the press to discuss without explicit presidential approval.[42]

The speed and ease with which Nkrumah's communication theories were abandoned after his departure were indications of his failure to use mass communications effectively. In any case, the majority of Ghanaians were happy to be rid of Nkrumah, and his views on news communication were largely discredited at the same time.

NEWS COMMUNICATION AFTER NKRUMAH

The coup d'état of February 24, 1966, had important consequences for public communication in Ghana. A neo-communist approach was replaced by an avowed desire to return the media to libertarian principles inherited from British institutions. The paradox was that this was being attempted by a military junta (the seven-man National Liberation Council), while almost all media were government-owned.

The three government dailies changed viewpoints overnight: one day they were extolling Nkrumah and the next day they were cheering his overthrow—without missing one day of publication. However, several top editors—Eric Heymann of the *Evening News,* Thomas D. Baffoe of the *Ghanaian Times,* and Kofi Batsa of *Spark*—were all detained briefly. These three were influential CPP members and recipients of free housing from Nkrumah. However, the papers themselves, as well as Radio Ghana and the Ghana News Agency, kept operating as usual with the same staffs right through the coup and the month of celebration that followed.

Censorship of outgoing press reports, initiated on September 8, 1962, was finally lifted seven months after the coup in September 1966, and a free flow of information was permitted. Bans on twelve foreign journalists, nine of them British, were lifted, including those against such well-known writers as Colin Legum of the *Observer,* Peter Younghusband of the *Daily Mail,* and Richard Beeston of the *Daily Telegraph.*[43]

Among the political prisoners released from Fort Ussher were Lutz Herold, a West German free-lancer under a 40-year sentence, and Kwame Kesse-Adu of the *Ashanti Pioneer.*

The two new Nkrumahist newspapers, the *Daily Gazette* and *Sunday Punch,* both just barely underway in early 1966 as "additional organs of the CPP," were promptly discontinued as was *Spark,* the ideological journal intended mainly for readership abroad.

The President of the National Liberation Council, Lt. Gen. Joseph Ankrah, told the heads of the fifty-odd diplomatic missions in Accra that the press in Ghana would now be free to express its political opinions and that criticism, "provided it was constructive," would also be allowed. He said the regime "is determined to open a new page in the journalistic ethics of Ghana."[44]

The new atmosphere of press freedom was enhanced by the repeal of the Preventive Detention Act of 1958, under which the ousted dictator had jailed without trial more than 1,800 people at various times, some for more than seven years.

Another significant development was the resurrection of the *Ashanti Pioneer*. Renamed the *Pioneer,* the paper reappeared on December 1, 1966, and promised to carry on where it had left off. Colonel Akwasi Afrifa of the NLC, in a message in the first issue, said:

> Those of us who carried out the coup did so in the firm belief to create the needed atmosphere for freedom of expression, the bedrock of all democratic institutions. We fought so that our newspapers should be free to begin this process of democratization. Liberty is here with us. But I have a feeling of disappointment and sometimes dismay when I see the quality of journalism that still lingers. I am aware that the press is owned by the government. But that is no excuse for mediocrity and sycophantic adulation.[45]

In July 1966 there appeared an important new publication, the *Legon Observer,* which would not be accused of "mediocrity and sycophantic adulation." It was published biweekly by a group of seventeen lecturers at the University of Ghana who fully supported the NLC—at least at first. The journal of opinion and news had much in common with such intellectual publications as *Transition* in Uganda and the *East African Journal* in Kenya, and soon reached a circulation of 10,000, with about 300 copies going abroad, mainly to Britain, United States, and Nigeria. Under its aggressive editor, E. Yaw Twumasi, and an all-Ghanaian editorial board that included K.A.B. Jones-Quartey, it was soon running critical and provocative articles appealing to Ghana's intellectual elite, so long muzzled under the Nkrumah regime.

These developments of the first year of the NLC promised a return to nominal press freedom. But later events soon dispelled the euphoria.

THE ABBOTT AFFAIR

The most disquieting episode for the press itself concerned the abrupt firing of four editors of three government dailies for criticizing the government's agreement with the Abbott Laboratories, an American drug firm, to take over and run a state-owned drug corporation set up originally by the Hungarians. Not only the three government papers but also the *Pioneer* and the *Legon Observer* were critical of the contract the government negotiated with Abbott. Finally, on December 14, 1967, four editors—Henry Thompson of the *Evening News,* John Dumoga and Oscar Tsedze of the *Daily Graphic,* and Moses Danquah of the *Ghanaian Times* —received brief letters from the Principal Secretary of the Ministry of Information summarily firing them. No reason was given, but there was little doubt that it was because of their criticism of the Abbott contract. (In the meantime, at the height of the controversy, Abbott pulled out of the agreement.)

The civilian Commissioner of Information, Kwabena Osei-Bonsu, resigned in protest and said the NLC's action in firing the editors was "irregular and impolitic . . . it jeopardizes the freedom of the press to which the NLC had irrevocably committed itself."[46]

In any case, the Abbott affair unsettled the morale of the news media which were still recovering from the years of strict controls under Nkrumah. One of the fired editors, John Dumoga of the *Graphic,* was saddened and disillusioned by the whole affair. An outstanding journalist, Dumoga had been in exile during part of Nkrumah's regime, working for the *Daily Nation* in Nairobi, and had returned as editor of the *Graphic* expecting things to be different. Dumoga said: "Generals Ankrah and Afrifa and all public men kept saying the press must be free and should speak out on public issues. So we did and then we found the old 'master and servant' relationship still existed. We were not warned, not accused of anything nor even told why we were fired. . . . Since the Abbott affair, the *Graphic* has done no serious writing on any public issues."[47]

The *Legon Observer,* outspokenly critical of the Abbott contract, soon ran into trouble with the judiciary. On January 8, 1968, twenty-nine persons associated with the university-based publication went on trial in the Accra High Court, charged with contempt of court. The charge stemmed from an article in the December 8, 1967, issue which criticized the court for delays in hearing cases. On January 22, Editor Twumasi and twenty-two university lecturers (all on the publication's board) pleaded guilty and apologized. (The six printers were exonerated.) The twenty-three were later fined 100 cedis ($98) each in this first direct clash between the government and intellectuals since Nkrumah's overthrow.[48]

While Ghana's government was in a transitional state from military to civilian rule, the media reflected this unsettled situation. There were rumors that the government wished to sell its three papers to private owners, but feared they would be purchased by some of Nkrumah's followers with funds taken from the government. The Ghanaian government and economy were in difficult financial straits, and this restricted the effectiveness of the media that had been so liberally financed under the old regime.

The *Daily Graphic,* with 130,000 circulation, and the *Sunday Mirror,* with 80,000, were still dominant and the only newspapers clearly making money. Still following the breezy tabloid style of the London *Daily Mirror,* the *Graphic* was the newsiest, most interesting paper around and was much like its one-time stablemate, the *Daily Times* of Nigeria. The only paper with classified advertising, it had more ads than the others together and carried comics, astrology, and other features from the London *Mirror.* Printed on excellent equipment and distributed by its own trucks, it sold about 30,000 in Kumasi, 17,000 in Takoradi, and 9,000 in the Volta region. Acting Editor Henry Ofori had an editorial staff of about sixty, including about twenty reporters scattered around the country. Most new reporters were trained on the job, but Ofori said the reporters were not as good as ten years ago. "Nkrumah killed off professional journalism and it will take years to recover," he said.[49]

The other morning paper, the *Ghanaian Times,* looked a lot like the *Graphic,* but lacked its quality, and at 60,000 was well behind in circulation. The writing was loose, headlines often misleading, and content at times irrelevant.

The other paper in the old Guinea Press stable, the *Evening News,* was barely surviving with a circulation of 15,000 to 20,000. The *News* was obviously losing money and was being carried by the *Ghanaian Times.*

Badly and carelessly written, it was a pale and ineffectual imitation of the two morning tabloids. More so than the *Graphic* and *Times,* it was almost completely lacking in useful information such as a calendar of local events, obituaries, movie ads, and radio and television logs. The *Evening News* ceased publication at the beginning of 1969 and was replaced several months later by a new daily paper, the *Evening Standard,* edited by Kofi Badu.

The *Pioneer,* the only independent or nongovernment daily, was still published in Kumasi by the Abura Printing Works, Ltd., and sold about 10,000 of its estimated 25,000 daily circulation in Accra. Under the same editor, A. D. Appea, that it had before being banned by Nkrumah, the *Pioneer* was again showing its old editorial independence. It criticized the Abbott contract, was the first to report the firing of the four editors, and kept pestering the NLC to explain the action. Kwame Kesse-Adu, the *Pioneer* editor "detained" by Nkrumah, was again with the *Pioneer* as its Accra editor.

The paper was badly in need of modern printing equipment and found it difficult to compete with the better-produced government papers. The management claimed it could sell many more papers if it had a better and faster press, but it lacked the money to purchase one. A typical issue carried only four pages with few ads. The *Pioneer* undoubtedly had a loyal following and was a quavering but determined voice for freedom of expression in Ghana. The *Pioneer* enjoyed an international reputation because it had always fought for its principles, and its editors had gone to jail for them. Along with the *West African Pilot,* the *Pioneer* typified the difficulties of publishing a daily newspaper in Africa that was independent of both government and foreign newspaper financing.

It should be emphasized that Ghana's daily press, like Nigeria's, was an indigenous African press, written by Ghanaians for that relatively small coterie of educated urban Ghanaians who followed public affairs and read newspapers to help them stay involved. Ghana's papers, as newspapers, lacked hard news, whether foreign or domestic, and provided little of the "service information"—local comings and goings, movie ads, radio and television logs, obituaries, and vital statistics— that newspapers can so easily and usefully report. But the Ghanaian press discussed—in a rather haphazard way—important public issues and reported what leaders of government, the professions, and business were saying about public issues. There was rather frank and full discussion of what the proposed new constitution should contain. This use of the press as a forum for public issues was an important plus for the Ghanaian press and one that set it off from the newspapers of francophonic Africa and North Africa.

The Ghana News Agency, despite cutbacks in its operations due to the national austerity, continued to be the most effective national news agency I observed in Africa. It did a professional job of gathering and distributing news from throughout Ghana as well as abroad.

A staff of 200 collected news from eight regional offices (each with teleprinter facilities) and redistributed it to all the news media, government offices, and the foreign embassies which subscribed to the service. The GNA had 30 reporters in Accra, 18 subeditors, and 6 in its overseas section. Twenty-four full-time staffers covered the news in the regions.

GHANA BROADCASTING CORPORATION (GBC)

Unlike Nigeria with its several overlapping radio and television systems, Ghana has had a single centralized broadcasting organization, all housed in the rambling "Broadcasting House" in Accra and responsible for radio, television, and external broadcasting. (Broadcasting House is actually a number of buildings surrounded by a wall topped with barbed wire. Since the abortive coup in April 1967 when the broadcasting station was briefly "captured," heavy security precautions were established and visitors had to identify themselves to armed soldiers at the gate.) Although there were numerous relay facilities, all sound and video programs were originated in Accra and broadcast from there.

GBC researchers estimated there were 450,000 radios in Ghana and a listening audience of over 4,000,000 persons. Ghanaians paid no license fee for a radio, but did pay five pesewas (about five cents) a month to use one of the 54,836 wired speakers found mainly in the bigger cities. Owners of television sets paid an annual fee of $10 a year, and GBC records in 1968 totted 6,500 television sets in use. Perhaps another 3,000 unlicensed sets were also operating, but television sets were expensive—about 300 cedis (about $300)—and well beyond the means of most Ghanaians.[50]

On October 29, 1967, the GBC reorganized its radio services. The new first service, GBC–1, carried radio programs in the principal Ghanaian languages and was intended primarily for rural listeners. Much traditional music was broadcast, too. The service devoted as much as two hours and fifteen minutes daily to news coverage in the local languages of Ga, Akan, Hausa, Ewe, Nzima, and Dagbani. Major news bulletins in English at 7 a.m. and at 1, 2, and 6 p.m. were also relayed on GBC–1.

GBC–1 was on the air during daylight hours and at 8 p.m. was replaced by the new GBC–3, which broadcast in English until

11 p.m. or close-down time. Modeled on the Third Programme of the BBC, GBC–3 provided "serious" or high-brow programming —both musical and informational—for Ghana's urban elites.

Another program, GBC–2, was a commercial service, mostly in English on the air from 5:30 a.m. until 11 p.m. and featured, in addition to news and advertisements, popular music programs with such titles as "Bright and Breezy," "Tropical Magic," "Highlife," "Pops Inn," "Highlife All the Way Till Nine," and "Low Lights, Soft Music."

News broadcasts were prepared by separate staffs for radio and television. The major English-language newscasts on radio were at 6 and 7 a.m. and at 1, 2, 6, 8, 9, and 10:30 p.m.

The GBC news bulletins faithfully imitated the formal BBC style. First several headlines were read, then the individual items with pauses between each, and then "the main points again." Although there was much emphasis on official news, radio also reported speeches, statements, etc., which often carried implied criticism of the government. As was more and more the case in tropical Africa, much attention was focused on Pan-African nationalist news such as stories relating to guerrilla or "freedom fighter" incursions in Rhodesia and Portuguese Africa.

Despite the 6,500 receiver sets in operation, television broadcasting was fairly inconspicuous in Ghana, and there was apparently little interest in the new medium. None of the daily newspapers, for example, carried announcements or logs of television shows. The only way to find out what was on was to buy a copy of GBC's *Ghana Radio and Television Times*. There were no television sets, for instance, in the large Ambassador Hotel, a major social center of Accra.

Television was on the air from 6 p.m. to 9:30 or 10 p.m. daily, with just two news shows: fifteen minutes at 7:30 p.m. and twenty minutes at 9:15 p.m. A GBC camera team filmed local footage, and the station received news film almost daily from Visnews in London. The news staff for television numbered fifteen, compared with sixty for radio news.

PROSPECTS FOR FREE EXPRESSION

The outlook for freedom of expression in Ghana in the years after the Nkrumah government was uncertain at best. Press freedom in Ghana depended on several factors: (1) How well the private or independent press could expand and prosper. The only two nongovernment publications of worth were the *Pioneer* and the *Legon Observer*, neither in a very strong position financially and both coming under increased pressure from government. (2) The independence of the courts and judiciary. Would they be able to legally protect press interests against political pressures? (3) Public opinion. How strongly would the 10 percent of educated Ghanaians insist on press freedom under the new civilian government?

Press freedom requires in large part a legitimate political opposition, so much depends on the success of the new civilian government. The first free elections since 1956 were held on August 30, 1969, and the second Republic of Ghana was launched under the most elaborately drawn constitution in postindependence Africa. The Progress Party of Kofi Abrefa Busia won a surprisingly easy victory and a majority of seats in the new National Assembly.

How well the new constitution works will largely determine whether there will be a renaissance of the Ghanaian news media and an improvement in their morale, public stature, and competence.

In the meantime, the independent press must somehow manage to hold on and increase its numbers. The tenuous hold it had was based in large part on British traditions and the fact that many educated Ghanaians and a handful of journalists felt strongly about democratic institutions and the key role that freedom of the press plays in representative government.

The immense economic problems that Ghana faced, mainly due to the prodigality of the Nkrumah regime, still stood in the way. In Africa, economic crises create acute political crises. The Abbott affair showed that a little press criticism in a country so precariously balanced can create a national crisis. This was indeed the paradox of press freedom in Africa.

In summary, for both Ghana and Nigeria, radio was the most important medium both in terms of people reached and the regularity of exposure. The GBC in Ghana and NBC in Nigeria were particularly important in reaching the illiterate majority in the rural areas where exposure to the press and cinema was slight to nonexistent. There was some evidence that radio was considered more reliable than the press, in part because of the oral tradition.

The audience of the printed word was much smaller, of course, but it included the highest proportion of the educated and politically aware. This group also apparently made considerable use of foreign radio stations, especially the BBC and to a lesser extent, Voice of America.

Although of minimal importance as a news medium, the cinema is popular in West Africa. In February 1967 there were 157 theaters in Ghana which attracted some 280,000 viewers weekly. Commercial American, British, Indian, and Egyptian films were popular. In Accra, for instance, available evidence indicated that 40 to 50 percent of the adult population (fifteen years or older) attended the movies at least once a month, while nearly 30 percent attended at least once a week. Newsreels provided the primary or only exposure to foreign news for about one of every seven residents of Accra.[51]

Despite their many problems, however, Ghana and Nigeria have many things going for them. Their greatest asset is their people—intelligent, energetic, lively, and often well educated and literate.

And in the increasingly important area of news communication, Ghanaians and Nigerians, not European nationals, long have had control over the direction of their press and broadcasting facilities. The duration and nature of this involvement have given them a decided advantage over their French-speaking neighbors in West Africa.

9

||||||||||||||||||||||||||||||||||||||||||||||||||||||||||||||||||||||

LINGERING INFLUENCE
OF FRANCE:
IVORY COAST AND SENEGAL

FRANCE has had a long and intimate relationship with a great portion of West Africa. Within a 60-year span (1857–1918), by diplomacy and military power, it acquired an area eight times the size of France over which it sought to establish one law, one government, and one language. French authority and culture became the unifying links of the new empire, and these influences had a profound and lasting influence on the region's news media.

Very early the French began to form a native elite, called *évolués,* who learned the French language and proved receptive to French culture. It was this group that was to provide, along with the resident Frenchmen, both the audience and the few journalists for the news media.

French-influenced West Africa covers a broad expanse—some 1,844,000 square miles, almost one-sixth of the African continent —and includes eight countries which formerly made up the Federation of French West Africa: Senegal, Ivory Coast, Mauritania, Mali, Guinea, Upper Volta, Niger, and Dahomey. A complex array of 200 ethnic groups are included in the 26 million people spread thinly over this mostly arid region. Some 120 languages and hundreds of dialects are spoken. In a region of such diversity, one influence in common is that of the French colonial experience.

The former British colonies of Sierra Leone, Nigeria, and Gold Coast (Ghana) were surrounded by these territories of

French West Africa. Despite many geographical, economic, and cultural similarities of the two regions, the press and radio developed much more slowly in French Africa. Many factors contributed, but most were related to differences in French and British colonial policies.

For one thing, there were larger concentrations of Europeans in French Africa which, as in the Belgian Congo and British East Africa, led to the founding of European or "settler" newspapers in the main urban centers, such as Dakar and Abidjan. These papers catered to European interests, but were also read by *évolués*.

The French policy of selective, though intensive, education in French produced far fewer literates than in the British colonies. High illiteracy in French Africa was combined with generally thinner and more scattered populations and lower economic development.

What European press there was served to further the process of assimilation of the few educated Africans into the French culture. Most educated French Africans were far more at home in the French language and culture than were British Africans in the English language and culture.[1]

These "black Frenchmen" had access to the readily available French newspapers, magazines, and books, which came into *Afrique Noire* without taxation.

All this fitted into French colonial policy which favored direct rule from Paris and drew a few educated African elites into the apparatus of government. Félix Houphouët-Boigny, for example, served in five French cabinets before he became the president of the independent Ivory Coast.

French colonial policy did little to encourage indigenous African newspapers or even the conditions (such as adequate education or freedom of expression) that might make such papers feasible. The French were much harsher and more authoritarian than the British in their control of the local Africans, and until the middle 1930s, newspapers and journals could be published only by French citizens. Moreover, while the circulation of publications *from France* was encouraged, there was a tax on the import of printing machinery and newsprint into French Africa. This was a further deterrent to African newspaper development.

The only successful and lasting newspapers were published in Dakar, the administrative center of *Afrique Ouest Française,* where there was a concentration of European traders and colonial administrators. *Le Reveil du Sénégalais* was founded in 1885, *Le Petit Sénégalais* in 1886, and *L'Union Africaine* in 1896; but these were papers published by Frenchmen for other Frenchmen.[2]

BEGINNINGS IN ABIDJAN

In the Ivory Coast, perhaps more so than anywhere else in French West Africa, many small papers appeared and promptly disappeared. There was more capital available in Abidjan than elsewhere, even if the conditions for newspaper survival were not particularly good. Before World War II the papers were published almost entirely by European planters and merchants.[3] At that same time numerous *African-run* newspapers had been appearing in Nigeria and nearby Gold Coast for many years.

Abidjan had the distinction of being the first French African city with a newspaper owned and operated by Africans themselves. This was the *Éclaireur de la Côte d'Ivoire,* first printed in 1935 and an immediate success with African readers.[4]

The *Éclaireur* was one of the first anticolonial papers which, even after restrictions against African-owned papers were lifted, were slower to develop in French Africa because of the lower literacy and stricter government censorship.

F. J. Amon d'Aby wrote of the *Éclaireur:* "This journal had immense success in African circles. It led a campaign against the senior chiefs and against the police. It demanded measures of social reconstruction; it urged the cause of the unemployed and of African farmers who had been hit by the economic crises."[5] The paper had the added distinction of surviving awhile; most papers started in the Ivory Coast have not lasted long. Between 1928 and 1959 some fifty papers appeared and disappeared, often in the same year.[6] The number of papers increased sharply once Africans were permitted to publish them. As elsewhere in West Africa, Abidjan's papers were characterized by inadequate financing, poor editing, and small circulation.[7]

During the 1930s the Charles de Breteuil newspaper chain was launched in French West Africa and was the only group of its kind. *Paris-Dakar* started as a weekly in 1933 and became a daily in 1935. In 1938 *France-Afrique* (which became *Abidjan-Matin* in 1954) appeared in the Ivory Coast. *La Presse de Guinée* began in Conakry in 1954 and *La Presse du Cameroun* in 1955.

These de Breteuil papers were originally edited for European readers with the exception of *Bingo,* a popular picture monthly for urban African youth, started in Dakar in 1952.[8]

By independence nearly all of Abidjan's newspapers had gone under. The flurry of journalistic activity between 1945 and 1960, when thirty-six papers surfaced and submerged, was directly related to the highly fluid political situation when Africans were permitted for the first time to organize parties and to vie for political power. As in British West Africa, those seeking political access used newspapers to gain followings. By the time of Ivoirien independence in 1960, the Parti Démocratique de la Côte d'Ivoire (PDCI) of Houphouët-Boigny had eliminated all opposition groups and the diversity of the press declined with them.[9] One Ivoirien paper that persisted was de Breteuil's *Abidjan-Matin* which was the Ivory Coast's only daily newspaper for its first four years of independence.

So the inadequacy of the news media and the lack of an African journalistic tradition in French Africa were legacies of French colonial policies. The few who were educated were brought into the colonial establishment as black Frenchmen. This, of course, provided close communication and a common bond between educated French Africans and resident Frenchmen. Almond and Coleman wrote that this "suggests the existence of a marked discontinuity in communication between the African elite and the French African mass. Compared to British territories, this is probably true. On the other hand, most of the French African political leaders have emerged as effective mediators, as communications nexus." They pointed out that Léopold Senghor and Félix Houphouët-Boigny, for example, were able to communicate effectively with their Wolof and Baoulé compatriots, respectively, as well as their French associates in the French parliament.[10]

Most *évolués* were concentrated in Dakar, and later Abidjan, which became the administrative, commercial, and financial centers for French West Africa, and it was there that news communications took hold. Therefore the focus will be on these two highly developed urban centers of French-speaking West Africa, Abidjan and Dakar, capitals today of the Ivory Coast and Senegal, respectively.

The news media of the other six countries, particularly Niger, Upper Volta, and Mauritania, were markedly less developed.

NEWS MEDIA OF IVORY COAST

The Ivory Coast, about the size of New Mexico (127,000 square miles), has had more success than most of the other new African nations in coping with the challenges of independence which it won from France on August 7, 1960.

Its economic progress and political stability have been due largely to the influences of France, past and present. Those same influences have shaped and are still directing its system of mass communications.

Côte d'Ivoire, as this French-speaking state calls itself, has the usual basic problem of the new African polities: it must pull its diverse ethnic elements together into a viable nation. Its 3.8 million people are fragmented into 60 tribes and speak as many languages and dialects. President Houphouët-Boigny, himself a member of the Baoulé tribe (the largest, with about 800,000 members), spoke more frankly than most African leaders would when he said, "The Ivoirien nation doesn't yet exist. France left the Ivory Coast a mass of tribes unaware of each other's existence. We are only gradually breaking down tribal barriers."[11]

In Africa the city is where tribal barriers are beginning to fall away; but only 10 percent of Ivoiriens are urbanized and most of these live in Abidjan, the gleaming, modern capital of 350,000. There the mass media are concentrated; even radio does not extend effectively out to the steamy rain forests and savannahs where most Ivoiriens live by subsistence agriculture. With a 1965 per capita income of $186 and a literacy rate of 10 percent, there were only about 1.7 radio sets and 0.4 daily newspapers circulated per 100 Ivoiriens. The limited media mostly reach only the urban elites, both African and French, who by virtue of their work in government and commerce influence the lives of the illiterate rural majority. Since the elites speak French (their language of education), the media operate almost entirely in that language.

Certain media-related characteristics of the Ivory Coast, such as low literacy, low income, the urban-rural schism, low media usage, government control of media, and the extensive use by elites of a European language, are also widely found in other new African nations. In the Ivory Coast, however, other factors make its news communications different from those of its neighbors.

The Ivoirien model of mass communication is completely French. To understand the news media situation in this African state in its early stages of development and decolonization, one must appreciate the colonial and "neo-colonial" impact of metropolitan France on this former part of *Afrique Ouest Française.*

Côte d'Ivoire under Houphouët-Boigny has been an authoritarian and centralized one-party state very much dominated by that remarkable man. All mass media were either owned or directly controlled by his government, yet this suave authoritarianism was in many ways only a continuation of what Ivoiriens knew as a colony of France dating from 1895.

French influence was still extremely pervasive because Houphouët, a Gaullist, encouraged French aid and private investment as a concerted policy to aid national development. As a result, the Ivory Coast has enjoyed a rapid development. Its gross national product has increased 10 percent annually since 1960 and exports (it is the number two coffee producer in the world) and investments have been soaring. Some 250,000 Ivoirien families, producers of 97 percent of the coffee and cocoa, the major exports (others are wood products, bananas, diamonds, and manganese), received an average income of $500 per family, which is extremely high for black Africa.[12] Politically conservative Houphouët's unabashed francophilia and free enterprise economic policies were not ideologically fashionable in Africa during the 1960s. However, those policies have made the Ivory Coast clearly the most prosperous of the fourteen francophonic nations.[13]

On the other hand, Africanization has been much slower than elsewhere in West Africa. In the late 1960s there were over 30,000 Frenchmen in the Ivory Coast, twice as many as in 1958, and many held high-paying jobs that Ivoiriens envied.

Half the people in booming Abidjan were foreigners, mostly Africans from Dahomey and economically stagnant Guinea and Mali. Abidjan moved ahead of Senegal's Dakar, the old administrative capital of colonial French West Africa, as the economic, financial, and gradually the news communication center of francophonic Africa. In independent black Africa, much of it plagued by severe economic problems, military coups, and political instability, the Ivory Coast stood out as an exception. With continued political stability and economic growth, its prospects for news media development were good, too.

NEWSPAPERS

During the first decade of independence, the Ivory Coast has been a one-daily-newspaper country. The first lone daily was the French-owned *Abidjan-Matin* of the de Breteuil chain. Despite its monopoly position, the lack-lustre *Abidjan-Matin* was able to sell only about 2,000 to 3,000 of its 12,000 to 18,000 circulation to the interior of the country. One critic said of it: *"Abidjan-Matin was 'independent' by virtue of having no opinions at all.* It carried little real news and none of a controversial nature and was not even read by many of the educated elite. Its main appeal was in extensive sports coverage (in a sport-conscious nation where athletic competition seems to be one of the few forms of competition approved)."[14]

The ailing *Abidjan-Matin,* by prior arrangement, graciously committed suicide the day after the new government daily, *Fraternité-Matin,* appeared on December 7, 1964. The government created *Fraternité-Matin* for the same reasons other African governments have gone into newspaper publishing. As Editor-in-Chief Laurent Dona-Fologo put it: *"Abidjan-Matin* was doing badly and in need of money. And since private capital was not available to start another paper, the government felt that since newspapers are vital in a developing country, the government would start one of its own."[15] The Ivoirien government owns 51 percent of *Fraternité-Matin* and a large French publishing firm, Société Nouvelles d'Éditions Industrielle (SNEI), which produces *France-Soir, Réalités,* and many other publications in France, owns the other 49 percent. SNEI is a subsidiary of La Société Nationale des Enterprises de Presse (SNEP), a state enterprise originally set up in France after World War II to dispose of confiscated assets of newspapers that had collaborated with the Nazis.[16]

The same 51-49 percent ownership arrangement, with President Houphouët as board chairman, applied to the beautifully equipped printing plant, Société Ivoirienne Imprimerie (SII) which, in addition to *Fraternité-Matin,* printed *Fraternité,* the weekly party paper, and *Le Journal,* a monthly paper, plus some books and other publications.

The press run of *Fraternité-Matin* was about 20,000 to 25,000 daily, but its readership was probably much higher, since in developing countries newspapers are often read to groups of illiterates.

Outside the capital, Editor Dona-Fologo said, there were real distribution problems: a daily plane took copies to Bouake in the interior, but the time lag to other cities was about two to three days. Completely French in format, *Fraternité-Matin* was printed on a Goss offset press from Chicago and utilized the Monotype phototypesetting process. Graphically, it was one of the most attractive papers in tropical Africa. The editorial staff of eleven—six full-time and five part-time—plus four photographers, were all Africans. The only Frenchman working there was a makeup editor who handled the offset process.

The African staffers were all Paris-trained. Before independence the Ivory Coast had few home-grown journalists. In 1960 the only African journalists in the Ivory Coast worked for *Abidjan-Matin* and only one, Dial Diop, was a permanent staff member. But by 1962 the new government had 100 journalism students training in France, and since then they have been joining the various media.

Fraternité-Matin usually ran about eight full-sized pages, giving most attention to government, sports, and foreign news. There was also a page of Abidjan news, plus comics and feature material from France. In fact the publication in appearance could almost pass for a daily in a provincial French city.

Fraternité, the weekly organ of the only party, Parti Démocratique de la Côte d'Ivoire (PDCI), had a circulation of about 10,000. In Abidjan the tabloid was sold on newsstands, but it was distributed free around the country through the party apparatus. Started in 1959, it was a useful source of information about the party and the government.

The handful of Ivoirien journals (one daily paper, a daily mimeographed bulletin, two weeklies, and two periodicals with a total circulation of 47,180 in 1967) were aimed at the educated commercial and government elites, both Ivoirien and French. Not only was there no vernacular press, but more important, there was little emphasis on publications aimed at new literates. The news media were not committed to mass education, and there was no indigenous publication in simple language and with ample illustrations.

Yet a great deal of current reading matter was available on the newsstands. Metropolitan dailies arrived from France each day by jet and were on Abidjan newsstands alongside some 300 to 400 other French journals and periodicals. Resident Frenchmen and educated Ivoiriens turned as a matter of course to the French press for sophisticated commentary and coverage of world and African affairs. Local papers in French West Africa could only hope to supplement the daily influx from Paris. The profusion of foreign publications available was noteworthy for the lack of many in English or of publications from neighboring English-speaking countries. The educated Ivoirien is in essence a Frenchman; he looks to Paris as his cultural and intellectual home. He rarely knows English and takes only a casual interest in what is happening in anglophonic Africa. (Conversely, English-speaking

Africans pay little attention to happenings in French Africa.)

News collection, both domestic and foreign, was a major problem, and to facilitate news dissemination a government news agency, Agence Ivoirienne de Presse (AIP), was started in 1961 with the assistance of Agence France Presse. AIP became the sole receiver of news from abroad; daily news reports of AFP, Reuters, UPI, and Deutsche Press-Agentur went directly into AIP offices and then were redistributed by AIP's teletype service to about twenty customers, mostly foreign embassies plus press and broadcasting offices. Obviously AIP was in a gatekeeper position to censor news from abroad if it so desired, but this caused few objections since most journalists work for the government. The most pressing problem for AIP was to work out a way to collect news from its own hinterland. Telecommunications were poor outside the capital and the alternatives were slow and time-consuming. So far, efforts to increase the flow of news back and forth between Abidjan and the capitals of the five regions have been ineffective.

In Abidjan, AIP supplemented *Fraternité-Matin* with its own *Quotidien Bulletin*, a 20- to 25-page mimeographed summary of news from the wire services. This was delivered by runner and car to about 700 local subscribers and was, in effect, a second daily newspaper.

The AIP was under the Ministry of Information, which also directed radio and television broadcasting as well as photographic and cinema production services.

The oldest and still most pervasive means of spreading news and information was word of mouth. Travelers and itinerant traders carried news from Abidjan to outlying areas and from one small community to another. Major news could still be spread with considerable speed by runner or drums. Until fairly recently, virtually all important information, both current and historical, was transmitted orally, and as elsewhere on the continent, the oral tradition was a significant factor in the development of communication media. Here, too, trust in oral communication plus low literacy combined to make radio the only mass medium. (The French-language press was distinctly an elite medium.)

RADIO AND TELEVISION

Radio Abidjan broadcast on two services, Chaîne National and Chaîne Internationale. All four transmitters, both medium wave and shortwave, were in Abidjan.

The French style of broadcasting pervaded Radio Abidjan; a listener could easily imagine he was tuned to a Parisian station. Music was mostly French or French versions of American popular music. There was little indigenous music or even the popular West African "high life" music heard so frequently on Radio Nigeria and Radio Ghana. Announcers were both French and Ivoirien and spoke in excellent French. In fact all but 6 of 175 hours a week of broadcasting were in French. There was a very limited amount of news broadcast in nine of the vernacular tongues: Ebrié, Baoulé, Dioula, Mossi, Senufo, Bété, Gouro, Dida, and Attié.

In the late 1960s the number of radio sets was estimated at about 75,000, with an audience of about half a million adults. No license fees were required because the government wished to encourage radio listening.

Television broadcasting began on August 7, 1963, and as elsewhere, was well behind radio. Reception was limited to about 10 kilometers from Abidjan for the estimated 2,300 receivers and audience of about 12,000. Television was available only from 6 to 9 p.m. Officially, Ivoirien television was considered a medium of education, but in fact was an expensive status symbol, reaching a very limited audience.

News, however, played a prominent role on both radio and television. Radiodiffusion Télévision Ivoirienne (RTI), established as a public corporation on October 31, 1962, had a combined news staff headed by a veteran French newsman, Pierre-Jean Laspeyres. On television there was a nightly half-hour news show drawn from the wire service reports distributed by AIP plus filmed reports supplied by Visnews and UPI news film.

The daily fare of radio news consisted of three 15-minute newscasts, one 20-minute, and three 5-minute news shows. Laspeyres denied there was any direct government censorship of news. Management practices gave government little cause to step in. "After two years, I know pretty well what the government wants," Laspeyres declared. "And if I have any doubts as to how to play a story, I call the Minister of Information who passes on it."[17]

The primacy of radio as a communication medium was borne out by a 1961 public opinion survey of adults in Abidjan. Radio garnered the largest audience in terms of overall exposure and was accepted as the best source of information about world affairs. Movies ranked second in total audience size with American films accounting for the bulk of those seen. The daily and weekly press had more limited audiences than sound or film.[18]

Radio's dominant position, however, was primarily an urban phenomenon since most radio listeners in the Ivory Coast lived in the Abidjan-Grand Bassam coastal area. Most Ivoiriens were untouched by mass communications.

NONIDEOLOGICAL APPROACH

Unlike neighboring Mali and Guinea, there was little or no nationalism or political rhetoric in the press and radio of the Ivory Coast, and the great variety of foreign sources of information available to Ivoiriens made any meaningful distinction between "news" and "propaganda" somewhat vague. This was due in part to the French colonists, who did nothing to foster freedom of expression, and in part to the pragmatic, nonideological outlook of President Houphouët-Boigny.

During their brief history the Abidjan news media have had a narrow, parochial focus, and with most journalists working for the government, questions of press freedom seldom arose.

Although press freedom was guaranteed in the Ivory Coast constitution, a 1959 law for "strengthening the protection of public order" made it possible for the government to confiscate or ban any publication which, intentionally or not, "brings about a disregard of the laws of the country, or injures the morals of the population, or casts discredit on the political institutions or their working," or has content "as to make these consequences likely."[19]

The law has been invoked, and newspapers from France and other African countries have been banned or confiscated at times. Occasionally, particular issues of Paris-based publications such as *Le Monde* or *Jeune Afrique* were seized when they contained articles critical of the regime, but usually they circulated freely. Since there was no political opposition to the PDCI, there was no opposition press. There were no Communist papers, correspondents, or diplomatic missions until January 23, 1967, when the Ivory Coast recognized the Soviet Union. However, Ivory Coast broke diplomatic relations with the Soviet Union in May 1969. There was no Communist Party in the country, and Houphouët permitted no Chinese Communist activities.

The need for an independent press free to comment on and even criticize the government was not widely felt. A free press has never been known; negative criticism was considered irresponsible, and articulate critics were usually absorbed into the establishment by the President. If not, they left the country.

The Ivory Coast had, then, an unusual communications mix: a francophonic press and broadcasting apparatus closely tied to the government and party, and on the other hand, a wide variety of international news sources entering from outside—mostly from France. As one authority said:

> For the young, middle-ranking civil servant, Paris-educated and highly assimilated, Paris and other European capitals are the source of "news" whereas what the party paper, *Fraternité*, prints and much of what is on the radio are considered "propaganda." For the clerk in the small town in the hinterland who reads *Fraternité* or *Fraternité-Matin* and whose radio set, if he has one, picks up few understandable stations outside of Radio Abidjan, "news" emanates from the party and government; all else may be "propaganda." Beyond that, the concept of propaganda may not exist at all.[20]

Although the news media were directed to the urban elite, the government and party apparatus did provide informal news channels to the diverse peoples making up the Ivory Coast. At the local level the government administration (based on the centralized French system of prefectures and sous-prefectures) and the PDCI were practically inseparable, with the party acting as a check on bureaucratic failures and helping to gain public support for government programs. Also there were ethnic political leaders (traditional chiefs, etc.), often members of the National Assembly, who represented tribal interests and served as "influentials" or opinion leaders between their tribes and the PDCI leadership. In theory, all adults belonged to the PDCI, and at the village level, the tribal leader and the party leader were often the same person. The Ministry of Information frequently worked through the party and government structure to rally support and to popularize government programs. As mentioned, the party paper, *Fraternité*, was distributed nationally throughout the party bureaucracy.

It should be emphasized, however, that communicating effectively to the diverse peoples of the Ivory Coast was an extremely difficult task and the news media reached and were understood by only a small fraction of Ivoiriens. Hence, interpersonal communication was still very important.

The development of the Ivory Coast's news communications, as with its economy in general, continued to be patterned on the French colonial model in that the whole system was in the hands of the new government (which took over the monolithic colonial administration) either alone or in combination with French concerns. As long as Houphouët-Boigny remained as chief executive, the continued development of press and broadcasting within that neo-colonial framework appeared likely. After Houphouët, the outlook was uncertain; the political pressures were great everywhere in Africa to eliminate all influences of the former colonial powers, whether they be French, British, Belgian, or Portuguese. So far, more than most governments, the Ivory Coast has resisted these pressures and has prospered.

SENEGAL'S NEWS MEDIA

The Republic of Senegal shared many similarities with the Ivory Coast. Located at the most westerly region of Africa at Cape Verde on the bulge of West Africa, Senegal, though smaller in area—only 76,124 square miles—was similar in population, with 3,580,000 (1966 census). It, too, has been led by an outstanding African leader—President Léopold Sédar Senghor who was also a renowned poet in the French language. In 1958 Senegal became an autonomous republic in the French community. Senegal's diverse peoples are mostly Moslems, and of the numerous languages, Wolof and Peul (Fula) are the most widely spoken.

Dakar, one of the most attractive cities in all of Africa, no longer has the importance it had when it was the administrative capital of *Afrique Ouest Française,* but it is still a busy city of about 576,093 (1965 estimate). Today, Dakar is only the capital of Senegal, but its influence still extends beyond its borders to other French-speaking countries.

News communications in Senegal and the environment in which they operated were similar to the Ivory Coast. Both were conservative francophonic nations that retained close and cordial ties with France. They enjoyed many of the same advantages; they shared the same basic communication problems.

The differences in their communications systems were differences of degree, not of kind.

For example, Senegal did not have a government newspaper, although the idea was occasionally suggested. The only real daily paper was the *Dakar-Matin,* along with *La Presse du Cameroun,* the last of the Charles de Breteuil group. In the mid-1960s, the circulation of *Dakar-Matin* had dropped to about 18,000 and was a thin, innocuous publication which avoided controversy and faithfully supported President Senghor and his Union Progressiste Sénégalaise (UPS) party. Before independence it consistently backed French government policy and gave little encouragement to the African independence movement.

The editor, M. de Bergevin, denied that there was any government censorship of *Dakar-Matin*. "We censor ourselves. We know the straight line of the government and we follow it," said the editor, who has had more than twenty years experience in Senegal and was a close friend of President Senghor.[21] If *Dakar-Matin* disapproved of a government action it just kept quiet, or as during a 1962 crisis situation when the paper could not determine the official government line, it merely ceased publishing for several days until it found out. *Dakar-Matin* was essentially a paper without editorial opinions of its own.

But *Dakar-Matin* still played an important role in Senegal. It did not try to compete with the ubiquitous Paris papers, but provided information not available in them. Moreover, with about fifteen stringer correspondents in other cities, it did a far more effective job than the government news agency, Agence de Presse Sénégalais (APS), in reporting Senegalese news originating outside Dakar.

Ten years after independence, *Dakar-Matin* remained in form and content still basically a French newspaper, even though it claimed it was now oriented toward the Senegalese. But since the Senegalese *évolués* who read the paper were essentially French in outlook, the paper had not really needed to change. *(Dakar-Matin* ceased publication in 1970 and was replaced by a new national daily, *Le Soleil du Sénégal,* which published in the same printing plant but was mainly owned by the government.)

The only other "daily" in Senegal was *Info Sénégal,* a small mimeographed bulletin of news items culled from the foreign news services and distributed by APS to about 300 customers in the capital.

NATIONAL NEWS AGENCY

The national news agency, Agence de Presse Sénégalaise (APS) reflected the strong residual influence of Agence France Presse. APS sent out AFP first on its domestic wires (about 80 percent of APS's total foreign file was AFP), then transmitted some Reuters (20 percent), but little news from UPI which it also received.[22]

The Senegalese agency was started in 1959 with major help from AFP, which provided the equipment and trained several

Senegalese in France for news agency positions. APS had a staff of five in Dakar but had no journalists stationed outside the capital. As a result, this national news agency collected very little news beyond the city limits of Dakar.

APS was essentially a small government bureau for redistributing the news from several world news service agencies which it resold to customers in Dakar. Clients included newspapers, the radio station, a few embassies, the president's office, etc.

Besides *Info Sénégal,* the other official publications were *L'Unité Africaine,* the weekly party of the UPS; *Sénégal d'Aujourd'hui,* a monthly publication (circulation 2,000), with features on political leaders and their activities; and *Sénégal-Documents,* a quarterly covering economic development.

"AFRIQUE NOUVELLE"

The really significant publication, not just for Dakar but for *Afrique Noire,* was the Dakar-based *Afrique Nouvelle,* the biweekly of news and comment which was almost required reading for anyone trying to keep up with political developments in francophonic Africa.

The most intelligently edited news publication in French Africa, *Afrique Nouvelle,* was founded in Dakar in 1947 by the Catholic White Fathers and was widely read over all francophonic Africa. Although it always had a large percentage of Africans on its staff and was consistently sympathetic to African political aspirations, *Afrique Nouvelle* cannot be considered part of the indigenous press.

The conservatively made-up but well-illustrated tabloid was distributed by air throughout Africa—any other means would be much too slow. Circulation varied from 15,000 to 21,000. Of these, 3,000 to 4,000 copies were sold in Senegal, 4,000 to 6,000 in the Ivory Coast, and lesser quantities to all the francophonic countries as well as to France, the United States, and anyone interested in French Africa. Although a Catholic-owned publication, it is not religious in tone. Editor John Adotevi said, *"Afrique Nouvelle* doesn't support Communists, but it doesn't back capitalists either. It works for African construction and development, for the unity of Africa and works to prevent a takeover by either the extreme left or extreme right."[23] Although it circulates freely throughout *Afrique Noire,* at times specific issues have been confiscated in Guinea, Mali, and the Ivory Coast because of particular articles.

Religion was not a problem even though a great many of its African readers were Moslems. Father J. de Benoist, an able French journalist, was associated with it during its early years, but later *Afrique Nouvelle* was run primarily by Africans. Simon Kiba has more recently been director of its six-man all-African staff in Dakar and its stringers in other countries.

Its intelligent reportage and commentary on events in Africa, including anglophonic countries, gave it an influence with West African intellectuals that was difficult to exaggerate.

There were two other Dakar publications widely read in West Africa. *Le Moniteur Africain du Commerce et de l'Industrie*, a weekly commercial paper, was established in 1962. Another, *Bingo*, was established in 1952 by Ousmane Soce Diop and published by the de Breteuil family. This was a monthly popular magazine, profusely illustrated, and distributed widely in French Africa. Circulation was about 25,000.

However, as in Ivory Coast, there are few vernacular publications in Senegal or little printed material aimed specifically for the newly literate.

For size of audience, in Senegal, too, radio was the outstanding medium. Radio Senegal was well developed, perhaps because Dakar had been the center for broadcasting in the AOF for so long. There were two services—Chaîne Internationale, in French only and broadcast in both shortwave and medium wave, and Chaîne Nationale, much more an instrument of rural and urban community development with local emphasis. On the latter, regional news was featured and the regular national newscasts were repeated in Wolof, Toucouleur, Sarakolé, Serere, Diola, and Mandingue.

Five major news bulletins were broadcast each day, and on Chaîne Internationale the news was also given in English, Portuguese, and Arabic as well as French, but the same news was carried on both services.

By francophonic African standards, Senegal had a comparatively large number of radio receivers. USIA sources estimated the total in February 1967 at 220,000 as compared with 75,000 for the Ivory Coast. The government, interested in widely distributing transistor sets, imposed no license fees or taxes on radio ownership. There was also widespread group listening in villages where there were some 200 wired loudspeakers for that purpose.[24]

Unlike most African nations, Senegal did not leap blindly into television. Instead of launching a general television service, Senegal chose to go slowly and to assess the role of television by a five-year research project in experimental educational television in cooperation with UNESCO. Under a carefully controlled project started in 1964, all telecasting was in the Wolof language. For two days a week, various groups of up to seventy persons gathered around community television sets at social centers in Dakar to watch the programs lasting from fifteen to forty-five minutes. After the broadcast, at each listening center, an instructor initiated a discussion and asked questions about what had just been viewed. It was hoped that the experience gained from the five-year project would provide guidelines for both educational and general television for Senegal as well as elsewhere in Africa.[25]

In French Africa the old rule about the rich getting richer seemed to operate. Dakar and Abidjan were far ahead of other French-speaking African capitals in their news media resources, meager though they were by developed-nation standards. There was reason to believe they would not only hold the lead over Conakry, Bamako, Ougadougou, Niamey, Lomé, and Nouakchott, but extend it. But for the noncountry of francophonic West Africa, the real news center and mass communications capital still was located on the River Seine, thousands of miles to the north.

The French government under President De Gaulle maintained a strong influence through technical assistance and private investment in the media. This assistance was of major importance for news media development in *Afrique Noire*. Whether the lingering influence of France will continue in West Africa now that De Gaulle is gone is a question that can only be answered in the years ahead.

10

FROM SETTLER PRESS TO
ONE-PARTY MEDIA:
KENYA AND ZAMBIA

THE NEWS MEDIA of Kenya and Zambia represent another variant of press development. They have been evolving from newspapers and broadcasting formerly dominated by and subservient to European interests toward "Africanized" news media controlled by the new one-party governments. Yet despite the threats of nationalization and thinly veiled official hostility, the foreign-owned newspapers have managed to survive into the postindependence period and have dominated the printed news in these two former British colonies.

IMPORTANCE OF SETTLERS

While West Africa counts the years of extensive contact with Europeans by the hundreds, British East and Central Africa (today's new nations of Kenya, Zambia, Uganda, Malawi, and Tanzania) can look back on less than a century. It was only in the last years of the nineteenth century that Europeans, mostly Britishers, came inland in any large numbers, and it was Kenya that most attracted them. But unlike West Africa, which for centuries was considered the "white man's grave," the Europeans came in numbers and settled, often in the fertile highlands of Kenya. Thousands of Britons made Kenya their home (this was much less true in Uganda and Tanganyika) and soon "settler" newspapers appeared. Then, to provide cheap labor to build the railroad from Mombasa to Uganda the British began importing Asians, mostly Indians, who in time dominated the commercial life and petty trade of East Africa. They, too, started newspapers.

(The main influx of European immigration in the Rhodesias was not until after World War II and came chiefly from Britain and South Africa.)

Like the French colonial press, the settler press in East and Central Africa reflected and supported the interests of the white man in Africa. White Kenyans considered themselves an integral part of the British Empire, and their newspapers provided news from home and the empire. It was and still is a *news*-oriented press, unlike the African-run papers of British West Africa which were mainly polemical newssheets that grew to express grievances, and in time, to advance the cause of political independence. The settler press showed little sympathy for African aspirations.

The Africans were much affected by the incursions of white settlers and Asians. In Kenya those most directly involved were the Kikuyus, whose traditional lands were appropriated by British farmers. As a result of the abrasive contact and their grievances, the Kikuyus became politically activated and ultimately published their own vernacular newspapers which had a brief but turbulent history.

Kenya has not lacked for newspapers during the seventy-plus years since Europeans arrived. Felice Carter discovered that since the beginning of the century more than 400 different publications of all kinds were registered as newspapers in Kenya. Most were small, ephemeral sheets, often in vernaculars, and few lasted long.

The first newspaper, the *East Africa and Uganda Mail,* was published at Mombasa in 1899, but it and many of its successors survived only a few years. A number of papers have promoted European farming and commercial interests.[1]

THE "STANDARD" GROUP

The settler newspaper that long dominated the journalism of East Africa was the *East African Standard* and its group of newspapers—owned and staffed by, and published for, Europeans. The *Standard* grew up with the colony and was long the spokesman of conservative white settlers. It opposed African nationalist efforts and often criticized British government policies to further African independence goals.[2]

The *Standard* was started by an Indian Parsee, A. M. Jeevanjee, in Mombasa in 1902. He imported W. H. Tiller from England to produce the *African Standard* which incorporated the *Mombasa Times* and the *Uganda Argus*. Soon afterward, Jeevanjee's paper was purchased by the partnership of Mayer and Anderson, then proprietors of the Grand Hotel in Mombasa. Anderson was editor and his son, C. B. Anderson, retired as board chairman in 1966.[3] Soon after its first weekly appearance on November 15, 1902, the name was changed to the *East African Standard*.

In 1910 the *Standard* followed the government to Nairobi, and the *Mombasa Times* was revived to cover the coast area. In 1923 the *Standard* bought out its opposition, the weekly *Leader of British East Africa* and hired its editor, George Kinnear, who headed the *Standard's* editorial department until 1956, when replaced by Kenneth Bolton.

Other Kenyan publications in the *Standard* group were the *Mombasa Times* which ceased publication in 1966, and *Baraza*, a Swahili weekly, started in 1939 with governmental encouragement. Editorially independent of the *Standard, Baraza* since 1945 had consistently advocated African political activity.[4] Other papers of the group were the *Uganda Argus,* started in Kampala in 1955, and the *Tanganyika Standard,* founded in Dar es Salaam in 1930. These sister papers shared wire services and correspondents with the Nairobi paper. (The paper in Dar was nationalized by the Tanzanian government in 1970.)

Asians started papers of their own to support the interests of *their* community. After 1945, radical Indian-owned papers such as the *Colonial Times, Daily Chronicle,* and *Tribune* supported African nationalist activities.[5] In fact, an Asian press of some size and influence developed, mainly in Kenya and Zanzibar. Among those more widely circulated were the *Kenya Daily Mail,* the *Observer,* the *Colonial Times,* the *Daily Chronicle,* and the *Goan Voice.* The first two appeared in two editions, Gujerati and English; the last three in English only. At one time their combined circulation was about 25,000.[6]

The government and missionaries provided some publications for African readers. However, the first African-owned paper was *Mwigwithania* ("work and pray" in Kikuyu), published in 1928 by the Kikuyu Central Association. It was edited by a young man named Johnstone Kamau, later to be known as Jomo Kenyatta.[7] It backed nationalist demands for land and ceased publication in 1934 when Kenyatta went back to England.

In 1945 Henry Mworia started *Mumenyereri,* the first of a

number of African vernacular papers that developed in the postwar years largely as outlets for the political and economic grievances of the energetic Kikuyus. By the time of the Mau Mau Emergency, there were about forty of these "violently written papers, mainly in Kikuyu, mainly mimeographed, mostly highly seditious and taking a bitterly anti-White, 'Quit Kenya' line."[8] They went largely unchecked because few Europeans could read Kikuyu and the colonial government failed to keep much of a watch over them.

VERNACULAR PAPERS SUPPRESSED

Most of these papers were suppressed under the declaration of The Emergency in October 1952. Those regulations empowered the government to prevent the printing of any material prejudicial to public order, and gave the right of search and seizure to any police or administrative officer. Had there been some effort by the colonial government to guide and direct these publications, an indigenous African press might have developed and persisted. Instead, they were ruthlessly suppressed.[9] In any case, this rapid development of a communication network among the Kikuyus has been called one of the critical factors in the nationalist buildup that resulted in the Mau Mau movement. The seditious Kikuyu newssheets certainly fostered social and political cohesion among the Kikuyus, and in this instance the press played an agitational role similar to that of the African press in British West Africa.

But at the same time, the vernacular newspapers had fostered anti-British feelings and encouraged terrorist uprisings. After the British government closed down almost the entire vernacular press, even the European and Asian journalists felt the restrictions of government censorship and suppression. Norman Miller pointed out that a double standard of press freedom existed in colonial Kenya: "In England the tradition of a free press is sacred; in the colonies, statutes and ordinances permit strong government control. Yet officially both England and the colonies are under the same laws. Kenya is a classic example of this double standard and the problem it creates."[10]

The Emergency regulations lasted until 1960, and the Kenyans' experience of a controlled press did not promise much for a free press after independence. Miller added: "In Kenya (under colonial rule) there is nothing in the African experience to indicate that press controls are not strictly a political expedient. It would, therefore, seem unrealistic to conclude that an African-run government will be more liberal in press policy or more considerate than has been the case with the Colonial administration."[11]

In 1952 the Government Information Department sponsored the formation of the Kenya Vernacular Press Company which provided the technical and financial backing for newspapers in Luo, Kikuyu, and Swahili. Assistance in organizing a vernacular press had also been one of the functions of the East African Literature Bureau which published a weekly magazine, *Tazama*, in Swahili.[12] Vernacular papers, as well as political activity, were greatly helped along in East Africa by Swahili, which while not a true *lingua franca*, is widely spoken throughout East Africa.

The last major element of the Kenya newspaper picture was added in 1959 with the appearance of new "European" interests —the East African Newspapers (*Nation* Series), Ltd., which presented the first real challenge to the dominance of the *Standard* group. First, in February 1959 there was launched a small Swahili weekly, *Taifa Kenya,* and then a Swahili daily, *Taifa Leo* ("Nation Today"). The English-language *Daily Nation* and *Sunday Nation* both appeared by 1961. The East African Newspapers, which included a large modern printing facility, were financed by the young Aga Khan with some help from Lord Thomson, the British publishing magnate, which was later withdrawn. From the beginning, the *Nation* papers identified with African nationalist aspirations.

By the time of Kenya's independence in 1963, these two European-owned newspaper groups, the *Standard* and the *Nation,* completely dominated the newspaper scene. The virtual nonexistence of an established independent African press meant that many Africans read the European papers. The Africans have preferred reading the independent settler papers to those published for them by government or missionary groups, in part because they were better papers. Almond and Coleman pointed out that the political effects of these European colonial newspapers were somewhat mixed:

> They are essential media for communication within the European community and for the functioning of that community's near autonomous political process. . . . There are also media furthering African acculturation to European models in style, dress, speech, tastes and social norms and to that extent they further emulative urges and a measure of emulation. . . . But they have also been instruments for ceaseless affirmation of white suprem-

acy and no group feels their anti-African editorials or slanted news more avidly than do the Africans. . . . Thus, the papers serve as agencies of alienation, reminding the educated African daily of his subordinate role and confirming in his mind the hopelessness of his political future.[13]

The years of conditioning by the settler press were to profoundly affect the attitudes of the new African government after independence came in the early 1960s.

INDEPENDENT KENYA: MODERATION UNDER KENYATTA

Uhuru (Swahili for "freedom") came to Kenya on December 12, 1963. One year later independent Kenya proclaimed itself a republic under a one-party government, and all political opposition was quietly merged into the Kenya African National Union (KANU), the ruling party headed by President Jomo Kenyatta.

During its first decade of nationhood, the energetic new East African government drastically reorganized Kenya's settler-oriented system of mass communications. As a result, the news media have been brought under either direct or indirect control of the one-party government. Yet because of democratic elements within the young government and the enlightened leadership of Kenyatta, Kenya had a media system that falls between the usual classifications, embodying characteristics of both libertarianism and authoritarianism. Moreover, European influences still permeate the news media.

The political stability and steady progress of the republic's first seven years generally proved beneficial for mass communications. Unlike some African nations, things were getting better for the news media in Kenya in many respects, though there were still many problems and occasional crises.

As under British rule, the Europeans and Asians continued to dominate the modern sector of society and were the biggest users of mass communications. In 1965 about 43,000 of the 53,000 Europeans, mostly British, who lived in Kenya before independence, still remained. By 1969 the number of Europeans was estimated at 125,000; however, most newcomers were not, as before, permanent settlers on the land, but more transitory commercial employees. (For example, the number of American companies in Kenya rose from twelve to seventy in a few years time.) There were about 188,000 Asians in Kenya.

In fact, the cosmopolitan capital of Nairobi, its population over 400,000, was more of a European and Asian city than an African one. Now the center of the flourishing East African tourist industry, Nairobi has long been the commercial and financial hub of East Africa. Its excellent communications and airline connections also helped make it the news communications center of East Africa, and this, combined with a salubrious climate (near the equator at about 5,452 feet), explains why it had the largest concentration of foreign correspondents anywhere in Africa.

Except for radio, few of Kenya's 10,209,000 citizens (1969 estimate) were touched by mass communications. Divided into forty tribes, most live not in Nairobi, Mombasa (population 180,000), or other cities, but in their tribal districts. Seventy different languages and dialects are spoken by these people.

Since only a limited number of the African population can communicate in English and about 25 percent in Swahili, the news media, which rely heavily on these two languages, are perforce elite media.

The news media are European phenomena, and although they are undergoing Africanization in Kenya, the imprint left by seventy years of British domination of the press, and later broadcasting, remains strong and pronounced. Although under increasing government pressure, the press was still mostly owned by two foreign companies which between them controlled the two English-language dailies, a Swahili daily and weekly, and two English-language Sunday papers.

TOWARD GOVERNMENT CONTROL

One of the early decisions of the new Kenyatta government was to assume greater control of mass communications and to minimize the European influences which had so long rankled so many Africans. This desire to "Kenyanize" such a sensitive institution was certainly understandable, and it was a policy strenuously pursued by the first Minister of Information, Achieng Oneko, who was closely allied politically with Oginga Odinga, former vice-president and once considered a possible successor to Kenyatta before he bolted KANU in 1966 to form his Kenya People's Union. Both Oneko and Odinga were considered sympathetic to the Soviet Union and Red China and were reportedly well financed by Communist sources. A decidedly pro-Communist bias showed in Kenya's communications during the period these two men had influence in the Kenyatta government.

Control over news was exercised from Oneko's Ministry of Information, Broadcasting and Tourism (tourism was later placed in another ministry with wildlife), and he paved the way for Communist nations to provide equipment, funds, and training for government activities in mass communications.

The ministry had two major departments: the Voice of Kenya, which included both radio and television broadcasting; and the Information Department, which encompassed government press and information services, as well as the new Kenya News Agency (KNA). Outside Nairobi, the Information Department had a senior information officer in each of Kenya's seven regions who distributed information and publications and also gathered news for the KNA.

In its first years the KNA represented the most controversial aspect of the new government's information policies. Russia and Czechoslovakia assisted in the development of the agency. Even before *uhuru,* several young Kenyans were receiving news service training in a castle near Prague from the Czech news agency, Ceteka. For the first several years of KNA operations in Nairobi, a Czech journalist, Zdenek Kubes, worked as an editorial advisor to the new agency. Russia provided, without charge, the technical assistance, teleprinters, and excellent radio-receiving equipment to pick up news beamed to East Africa, as well as a resident technician in Nairobi to keep the machines working.

In line with its official policy of nonalignment between East and West, the government decided KNA would take only two world news services, Reuters and TASS, the latter provided without charge. This gave KNA a virtual monopoly on incoming news and placed the government squarely astride the news flow.

After the ouster of Oneko as minister of information in June 1966 and his replacement by James Osogo, the KNA modified its operations a good deal. Kubes, the Czech advisor, was deported in March 1966, and the pro-Communist influence in the national news agency almost disappeared. In addition to Reuters and TASS, KNA started receiving AFP and UPI reports as well. Also, there was much less tampering with incoming news reports. A spokesman for the Ministry of Information admitted that KNA, originally designed to provide news for radio, was "not started in a proper manner." He said that later there was much more balance in its international news reporting. However, KNA was still an underfinanced and understaffed operation and failed to cover news of Kenya adequately.[14]

VOICE OF KENYA

The continued shortcomings of KNA had implications for radio and television news because KNA was the sole newsgathering organization for the government's Voice of Kenya, the major mass medium.

Broadcasting was started in 1927 as a service for British settlers and was the first such operation in tropical Africa. Television broadcasting came in October 1962 and went through a commercial phase until April 1964, when the new Kenyan government decided to take direct control of both sound and television transmissions. Before 1961 all radio broadcasting, except the British East Africa Command's Forces Broadcasting Station, was controlled by the colonial government's Kenya Broadcasting System (KBS). In late 1961 the colonial government established a new corporation, the Kenya Broadcasting Corporation (KBC), as an independent public service body, much along the lines of the BBC, to run radio and television.

The KBC, organized before Kenya's independence, was not fated to survive long, if only because it was identified with settler interests. One incident will illustrate the tensions under which the KBC operated during the first months of independence. On March 8, 1964, the KBC played "Rule Britannia" in a songs-of-the-sea medley on radio. A listener telephoned the studio complaining that "Rule Britannia" was an offensive tune and an insult to Mr. Kenyatta and the government. A European announcer promptly broadcast an apology.

Besides the Africans' political suspicions, the KBC television operation proved costly; it lost £104,086 during its first year of operation.[15] Moreover, the Kenyatta government resented the corporation's lack of interest in African affairs. The KBC aimed all of its television programs, done solely in English, at Europeans and Asians, who incidentally owned the great majority of TV sets (and still do). Later, faced with the threat of nationalization and attempting to head it off, the KBC tried to make its offerings more attractive to Africans by introducing some Swahili-language programs and by appointing Africans in more than token numbers to positions of responsibility.[16]

Since July 1, 1964, when the Kenya Broadcasting Corporation officially became the Voice of Kenya (VOK), the young government has taken the full responsibility of developing these two major media of communication. Radio was by then well established and a going concern, whereas television was still getting started, was expensive to operate, and reached only a fraction of radio's audience. Television was still the headache.

Revenue for broadcasting comes from three sources: annual license fees for radio and television sets, advertising revenue, and direct subventions from government.

Radio, beamed to an estimated 500,000 receiving sets and an audience of 3½ million, was the nearest thing to a mass medium. Even though radio listening was much higher in urban areas, the audience in the outlying districts was still significant, more so than in many other new African states.

To serve this audience, VOK at first provided three full services—English, Swahili, and Hindustani—plus some regional broadcasts in twelve vernaculars. However, the Hindustani service was later dropped and two hours of Hindustani were added to the vernacular service. The reduction of the full Hindustani service from seventeen hours daily to just two hours was a deliberate slap at the politically unpopular Asians who have been under increasing pressure from the government to identify themselves more closely politically and economically with Kenya. Recently, the VOK consisted of the National service on the air in Swahili from 6 a.m. to 11 p.m. and the General service in English, also from 6 a.m. to 11 p.m., plus various vernacular broadcasts.

On its fourth birthday, television was still far behind radio. Of the estimated 14,000 receiver sets in 1968, about 5,500 were owned by Europeans and 5,500 by Asians and only about 2,500 sets belonged to Africans.[17] In addition, 500 community television sets were in operation, with a total weekly audience of about 500 to 600 per set, according to VOK officials. Television reception was largely confined to greater Nairobi, Mombasa, and the Kisumu area on Lake Victoria.

Radio reception was excellent all over Kenya, with the exception of the thinly populated Northeast.

The BBC influence has remained strong in broadcasting, and was most apparent in the news presentation style which followed the BBC format of giving the headlines, the individual news items, and then a repetition of the headlines.

The VOK's news staff gathered no news of its own, but relied entirely on what was provided by the KNA, located across Nairobi in Jogo House. The Ministry of Information deemed it "needless duplication" for both the news agency and the broadcasting station to gather news.[18] However, it was possible that there were security or political considerations as well, for whoever controlled the radio and television station would not then control the news-gathering apparatus and vice versa.

Between visits in 1965 and 1968, I noted a marked improvement in VOK newscasts, which earlier suffered from the usual monotony and dullness that comes from a surfeit of self-serving government handouts. By 1968 the news programs laid more stress on hard news and were no longer merely a transmission belt for government releases. However, the comings and goings of President Kenyatta and his chief ministers and what they said still received, as they should, ample attention. Moreover, the VOK gave more prominence than before to international news which came mainly from Reuters, plus some from AFP, UPI, and TASS.

Yet, the VOK persisted with the earlier policy of withholding any news considered unfavorable or unflattering to Kenya or countries friendly to Kenya, even though such news might be fully reported in the newspapers. This policy was in keeping with Kenya's interpretation of a proper nonalignment position. For instance, until 1968 news of the Vietnam War was not reported on radio at all. And in mid-1968 when Oscar Karbona, former foreign minister of Tanzania, was regularly criticizing President Julius Nyerere from various places abroad, stories quoting Karbona appeared in the Nairobi papers, but not on VOK.

It was VOK policy to stress development news, so such items as new hospitals and schools and various self-help projects received a good deal of attention. Conversely, few negative news items such as crime, tribal frictions, and violence were reported.

Radio newscasts were given daily at 7 and 9 a.m. and at 1, 4, 7, 9, and 11 p.m. on both English and Swahili services. News was also broadcast for fifteen minutes daily in each of twelve vernaculars—Masai, Kikuyu, Luo, Kikamba, Somali, Borana, Kalenjin, Luluhya, Mero, Teso, Kimeru, and Hindustani.

On television the news *(habari)* was given for fifteen minutes in Swahili and then later for fifteen minutes in English.

Although the VOK was ostensibly almost completely Africanized, behind the scenes American and British experts were playing important roles in the day-to-day operations of both media.

With the decline of pro-Communist influences in both KNA and VOK, the news flow to the Kenyan public was considerably improved, even though a significant segment of news was never aired because of the government policy against broadcasting "bad news" about itself or its friends. As long as it controlled the news of both radio and television, the government felt no need for a newspaper of its own. But that did not mean the government was reconciled to continued European control of the press.

THE PRESS

The daily and periodical press of Kenya was not under direct government control; further, there were no government papers. For, despite the push for "Africanization" of the news media, the European-owned newspapers continued to dominate the printed press as they did under colonial rule. All adapted themselves to the constraints of publishing under one-party African rule.

Looked at objectively, the major publications in Nairobi—*East African Standard, Daily Nation, Sunday Nation, Taifa Leo, Baraza,* and the *Reporter*—are among the very best *news*papers in tropical Africa. These papers have enjoyed an unusual amount of freedom for contemporary Africa, but it is still a press controlled by the Kenya government, albeit in a light and indirect manner.

Doyen of the Kenya press was the *East African Standard,* the oldest daily in Kenya, and dominant paper of the *East African Standard* group. In May 1967 the *Standard* group was purchased by Lonrho, a British firm with diverse investments in Africa, which acquired a majority interest at a cost of more than £1,000,000. This price, however, included a lucrative commercial printing and packaging business.[19] Although the new ownership exposed the *Standard* group even more to the charge of foreign ownership (most of its previous European shareholders at least resided in Kenya), there was no change in either staff or policies. The paper's typography and makeup were changed, however, giving the paper a drab and conservative appearance.

Although long the spokesman of the conservative white settlers, the *Standard* since independence uncritically and even obsequiously supported the Kenyatta government and regularly ran its press releases. A broadsheet daily, the *Standard,* with 33,774 average daily sales as of December 1967, was still ahead of its tabloid rival, the *Daily Nation,* whose comparable circulation was 30,121. The *Standard's* weekend edition on Friday, which included a magazine section, had a circulation of 44,508, while the *Sunday Nation's* circulation was 39,343.[20]

The *Standard's* bigger Friday edition was originally intended for up-country areas when poor communications made it impossible to get the *Standard* daily. Bulging with features, women's page items, church notices, a children's page, and radio and television logs, it later served mostly an African audience who could not afford the daily paper. One distributor who sold seven copies of the Friday *Standard* in an impoverished rural area estimated that about seventy people became acquainted with the contents of each copy. The copies were sold to officials such as the District Commissioner, local school teachers, or the owner of the local duka (Asian store). The papers were read aloud, translated, and explained in the village compounds.[21]

About two-thirds of the *Standard*'s circulation was outside Nairobi, while the *Nation* was aimed mainly at the urban African. A 1967 readership study conducted by the *Standard* showed that African readership of the daily paper was 42 percent, European 34 percent, and Asian 23 percent.[22]

U.S. Information Agency surveys in East Africa have found that of newspaper readers with some secondary education and above, 51 percent read the *Standard* and 50 percent read the *Nation*. A much smaller percentage of educated Kenyans read the Swahili papers.

Lesser educated persons tended to read the *Taifa Leo, Baraza,* and *Taifa Kenya*—the Swahili papers—and as education and social status went up so did readership of English. This was especially true for books and more sophisticated fare.[23]

Although less lively appearing than the *Nation,* the *Standard* carried a greater volume of news and, by African standards, had a large editorial staff (about twenty-five) to report the news. However, that staff was still essentially European; in 1968 there was just one African subeditor. The *Standard* also maintained an office in London. The paper was distributed all over East Africa and was sent by air to Dar and Kampala.

Although it still gave a good deal of attention to the European community—social affairs, horse shows, agricultural fairs, and news from Britain—the *Standard* did adapt to the new Africa and did report news and comment of interest to the black majority. And it gave full and accurate coverage of government news, especially from parliament and the various ministries; hence, there has been little need for a government newspaper.

The *Standard*'s Swahili weekly, *Baraza,* with a circulation of about 58,000, was the largest weekly in East Africa, with many readers in Tanzania. Much of its success was due to its editorial independence from the *Standard,* although the two papers shared printing, advertising, and distribution facilities. Its all-African staff (unusual for any paper in East Africa) was headed by Francis

Khamisi, who said he had full editorial freedom and felt no conflict in working for a white ownership. Its readership came primarily from the rural areas, and it maintained a string of part-time correspondents throughout Swahili-speaking East Africa.[24]

THE "NATION" PAPERS

The Aga Khan's East African Newspapers (Nation Series), Ltd., publishing enterprise, which included a large commercial printing operation, has provided real competition for the Standard group. But successfully establishing their four papers, Daily Nation, Sunday Nation, Taifa Leo, and Taifa Kenya, required the overcoming of many obstacles. As the first rotary offset daily in Africa, there were numerous technical problems. There were the peculiarly African difficulties: heavy rains that flooded the printing works; flying ants in the ink ducts; eight Land Rovers used for distribution were written off in the first six months; one man drowned when his vehicle was swept off a bridge during the long rains; another car was charged by a rhino; and at times elephants blocked delivery trucks on the road to Mombasa.[25]

But with able management, the Nation papers overcame these, plus a number of erratic missteps. One plus was that from the beginning the papers gave full editorial support to the cause of African self-government in Kenya. However they did not hesitate to criticize African political leaders and this caused trouble from time to time. The Nation papers tried to Africanize their staffs as quickly as possible; that they have been unsuccessful is due largely to the continuing problem of training and then holding good African journalists. In 1968 Europeans still provided the backbone of the editorial staff, although the Nation has had two able African editors, Hilary Ng'weno and later, George Githii. But both were in a sense figurehead editors; they wrote the daily "leader" or main editorial, put together the editorial page, answered the phone when government officials called to complain about something in the Nation, and represented the paper officially. However the day-to-day work of producing the paper was carried out by expatriates.

The tabloid Nation was bright, interesting, newsy, and intelligently edited. Like the Standard, the Nation has followed a policy of basic support for the Kenyatta government, but has criticized certain aspects of government. The Preventive Detention Act was criticized by the Nation as was the contemplated purchase of a Rolls Royce car by the mayor of Nairobi, who later decided against buying it. The *Nation*'s exposure of corruption in a scandal over corn marketing led to dismissal of a cabinet minister. However, the two papers only go so far in their criticisms, and Githii said, "We still have a long ways to go before we have real freedom of the press in Kenya, maybe twenty or thirty years."[26]

The *Nation*'s sister daily, *Taifa Leo,* played an important role in Kenyan public opinion because it was the only Swahili daily. Under the editorship of Boaz Omori, *Taifa Leo* shared the reporting staff of the *Nation,* but had its own subeditors and translators and was generally more Africanized if only because few expatriates know Swahili. It was a smaller paper—usually about eight pages as against twenty-four for the *Nation*—and the news was handled in a more simplified and sensational fashion, because Swahili readers tend to be less educated.

Although Swahili readership was increasing, along with English, it was still a "stepping stone" language. Once their English was good enough, Africans began reading the more prestigious English-language press.[27] Swahili papers had a continuing problem of holding onto educated readers. Because English had precedence in the higher levels of education, its influence tended to spread downward from the top.

Taifa Leo's circulation recently jumped from 17,000 to 25,000 as of June 1968, and circulated, along with the *Nation,* in the main areas of population: Nairobi, Mombasa, and the Central Province. Readership was particularly high among the politically sophisticated Kikuyus. Trucks left Nairobi at midnight for Mombasa on the coast and Kisumu on Lake Victoria, and the papers were on sale by 6 a.m.

The *Nation* Sunday papers were basically weekend editions of the English and Swahili papers. The *Sunday Nation*'s circulation in 1968 was 39,343, while the three separate Swahili editions, which went to Uganda and Tanzania as well as rural Kenya, had a combined circulation of 64,717.[28]

Kenya's newspapers enjoyed wide readership in neighboring Tanzania and occasionally came under restrictions by the Tanzanian government. In October 1968, four papers—*Daily Nation, Sunday Nation, Taifa Leo,* and *Taifa Tanzania*—were banned following the publication of a report two weeks earlier that seventy-five tribesmen in the Kilimanjaro area of northern Tanzania were arrested for disloyalty. M. Kangero, a Tanzania reporter for the *Daily Nation,* was remanded on bail, charged with publishing false news likely to cause fear and alarm. In the same month, *Baraza* was banned on the island of Zanzibar where it regularly sold 1,600 copies.

Some of the English-language magazines and journals have been quite outspoken. The *Kenya Weekly News* (circulation 7,000) was a very independent journal under its long-time editor, M. F. Hill. But after Hill's death, the Nakuru agricultural paper was sold to the *Standard* group and lost much of its vigor.

The *Kenya Weekly News* was finally closed down in the fall of 1969, and the passing of the "Green 'Un" was indicative of changes in Kenya. Published in Nakuru for over thirty-five years, it was dependent on a dwindling number of white settlers for subscriptions and advertising. The last issue, the 2,276th for the weekly, was devoted primarily to coverage of the Nairobi agricultural and trade show.

Kenya's one remaining independently owned national English-language paper, the *Sunday Post,* was still holding on with a circulation of about 16,000, although it had been hurt by competition from the *Sunday Nation.*

The *Sunday Post,* owned by the English Press, Ltd., and published since 1935, was unusual in Kenya (and in Africa, for that matter) in that it was a public company whose shares could be bought on the local stock market; it was 94 percent Kenyan-owned. However, as of 1966 not one black Kenyan had availed himself of the opportunity to buy stock in the company.[29]

The most important fortnightly publication was the *Reporter,* founded in April 1961 by its editor-owner, Henry Reuter. The *Time*-style news magazine had a circulation of about 10,000 throughout East Africa and also went to universities and Kenyan students abroad. From its inception, the *Reporter* has been surprisingly outspoken and critical of government in its news coverage—consistently more so than the daily press. For example, note the following item: "*Objectivity.* Told that a 'certain Asian' in Nanyuki was uncooperative and did not respect the Kenya nation and its leaders, Information Minister Mr. Achieng Oneko told a recent public rally: 'A full investigation into this complaint will be made by the Government, and as soon as the facts are known immediate action will be taken against this Asian.' "[30]

Reuter said that the periodical press was freer because the government considered it much less influential than daily papers and hence did not badger it as much.[31]

Although there have been numerous Indian-language papers in Kenya's history, there was only one remaining—*Africa Sa-*

machar, a Gujerati weekly with 18,000 circulation spread over East and Central Africa. It claimed 8.4 readers per copy. Started in 1954, it was the only Asian paper that caught on with the large Asian community. Most of the others did not exceed 4,000 or 5,000 circulation.

There were also a few religious, professional, commercial, and government publications, two English-language regional periodicals with circulations of about 2,000, and two Arab papers in Mombasa with circulations of about 2,000 and 500 each.[32]

A popular religious publication, *Target*, a weekly which together with its Swahili counterpart, *Lengo*, had a circulation of almost 20,000, came under government attack in December 1968. Attorney General Charles Njonjo threatened to close down *Target* because it criticized the growing gap between rich and poor and the divisions within the ruling KANU party. The government was finally persuaded to allow the paper, sponsored by the National Christian Council of Kenya, to carry on but insisted that the British editor, Rev. John Schofield, be fired.

Largely because of the increasing ascendency of the *Standard* and *Nation* papers, periodicals published by Africans in the vernaculars have not been able to sustain themselves.

When Odinga still had political influence, three anti-West, pro-Communist papers, *Pan Africa* (a monthly in English), *Nyanza Times* (a Luo weekly), and *Sauti ya Mwafrika* (a Swahili weekly), were financed by Communist sources. All three were badly produced and mostly filled with anti-American diatribes. Their street sales never amounted to much, and by 1968 their subsidies had dried up and all three had disappeared.

The lack of local capital, problems of distribution, high cost of newsprint, and the dearth of trained African journalists combined to make it difficult for Africans to launch and sustain publications of their own. And this, of course, remained the greatest shortcoming of the press of Kenya—the near total lack of completely African publications. Foreign capital and expertise were still required.

PRESS AND GOVERNMENT RELATIONSHIPS

The lack of indigenous newspapers was undoubtedly a source of the continued tension between press and government and yet relationships had generally improved. Much of the credit goes to the moderation and good sense of President Kenyatta, who better than most African leaders understood the value of a free press, and also to the restraint and responsibility exercised by journalists themselves.

Despite the government's pressures toward political conformity and its sensitivity to criticism, there was a desire among many government leaders to maintain freedom of expression. It was a value highly prized by British-educated journalists and lawyers in and out of government. A respected journalist in Nairobi told me in 1965 that the press is about 51 percent free. "A great deal," he said, "depends on what happens during the next several years. If the young government can somehow get through this period and provide itself with a firm foundation, then there is hope that freedom of the press will prosper and expand." Under Kenyatta's leadership this was happening and the press was beginning to establish itself as a viable institution.

Henry Reuter said in 1967, "At present there is a great deal of press freedom in Kenya, despite the occasional pressures, and I believe, personally, that as things appear at the moment, this freedom will expand rather than contract as the economy grows and the government matures."[33]

However, the press in Kenya was not a free press by the standards of Western Europe and America. The press was controlled in that it knew full well, by informal and unwritten agreement, just how far it could go in criticizing the regime or in reporting information "embarrassing" to the government. While some criticism was permitted, no one dared use the printed word for direct attacks on Kenyatta himself or any program or action he strongly advocated. In May 1968 when President Kenyatta was taken ill while in Mombasa, no Kenya paper reported his illness for several days, even though the essential facts were well known to the press.

And as yet, freedom of the press does not enjoy any substantial protection of the law; it exists at the whims of officialdom. The Constitution guarantees freedom of the press and expression, and there are no restrictive press laws on the books. But should the government suppress a Kenya newspaper (something which, to it credit, it has not done), there are no real legal mechanisms or procedures by which the paper can seek redress; it certainly cannot appeal to the Constitution. And if the government pleads "national interest" or "national security," then no reasons for the suppression need be given any more than in cases of individuals expelled from the country for the same reasons. For the fact is there is no substantial body of either written law or case law to protect the press against arbitrary government action. The main line of defense for the press is public opinion and the public's faith in the Constitution, and in Africa this does not as yet represent much of a bulwark for a free press.

The Kenya Parliament played a rather ambiguous role vis-a-vis press and government relationships. The press was free to report whatever was said in Parliament and this enabled the papers to carry a lot of discussion of public issues, including outspoken criticisms of particular policies and government ministers. But often the press itself came under attack from MP's, some with little sympathy for press freedom.

In February 1965 the Senate passed a motion urging the government to introduce a bill "compelling" newspapers to assist in the task of nation-building. A spokesman for the Ministry of Information fended off the proposal saying, "I can assure you that we keep a very close watch indeed on what the papers publish, and we would be very firm indeed if we thought that any publication or group of publications was deliberately setting out to undermine the nation's efforts at nation-building." Unfortunately, almost any kind of criticism could be construed as an effort to undermine nation-building, and as indicated, the papers did little real criticizing.

During one Senate session, the government-owned radio and television stations were criticized for giving more coverage to the lower house than to the Senate. The fact that the National Assembly, which had more power and from which cabinet ministers were drawn, was more newsworthy, did not enter the picture. The Senators wanted equal time regardless.

Although it was capable of such views, the Parliament was also an important stronghold of free expression and political dissent. Although Kenya was essentially a one-party state, the backbenchers criticized the government freely and during the question period (borrowed from British practice) asked searching questions of cabinet ministers. Kenyatta himself was not immune from embarrassing questions in Parliament. The proceedings were fully reported by the newspapers, especially the *East African Standard*. The Voice of Kenya also reported "The Day in Parliament" each evening. As long as there was this political diversity within the government itself, press freedom was given an additional boost.

But source after source in Kenya's press emphasized to me that it was the informal controls—the unwritten agreements of how far the press could go—that really restricted the press. One top journalist said, "They've established these unwritten rules of conduct and have managed to let us know what they are." This was usually done by phone calls to the editor from top people in government. In earlier days, the information ministry would call in editors for group meetings.

Sometimes blunt public warnings came from high government officers. On January 14, 1969, the government warned the newspapers of Kenya to cease "highlighting and sometimes exaggerating" its programs to break the grip of Asians on trade lest the press finds itself next to be purged of its non-African elements.

"It is a matter of regret that even after five years of independence from Britain, a section of the influential local press is still inclined not to effectively promote the interests of the country in general," the government announcement said.

(Only two weeks before, the newspapers in Nairobi were reprimanded by Vice-President Daniel Arap Moi for carrying photographs of the Rhodesian flag along with an article about its being hoisted above Rhodesia's mission in London.)

"The local press is expected to positively identify itself with the aspirations and the wishes of the people of this country," the statement said. "Indulgence in excessive sensationalism, highlighting and sometimes exaggerating certain issues, can only be viewed as a negative contribution. It should not be surprising, therefore, if action is taken to remedy this situation," the statement concluded.

In an editorial the next day, the *East African Standard* reiterated its support for the government's policy to make it easier for Africans to get into commerce but asked where the paper had gone wrong in reporting the matter. "Government and ministerial statements have been published daily, though the criticism that publicity has also been given to complaints cannot be answered since it is true," the *Standard* said.[34]

The assassination of cabinet minister Tom Mboya in July 1969 produced political repercussions which brought the most serious threat to the press since independence nearly six years before. Three British journalists—all of whom had worked in Kenya for several years—were summarily deported for unspecified reasons. They were Eric Marsden, acting editor of the *East African Standard,* Alan Chester, head of the *Standard* syndication office, and Michael Chester (no relation), news editor of the *Daily Nation.*

Peter Gachathi, Director of Information, went out of his way to observe, ". . . local newspapers, by virtue of being foreign-owned and controlled, are particularly susceptible to representing interests which may run counter to those of the people of this country." Warning the press not to create alarm and despondency or to print sensational events, Gachathi said: "The Government will not tolerate the activities of self-appointed guardians of Kenya's who, paradoxically enough, are also champions of disunity."[35]

In such a highly charged political atmosphere, the press apparently could do nothing right, and being foreign-owned, became an obvious scapegoat.

As long as these informal, extra-legal threats persisted, real press freedom in Kenya was somewhat illusory.

Some wariness and suspicion of the press stemmed from official government policy that mass communications, particularly newspapers, should be Kenyanized (i.e., run by black Africans) as soon as possible.

But six years after independence, the major papers were still owned and mostly staffed by Europeans. There was still a continuing, serious shortage of educated and journalistically trained Kenyans. In a country where trained and educated people are generally scarce, a good journalist—especially one who can write and express himself effectively—can easily command a more prestigious and high-paying job in government or public relations.

Real freedom of expression and adequate numbers of African journalists will probably only be realized as the more basic problems of illiteracy and poverty are to some extent overcome. Cosmopolitan Nairobi has given Kenya an excellent system of news communications, but it was not an indigenously African one as were those of Ghana or Nigeria. Kenya does not yet have mass audiences of Africans who effectively use the media and who constitute an informed public opinion.

In any case, its newspapers, broadcasting, and periodicals were much better than one would expect for a nation at its level of development. Foreign ("neo-colonial," if you will) influence in the news media helped to bring this about, as did the moderate government of Jomo Kenyatta.

ZAMBIA: NEWS MEDIA ON "LINE OF RAIL"

The new Republic of Zambia attained its independence from Britain on October 24, 1964, almost a year later than Kenya, and the two former British colonies had much in common. Both were led by able leaders whose governments became increasingly one-party regimes, in part due to rising tribal tensions. Both new nations inherited media systems forged and dominated by Europeans and in which Africans had had near nonexistent involvement.

The Europeans, mainly British and South Africans, came much more recently to Zambia and did less to develop the nation, but the former Northern Rhodesia had one great assest in its quest for modernity: copper.

What modernity and "advantages" of civilization that the new nation in south-central Africa enjoyed were clustered along the spinelike "line of rail" that bisected the Texas-sized country from the southern border at Livingstone to the rich Copperbelt near the Congo border. What colonial development there was came from efforts to establish infrastructure necessary to mine copper and transport it out through Southern Rhodesia. The vast areas to east and west were largely unchanged and were hardly touched by mass communications.

Zambia's inadequate mass media facilities reflected the mining configuration and these general conditions: the dominance of Europeans and Asians in the small modern sector, lack of educated Zambians, the orientation to and economic dependence on southern Africa, and decentralized urbanization due to the scattered mining towns. Strategically located on the guerrilla warfare frontier between white-dominated southern Africa and the independent black nations to the north, Zambia was trying to reorient itself to East Africa.

The meager audience for mass communications (including most of its 15 to 20 percent literates) was concentrated along the line of rail. Newspapers were quickly and easily distributed along this area but not beyond into the hinterlands. Not even radio, Africa's one mass medium, was an exception. Due to low transmitting power, lack of receivers, and the babel of thirty vernaculars, spoken by the over four million Zambians, few beyond the line of rail could hear "Lusaka calling."

This independent republic within the British Commonwealth was led by one of Africa's outstanding leaders, President Kenneth Kaunda. Kaunda's United National Independence Party (UNIP) won the preindependence national elections, but was challenged later by other political groups in an atmosphere increasingly charged with tribal rivalries.

In Zambia's first general elections since independence, held on December 19, 1968, Kaunda and UNIP were returned to office for five more years by an overwhelming majority.

Zambia's economic potentialities stemmed from great mineral resources, especially copper. In 1967, 606,436 tons of copper were produced with a value of 454,047,506 kwachas (1 kwacha = $1.40). The immense ore reserves on the Copperbelt exceeded 883 million tons, making Zambia the world's third largest producer and second largest exporter of copper. Zambia's underground wealth gave her a substantial economic advantage over other new African nations; the gross national product of the cash economy in 1962 was $555 million, half of it from mining, chiefly copper but also cobalt, lead, zinc, and manganese. In 1968 exports totaled $655 million, while imports were $483 million.

But six years after independence, these assets were barely developed, and the nation still faced difficult problems. More so than Kenya, land-locked Zambia was sorely neglected by her colonial rulers, and unlike West Africa, her peoples did not have sustained contact with Europeans until the late nineteenth century. Victoria Falls, on the Zambezi River between Zambia and Rhodesia, was not seen by a white man until David Livingstone arrived there in 1855. Cecil Rhodes, in 1888, obtained mining concessions from the King of the Matabeles and soon sent in settlers. Rhodes's British South Africa company controlled the area from 1889 until 1924 when the British government took it over as a protectorate. But the potentialities of copper mining were not realized until the late 1920s, and Northern Rhodesia's limited development was a by-product of efforts to exploit the mineral resources.

From 1953 to 1963 the Protectorate was in the Federation of the Rhodesias and Nyasaland. The peoples of Northern Rhodesia benefited little either in terms of education, health measures, or community development. So by independence, a basic problem common to all fields was the desperate lack of trained personnel and even of persons with secondary education available for immediate employment or for further training. In 1964 it was estimated that there were not more than 100 Africans in Northern Rhodesia with university degrees, nor more than 1,000 with the school certificate awarded after four successful years of secondary education.[36]

The European population of about 70,000 remained fairly constant; the whites and the 8,000 Asians still controlled the commercial life. The rich Copperbelt was largely in the hands of two great foreign mining combines, the Anglo-American Corporation and the Roan Selection Trust (RST), which were recently nationalized. Like Kenya, most businesses large and small were controlled by non-Africans, despite efforts by Kaunda to nationalize some of the foreign-owned enterprises. Kaunda noted in 1968 that not one business on Cairo Road, Lusaka's main business thoroughfare, was in the hands of a black Zambian. Until there was, this would remain a potentially explosive issue.

Zambia's inadequate media facilities reflected the country's general underdevelopment. There was one independent daily paper, the *Times of Zambia* (circulation 34,000), and a government-owned weekly paper, *Zambia Mail* (circulation 30,000), which changed from weekly to daily publication in 1970. The one radio station in Lusaka with five AM transmitters along the line of rail broadcast to 120,000 receivers and an audience of about 730,000. Two television stations broadcast about four hours daily to about 13,000 receivers and an audience of 91,000. (These totals come from government sources and may be quite high.) There were 61 commercial cinemas with 13,570 indoor seats. In an effort to expand news flow, the government started the Zambia News Agency (ZANA) in 1969.

Almost all of this media system was under the control of the Zambian government, and in 1968 the government was moving to bring the independent daily and Sunday papers under some kind of quasi-public control, if not actual nationalization. This policy was also indicative of the lack of a Zambian tradition in journalism and communications because historically the meager press and broadcasting were monopolized by European expatriates.

EARLY NEWSPAPERS

The press in the Rhodesias was essentially an extension of South African publishing interests. The Argus group followed Cecil Rhodes across the Limpopo River in 1891 when Argus bought a duplicated weekly called the *Mashonaland Herald and Zambesian Times* (produced in Fort Salisbury), brought in printing equipment, and changed its name to the *Rhodesia Herald* in 1892. The paper claimed to have invented the country's name, since the *Rhodesia Herald* began publishing three years before the country was so named by a reluctant Cecil Rhodes.[37] Argus, through its subsidiary, the Rhodesian Printing and Publishing

Company, enjoyed a near-monopoly in the region, and in Rhodesia still owned the *Rhodesia Herald, Sunday Mail, Bulawayo Chronicle, Sunday News,* and *Umtali Post.*

The Argus Company entered Northern Rhodesia in 1951 when it purchased the weekly *Northern News* from Sir Roy Welensky and within two years turned it into a daily newspaper, the first for the Protectorate. Five years later, it had a circulation of 20,000 a day. Published at Ndola, it became the most powerful news medium in the years prior to independence.

Lusaka's first newspaper, the weekly *Central African Post,* was launched as recently as 1947, by Dr. Alexander Scott. In 1957 the Argus group bought the *Post* and by the time it expired in 1962 was published thrice-weekly and circulated about 3,600 copies.

In February 1960 Dr. Scott also had a hand in starting the weekly *African Mail,* with financial help from David Astor, editor of the London *Observer,* who put up half the capital. Richard Hall, who had served in the Northern Rhodesian government as assistant information officer, supervised the editorial operation, and Titus Mukupo, an outstanding African journalist, strengthened the staff as did Kelvin Mlenga, who was later editor. The *African Mail,* renamed the *Central African Mail* in 1962, was openly against the Federation and took a pro-African stance by supporting "one man, one vote," the motto of Kaunda's United National Independence Party. This liberal, pro-African weekly, which also had an edition in Southern Rhodesia for a while, was relatively successful, attaining 21,000 circulation just before independence. Still it was no match for the daily *Northern News.*

After independence, the newspaper picture changed quickly. In 1964 a large brewing company, Heinrich's Syndicate, started a daily, *Zambia Times,* and a weekly, *Zambia News,* on the Copperbelt. But the daily ceased publication after three months and a change of ownership—at a loss of about £200,000.[38]

In November 1964 an important new factor was added to the Zambian newspaper scene. On November 12 Lonrho, formerly the London and Rhodesian Mining and Land Company, which long had had mining, land, ranching, and other interests in all three countries of the Federation, bought control of Heinrich's and with it, the *Zambia Times* and *Zambia News.*[39] Then in December 1964 Argus sold the *Northern News* to Lonrho; that made Lonrho the owner of the only two dailies and Sunday paper in Zambia.[40] Actually President Kaunda was responsible for Lonrho's buying the Argus paper. He had urged Lonrho not to scrap its newspaper interests, and Lonrho's directors responded by buying the *Northern News* for £200,000 and renaming it the *Times of Zambia*. Lonrho also bought both the *Livingstone Mail*, a small weekly which had been publishing continuously at the border city at Victoria Falls since 1906 and a financial monthly, *Business & Commerce*, based in Lusaka. (This is the same Lonrho that was major owner of the *East African Standard* group.)

The *Northern News* emerged in July 1965 as the *Times of Zambia*, with Richard Hall as editor.

In the meantime the *Central African Mail*, which did so well before independence by riding the crest of the pro-nationalist movement, had begun to founder, having lost its *raison d'être*. At about the same time, the Zambian government decided it needed a newspaper of its own, so when the *Mail* found itself in financial difficulties, the government bought it on July 30, 1965. Kelvin Mlenga, possibly the outstanding journalist in Zambia, was editor of the *Mail* from 1962 until the government purchase and then continued until January 1967 when he was replaced by William Dullforce, a Briton.

With the entry of Lonrho as publisher of the daily *Times of Zambia* and Sunday *Zambia News*, and the government's purchase of the *Central African Mail* (renamed the *Zambia Mail* and turned into a biweekly by October 24, 1967), the newspaper situation in Zambia became somewhat stabilized.

It should be emphasized that the development of the press in Northern Rhodesia was essentially a European activity. Africans living in the Protectorate—the future Zambian citizens—had almost no involvement in journalism. The meager beginning of African journalism was the *Bantu Mirror* of Bulawayo in Southern Rhodesia which began in 1936 and circulated across the Zambezi into Northern Rhodesia. However, the *Bantu Mirror* did not employ any reporters nor did the *African Weekly* (1943) for the first ten years. Workers merely clipped "African" news out of the Argus papers and translated the clippings into the vernaculars.[41]

Kelvin Mlenga told me he was offered a job on the *Rhodesia Herald* in Salisbury in 1960 and had he accepted he would have been the first African from Northern Rhodesia employed on a European paper. He chose instead to work for the *Daily News*, a Lord Thomson paper in Salisbury which was later suppressed by the Southern Rhodesian government.

What few Africans did work later for papers in Northern Rhodesia were usually from Southern Rhodesia where educational opportunities were much better. It is important to realize that Zambia began independence in 1964 with an almost complete lack of experienced and competent *Zambian* journalists.

THE PRESS SINCE INDEPENDENCE

In the years since independence the *Times of Zambia,* as the only daily, has been the dominant newspaper voice just as its predecessor, the *Northern News,* was in preindependence days. Soon after Lonrho took control, the *Times* acquired both a new web offset press, which greatly improved its technical appearance, and a first-rate editor, Hall, who knew Zambia well and was a close friend of President Kaunda.

Hall's policy was to make the *Times* a paper in tune with independent Zambia. This did not always prove to be an easy goal to reach; for one thing, many Zambian officials assumed that Lonrho was dictating *Times* policy, whereas in fact Lonrho interfered very little.

With a capitalization of £430,000, the *Times* was printed at Ndola on the Copperbelt where most of its 40,000 to 48,000 readers were located.[42] However, most news was generated in Lusaka over 200 miles away. The *Times,* therefore, maintained a bureau in Lusaka, headed by Political Editor Derek Taylor, who filed stories by telex to Ndola. Each morning two high-speed trucks brought copies of the paper to Lusaka.

The *Times* felt keenly the lack of experienced journalists. Eight expatriate senior journalists were the backbone of the *Times*'s staff. In addition, there were fourteen Zambian reporters and one Zambian news editor. The *Times* had tried to conduct on-the-job training, but personnel shortages and the constant pressures attendant on producing a daily paper made this difficult.

The *Times* admitted that it could cover the line of rail area only from the Copperbelt to Livingstone. Into the eastern and western areas, the *Times* sent neither reporters nor copies of the paper.

Although the *Times* claimed that over half of its readers were Zambians (the reverse was the case with the *Northern News*), the news and feature content seemed oriented more toward Europeans. The *Times* was typographically attractive, well made up, and made excellent use of pictures. It carried a respectable amount of advertising, especially "smalls" or classified advertising.

As Zambia's only independent daily, and owned by a British conglomerate at that, the *Times* was subject to a fair amount of government pressure.

There was no outright censorship of the *Times,* although on occasion Kaunda asked the *Times* not to print stories which might have caused antiwhite riots on the always-volatile Copperbelt.

The *Times* obviously engaged in a good deal of self-censorship. For the first several years, Hall and his editors decided not to carry anything about tribalism—a potentially explosive problem in Zambian politics. The rationale of the expatriates running the *Times* was that they were caretakers of the Zambian press (until it was fully Zambianized) and that as Europeans they did not really understand the causes of tribalism anyway.[43] Such a policy was perhaps sensible for a foreign-owned paper to follow, but it did not prevent the *Times* from being attacked by politicians and others.

During a famous hassle in February 1967 over the unwholesome turkey given as a gift to the wife of Vice-President Reuben Kamanga by an alien butcher, Carlo Ottino, which set off a small riot, the *Times* came under attack for its editorial support of the judiciary and its criticism of the "young fools" and "party thugs" who hurled bricks and stones at the butcher's windows. UNIP Youth Brigade delegations then demonstrated outside the offices of the newspaper. One placard referred personally to Editor Richard Hall: "Hall of Times of Lies is a mental home candidate for calling us stupid. Hall why can't you control your stupid journalists, some of whom are spies."[44]

The paper was accused by the ruling UNIP of "fostering alien elements."

A police guard was provided for the newspaper offices and Hall's home. During the colonial era, Hall was vilified by whites for his ardently pro-African position. In any case, such incidents and harassment may have been one reason that Hall had left Zambia by early 1968, although he was still carried at salary as editor for a time.

As a foreign-owned enterprise, the *Times* has come under increased pressure from the government. As a result of President Kaunda's takeover of some business firms in April 1968, the Lonrho organization apparently stood to lose more than most. In 1967 Lonrho earned pretax profits of £3.3 million, and possibly the company's most profitable investment was Heinrich's Syndicate properties, which included the *Times of Zambia* and the monopoly to brew Chibuku (an African-type beer).[45] Although the government denied it wanted a controlling interest in the newspaper and a share of the profits, the government obviously did want to diminish Lonrho's influence over Zambia's only daily newspaper.

On August 19, 1968, Lonrho announced the appointment of President Kaunda's press secretary, Dunston Kamana, as editor-in-chief of its Zambia newspaper group. Negotiations on a possible government takeover of the group continued.[46]

Zambia Newspapers, Ltd., publishers of the *Times,* also published at Ndola the nation's only Sunday newspaper, the *Zambia News,* with a circulation of about 30,000. With much the same typographical format as the *Times,* the *Zambia News* carried a lot less hard news, relying instead on lightweight features, cheesecake photos, and trivia syndicated from British sources. It contributed little to public enlightenment and was handicapped by the difficulties of distribution on Sunday when the business districts of Zambian cities were deserted.

At its excellent Ndola printing plant, which also did commercial printing, Zambia Newspapers, Ltd., printed *Business & Commerce,* a monthly business magazine; the *Livingstone Mail,* its small tabloid weekly with about 2,000 circulation; and the *Miner,* a house organ for the giant Anglo-American Corporation.

THE "ZAMBIA MAIL"

The *Times*'s principal rival in Zambian journalism was a much different sort of publication. The government-owned *Zambia Mail,* published since October 24, 1967, in Lusaka, sold from 34,000 to 36,000 copies, depending on the weather and the page-one news. Unlike the *Times,* the *Mail* carried little foreign news (it did not even subscribe to Reuters, but bootlegged it from the Zambian Information Service). It concentrated instead on Zambia, particularly news relating to government affairs, the comings and goings of government and party officials, and features about Zambians. The *Mail* made little effort to cover news of interest primarily to expatriates and was attuned to the reading interests of the urban Zambian.

The *Mail* had the obverse of the *Times*'s distribution problem: the paper was published in Lusaka, the principal news center, but most readers were located in the scattered townships of the distant Copperbelt. Two vans carried about 22,000 copies to the Copperbelt daily in an effort to reach the mine employees before they went to work.

As a government paper, the *Mail* was under more pressure to distribute to the remote bush areas despite the lack of potential readers and the difficulties of getting the papers there, and like government papers elsewhere in Africa, the *Zambia Mail* had its difficulties with its employer, or more specifically with certain party and government officials.

Many problems arose because government officials in Zambia, as elsewhere in Africa, needed to be educated as to the difference between news and comment and to realize that a straight news story about one politician or his party was not an effort to "divide the nation." The reading public, at all levels, must learn not to equate news with comment or, especially, advocacy. In any case, the African government newspapers, as with the suburban community paper in America, must constantly seek consensus and avoid issues or news which divide the body politic. It was a difficult path to follow and usually did not result in a very newsworthy journal.

An important supplement to the general press was provided by the five house organs published at varying intervals by the mining Companies on the Copperbelt reaching a combined circulation of 73,500. One of the best was the Anglo-American Corporation's *Miner*, a 24-page offset tabloid, job-printed by the *Times of Zambia* at Ndola. News and features about the employees, black and white, of the giant concern, were professionally handled and well illustrated. One page of news was in the Bemba language.

Another publication, *Roan Antelope*, was published in Luanshya by the Roan Selection Trust. Also an offset tabloid, the *Roan Antelope* carried the same kind of company news and personal features as did the *Miner*. Such publications avoided controversial topics and general news, but they were undoubtedly an important modernizing influence among the newly literate and newly urbanized Africans on the Copperbelt, the real crucible of modernization in Zambia.

ZAMBIAN INFORMATION SERVICE

The only newspapers that went beyond the line of rail were the six provincial papers published by the Zambian Information Service in vernaculars. These had a combined circulation of

70,200. Typical was *Tsopano* in the Nyanja language for readers in the Eastern Province. Most stories were datelined Chipata, a provincial city near the Malawi border and a center for Nyanja speakers. Another was *Imbila,* published at Kasama in the northeastern part of the country every Thursday and sold like the others for two ngwees (about three U.S. cents). The format of all these papers was similar: an offset tabloid of about twelve to sixteen pages, amply illustrated, and full of local government news, as well as the activities and pronouncements of President Kaunda and other national leaders.

These papers were important if only because they reached literate Zambians in rural areas who rarely saw the *Times* or *Zambia Mail,* and they pointed up the important role of the Zambia Information Service in a nation so lacking in communications media.

The ZIS was under the same ministry (Presidential Affairs) as the *Zambia Mail.* The ministry, directly answerable to President Kaunda, also was responsible for the Zambian Broadcasting Services and the Provincial and District governments. The ZIS was divided into two main divisions, Public Relations and Production Services.

Public Relations produced the six provincial newspapers, as well as a national magazine, *Nshila* ("The Way"), and a prestige magazine, *Zambia,* designed for distribution abroad through Zambian embassies.

Production Services included a Film Unit which produced a newsreel, "Focus on Zambia," every two weeks and occasional documentary films. It would have done more if it had had an adequate staff. A Graphic Arts Unit made visual aids and exhibits for fairs and exhibitions at home and abroad.

ZIS recognized the importance of spreading the basic governmental message of "One Zambia, One Nation" to the farthest corners of the Republic, and to do so it used a fleet of 40 campaign vans, each equipped with a public address system and a film projector.

Zambia did not have a national news agency (mainly because of a lack of trained Zambians to staff it) until the Zambia News Agency was formed in early 1969. The new ZANA grew out of ZIS. Before then, the ZIS performed the functions of such an agency to a considerable extent. The only news coverage of rural Zambia was provided by the Provincial Information Officers in each of the eight provinces and thirty-seven district officers who sent in information to the ZIS in Lusaka. The information was then distributed to the news media. This was the only systematic gathering of information from the rural areas.

Compared to information services in Ghana or Nigeria, ZIS was underdeveloped and undermanned. The government was anxious to expand its information services, but the lack of trained and experienced Zambians to staff the ZIS was the main stumbling block to expansion.

RADIO AND TELEVISION

Broadcasting services were controlled by the government within the Ministry for Presidential Affairs. Zambia followed the usual broadcasting pattern in Africa: radio was much more highly developed than television, with more programming reaching a larger and more dispersed audience.

Radio played a key role in this nation where mass communications were such recent phenomena. The first paper *primarily* for Africans, *Mutende,* was not launched by the government until 1936 and did not reach its peak circulation of 18,000 until World War II.[47] An experimental broadcasting service was set up in Northern Rhodesia during the war to carry news of the hostilities and especially to broadcast messages to families of the Northern Rhodesia regiment. The service by 1946 was unique in Africa in that programs were broadcast almost exclusively for Africans and was also heard in Nyasaland and Southern Rhodesia. In 1949 the introduction of the cheap "Saucepan Special" wireless receiver, by Harry Franklin, then Director of Information, brought the service within reach of many more African listeners. The "early days" of radio were engagingly recounted in the book, *Wayaleshi: Radio in Central Africa.*[48] Until that time the great majority of the seventy tribes had little contact with *any* modern means of communication.

Television transmissions started in Northern Rhodesia in 1961 on the Copperbelt at Kitwe as an extension of the services of Rhodesia Television, Ltd., in Southern Rhodesia. The service was financed by advertising and controlled by the company at Salisbury. On independence, responsibility for the services was assumed by a new company, Zambia Television, Ltd., the government nominating a member to sit on the board of directors. An experimental service was introduced at Lusaka in December 1965 in temporary premises of the Zambia Broadcasting Corporation. Finally the new government took over complete control of all television services in 1967 as a division of the Department of Broadcasting. For a while, Kitwe and Lusaka were each telecasting separate programming, but after the two transmitters were joined by a microwave link, the programming became identical. A third transmitter link was added at Kabwe (Broken Hill).

Broadcast financing came from license revenues, commercial advertising, and government subventions. Licenses were renewable each year. A combined sound and television license cost ten kwachas ($14) and a sound license only, two kwachas ($2.80). The ZBS claimed in 1968 that there were 120,000 radios in Zambia and 13,000 television sets.[49]

Radio Zambia ("Lusaka calling") broadcast in English and in seven Zambian languages on two channels, a Home Service and a General Service, from 5:45 a.m. until 11 p.m. on weekdays and from 7 a.m. to midnight on Sundays. The General Service was given over primarily to English-language broadcasts with some programs in Chibemba and Chinyanja at off-peak hours to give wider exposure to these two major languages which were also carried on the Home Service. The Home Service broadcast almost exclusively in Zambian languages, the exceptions being news in English relayed from the General Service.

Despite its strategic location on the border between independent black Africa and white-controlled southern Africa, Radio Zambia had no international broadcasting even though its airwaves were bombarded with broadcasts from Rhodesia Broadcasting Corporation and Radio South Africa. Zambia just did not have the staff to participate in this form of international political communication as yet. However, it may soon have the facilities. In March 1970 the New China News Agency reported that Communist China and Zambia had agreed that the Chinese would construct a broadcasting station in Zambia.

The language pattern on radio, which was related to the population divisions by tribe and area and to the relative language comprehension in urban and rural areas, in hourly terms for each week, is shown in Table 10.1.

All news bulletins for both radio and television were prepared in the Lusaka studios. More than twenty news and "newsreel" broadcasts were carried daily on both radio services in English and the seven major Zambian languages. A staff of nine journalists prepared the major English bulletins broadcast on the General Service at 7 a.m., 1:15 p.m., and 8 p.m., and the shorter bulletins at 6 a.m., 8 a.m., 6 p.m., 10 p.m., and 11 p.m.

For the Home Service, the English-language bulletins were

TABLE 10.1: Languages Used on Radio Zambia

Language	General	Home	Total Hours for Week
English	96	3	99
Chinyanja	12	20	32
Chibemba	12	20	32
Chitonga	...	22	22
Silozi	...	22	22
Kikaonde	...	11	11
Luvale	...	11	11
Lunda	...	11	11
	120	120	240

rewritten and translated into the seven main vernaculars and broadcast three times daily—early morning, noon, and evening in each language.

Local observers agreed that the quality of news on Radio Zambia was very low. (I found it the least professional of any country included in this study.) The news bulletins were poorly edited and badly read. (The announcers usually sounded as though they had not previously seen their scripts.) Major world, and even major Zambian, stories went unreported, and tendentious or openly propagandistic stories, lacking the most obvious kinds of substantiation or even attribution, often made up at least half of the news broadcasts.[50]

Most newscasts began with the words, "President Kaunda today. . . ." This practice had a certain logic—the Zambian people should know what their leaders were doing and saying—but the practice was overdone, very possibly to the embarrassment of President Kaunda himself.

Persons interviewed in Lusaka agreed that the problem was basically one of personnel. Until better educated and more sophisticated journalists were preparing the newscasts on Radio Lusaka, there was little reason to expect improvement.

The news on television was of about the same quality but less extensive: there was just one 10-minute bulletin nightly.

For local film coverage there were two cameramen in Lusaka and two more at Kitwe, whose main function seemed to be to follow the President and important government officials around. Television news was very short on skilled writers, subeditors, and reporters. Until they were available, news programs, much less documentaries and special reports, would be circumscribed on television.

The main concentration of viewers was on the Copperbelt, with Lusaka and Kabwe expected to provide an increasing number of viewers. However the high costs of receiving sets and the difficulties of transmitting beyond the line of rail would undoubtedly restrict television expansion for some years to come.

Training is the overwhelming need of the news media as it is in other sectors of modern life in Zambia. A 1964 UNESCO study made the point that "there is a serious shortage of trained African personnel in every field in which communication skills are required."[51] That need is still great and will continue for some time to come. The government and educational leaders of Zambia, however, are well aware of the problem and are working to eliminate it.

In some ways the lack of Zambians with communications skills was reflective of the general deficiencies in education in the young nation. But it was also indicative of the lack of a Zambian tradition in journalism and communications because historically the press and broadcasting were monopolized by expatriates. As recently as 1964, Radio Zambia's technical staff consisted of twenty-one Europeans, but only one trained and nine trainee African technicians.

In mass communications, as in other sectors of modern life, the young Republic of Zambia started well behind the other nations included in this study. The problems everywhere were similar, but Zambia had further to go and fewer modern persons to take it there. But if the mineral riches of Zambia could be effectively harnessed to the great task of modernization, Zambia had the possibility, indeed the probability, of catching up with the other new black nations.

In retrospect, one of the great disservices of the settler newspapers and broadcasting in Kenya and Northern Rhodesia was that they did not involve many Africans as either journalists or members of the audience. The new one-party governments of Kenya and Zambia were finding it no easy task to refashion these instruments of communication to more effectively serve the new African governments.

In both nations there was serious question whether the libertarian tendencies in their news media could somehow ride out the contemporary political storms and take root in the one-party governments. If they can, then something new in mass communication will have come out of Africa.

11

||||||||||||||||||||||||||||||||||||||||||||||||||||||||||||||||||

AN IMPORTANT EXCEPTION:
SOUTH AFRICA

THE REPUBLIC OF SOUTH AFRICA presents the exceptional situation on the continent in political control as well as news communications. The prototype of the European or settler press developed
in South Africa, and unlike its counterparts in French and East
Africa, it prospered and became the entrenched spokesman for the
white minority controlling that troubled land.

South Africa had the finest and most pervasive news media in
Africa, but it was essentially a European system of communication.

South Africa was the white man's redoubt on the continent
where 3.6 million "Europeans" (both English- and Afrikaans-
speaking whites) completely controlled the political and economic
destinies of some 13 million black Africans, 1,900,000 "Coloureds"
(admixture of East Asians, Europeans, and Hottentots), and 74,000
Asians.

In that complex multiracial nation of 19 million, a dramatic
struggle was being played out—a struggle that the rest of the
world, both white and colored, was watching with growing interest and apprehension. The over 15 million non-Europeans were
still in actuality colonial subjects of the white minority and were
largely debarred by custom and law from playing a part in the
building of the nation to which their abilities and ambitions entitled them. They were outsiders in their own land. The Africans
or "Bantus" could not vote in any national election, work outside
their "reserves" without a permit, remain in the big cities for
more than seventy-two hours without permission, join organized
labor unions or go on strike, attend a white man's theater, sit on

a white man's bench in a park, ride on a white man's bus, or even buy a postage stamp from the same post office window.

South Africa's "solution" to multiracial problems was known by the familiar and noxious term "apartheid," or its euphemism, "separate development." The development of South Africa's mass communications had been partly shaped by the multiracial aspects of South African life.

And the ever-increasing restrictions on political activity and freedom of expression directly affected the news media. Yet despite the growing authoritarianism, the white man's freedom of the press, while increasingly hobbled, still showed signs of life.

Historian Leo Marquard summarized South Africa's plight very well: "Whether South Africa will sink into oblivion, a classic example of a multi-racial society that failed, or become a force for the maintenance of civilized standards and culture on the continent of Africa, depends primarily on whether her white rulers can associate their non-white subjects in a national state that is representative of all its inhabitants."[1]

The prospects were not very encouraging in that beautiful, bountiful, but troubled land. The mass media, which could help bridge the differences, only tended to emphasize the discontinuities.

The linguistic cleavages of South Africa complicated the communications problems. Among the 3.6 million whites, about 37.3 percent had English and 58 percent had Afrikaans as their mother tongues. Afrikaans and English were also widely used by the nonwhite groups, especially in urban areas.

Among the Africans, the two major first languages were Xhosa and Zulu, each having about 3 million speakers. This meant that among the total population more spoke each of these two tongues than either English or Afrikaans. Other major languages were South Sotho, Tswana, Sepedi, Shangaan, Swazi, Ndebele, and Venda.[2]

It should be emphasized that the mass media system of South Africa was essentially a European system which in conception, economics, and political theory had much more in common with that of England or Western Europe than with other countries in black Africa. The white man owned and controlled almost all mass communications, which were designed primarily to serve European needs and interests. The Africans, Coloureds, and Asians were much poorer served, and had just a few publications designed especially for them, and these were white-owned and managed. They had access to *some* of the European media, but were barred from others, especially movies and books.

No nation in Africa approached South Africa in the range and scope of mass communications resources. For example, there were some 600 printing, publishing, and allied companies, concentrated mainly in Johannesburg, Durban, and Cape Town.

JOHANNESBURG IS MEDIA CENTER

The hub of mass communications in South Africa was Johannesburg—that bustling metropolis that was simultaneously the largest "European" city in Africa as well as possibly the largest "African" city. The government itself would not acknowledge how many hundreds of thousands of Africans were packed into Soweto and the other townships ringing the city. The townships were a great melting pot for the modernization of tribal Africans with all the attendant social problems of crime, alienation, family disintegration, etc., that go with urbanization. In Johannesburg were located the major newspapers, the South African Broadcasting Corporation, the South African Press Association, and other facilities. About 500 newspapers, periodicals, and journals of all kinds were published throughout the Republic; the number of employees in the industry exceeded 22,000.

Of the twenty-one daily newspapers, fifteen were printed in English and six in Afrikaans. Five Sunday newspapers were published in Johannesburg and one in Durban. The press of South Africa—at least, the English-language part of it—was the finest to be found on the continent. No papers elsewhere could compare with the three great Johannesburg papers—the *Rand Daily Mail,* the *Star,* and the *Sunday Times.* But to reiterate, these were European papers, the products of the affluent, industrialized white segment of society and were not those of a "developing" nation.

About 130 newspapers were published weekly or two or three times weekly. The majority were published in either of the two official languages—only a handful were in Xhosa, Zulu, or Gujerati. The estimated circulation of English-language newspapers and periodicals was about 2,200,000 against 1,700,000 of Afrikaans publications, even though English was the home language of only about 37 percent of the whites.

Despite apartheid, South Africa's economic boom was bringing about a measure of economic integration as nonwhites provided more and more of the manpower needed to run the economy. As a result of their increasing purchasing power and literacy, the number and circulation of newspapers and journals catering to the "black bourgeoisie" rose steadily. More than thirty were published in 1967 for nonwhites, including the *World* of Johannesburg, fourth in circulation of *any* daily, and the *Post*, a multi-edition Sunday paper with nationwide circulation.

In broadcasting as well, South Africa led the continent. The government-controlled South African Broadcasting Corporation (SABC) produced fourteen different services or programs: six for Europeans, seven for Africans, and one external. There were more than three million radio receivers and the audience was estimated at over ten million. Nigeria had a larger total audience, but SABC came closer to saturation of its potential audience. In 1969 the government continued to resist considerable public pressure for a general television service. However, there were over 200 licenses issued for closed-circuit television. Denied the doubtful benefits of television, South Africans went to the movies at the rate of about one million per week. In 1967, 35mm theaters numbered 754 and 16mm theaters 2,750, with a total seating capacity of 400,000.[3]

HOW SOUTH AFRICA DIFFERS

Not only did it have more of everything, but South Africa's news media differed significantly from those of most other African nations:

● Daily newspapers were firmly based in private enterprise and were often quite profitable business ventures. This gave them an economic independence—a place in the business community—and a strong base from which to oppose government policies. For the white minority, the press was a true "mass medium" and more influential than radio.

● There was no official or government-owned newspaper in South Africa. However, boards of directors of the Afrikaans papers were sprinkled with cabinet ministers, and the Afrikaans press, to a paper, was pro-government. The English press, in varying degrees, was in opposition to the ruling Nationalist party.

● There was no public television service.

● There was no government news agency. The only news

agency, South African Press Association (SAPA), was a cooperative owned by the daily and weekly papers much as the Associated Press was owned in the United States.

● The South African press enjoyed the protection of law, and despite much recent legislation closing off important areas of news access, the press in South Africa was still the freest in all of Africa, and the English-language press, at least, was the most outspoken and critical of government leaders and policies. (This freedom of expression was not enjoyed by nonwhites nor by persons not owning newspapers.)

● Concomitantly, there was a more thorough and pervasive border censorship of incoming books, magazines, and motion pictures than anywhere else in Africa.

These characteristics helped make South Africa the exception. Yet, its news media system also shared some similarities with most others in Africa:

● Linguistic cleavages created many communication discontinuities and necessitated the use of numerous languages in the media, thus reducing communication effectiveness. Important segments of the population, especially the Africans on rural or tribal reserves, were not effectively reached by mass media.

● The powerful medium of radio was under government control and used to support and implement government policies.

● The independent press was under increasing pressures from government officials who, as elsewhere in Africa, tended to equate criticism with disloyalty and dissent with sedition, or at least as a threat to national security.

● The government recognized the importance of propaganda and political communication. The South African Information Service was a highly sophisticated and well-financed arm of government policy, as was the "Voice of South Africa," the powerful external radio station.

HISTORY OF THE PRESS

The burden of history hangs heavily over all aspects of life in South Africa and the modern news media have evolved out of the interplay, and conflict between ethnic groups. The presence of Dutch-descended Boers and British meant that the European press became linguistically bifurcated—into Afrikaans and English-language publications. Another communications chasm developed between the Europeans and "non-Europeans"—the catch-all phrase for the South African majority of black Africans, Coloureds, and Asians. These economically deprived and politically submerged peoples have long had publications of their own, but they have always been circumscribed and restricted by the dominant white minority.

The press was started in Cape Town, locale of the original Dutch settlement in 1652, and in time penetrated northward so that the newspapers today in Rhodesia and Zambia still show South African influences. Although the Dutch settlers arrived first, the English speakers have the longest press tradition—the highly political Afrikaans papers did not emerge fully until the twentieth century.

The *Cape Town Gazette and African Advertiser,* a bilingual (English and Dutch) publication, was started in August 1800 and may have been the first paper on the African continent south of Egypt.

A more interesting historical question is why did it take the Cape Colony so long to establish its first newspaper? After all, the settlement had been there for 158 years before the *Gazette* first appeared, and in the American colonies Benjamin Harris's *Publick Occurrences* was published in Boston in 1690, some 110 years before the Cape Town *Gazette.*[4]

The first of many conflicts between press and government occurred in 1824 when the *South African Commercial Advertiser* first appeared in the Cape under the editorship of James Fairbairn and Thomas Pringle. After the paper criticized the living conditions of British settlers brought to the Eastern Cape in 1820, the government of Governor Lord Charles Somerset suppressed it. The owner, British-born printer George Grieg, waged a long battle both in London and in South Africa against this government repression. His cause was finally won on April 30, 1828, when a new colonial secretary sanctioned a press law for the Cape based on English law. Publishers were to deposit £300 plus £300 in guaranties with the government and they were then free to publish, subject only to defamation law. South Africa's tradition of freedom of the press dates from this law.

Other papers soon appeared elsewhere. Partly in response to attacks from the *Advertiser,* the Dutch-speaking community in Eastern Cape by 1830 had a paper of its own, *De Zuid-Afrikaan,* which spoke for the proponents of slavery. This paper and its successor, *Ons Land,* became the forerunners of what Afrikaners consider to be the "true South African national ideal." The *Friend of the Sovereignty*, launched in Grahamstown in 1850, moved to Bloemfontein two years later, and as the *Friend*, it continues to publish today.

The first paper printed in Afrikaans, as distinct from Dutch, was *Di Patriot*, launched in 1875 as the spokesman for the Society of True Afrikaners "to stand up for our language, our nation, and our people."[5]

Two significant press developments occurred in urbane Cape Town where the *Cape Argus* began in 1857 and the *Cape Times* in 1876. In these two pioneer papers, the two great contemporary English-language newspaper chains, Argus and South African Associated Newspapers (SAAN), had their beginnings.

In style, professionalism, businesslike competence, and worldly orientation, these papers bore heavily the imprint of British journalism. The English-language papers' long marriage of convenience with mining financial interests probably began in 1881 when Cecil Rhodes put up the money so the *Argus* editor, Francis Dormer, could buy control of the young paper from Saul Solomon, a printer and member of the Cape Parliament. By 1880 the *Argus* was a daily and was receiving news from Reuters over the recently laid cable from Europe. The front page was usually devoted to overseas news.

With the discovery of gold in the Transvaal in 1886, the *Argus* opened a branch in the frontier mining camp of Johannesburg. By 1889 the *Argus* acquired the *Star*, which was founded in Grahamstown and transported by ox-wagon, press and all, to Johannesburg in 1887. After purchase of the *Star*, the Argus Printing and Publishing Company was formed, and by 1891 many of the great names of gold mining, including Solly Joel and Barney Barnato as well as Rhodes, were Argus shareholders. The *Star* soon went daily, and in 1893 introduced rotary printing and linotype setting. Its large capital resources as well as pooled journalistic and technical facilities gave Argus a big advantage over rivals.

Another significant date in South African journalism was 1902, just after the Boer War, when the *Rand Daily Mail*, destined to become a keen rival of the *Star* and in time a lonely voice of white liberal conscience, was founded. Its first editor was Edgar Wallace, the prolific popular novelist, who had served as a British officer in the Boer War. The *Sunday Times*, founded in 1906, has always held a unique position in South African journalism; for years it returned a profit of 7,000 percent to stockholders on the original investment. Yet all production was hired from the *Rand Daily Mail,* which benefited from the rental charges.[6]

Between the two, the *Rand Daily Mail* and the *Sunday Times,* numerous journalistic innovations such as imaginative makeup, ample illustrations and photographs, and breezy features were introduced into South Africa. In time, the *Cape Times, Rand Daily Mail, Natal Mercury* (begun in 1850), and the *Sunday Times* cooperated in the exchange of materials and were joined later by the *Eastern Province Herald* and the *Evening Post* of Port Elizabeth to form the South African Associated Newspapers. The SAAN provided a counterpoise to the dominant Argus group, which in 1903 had acquired interest in the Central News Agency, which eventually monopolized newspaper distribution in South Africa. Other papers brought into the Argus fold were the *Friend* in 1917, the *Natal Advertiser* in 1918 (which later became the *Natal Daily News*), the *Diamond Fields Advertiser* of Kimberley in 1922, and the *Pretoria News* in 1930.

AFRIKAANS PRESS

Unlike these British-influenced papers which developed as commercial and professional publications, well-financed by mining interests, the Afrikaans press was from its beginnings a partisan instrument, designed to give expression to the growing political aspirations of the Afrikaners. These were the descendants of the original Dutch settlers, who, though defeated by the British in the Boer War, finally wrested clear political power from the English speakers in 1948 when the National party took control of South Africa—a control maintained to this day. As with the indigenous agitational press of British West Africa, journalism became for the Afrikaners a means to an end—political influence. In 1915 *Die Burger* was established in Cape Town under the editorship of Dr. D. F. Malan who was to become prime minister in 1948. This was followed closely by *Die Volksblad,* started the same year in Bloemfontein and later taken over by *Die Burger.* Also in 1915 *Ons Vaderland* (later to become *Die Vaderland*) appeared in Pretoria, the heartland of Afrikanerdom. In 1937 *Die Transvaler* started in Johannesburg under the editorship of yet another future prime minister, Dr. Henrik F. Verwoerd.

Until recently the Afrikaans papers were poorly financed, lower in technical quality than the English papers, and much smaller in circulation. They ignored world news, concentrating on South African events. But political partisanship rather than news was their mission and Afrikaner cabinet ministers, present, past, and future, have always been well represented on the boards of directors of the Afrikaans papers.

The Afrikaans press was a key factor in the resurgence of Afrikaner nationalism in the 1930s, and some say the National party would never have gained power in 1948 if it had not been for the close and continued support of the Afrikaans papers. The Afrikaners, traditionally rural and agrarian, have long been suspicious of and annoyed by the more sophisticated and urbane English press. They have clung to their own papers which voice Afrikaner nationalism and culture and have, with minor deviations, provided a solid front of Nationalist party support.

South Africa's sizable Indian community, concentrated in the Natal area, has enjoyed a long press tradition. In 1906 Mahatma Gandhi founded the *Indian Opinion,* a paper in English and Gujerati which defended the interests of the Indian traders and espoused his ideas on passive resistance. After Gandhi returned to India the paper was edited by his son, Manilal, and after his death in 1958 it was published by Manilal's widow.[7]

The beginnings of a native African press in South Africa came from the mission papers, often in vernaculars. The *Isigidimi SamaXosa* (the *Xhosa Express*) was sponsored by the Lovedale Mission in the Transkei and edited by John Tengu Jabavu until he was dismissed for press criticism of members of the Cape Province Parliament.[8] In 1884 Jabavu started his own paper, *Imvo Zabantsundu (Native Opinion),* printed in both English and Xhosa, which urged African political and educational advance. Although its control and purposes have long since changed, the paper has persisted. *Um Afrika* was published by a Catholic mission, beginning in 1888.

Of the five major African newspapers in 1914, only two of them, *Imvo* and *Ilanga Lase Natal* (the *Natal Sun*) (begun in 1906 by a Methodist minister, Dr. John L. Dube), lasted until the 1960s. The others were *Izwi la Bantu,* established by the Rev. Walter Rubusana, a founder of the African National Congress, in opposition to *Imvo; Ikwezi le Afrika,* begun in 1902 by the Church of England; and *Abuntu Batho,* organ of the African National Congress. *Abuntu*'s first editor was Dr. Pixley Isaka ka Seme, and under him the paper played a leading role in the ANC's first political campaign—against the Lands Acts of 1913 depriving Africans of land rights outside the reserves and against the proposal to extend the pass system to women. The paper lasted until 1932 after which the ANC never again published a paper of its own.[9]

The political and economic repression of the nonwhite majority in South Africa has stifled and stultified an indigenous press speaking for the growing black bourgeoisie. An increasingly repressive government has systematically suppressed, censored, and harassed the nonwhite press over the years so that by the 1960s only one newspaper not owned by Europeans was catering to the non-European majority—the *Leader,* an Indian-owned paper in Durban.

Without the economic power of the large English papers or any effective political rights, the nonwhite press that had flowered in the early twentieth century enjoyed none of the freedom which the European press so highly prized.

Two periodicals of importance to the non-Europeans have been the two monthly illustrated magazines, *Drum* and *Zonk,* both published in Johannesburg for African readers but edited and owned by Europeans. In their heyday in the 1950s, both carried a high proportion of sporting and social news and specialized in adapting European advertising techniques to a fast-growing market of African consumers. *Drum* did much to expose scandals in the Native Administration without committing itself to an active political line—something the government would never have permitted. In 1954 *Drum*'s circulation was said to be 75,000 in the Union and 12,000 in West Africa.[10] Two distinguished former editors, Anthony Sampson and Tom Hopkinson, have each written of their careers with *Drum.*[11]

The history of the press in South Africa faithfully mirrors harsh political realities. Given the proper conditions of political and economic equality, the nonwhite press might have become the most vigorous and effective of any indigenous press system on the continent. But this the white minority government did not permit; hence, the story of the South African press has been essentially one of a highly evolved European settler press, divided linguistically into two prosperous but mutually antagonistic groups. Since the Afrikaners have monopolized political power since 1948, their papers have enjoyed great influence among the Afrikaner political elite. The English papers, though still the finest and most prosperous in Africa, have experienced decreasing political influence and have seen their independence and press freedom progressively curtailed.

THE PRESS TODAY

Because of its past, the newspaper press of South Africa became divided into three distinct groups: the English-language press, the Afrikaans press, and the non-European press. The cleavages were such that it had been indeed a case of different voices speaking different messages to different audiences. There was a small overlap audience and there were signs that the overlap was growing, at least as the English and Afrikaner whites tended to become more bilingual and to move together politically into a more cohesive white society. The great bulk of the news press did not address itself to the interests or needs of the nonwhite majority.

In 1968 there were fifteen English-language dailies, with an aggregate circulation of about 700,000 copies a day, compared with six Afrikaans dailies (including the new *Hoofstad* in Pretoria), selling about 170,000 copies daily. The *World* was the only daily edited specifically for African readers.

The major dailies and their circulations as of January 1968 were Johannesburg: the *Star* (English), 179,000; *Rand Daily Mail* (English), 111,000; *Die Vaderland* (Afrikaans), 56,000; *Die Transvaler* (Afrikaans), 37,000; *World* (English), 82,000; *Daily Bulletin*, 20,000; Cape Town: the *Argus* (English), 103,000; *Cape Times* (English), 65,000; *Die Burger* (Afrikaans), 52,000; Durban: *Natal Daily News* (English), 82,000; *Natal Mercury* (English), 65,000; Pietermaritzburg: *Natal Witness* (English), 15,000; Port Elizabeth: *Eastern Province Herald* (English), 28,-000; *Evening Post* (English), 27,000; *Die Oosterlig* (Afrikaans), N.A.; Pretoria: *Pretoria News* (English), 18,000; *Hoofstad* (Afrikaans), N.A.; East London: *Daily Dispatch* (English), 23,000; Bloemfontein: *Die Volksblad* (Afrikaans), 32,000; the *Friend* (English), 9,500; Kimberley: *Diamond Fields Advertiser* (English), 7,000.[12]

There were six Sunday papers in South Africa and while all but one, the *Sunday Tribune* of Durban, were published in Johannesburg, all were distributed nationally: *Sunday Times* (English), 396,000; *Post* (English for nonwhites), 224,000; *Dagbreek en Sondagnuus* (Afrikaans), 212,000; *Die Beeld* (Afrikaans), 196,000; *Sunday Express* (English), 182,000; and *Sunday Tribune* (English), 132,000.

Group or chain ownership has long been a prime characteristic of the South African press. The largest was the Argus Printing and Publishing Company, which directly or indirectly through subsidiaries, controlled the *Star,* the *Cape Argus,* the *Natal Daily News,* the *Diamond Fields Advertiser,* the *Friend,* the *Pretoria News,* and the *World.* In addition, it owned such leading periodicals as *Personality* (circulation 116,968), *Femina* (circulation 92,173), and the *Farmer's Weekly,* as well as others.

Argus moved into the magazine publishing field in a big way in March 1968, when its wholly owned subsidiary, Friend Newspapers, merged with Republican Publications, a Durban magazine publishing company. Republican was owner of the *Star* group of magazines including *Scope,* an English-language general magazine of 51,923 circulation, *Star,* a general magazine in Afrikaans with 99,128 readers, *Keur, See,* and a number of photo-story magazines which were popular in South Africa. Argus was owned by mining financial interests, particularly Central Mining and Rand Mines, two of the biggest gold mining operations on the Rand. In 1963, of the eight directors of the company, four were also directors of major mining companies.[13]

All Argus papers were essentially branches; they shared offices abroad and each was connected to the others by telex. The group claimed that "every day more than 500,000 copies of Argus's nine daily newspapers (including two in Rhodesia) are read."[14] This gave Argus a very significant fraction—almost one-seventh— of all daily newspaper circulation on the continent.

Second largest combine, but well behind Argus, was the South African Associated Newspapers, Ltd. (SAAN), which controlled the *Rand Daily Mail,* the *Sunday Express,* the *Sunday Times, Eastern Province Herald,* and the *Evening Post.* In addition, these and other English-language morning papers (the Argus papers were mainly afternoon papers) were grouped into a loose association for purposes of sharing some staff and material, and known as the South African Morning Newspapers.

Among the Afrikaans press, Nasionale Koerante Bpk., a subsidiary of Nasionale Pers Bpk., owned *Die Burger, Die Volksblad, Die Oosterlig,* and *Die Beeld.* Another subsidiary, Nasionale Tydskrifte, owned several important magazines, including *Die Huisgenoot* (circulation 155,443), *Die Landbouweekblad, Die Jongspan, Sarie Marais* (circulation 137,038), and *Fair Lady* (circulation 99,345).

The Afrikaanse Pers published the *Dagbreek, Die Vaderland,* and owned half of the English-language *Financial Gazette.* In addition it had joined with Voortrekkerspers, publishers of *Die Transvaler,* to launch in 1968 an Afrikaans daily in Pretoria, *Hoofstad* ("Capital City").

During one period, Argus and SAAN were often accused by their Nationalist party critics of monopolizing the press; it was a charge with some validity. However, after the later upsurge of the Afrikaans press, which had been growing both in circulation and advertising faster than the English press, the talk died down.

The language barrier between the English and Afrikaans papers was also a political barrier. While the English-language press, to a greater or lesser extent, was "in opposition" to the Nationalist party, all the Afrikaans papers not only supported the Nationalists, but have been "an instrument of nationalism, enhancing the cohesiveness of the Afrikaner community and largely insulating its readers from the liberal, cosmopolitan and antigovernment attitudes to be found in the English press. To a degree hardly equaled by the press in any other Western country, all five (now six) Afrikaans daily newspapers, beginning with the publication of *Die Burger* in Cape Town in 1915, were closely allied to political party leadership."[15] Although efforts had been made, there was no successful English-language newspaper supporting the Nationalists nor any Afrikaans-language newspapers "in opposition."

AFRICA'S LARGEST NEWSPAPER

The *Star* of Johannesburg, leading paper in the Argus group, was the largest daily newspaper on the continent. It had the largest circulation (179,000 copies daily in early 1968), carried the most news, and had the greatest advertising linage. Its editorial staff of fifty-four reporters and fifteen subeditors, plus various specialists for sports, women's news, finance, etc., put out its daily product in a large, modern plant at 47 Sauer Street that would have done justice to any prosperous American newspaper.

The Argus papers' unusually good coverage of sub-Saharan Africa was largely due to its Argus Africa News Service which was started to give its papers news of Africa it could vouch for. Headquartered in Johannesburg and with a suboffice in Salisbury, the Africa News Service maintained full-time staffers in Salisbury, Lusaka, Blantyre, Nairobi, and Dar es Salaam, and sent in reporters wherever news was breaking elsewhere. The news service also maintained several stringers in other African capitals.

In addition, the Argus papers maintained and shared offices in London, New York, and Washington. These overseas news sources enabled the *Star* to publish comprehensive foreign news and earned it a reputation as the New York *Times* of South Africa. However, the sharing of news and correspondents, both foreign and domestic, meant that the several Argus afternoon papers—the *Star, Cape Argus, Natal Daily News,* the *Friend,* and *Diamond Fields Advertiser*—often looked very much alike on any given news day.

The *Star* has consistently played the role of an Opposition paper since the Nationalist party came to power in 1948. Its "leaders" (editorials) have been consistently liberal and anti-apartheid. However this did not usually carry over to its news columns; it tended to present news the way the average English-speaking South African would like it. And the average English speaker was going along more and more with Nationalist policies, as the parliamentary elections show, and did not like to be reminded too frequently of the unpleasant political and social realities of apartheid.

The *Star*'s morning competition, the *Rand Daily Mail,* much more consistently opposed the Nationalist party both in editorials and news columns. More than any other South African paper, the *Mail* was the voice of liberal dissent, and this was due in large part to its famous editor, Laurence Gandar. About 8,000 copies were sold directly in the African townships of Johannesburg, and an indeterminate number of copies were sold to nonwhites in street sales. To some extent the *Mail* did bridge the racial barrier that apartheid had widened. It did concern itself with the mounting social and economic problems of the Africans, and its stronger nonracial, antigovernment position may have been one reason its circulation lagged behind that of the *Star.*

For its persistent fight against South Africa's racial policies, the *Rand Daily Mail* received in 1966 the World Press Achievement Award of the American Newspaper Publishers Association.

While the paper was being the most effective white voice against apartheid, its circulation dropped from 125,000 in 1961 to 111,000 in 1968. As a result, a majority of SAAN board members attempted to ease out Gandar, reasoning that a less liberal outlook would improve business. Gandar won a compromise; he was elevated from editor to editor-in-chief, a position which permitted him to retain a free editorial voice, but he relinquished active direction of the newspaper to a subordinate chosen by himself, Raymond Louw. In 1968 Gandar's editorials were as outspoken as ever. As he put it, "We are helping to keep alive the small but vitally important liberal spirit among the whites—helping them to feel they're still in the fight." There was some question as to how long the fight could go on. Asked how many members of the SAAN board had called to congratulate him on the ANPA award, he smiled and replied, "Only one—an alternate."[16]

THE SUCCESSFUL "SUNDAY TIMES"

The *Mail's* stablemate, the *Sunday Times,* located in the same new building in Johannesburg, shared some of its antigovernment liberalism.

Sunday papers were the only national papers in South Africa, and the *Sunday Times,* with 396,000 circulation in 1968, was the most successful by far. The *Sunday Times* was available on the morning of publication from Seapoint in Cape Town to Salisbury, Rhodesia. The paper was published in Johannesburg, but mats were flown to Cape Town and Durban where the paper was rolled on the presses of the *Cape Times* and *Natal Mercury,* respectively, which were idle on Saturdays.

The *Sunday Times* was a peculiarly South African institution which grew up with the country and had the unusual distinction of having a 60–40 split between English and Afrikaans readers. Its nonwhite readership is only about 3 to 5 percent. "Our enemies say it's about 25 percent, but we only wish it were that high," said Joel Mervis, the editor.[17]

The *Sunday Times* shared the overseas services of the other SAAN papers but could not share domestic sources because of its different news cycle and because it competed with those papers. In editorial content the *Sunday Times* was a strange melange of lurid Sunday-supplement sensationalism and crime news, a few stories aimed at Afrikaans readers, and a solid budget of thoughtful intellectual fare for the discriminating reader.

The *Sunday Times,* a thoroughly successful publication, bulging with advertisements, like the *Rand Daily Mail,* has gone through a number of legal hassles with the government, particularly over stories relating to conditions in the prisons.

The *Sunday Times,* the *Rand Daily Mail,* and a few other English papers were much more liberal than most of their reading public, reminding it of certain unpleasant realities in prosperous, affluent South Africa. This was a most important (if dwindling) press function in South Africa, since the government dominated the Afrikaans press; censored all incoming books, magazines, and movies; and controlled the news and commentaries on Radio South Africa.

Prime Minister B. J. Vorster once told Mervis at a social gathering, "You (the English-language press) have no political power." Mervis replied, "But you, Mr. Vorster, have no literary power."[18] And, in the long run, the power of the pen may be more important—if it survives.

Die Burger of Cape Town was generally considered the best and relatively most liberal of the Afrikaans papers—because it was more sophisticated and intelligently edited—and was possibly the most influential. The Afrikaans press had considerable political influence in that the Nationalist politicians paid close attention to what these papers advocated. On the other hand, the ruling Nationalists generally showed distrust and even animosity for the opposition English-language papers.[19]

In the late 1960s a phenomenon new to Afrikaans journalism was observed: the papers began to criticize one another quite vigorously on occasion. Between the two Sunday papers, *Die Beeld* and *Dagbreek,* for instance, there was no love lost at all. There were political differences between the two, but basically it was an economic fight, a battle for circulation with no holds barred. The argument became so intense in 1967 that the Prime Minister felt constrained to resign as chairman of the *Dagbreek* group lest he become too closely identified with one side, either ideologically or economically.[20]

The recent ideological splits, or at least disagreements, between the "verkramptes" (the hard-line extreme right wingers) and the "verligtes" (the more liberal wing, comparatively speaking, of the Nationalist party) were often aired in the press as in the exchanges between *Die Beeld,* a "verligte" mouthpiece, and *Dagbreek,* which inclined toward the "verkramptes."

In Johannesburg *Die Vaderland* was a reactionary "verkramptes" paper, which in its editorials was often anti-British, anti-United States, and antisemitic. By comparison, *Die Transvaler,* by supporting more moderate measures, was able to consider itself comparatively enlightened if not "liberal."

The English-language papers enjoyed playing up these Afrikaans press feuds, and there was some wishful thinking that they presaged a fundamental split within the Nationalist party. Other observers disagreed, convinced that on any fundamental issue, such as a direct challenge to apartheid policy, the Nationalist party—and its press—would always present a solid front to its opposition. *Die Burger* and *Die Vaderland* were generally considered the two leading Afrikaans papers and were not far apart in circulation.

But *Die Transvaler* was in many ways more typical of the

Afrikaner press. This morning Johannesburg paper had a circulation of only 37,000 and most of that was outside Johannesburg (still mainly an English-speaking city) in the small towns and "dorps" along the Witswatersrand or "Reef" where many Afrikaners lived. Designated as the "Official Newspaper of the National Party," it carried notices of party meetings, official announcements, promotions, etc., but stayed out of the "verkramptes-verligtes" feuds. Several cabinet ministers were on the board of directors of this paper started by Dr. Henrik Verwoerd. Its news editor, Hennie Kotze, said: "We compete with the *Rand Daily Mail* for hard news in the morning and with *Die Vaderland* for Afrikaans cultural news in the afternoon." Bilingual white South Africans were tending more and more to read one of each type of paper daily.[21]

The Afrikaans journalists, of course, had important differences of opinion with their English counterparts. Most, for instance, thought that the various laws restricting political activity and news access were quite necessary and did not hamper the press.[22] However, at the associational and business levels, the Afrikaans and English editors and publishers cooperated quite effectively in both the South African Press Association and the Newspaper Publishers Union.

NEWSPAPERS FOR AFRICANS

For black Africans, the press—in whatever language—has contributed to the overriding of tribal differences and the promotion of Westernization. Newspapers intended mainly for Africans have long been published in the vernaculars or in English or in both. Although there were still some small vernacular newspapers, English had become the prevailing medium in the so-called Bantu press. As Africans became increasingly involved in the modern economy, they produced more newspaper readers able to buy products advertised in newspapers. Some Africans were reading the *Star* and *Rand Daily Mail,* and many more were reading their "own" publications, the *World* on weekdays and the *Post* on Sundays, two of the fastest growing papers in South Africa and two highly fascinating examples of journalism.

The masthead of the *World,* a sensational tabloid edited for the million or so Africans concentrated in the townships on the edge of Johannesburg, said it is "Our Own, Our Only Newspaper." It was not quite that, but it tried to be. The Argus group, through its subsidiary, World Printing and Publishing Company, took over the *World* in 1963 when its circulation was only 11,000. In early 1968 circulation had climbed to 82,000, making it the "fastest growing daily in South Africa" and fourth in circulation of all dailies.

The *World*'s circulation soared by offering its readers a steady diet of crime, sex, death, and various kinds of sensation—all presented from the viewpoint of the urban African. The *World* put out five editions daily—all sold on the streets and promoted by large posters or "bills" with oversized headlines proclaiming the day's lead story: "Wire-bound Corpse Was Throttled, Township Court Told," or "Lovers, Who Died Together, Are Buried Side by Side." Life was violent and death ever present in Soweto (a segregated African housing area outside Johannesburg), and the *World* reflected this in its coverage. Funerals of prominent African "tycoons" or "socialites," as they were called, were major social events and big stories for the *World*. Street sales increased greatly if there was a lurid local story and were depressed by bad weather.

The *World* tried hard to identify with the urban African. All reporting and writing were done by Africans, including several who previously had worked for *Drum,* and the paper's editor was an African, Tom Moerane. However, the news editor and the five subeditors were all Europeans. "We would like to have an all-African staff but we do not have the trained editors yet," said Charles Still, the white managing director of the *World*.[23]

Not unexpectedly, the *World* tended to shy away from politics ("Africans aren't interested," said Still) for fear of running afoul of the government or of breaking any of numerous laws restricting news coverage. "Our main purpose is to stay open and to make money, while producing a paper that urban Africans can identify with," said Still. Using the *Daily Mirror* of London as its "bible," the *World* appeared to be doing well. The paper was definitely not edited for the professional or educated class which was small and probably preferred the *Star* or *Rand Daily Mail.* But despite its sensationalism and emphasis on crime and sex, the *World* probably substantially helped the detribalized African to understand and find himself in the modern, violent, nonwhite segment of Johannesburg.

The *World*'s main competition came from the *Post,* a Sunday paper edited not only for the Africans, but for Asians and Coloureds as well. The *Post* gained 90,000 in circulation in 1967, moving it up to 235,000, in second place in the Sunday field behind the *Sunday Times.* The *Post* and *World* were prospering because the market for nonwhite readers was far from being met. And that readership represented a fast-growing consumer market.

Because of animosities and jealousies among the nonwhite groups, the *Post* published five distinct editions all printed in Johannesburg on a high-speed Italian offset press.

On Wednesdays the *Post* published its East and West Cape editions which were heavy with news about Coloureds. On Thursdays were published the Natal edition, designed for the large Indian population in Durban, and the Reef edition. On Saturdays, the whole paper was practically made over again and was filled primarily with news of black Africans for the large readerships in the townships of Johannesburg. In effect, then, separate editions were published for the Coloureds, Indians, and Africans. Indian reporters supplied news from the Natal area and Coloured reporters sent in news from the Cape. The Johannesburg reporting staff was all-African (white reporters could not get access to the townships anyway), but the editing and make-up was done by Europeans.

The news formula was much like that of the *World:* heavy on the "basics" of sex, crime, violence, and social upheaval. The *Post,* too, avoided politics, but it could and did publicize many of the gnawing social problems faced by nonwhites that were largely neglected by the European press. The *Post* tried, for example, to publicize the numerous cases of "endorsing out," whereby if a head of a household was either out of work, dead, departed, or divorced, the mother and children were evicted from their home in Soweto and sent back to their tribal reserves.

The *Post* was published by Post Newspapers (Pty.), Ltd., and printed by another corporation, Trinity Printing and Publishing Company, which also published *Drum* magazine. *Drum* was the most famous of publishing ventures "for Africans" by European publishing interests anywhere on the continent. During its heyday *Drum* became quite a success, especially with the urbanized Africans in Johannesburg, as well as Nigeria and Ghana. Relying heavily on pictures, *Drum* covered everything from witchcraft to shebeens (illegal African drinking houses) to crime and even the Sharpville riots, of which it published some remarkable photographs. It also had East and West African editions. *Drum,* in fact, set the style of journalism that the *Post* and the *World* so successfully emulated.

However, in April 1965 the South African *Drum* was discontinued by publisher James R. A. Bailey, and it became merely a color supplement to the *Post*. In April 1968 *Drum* reappeared as a full-fledged monthly magazine and was printed on a new gravure press acquired by Trinity printing. The resuscitated *Drum* had many of its old features, including the "Dear Dolly" advice column ("Will I Die for Loving Mum-to-Be?") and its typical picture stories on such phenomena as the "Skyline Locations" (social life of the 90,000 African domestic servants permitted to "live in" downtown Johannesburg), "What Makes our Moffies Tick?" (the Coloureds' homosexual society in Cape Town), and a feature on an Indian faith healer in Pretoria. It remained to be seen whether *Drum* could recapture its old readership. To help do so *Drum* had three distinct editions: a Transvaal edition for Africans, a Natal edition for Indians, and a Cape edition for Coloureds. In 1969 *Drum* acquired its first nonwhite editor, G. R. Naidoo, a South African Indian.

There was a fairly wide range of publications for nonwhites, but far fewer in numbers than those serving the white minority. In the Natal area, World Printing and Publishing Company (Argus) published a weekly, *Ilanga Lase Natal*, in Zulu and English, with 30,000 circulation. The large Xhosa-speaking population in the Transkei area was served by *Um'thunya* at Umtata, *Imvo Zabantsundu* at King Williams Town, and *Izindaba Zabantsundu*, a weekly in the eastern Cape.

It was significant that Afrikaner publishing capital has been involved in a number of ostensibly neutral, but in effect, progovernment publications. Afrikaanse Pers, for example, published *Bona*, a feature monthly magazine much like *Drum*, with separate editions in Xhosa, Zulu, Sotho, and English, and a total circulation of about 90,000. The government distributed copies free in the African schools.

The Cape Coloureds had two weeklies of their own in Cape Town, the *Cape Herald* and *Die Banier*. In Durban there were two weeklies for Indians, the *Graphic* and the *Leader*.

Possibly the most telling fact about the nonwhite press in South Africa was that only one publication, the *Leader* (10,000 circulation), a weekly for Indians in Natal, was *owned* by a nonwhite. *Die Banier*, an Afrikaans-language weekly for Coloureds, ceased publication in 1966, leaving the *Cape Herald* the only paper edited specifically for Coloureds. However, it was owned and published by three Afrikaners. Started in 1965, it relied heavily on stories about sex, crime, and popular culture. The

Cape Herald editor, Howard Laurence, said that the Cape Coloureds identified with American Negroes and showed high interest in U.S. civil rights news. There was little opportunity or training for Coloureds who wished to go into journalism. Laurence said that when he told his mother he wanted to become a newspaperman, she said, "Why do you want to do a white man's job?"[24]

The *Moslem News* was a small fortnightly published in Cape Town for the Moslems in the country.

If the nonwhite press were owned by nonwhites, it would probably be even more restricted in its activities by the government. Editors of nonwhite papers said there was much they could report but they did not dare. If they did, they risked government retaliation which usually began with a visit from the Special Branch asking what they *really meant* by the disputed story.

The inadequacies of the meager nonwhite press illustrated the communication breakdowns in South Africa. These papers were in a position to report the real views and problems of the nonwhite majority, but were not permitted to do so. And the white press, more and more, tended to look the other way.

The South African Information Service (SAIS) published an array of monthly newspapers and magazines for the African population; these, of course, only reinforced government policies. Among the monthly government newspapers were *Ikwezi Lase* (Morning Star) in Xhosa for the Transkei, *Izindaba* (Case or Discussion) in Zulu for Natal, and one in the Southern Sotho language.

The government also produced monthly publications in the major African languages, designed for the principal "nations": *Intuthuko* in Zulu, *Inkqubela* in Xhosa, *Tswelopele* in Southern Sotho, *Twelelopele* in Tswana, *Mbvela-Phanda* in Venda, and *Nhluvuko* in Tsonga. These papers were all distributed free by mailing lists or through schools and organized groups. "News" for these government publications was gathered by information officers in the field and sent in to Pretoria where all the papers were published.

The SAIS also published *Alfa* in English and Afrikaans for Coloureds in the Cape area, and *Fiat Lux* in English for Indians in Natal.

If it is true that *some* newspapers are better than *none,* then these publications served some kind of purpose in providing printed matter to the great nonwhite population of the Republic.

The government's purposes were much like its vernacular radio broadcasting—to perpetuate and accentuate apartheid policies.

NEWSPAPER PRESS UNION

Apartheid and tradition kept the two major newspaper organizations, the Newspaper Press Union of South Africa and the South Africa Press Association, exclusively white. Even papers like the *Rand Daily Mail,* which were nonracial in editorial policies, went along with this situation. They had no alternative.

The Newspaper Press Union (NPU) was in many ways unique in Africa. It was a trade organization or lobby of the white publishers of South Africa and filled much the same function as the American Newspaper Publishers Association in the United States. It represented the twenty-eight papers (mostly dailies) of the nine major urban areas, ninety-one provincial newspapers, and forty-eight magazines, trade journals, and periodicals, including all the major consumer magazines. To qualify for membership in the NPU, the *entire* directorate of a publication must be composed entirely of Europeans. Under a 1923 law, the NPU was empowered to represent the entire newspaper industry, and its rules and regulations applied, with the force of law, to all other publications not in the NPU.

The NPU's major editorial activity involved its Board of Reference which was established in March 1962 as a kind of press council. By adopting its voluntary Code of Conduct and the Board of Reference to enforce it, the NPU won exemption for all of its member publications from the Publications Control Board, the national censorship board, set up in 1963. (The Afrikaner publishers' help in winning this exemption from Parliament was a good example of NPU's power as a lobby for white newspapers.) However, in 1968 the government said it was considering extending the censorship law to all daily and Sunday papers.

The Board of Reference had three regular members: a retired judge of the Supreme Court and one retired and prestigious journalist each from the Afrikaans and English press.

The board considered "alleged infringements of the Code of Conduct in respect of matter appearing in South African publications or matter originating in South Africa and appearing in overseas publications."

The Code of Conduct itself was a straightforward listing of

about a dozen points of journalistic ethics, such as "News reports should be free from coloring, slanting, or emphasis," and "No willful departure from facts either through distortion, significant omissions, or summarization."

The most controversial clause of the code was the last one: "Comment should take cognizance of the complex racial problems of South Africa, the general good and the safety of the country and its peoples."

By early 1968 the Board of Reference had heard only about fourteen cases, a disappointing number to journalists who had hoped the board would function effectively both to uphold press freedom and to improve press performance.

In the first case before it, a Nationalist M.P. complained about an antigovernment letter which the *Star* had published. The board rejected the complaint.

Later a United Party M.P. complained about a report in *Die Transvaler*. The complaint was upheld. In another, the Black Sash, an antigovernment women's group, complained about a caption to a photograph in *Dagbreek an Sondagnuus*. The board found the complaint well founded and issued a reprimand.[25]

The Board of Reference had no teeth, no punitive powers, but all members of the NPU, including the erring paper, agreed to publish findings of the board.

The Board of Reference had not been influential mainly because it had not been used much. However, it probably was effective in inhibiting somewhat the Nationalist politicians in their outspoken criticisms of the English press. They were invited to bring their complaints against the English press to the board, but seldom did.

There were conflicting opinions about the worth of the Board of Reference. Some thought it was only a sop to the government's Press Commission. The South African Society of Journalists denounced the code as a form of self-censorship and instructed its members to ignore it.[26] The "self-censorship" aspect of the code was pointed out in one of the first cases heard. A complaint was made against two statements in a signed article in the *Sunday Express*. The article alleged that the government employed the political police to restrain and silence almost every form of outspoken protest and that this feeling was not expressed with more vigor because men were afraid of the personal consequences to themselves or their jobs. The board found "that the article complained of contains both overstatement and unfair comment and that the newspaper failed in its duty to avoid these violations of the code of conduct."[27]

There was no direct connection between the NPU and SAPA, the cooperative news service, but the board of directors of the NPU was in 1968 identical to that of SAPA, which was the only completely nongovernmental news agency in Africa.

The South African Press Association was founded on July 1, 1938, as a cooperative newsgathering and distributing agency to take over the business of the Reuters South African Agency, which had been a partnership of Reuters and certain South African newspapers. SAPA was nonprofit and owned and controlled by its members. The founding members of the association numbered twenty-eight newspapers, seven of them Afrikaans. In the late sixties about forty newspapers, two broadcasting systems, a television system, and three international news agencies (AP, Reuters, and AFP) subscribed to its services.

SAPA's foreign news came to Johannesburg from Reuters and Associated Press via transcontinental radio-teleprinter channels from London and New York. Southern African news was supplied by its member newspapers, staff men, full-time and part-time correspondents, and subscribers within its territory. Most news came from member newspapers which were obliged to give SAPA any routine stories. SAPA claimed that it received no subsidies from any quarter, and I found no reason to doubt this.

PRESS AND GOVERNMENT RELATIONSHIPS

The complex topic of freedom of the press in South Africa was just one aspect of the much bigger subject of political liberties. It is not possible here to go into all its ramifications. As was said before, the European press—English and Afrikaans—enjoys more freedom than in any other country of Africa, *but* this freedom is not enjoyed by the nonwhite majority or its press; further, there was good reason to believe that the white man's press freedom was being whittled away along with his other liberties.

As an inheritor of British institutions, South Africa had a long tradition of press freedom, going back to the early nineteenth century, and until World War II that freedom was expanding. South Africa operated under a rather unique system of Roman-Dutch law, veneered with some aspects of British legal traditions. The legal system gave great power to the Minister of Justice, who

could (and did) act in an arbitrary manner, and individual journalists or newspapers lacked the usual procedural safeguards to
challenge in the courts infringements on their civil liberties.

No legislation in South Africa was aimed solely at circum-
scribing the freedom of the press. There was much concern in
May 1967, therefore, when the new Prime Minister, John Vorster,
proposed in a speech that there be legislation which would enable
the government to act against papers publishing "false or distorted
reports" and to compel journalists to reveal their sources on demand. The political correspondent of the Johannesburg *Star*
wrote that the proposed law would "virtually preclude newspapers
from publishing anything but official information about the
Government and its activities."[28] However, the government had
second thoughts, and the plan to legislate against "ascertainable
lies" was postponed, if not dropped. Vorster himself indicated it
might be difficult to define an "ascertainable lie."

But Vorster did not really need his threatened Press Bill.
After twenty years of Nationalist party rule, the South African
press was bound hand and foot by various statutes which restricted
the activities of newspapers both directly and indirectly. There
was a steady encroachment on the rights of the South African
individual, especially the nonwhite. The press suffered con-
currently, and there was a maze of laws whose effect was grossly
to inhibit the right of the public to know what was going on. In
many areas of news the press was either expressly forbidden to
publish, or as a result of certain laws, was afraid to publish.

LAWS RESTRICTING ACCESS

These were some of the laws which most severely restricted
press freedom and were the most unjustifiable:[29]

1. Official Secrets Act, No. 165 of 1965.

The Official Secrets Act made it an offense to publish or
communicate in any way or for any purpose prejudicial to the
safety or interests of the country any information relating to military matters. This kind of law was found in many countries. But
under the 1965 amendment, the scope of the Act was extended to
"police matters," which were defined as meaning "any matter relating to the internal security of the Republic or the maintenance
of law and order by the South African Police." This covered any-

thing and everything to do with the police. In fact, no one, except possibly a few in government, even knew what was prohibited under it.

2. Defense Amendment Act of 1967.

This Act placed a blanket ban on publication of news about defense matters. Any and every item of such news must be approved for publication by the Minister of Defense or a designated officer. Late in 1967, for example, a golfer in Port Elizabeth looked up as a jet trainer flew overhead. From the plane fluttered a pair of trousers followed by a tie, which landed near the golfer. The press found it necessary to refer the story to the Defense Department for permission to publish. That was where the danger of the Act lay: its terms were so broad that newspaper editors, rather than take a chance on even a ridiculous story of this kind, chose to consult the Minister—who then decided whether the public could read about it.

3. Native Administration Act, No. 38 of 1927.

One of the few laws inherited by the Nationalists, it provided that "any person who utters any words or does any other act or thing whatever with intent to promote hostility between Natives and Europeans shall be guilty of an offense." The possibility of a prosecution for printing inflammatory speeches by whites against nonwhites virtually did not arise. But the reverse did—and this law was long a headache for newspaper editors. Where the slightest possibility of a prosecution existed, the natural tendency was for the editor to drop the story.

4. Riotous Assemblies Act, No. 17 of 1956.

First enacted in 1914, this law contained provisions similar to the Native Administration Act, except that it went further, giving the government the power to ban a newspaper which was "calculated to engender feelings of hostility between European inhabitants of the Republic on the one hand and any other section of the inhabitants of the Republic on the other hand." Here, again, editors had to employ self-censorship, and they seldom took a chance.

5. Public Safety Act, No. 3 of 1953.

On declaration of a state of emergency, the government had total powers of control over every aspect of life in the country, including the right to close down newspapers and prohibit printing, publishing, or dissemination of any matter.

6. Criminal Law Amendment Act, No. 8 of 1953.

This was the "incitement law," whereby it was an offense for any person to use language or act in any way calculated to contravene the law by protesting against any law. It meant that if an African took part in a strike, he committed an offense. But if he was also charged with having taken part in the strike in order to protest against apartheid, then it became a far more serious offense. And if a newspaper published the bare fact that a strike was about to take place, or was taking place, then it opened itself to a charge of incitement—and the penalty for the editor included imprisonment for up to five years and/or a whipping of up to ten strokes. A nationwide stoppage of work by Africans could disrupt all of South Africa without the press being able to tell the public about it in advance.

7. Suppression of Communism Act, No. 44 of 1950.

Ostensibly aimed at Communism, the wide powers in this Act have been used both against Communist and non-Communist opponents of the Nationalists. It gave the government power to ban newspapers which it deemed to be spreading Communism. The definition of Communism was a wide one. It also gave the government power to ban attendance at gatherings—and later amendments prohibited newspapers from publishing any statement by a banned person, whether he was alive or dead, without permission of the Minister of Justice. Still another amendment gave the government the power even to prohibit the publication in South Africa of the statements of people who had left the country.

In 1968 there were some 700 "banned" persons, whose views ranged from Communism through African Nationalism and Pan-Africanism to liberalism and moderation. A wide segment of opinion was thus silenced and the public could not, unless the Minister consented, know the views of much of the opposition.

8. Prisons Act, No. 8 of 1959.

It was an offense to publish any information about prisons, knowing such information to be false or without taking reasonable steps to ensure that the information was accurate. The burden of showing that reasonable steps were taken rested on the person charged. It was under this law that a prolonged prosecution of editors Laurence Gandar of the *Rand Daily Mail* and Joel Mervis of the *Sunday Times,* and a *Mail* reporter, Benjamin Pogrund, took place. The original stories on the brutal conditions in South African prisons were printed in June and July of 1965. The *Mail* was raided by security forces four times and Gandar was subjected to legal harassment, had his passport withdrawn, and finally was charged, along with Pogrund, with publishing false information about prisons. On November 1, 1968, the actions against Gandar and Pogrund finally came to trial. Charges against Mervis and two others were withdrawn. On conviction, the maximum penalty would have been a fine of 200 rand ($280), or imprisonment for a year, or jail without the option of a fine.

Outside South Africa there was a good deal of concern over the Gandar-Pogrund trial. The International Press Institute at Zurich sent a qualified observer to the trial, which was considered significant because it was an apparent effort by the Nationalist government to retaliate against the editor (and newspaper) who had been the most outspoken critic of its policies. In a letter to *IPI Report* in December 1968, Sean McBride, Secretary-General of the International Commission of Jurists, wrote:

> Inevitably, discriminatory laws lead to the erosion, one after the other, of the elements of the rule of law, including those which are related to the policy of apartheid. We fear that the Gandar trial represents a further step in this process of erosion, this time directed against the freedom of the press. The *Rand Daily Mail* has criticized the policies of the South African government and dared to publish information which displeases the authorities, hence it must be silenced. Instead of suppressing it openly, an attempt is being made to prosecute it out of existence. In this manner, the *Rand Daily Mail* will be effectively silenced and the rest of the South African press will be intimidated into subservience. In our view, it is the freedom of the press in South Africa which is now at stake in the Gandar trial.

The lengthy and expensive trial ended on July 12, 1969, with convictions of the defendants. Gandar was fined $278 or six months imprisonment; Pogrund was given a six months suspended sentence; and the *Rand Daily Mail* was fined $417. Although the sentences were lighter than expected, the government had made its point—it had intimidated the English-language press. A few hours after his conviction, Gandar printed a front page editorial in the *Rand Daily Mail* defending the principles of a free press.

However, in September 1969, Gandar announced that he was leaving South Africa for two or three years to work in London on a special assignment, the details of which he did not disclose.

9. Extension of University Education Act, No. 45 of 1959.

Students at nonwhite universities were prohibited from giving statements to the press without their rector's permission. The stifling effect on news access was obvious.

10. Laws controlling the entry of whites into African Reserves and urban townships.

These gave authorities a large measure of control over the access of the press to large areas of South Africa. Any newsman who wrote about these areas could be blacklisted from entering them. Moreover, the mere fact that entry required permission meant that control was exercised over what the public could read.

11. Unlawful Organizations Act of 1960.

Although the government already had the power under the Suppression of Communism Act, it chose to legislate specially to ban the African National Congress and the Pan-Africanist Congress in 1960. The two groups were then the only spokesmen for the African people. Nothing about their policies or viewpoints could be published. If either of them should issue an underground pamphlet, as they sometimes did, the press could not divulge the pamphlet's contents.

12. 180-day detention without trial.

This placed an even greater inhibition on a newspaper's enthusiasm for publishing any story that might possibly incur the ire of the authorities. If there was any risk at all of police interest —drop the story was the immediate instruction, as indeed it must. Newspapers no longer had any choice.

The cumulative effects of these laws were to make access to news of major segments of life in South Africa extremely difficult and hazardous for the press. It affected government officials who, because they knew their superiors might disapprove, were reluctant to talk to the press. "Leakage" of news from government sources almost never occurred. Also, this reticence spread to the public at large and there was a generalized fear of giving information about a range of subjects both "safe" and "unsafe" to the newspapers.[30]

Numerous instances could be cited of application of these laws against newspapers, and of course, their power to inhibit the press was extremely pervasive.

THE PRICE OF OPPOSITION

But the fact remained that there were still some newspapers in South Africa which did speak out. In their news columns they might no longer publish all that they would wish to, but in their editorials they continued to oppose Nationalist policy. The price of opposition was harassment; these several examples were culled from *IPI Reports:*

● Mike Norton, editor of the nonwhite Sunday *Post,* was arrested and sentenced to four days imprisonment for refusing to divulge the source of his information for an article. He was sentenced to a further eight days when he still declined to name his sources and was jailed for a third time for the same reason. He was released after almost three weeks in jail.[31]

● Marcus Ngani, African editor of the weekly *Um'thunya* in the Transkei, was arrested in his office in Umtata and taken to Port Elizabeth. The police gave no reason for his arrest.[32]

● Police raided the offices of the *Sunday Times,* following the paper's exposé of the Broederbond, an Afrikaner secret society.[33]

● Three members of the Security Branch of the South African police raided the offices of the Port Elizabeth *Evening Post.* For an hour and fifteen minutes they inspected the reference books, filing cabinets, desk papers, clippings, letters, and various journals in the office of the editor, J. G. Sutherland.[34]

● Mrs. Margaret Smith, a reporter for the *Sunday Times,* was released in early 1965 after being detained under the 90-day law since November 11, 1964. She was not charged.[35]

● Imam Abdullah Haron, 44, editor of the *Moslem News,* Cape Town, and an outspoken critic of apartheid who was arrested in May 1969, died in prison from "natural causes," according to the government. The statement met with "widespread disquiet" among South Africa's large Moslem community.[36]

Yet, despite such harassment and the deterrent effects of the laws, the English-language press was still more outspokenly critical of government than any other press on the continent. It was ironic that the Opposition English press, which did exercise its freedom to criticize government, had little real political influence because of the near dominance of the Nationalist party which was backed by an increasing number of English speakers. But the Afrikaans press, which did not exercise its right to criticize and gave mostly obsequious support to the government, enjoyed real political influence because it spoke for important factions in the Nationalist party.

Why did the English-language press enjoy this limited freedom, even though it was a special and privileged kind of freedom belonging only to them? There were several reasons.

The government knew it would greatly damage its already tarnished image abroad if it suppressed outright the English papers. And because of the myriad of laws restricting access to news of politically sensitive subjects, there seemed little need to suppress any major newspaper. The Nationalist government was doing so well—overwhelmingly supported by whites while the country was enjoying a prolonged economic boom—it could afford to be somewhat tolerant. Further, it was said the Nationalists did not mind a certain amount of political give-and-take in the English press since they were so entirely in command anyway.

Also, it should be remembered that the major English-language papers, especially those in the Argus and the SAAN groups, represented important economic power in South Africa, including the great mining complex Anglo-American Corporation, headed by Harry Oppenheimer. The government was understandably reluctant to clash head-on with such power unnecessarily. And so far, it was not necessary. Because of their financial backing, the English-language papers had a respectability that the various small opposition newssheets of earlier years lacked. It was quite easy for the government to ban the latter as "Communist."

And finally, credit should be given to the numerous dedicated and courageous journalists on the English-language papers—people like Gandar, Mervis, Anthony Delius, Stanley Uys, among others, who really believed in freedom of the press and were willing to fight for it.

The Nationalists' disapproval of English-language newspapers extended to those published in the United States and Britain as well, at least to those which disapprove of apartheid. Typical was a comment made in a senate debate by Dr. Albert Hertzog, former Minister of Post and Telegraphs. News entering South

Africa, he said, was "sifted" by Communists employed at Reuters's London office. For this reason, in his view, South African newspapers could not always be blamed for the distorted overseas news they published, but it was their fault if they still made use of agencies like Reuters. Reuters, of course, denied the charge.[37]

Restrictions were often placed on foreign correspondents in South Africa, and Johannesburg, therefore, was not the international news center for southern Africa that it could be. It was just too difficult for the foreign correspondent to work there unhampered.

By way of illustration, these few items from the *IPI Report* indicated the problems encountered by foreign journalists in South Africa:

● Anthony Lukas, New York *Times* correspondent in Johannesburg, was searched by security police at Jan Smuts airport. Police seized the draft of a magazine article, photographs, letters, and a book banned in South Africa. The papers and the book were returned to him a few days later, and he left the country.[38]

● The government informed Joseph Lelyveld, another New York *Times* correspondent, that his visa would not be renewed and that his permit would expire on April 28, 1966. No reason was given. (The *Times* has not had a resident correspondent in South Africa since.)[39]

● Gordon Winter, a British journalist, who was detained pending his deportation, was released for seven days to wind up his affairs. No reason was given for the order.[40]

Such incidents explain why there were only about a dozen foreign correspondents in South Africa and some of these were not full-time. Associated Press had one American staffer and two South Africans, UPI's bureau was run by an Australian, AFP had three Frenchmen, and DPA one German. A stringer covered for *Time* and the New York *Times*, which each once maintained full-time staff correspondents. Resident correspondents were given little help by the South African Information Service, which went out of its way to cooperate with "approved" visiting correspondents (i.e., ones likely to be sympathetic to its apartheid policies).

This, of course, was related to the South African government's efforts to promote its image abroad and to "protect" its public at home from unfavorable information originating overseas.

PUBLICATIONS CONTROL BOARD

A major mechanism of this "thought control" is the Publications Control Board, which was set up by legislation in 1963 to pass on books, motion pictures, magazines, and periodicals, both foreign and domestic. From the time the board was instituted in November 1963, after the enactment of the Publications and Entertainments Act, until 1968, more than 11,000 books had been banned. That averaged out to two books being banned a day, and the rate was said to be going up.

Most of the banned books fell into the category of works that might "pervert" the minds of the Africans because they discussed race or violence or were sexually provocative by the Calvinistic standards prevailing among many Afrikaners in government. Paperbacks were examined especially, because they were cheap enough for the black man's pocketbook.[41]

Thus South Africans of whatever color were denied access to a great share of the important books being published in the English language.

The censors were especially wary of anything with the words "sex" or "black" in the title, so it was to be expected that a customs official would hold up all copies of "Black Beauty" for some time, until he learned that it was a children's story about a horse.

Censorship extended just as stringently to imported motion pictures, all of which had to bear a stamp of approval from the board to be shown. Bill Edgson, film critic for the Johannesburg *Star*, noted that almost all the films receiving top honors in the 1968 Academy Awards from Hollywood—"In the Heat of the Night" (best film and best actor), "Guess Who's Coming to Dinner" (best actress), "The Graduate" (best director), and "Bonnie and Clyde" (best supporting actress)—were banned in South Africa. One exception was "Dr. Doolittle," which won the award for the best song.[42]

Films were often classified according to the racial status of the theater audiences, which in South Africa were always segregated. Certificate B permitted showing to "whites only," while Certificate C admitted "Coloureds" under the classification "whites and nonwhites, excluding Bantus." Certificate D required cutting or alteration before a film could be shown, and the cutting of racially "disturbing" scenes was very common. The American film "South Pacific" was cut almost beyond recognition because of its racial implications.⁴³ Another Hollywood musical, "Finian's Rainbow," was banned in 1969.

BROADCASTING

The government had no difficulty in controlling the other major medium—radio—because the South African Broadcasting Corporation (SABC), organized in 1936, was directly responsive to the views of the ruling Nationalists. As the Nationalists had no English-language newspaper that spoke for them, it was said in South Africa that the English-language service of the SABC was the mouthpiece of the Nationalist party. In both news and commentaries, SABC consistently parroted the government line.

As would be expected in the wealthiest nation in Africa—and one still without general television—radio broadcasting was a highly developed medium that compared favorably with any system in Western Europe. The SABC offered no less than fourteen program services—six for Europeans, seven for Africans ("Radio Bantu"), and a highly sophisticated external service in nine languages: English, Afrikaans, French, Portuguese, German, Dutch, Swahili, Zulu, and Tsonga.

Nationally there was the English service, the Afrikaans service, a commercial service called Radio Springbok (alternating in both English and Afrikaans), and three regional commercial services—Radio Highveld, Radio Port Natal, and Radio Good Hope.

Radio Bantu's services were directed at the various "nations" or linguistic groups among the Africans. The expansion of the Xhosa service into a full program, broadcasting eighteen hours daily, resulted in the seven language services of Radio Bantu being on the air almost eighty hours a week. Every day the Zulu, Southern Sotho, and Xhosa services were on the air for eighteen hours each, the Northern Sotho and Tswana services for twelve hours, and the Venda and Tsonga services for two hours.

About 95 percent of Radio Bantu was broadcast on FM, which was interesting because it suggested a subtle form of censorship: an African with an inexpensive FM transistor was not likely to be able to afford a shortwave receiver as well. Thus, the chances he would turn to the international broadcasts beamed on shortwave to South Africa were fairly remote.

South Africans paid an annual license fee of R 5.50 (one

rand = $1.40) for the first radio and R 1 for each additional set. In 1968 there were about 1.5 million licensed radio sets, plus probably many more unlicensed transistor receivers, giving a total of about 3 million. Despite the government propaganda that pervaded all the news and public information shows, radio was widely listened to in South Africa, reaching an audience estimated at 10 million.

Johannesburg was the administrative center for Radio South Africa. Regional operations at Cape Town, Grahamstown, Port Elizabeth, Durban, Bloemfontein, Pretoria, and Kimberley prepared local and regional programs, including news, but about 90 percent of the broadcasting originated in Johannesburg. The three national services were all in AM, FM, and shortwave and could be picked up anywhere in the Republic.

News on the SABC was the most extensive operation of its kind in Africa. One hundred sixty news bulletins were broadcast *each day* on the various domestic and external services, plus another forty-eight on Radio Bantu, giving a daily total of 208 bulletins daily. Some news bulletins were regional, others national.[44]

News was prepared by a staff of 140 journalists. (The total SABC staff was about 2,300 of which 1,700 were whites and 600 nonwhites.)

For foreign news, the services of AP, UPI, DPA, AFP, Reuters, and SAPA were used. Domestic news sources were SAPA, a corps of SABC staffers who reported regional news and covered for national stories, plus an estimated 1,200 part-time stringers scattered around the country.

News on the air was professionally handled and followed the familiar pattern of a BBC news broadcast. In fact, the external service had been accused of imitating the BBC Overseas service so that foreign listeners would think they were tuned in to that highly credible source. Other than in the selection of news items, there was little obvious bias in news presentation.

The most controversial programs were the daily "Current Affairs" commentaries. The SABC's Annual Report said rather candidly:

> The talks are offered as an SABC editorial in which, from a South African [i.e., Nationalist party] point of view, positive comment is made on the affairs of the day. The broad objectives are (1) to project a true picture of South African motives, policies, problems, achievements, and goals; (2) to give constructive guid-

ance to listeners on the innumerable situations which are continually developing at home and abroad and which affect the fate of the nation; and (3) to counteract influences which are hostile to South Africa and which seek to undermine the South African pattern of society.[45]

In any case, the "Current Affairs" talks infuriated a good many South Africans of all colors who saw them only as blatant self-serving propaganda to defend and justify the controversial policies of the ruling Nationalist party. Any claims that SABC was an independent public service free of political influences and comparable to the BBC are rendered meaningless after one listens to a few "Current Affairs" talks. Titles of a few such talks broadcast in 1967 were "Liberals in the American State Department," "Guevara in Africa," "A Pertinent Reminder About Communism," "The Crux of Ghana's Problems," "A Sordid Chapter in American Degradation," "Chinese in Zambia," "Terrorists in Malawi," "Subversion at Universities," and "Focus on China in Africa." "Current Affairs" must be heard to be appreciated fully. The program was, in truth, the Nationalists' editorial page—an effort to influence the many English-speaking South Africans who did not read an Afrikaans newspaper.

The influence of sound broadcasting was greatly enhanced by the fact that the Nationalist government steadfastly refused to permit general television, which it seemed to regard as a corrupting influence from outside, mainly the United States and Britain, from which would come the great bulk of programming if and when television were allowed. To some extent it also reflected the Afrikaner resentment of the fact that popular culture in South Africa was predominantly American, and to a lesser extent, British. South Africans through records, popular music, motion pictures, and magazines were keen fans of the mass culture of America. Television would only increase the trend.

The government certainly opposed general television because the Afrikaans language, an important pillar of Afrikanerdom, would be swamped by the English-language programs. Even a country as advanced as South Africa would find it difficult to produce all its own programming. Dr. Hertzog, who as Minister of Posts and Telegraphs long blocked television, said: "Overseas, money power has used television as a deadly weapon to undermine the morale of the white men, and mighty empires have been destroyed in 15 years."[46] In the meantime, on weekends, people in Johannesburg and elsewhere rented and screened Hollywood films which, said one wealthy young stockbroker, "may not be as good as television, but at least we don't have commercials." It was not unusual for Johannesburg suburbanites to exchange rented or borrowed films with their neighbors and in this way see three or four films over a weekend. This also meant that South Africa's electronics industry could have little growth.[47]

However, recent developments indicated the government possibly had already decided to install a general television system, perhaps in 1972. That was the year the new headquarters for SABC was scheduled for completion, and there were reports circulating in South Africa that the new buildings would be large enough for a television operation, and in fact had been designed that way. Also, it was expected that there would be by that time enough experience in the dubbing of English-language imported shows into Afrikaans. A team of West German technicians was said to have completed the installation of television equipment in the headquarters of the SABC. Also, a SABC film unit set up two years before had built up a stockpile of more than 200 canned programs in both English and Afrikaans.

Mass communications in the Republic of South Africa were indeed the exception in Africa, and they reflected the tragic social and political problems that were pushing that bountiful land to the edge of the abyss. It was a sad thing that mass communications were being so little used to help ameliorate or head off the ominous racial holocaust that seemed destined to ignite at the southern end of the continent.

12

‖‖

CONCLUSION

AFRICA'S "MUFFLED DRUMS" come in many sizes and beat out greatly contrasting and varied messages. There are exceptions and special cases, professional practitioners and unskilled trainees, going concerns and shaky enterprises. But taken all together, the African media situation does form a generalized picture.

Of the world's continents, Africa is the least endowed with news communication resources: fewer newspapers and periodicals, fewer broadcasting transmitters and receivers, and fewer cinemas. These scarce news media serve the few educated elites, usually about 10 percent or less of the people, who are clustered in the cities. They do not yet begin to reach the common man, except for radio which, thanks to the ubiquitous transistor, is picked up in the countryside. However, language diversity and economic problems circumscribe listening, and radio in most places is not a true mass medium.

The plight of Africa's news media is directly related to the circumstance that they are a Western import—a by-product of European colonialism. The printed word and broadcasting came from outside with the European incursion. Neither journalism nor mass communications were indigenous to African societies.

And today, despite political independence for most of the continent, European influences still pervade news communication. Most programs on television and films shown in cinemas are produced in Europe and America. For news about themselves and the outside world, Africans are largely dependent on European correspondents and news services, principally Reuters and Agence France Presse. Newspapers flown in daily from Europe are widely read in African capitals, often outselling local publications.

European interests still own a number of newspapers in Africa and have been involved in establishing government papers and radio and television facilities. Some places in Africa are entirely dependent on such outside media support and it is apparent that such assistance must continue if the news media are to expand.

Yet at the same time, the need to "Africanize" the news media in both content and personnel is very real. Much more of the news and entertainment in mass communications must be prepared by Africans themselves and be intended primarily for African audiences. This necessarily involves a continued effort to train many more mass communicators. Until Africans themselves, and not Europeans, completely control the instruments of communication, the media are certain to be resented not only by government officials but by the public itself.

Historically the political function of the news media has been of crucial importance in their evolution. The European settlers and colonial officials used their own newspapers and radio stations to reinforce and support their political objectives. The indigenous African press, built on European models, evolved as a political instrument, an organizational tool for molding a political organization, and in time, played a role in the struggle for independence.

Politics were the *raison d'être* for much of the preindependence African press. In only a few places did the press function primarily as a *news* medium or serve an economic purpose. Seldom was the press, whether European or African, a successful business enterprise; a notable exception was the English-language press of South Africa.

The Western model of the newspaper as a profit-making enterprise, independent of government, and supplying the public with reliable and objective news and public information is seldom found, although many African journalists aspire to such a news press. Economic and social factors—poverty, illiteracy, economic structures, linguistic and ethnic diversity—have combined to inhibit such media development.

Hence the new African governments have played a major role in the ownership and control of the news media. In many African capitals the government is the only institution capable of supporting the media. Government control and the push toward "Africanization" are understandable and necessary steps in the transition from neo-European to indigenous national media systems. The numerous examples of cooperative endeavors in press and broadcasting between European enterprises and African governments characterize this transition period.

Like governments everywhere, African politicians are suspicious of and hostile to press criticism, especially from foreigners, and believe the news media should support the goals of national development and political integration. Therefore, in crisis situations—and these have been numerous in the turbulent sixties—the news media are often silenced or are otherwise ineffective in supplying reliable news.

Although African leaders usually recognize the importance of mass communication, the media's role in national development is as yet neither clearly defined nor effectively implemented. The proposition that "if there is communication, there is development, and if there is development, there is communication" is understood in principle. But immediate pragmatic and political considerations appear to be more decisive in the uses and controls of the news media than are explicit development goals.

Undoubtedly the comparative handful of Africans who do attend to the news media are better informed and more useful citizens for it, and therefore, in a cumulative behavioral sense, the nation itself profits.

For example, the nation of Kenya undoubtedly is being assisted in its steep climb toward modernity by the fact that a few thousand Kenyans read and react to the *East African Standard* and the *Nation* papers, listen to news on "Voice of Kenya," watch some television, and see an occasional motion picture. All African nations sorely need more "modern," effective citizens and the news media do assist in producing them.

News media are playing an important role, too, at the international level. African peoples, once so isolated from each other and from the outside world, are being increasingly pulled onto the stage of modern world history, in part through the news media. Thus it is significant that an increasing number of Africans read foreign newspapers, listen to international broadcasts, and see television and film content from Europe and America. The world is moving willy nilly toward a rudimentary world community, held together in part by mass communications; and Africa, despite its media deficiencies, is being drawn into it. But perhaps more important, educated Africans are learning more about their neighbors and events elsewhere in Africa through the news media. This has important implications for the future of the continent.

The prospects for improving the news media and expanding their audiences are intimately associated with the general prospects for social, economic, and political development. Studies on the role of media in national development convincingly show that mass communications will expand along with the general process of modernization. In a general way, more facilities for news communications and the modern, empathetic people to use them will come with more education, more literacy, a greater gross national product and higher per capita income, and more industrialization. Such has been the case elsewhere in the world.

Moreover the relationship is a reciprocal one; mass communications are both an agent and an index of social change. Mass communications can help speed the process of social change by more efficiently distributing essential information and involving more of the public in the tasks of nation-building and participation in the modern world. The news media can help bridge the great chasms that separate the few modern persons in African cities from the many traditional Africans living in mud-hut villages or leading nomadic lives, virtually cut off from the urban population by the nearly insurmountable barriers of language, ethnicity, and profound cultural differences. Inadequate as the news media still are, they undoubtedly play an important role in helping to hold together the fragile new nations.

So as Africa modernizes, its news media will grow and flourish. But anyone who studies Africa today must be impressed by the enormity and the complexity of the problems encountered. Poverty, lack of economic potential, political instability, linguistic and ethnic fragmentation, illiteracy, and other factors can and do combine to slow and confound the process. Yet the trend is clear: African societies are moving, however differentially and irregularly, from traditional communication systems to modern media systems of communication. The oral point-to-point or person-to-person methods of traditional social organizations are slowly giving way to and combining with mediated communication. The direction is distinctly one way: from traditional to modern news communication. Africa has opted for the modern world, and mass communications will speed and ease the transition and are themselves a product of the process. But it is not an easy nor a regular process.

The news media will continue to be "muffled drums" for some time to come. Because of economic, social, and political constraints, the printed and electronic word will still be muted and indistinct.

In most places the newspaper, radio, television, and cinema will be directly or indirectly controlled by African governments. The outlook for freedom of expression is not promising because the necessary conditions are generally lacking. In Nigeria and South Africa, the two nations enjoying the greatest press freedom in the mid-sixties, that basic political right was markedly diminishing as the decade ended.

What the West in its culture-bound way calls "freedom of the press" will become widespread only when shaky political structures evolve to where they provide for legitimate political oppositions, rule of law, and legal protection of civil rights; and when economic structures will permit much higher per capita incomes, accumulation of savings, and private investment in mass communication enterprises. A free press in the Western sense is basically a press independent of government, and this is still a distant prospect for Africa.

In the meantime, African governments will use the mass media for the difficult tasks of establishing national unity and modern economic and social institutions.

Mass communications can be used to help improve regional cooperation, which has been recognized as a high priority need. Most nations are too small, in terms of effective populations and necessary resources, to deal with problems of development alone. The mass media can be of real use in establishing the links that make regional cooperation meaningful.

Communication satellites will provide intra-African links, as will the increased exchanges across borders of printed matter, radio and television programs, and locally produced motion pictures.

The flow of international communication into Africa will undoubtedly increase. Whether it comes from the commercial and private sectors—newspapers, books, films, television programs —or from official foreign sources (i.e., political communication), the increased input will probably be on balance a good thing since it will increase Africa's involvement with the greater world and supplement the news and information emanating from local news media.

Some find it difficult to be anything but pessimistic about Africa's prospects for becoming a prosperous, stable, and peaceful region of the world. But there are grounds for hope.

In almost every aspect of human endeavor—education, public health, establishment of modern institutions—there has been progress since the early 1950s, when most of the continent was still under colonial rule. Even the turmoil and dislocations of the sixties can be considered indicators of change, as efforts to deal with overwhelming problems.

In the great human drama being played out in Africa, the news media have many roles to play: to aid in nation-building, to inform and edify individual Africans, and to explain Africa to an outside world that is still too ignorant and unsympathetic.

APPENDIX: TABLES ON MASS MEDIA

TABLE 1: Demographic Characteristics

	Area (sq. mi.)[a]	Population (est.)[a]	Year of Independence[a]	Percent of Literacy[b]	Total GNP (US$ mil.)[c]	GNP per Capita[c] (US$)
Algeria	920,000	12,102,000	1962	15	2,709	220
Angola	481,352[d]	5,225,000[e] (1966 est)	. . .	3	909	170
Botswana	220,000	576,000	1966	20	34	60
Burundi	10,747	3,300,000 (1968 est.)	1960	n.a.	154	50
Cameroon	183,381	5,100,000	1960	10	478	110
Central African Republic	238,224	2,088,888 (1965 census)	1960	15	161	110
Chad	495,753	3,500,000 (1967 est.)	1960	5	222	70
Congo (Brazzaville)	132,050	1,000,000 (1966 est.)	1960	20–25	151	180
Congo (Kinshasa)	905,563	14,500,000	1960	50–60	1,007	60
Dahomey	44,695	2,462,000 (1967 est.)	1960	5	183	80
Ethiopia	457,266	23,000,000 (1966 est.)	[f]	5	1,357	60
Gabon	102,089	630,000 (1968 est.)	1960	10–15	187	400
Gambia	4,004	315,000 (1963 census)	1965	10	30	90
Ghana	91,844	7,841,000 (1966 est.)	1957	20–25	1,851	230
Guinea	94,925	4,000,000 (1968 est.)	1958	10	289	80
Ivory Coast	124,503	4,000,000 (1965 est.)	1960	20	878	220
Kenya	224,960	9,365,000 (1965 est.)	1963	20–25	887	90
Lesotho	11,720	976,000	1966	40	49	60
Liberia	43,000	1,016,443 (1962 census)	1847	10	228	210
Libya	679,359	1,564,369 (1964 census)	1951	22	1,078	640

[a] The 42 Independent States of Africa," *Africa Report* 14:1, Jan. 1969, pp. 48–51.
[b] AID, *Selected Economic Data for the Less Developed Countries,* Statistics and Reports Division, Office of Program and Policy Coordination, Apr. 1968, p. 7.
[c] "Population, Total GNP, and GNP per Capita in US Dollars for African Countries and Territories, 1966," *Africa Report* 14:1, Jan. 1969, p. 19.
[d] Colin Legum, *A Handbook to the Continent,* p. 332.
[e] *UN Statistical Year Book 1967,* p. 79.
[f] Always independent except for Italian colonial period, 1936–41.

	Area (sq. mi.)[a]	Population (est.)[a]	Year of Independence[a]	Percent of Literacy[b]	Total GNP (US$ mil.)[c]	GNP per Capita[c] (US$)
Malagasy Republic	228,572	6,200,000 (1966 census)	1960	35	577	90
Malawi	36,000	4,042,400 (1964 census)	1964	5–10	206	50
Mali	464,875	4,500,000 (1968 est.)	1960	2	293	60
Mauritania	419,231	1,500,000 (1968 est.)	1960	1–5	139	130
Mauritius	720	884,000 (1968 est.)	1968	62	162	210
Morocco	171,305	14,342,000 (1968 est.)	1956	10–15	2,306	170
Mozambique ..	297,654[d]	7,040,000[e]	. . .	2	704	100
Niger	489,000	3,200,000 (1965 est.)	1960	1–5	268	80
Nigeria	356,000	55,670,052 (1963 census)	1960	30–35	4,895	80
Rhodesia	150,820[g]	4,580,000[g]	. . .	20	915	210[g]
Rwanda	10,169	3,300,000 (1968 est.)	1962	5–10	128	40
Senegal	76,124	3,500,000 (1966 est.)	1960	5–10	763	210
Sierra Leone ...	27,925	2,180,355 (1963 census)	1961	7	351	150
Somali Republic	246,201	2,580,000 (1966 est.)	1960	5	129	50
South Africa ...	472,685	18,298,000 (1966 est.)	1910	35	11,939[h]	576[h]
Sudan	967,500	14,100,000 (1967 est.)	1956	10–15	1,366	100
Swaziland	6,704	389,492 (1966 census)	1968	36	107	290
Tanzania	363,000	12,231,000 (1967 census)	1961	15–20	887	70
Togo	21,853	1,702,300 (1967 est.)	1960	5–10	166	100
Tunisia	63,000	4,457,466 (1966 census)	1956	25–35	905	200
Uganda	91,000	7,551,000 (1964 est.)	1962	20	782	100
Upper Volta ...	105,838	4,955,000 (1967 est.)	1960	5–10	268	50
Zambia	290,586	3,780,000 (1956 est.)	1964	20	704	180

[g] "Populations and Areas of the Countries of the World," *Britannica Book of the Year 1969*, p. 621.

[h] AID, *Selected Economic Data for the Less Developed Countries*, Statistics and Reports Division, Office of Program and Policy Coordination, Apr. 1968, p. 6. South Africa figures include Botswana, Lesotho, South West Africa, and Swaziland.

TABLE 2: Media Development in 43 African Countries (numbers per 100 people)

	Radio Receivers	Television Receivers	Daily Newspaper Copies	Cinema Seats
Algeria	16.5	1.3	1.6	1.7
Angola	1.9	0	1.0	0.4
Botswana	0.5	0	0	na
Burundi	1.1	0	0	0.2
Cameroon	4.4	0	0.2	na
Central African Republic	1.5	0	0.02	0.1
Chad	0.7	0	0.03	0.1
Congo (Brazzaville)	6.0	0.05	1.1	na
Congo (Kinshasa)	1.3	0.003	0.4	0.1
Dahomey	1.6	0	0.2	0.2
Ethiopia	0.9	0.03	0.2	0.1
Gabon	7.8	0.09	0.3	0.1
Gambia	4.7	0	0.5	0.6
Ghana	6.8	0.1	1.9	0.8
Guinea	2.2	0	0.2	0.3
Ivory Coast	2.0	0.05	0.5	0.7
Kenya	5.3	0.1	0.8	0.2
Lesotho	0.7	0	0	na
Liberia	12.6	0.2	0.6	1.1
Libya	12.1	0.4	1.0	1.3
Malagasy Republic	4.1	0	0.6	0.2
Malawi	0.4	0	0	0.2
Mali	1.1	0	0.1	0.3
Mauritania	1.5	0	na	0.01
Mauritius	10.9	0.5	7.2	6.2
Morocco	5.1	0.2	1.1	0.9
Mozambique	1.4	0	0.5	0.2
Niger	1.3	0	0.4	0.1
Nigeria	1.8	0.05	0.7	0.1
Rhodesia	3.6	1.0	1.7	0.2
Rwanda	0.7	0	0	na
Senegal	6.5	0.003	0.6	1.5
Sierra Leone	16.9	0.5	0.7	0.3
Somali Republic	5.0	0	0.2	0.8
South Africa	17.3	0	5.4	2.9
Sudan	2.3	0.08	0.8	0.5
Swaziland	1.4	0	0	0.2
Tanzania	1.5	0	0.4	0.2
Togo	1.4	0	0.6	0.1
Tunisia	8.6	0.1	1.5	1.3
Uganda	2.6	0.06	0.9	0.2
Upper Volta	1.1	0.002	0.06	0.2
Zambia	2.8	0.3	0.9	0.4
UNESCO Minimum[a]	5.0	2.0	10.0	2.0
AFRICA 1960	2.3	0.07	1.2	0.6
AFRICA 1965	4.3	0.1	1.0	0.5

Source: USIA, *Communications Data Book for Africa*, pp. 4–6.

[a] UNESCO minimum represents the bare minimum standard considered for "adequate" communications.

TABLE 3: Radio Broadcasting

	Number of Programming Stations	Radio Sets in Use[a]	Estimated Audience Size	Short-wave Transmitters	Medium-wave Transmitters
Algeria	1	1,900,000	7,600,000	4	4
Angola	16	90,000	880,000	30	19
Botswana	2	5,000	30,000	2	2
Burundi	2	55,000	330,000	5	...
Cameroon	4	210,000	1,000,000	3	4
Central African Republic	1	44,000	230,000	1	1
Chad	1	50,000	210,000	2	1
Congo (Brazzaville)	2	62,000	200,000	8	1
Congo (Kinshasa) .	8	200,000	1,900,000	16	2
Dahomey	1	50,000	320,000	2	2
Ethiopia	1	200,000	2,200,000	4	4
Gabon	2	50,000	120,000	3	2
Gambia	1	33,000	70,000	1	0
Ghana	1	450,000	4,051,200	14	0
Guinea	1	85,000	640,000	3	1
Ivory Coast	2	67,000	495,000	4	3
Kenya	1	500,000	3,500,000	6	3
Lesotho	2	2,675	40,000	2	1
Liberia	4	151,000	350,000	5	2
Libya	2	76,000	500,000	2	2
Malagasy Republic	2	308,000	1,400,000	3	3
Malawi	1	100,000	140,000	1	3
Mali	1	50,000	300,800	2	2
Mauritania	1	45,000	140,000	1	1
Mauritius	1	70,000	300,000	1	1
Morocco	3	820,312	3,000,000	6	7
Mozambique	6	185,000	1,000,000	27	10
Niger	1	75,000	180,000	3	1
Nigeria	7	1,260,000	8,400,000	17	12
Rhodesia	1	134,000	930,000	3	7
Rwanda	2	15,000	230,000	2	0
Senegal	3	265,000	1,600,000	4	2
Sierra Leone	1	330,000	1,480,000	2	1
Somali Republic .	2	140,000	1,500,000	4	0
South Africa	1	3,100,000	10,000,000	4	12
Sudan	2	300,000	1,900,000	2	3
Swaziland	2	12,000	20,000	0	2
Tanzania	2	135,000	1,500,000	4	6
Togo	1	35,000	140,000	1	1
Tunisia	2	400,000	2,275,000	1	4
Uganda	1	175,000	1,400,000	3	3
Upper Volta	2	80,000	490,000	2	2
Zambia	1	151,000	730,000	6	5

Source: USIA, *Communications Data Book for Africa*, pp. 46–61.
[a] *World Radio-TV Handbook 1969*, p. 246.

TABLE 4: Press and Periodicals

	Number of Dailies[a]	Estimated Circulation[b]	Total Number of All Publications[b]	Total Estimated Circulation of All Publications[b]
Algeria	3	185,000	39	213,000
Angola	4	52,000	27	89,000
Botswana	0	. . .	. . .	. . .
Burundi	0	. . .	6	17,000
Cameroon	1	10,850	26	25,990
Central African Republic	1	500	2	850
Chad	1	700	4	700+
Congo (Brazzaville)	3	9,000	14	39,000
Congo (Kinshasa)	6	53,000	36	162,500
Dahomey	2	3,500	10	11,500
Ethiopia	6	48,300	55	105,900
Gabon	1	1,500	5	5,000
Gambia	1	1,500	5	2,750
Ghana	4	140,000	13	272,000
Guinea	1	5,000	3	8,000
Ivory Coast	1	17,680	6	47,180
Kenya	3	73,000	74	341,900
Lesotho	0	. . .	4	11,000
Liberia	1	6,500	36	29,700
Libya	5	15,500	22	33,000
Malagasy Republic	6	62,300	39	160,330
Malawi	0	. . .	7	105,000
Mali	2	3,000	9	9,000
Mauritania	1	na	3	4,300
Mauritius	13	53,100	44	77,200
Morocco	8	135,000	40 (est.)	247,500
Mozambique	5	35,000	19	80,000
Niger	1	1,250	6	2,850
Nigeria	18	363,000	85	1,041,000
Rhodesia	2	66,600	25	237,100
Rwanda	0	. . .	6	27,000
Senegal	1	18,000	12	87,000
Sierra Leone	2	15,000	15	47,500
Somali Republic	1	4,000	9	10,000
South Africa	21	973,671	500	2,883,700+
Sudan	10	107,000	33	149,000
Swaziland	0	. . .	1	na
Tanzania	8	39,000	54	257,200
Togo	2	10,000	13	13,600+
Tunisia	5	68,000	29	171,500
Uganda	6	65,000	29	127,000
Upper Volta	2	3,000	4	5,000
Zambia	1	34,000	23	89,000+

[a] *Britannica Book of the Year 1969*, p. 638.
[b] USIA, *Communications Data Book for Africa*, pp. 66–68.

TABLE 5: Television Broadcasting

	Number of Programming Stations[a]	Volume of Telecasting[a] (hr. weekly)	Estimated Number of Sets[b]	Estimated Audience Size[a]
Algeria	3	30:10	83,064	980,000
Congo (Brazzaville)	1	16:45	1,000	14,400
Congo (Kinshasa)	1	10:30	7,000	2,000
Ethiopia	2	16:30	6,000	20–35,000
Gabon	1	10:00	1,200	1,600
Ghana	3	25:05	10,000	50,000
Ivory Coast	1	51:00	6,500	12,000
Kenya	1	35:30	14,500	76,000
Liberia	1	28:00	4,000	30,000
Libya	1	42:00	6,000	25,000
Malagasy Republic	1	15:00	na	na
Mauritius	1	24:30	11,000	6,000
Morocco	3	31:30	85,656	235,000
Niger	1	8:00	6	less than 100
Nigeria	5	180:00	53,000	400,000
Rhodesia	2	39:30	46,000	85,000
Senegal	1	1:45	500	1,000
Sierra Leone	1	33:30	3,000	15,000
Sudan	1	33:30	20,000	65,000
Tunisia	1	35:00	37,000	70,000
Uganda	1	30:30	9,000	30,000
Upper Volta	1	12:00	5,000	900
Zambia	3	37:30	17,500	91,000

[a] USIA, *Communications Data Book for Africa*, pp. 62–65.
[b] *World Radio-TV Handbook 1969*, p. 246.

TABLE 6: Cinema Facilities, 1960–65

	Indoor (16mm and 35mm)	Outdoor and Mobile Units	Total	Number of Seats	Weekly Attendance
Algeria	530	...	530	200,000	560,000
Angola	23	1	24	18,000	45,000
Botswana	6	1	7	1,600	1,000
Burundi	5	...	7	6,000	35,000
Cameroon	23	...	23	na	...
Central African Republic	4	...	4	2,000	7,600
Chad	7	...	7	4,000	25,000
Congo (Brazzaville) .	10	1	11	na	na
Congo (Kinshasa) ...	57[a]	210[b]	267	17,500	105,000
Dahomey	3	2	5	4,700	na
Ethiopia	18	2	20	15,250	8,000
Gabon	2	2	4	600	na
Gambia	7	5	12	2,000	na
Ghana	72	85	157	58,000	280,000
Guinea	20	2	22	10,000	na
Ivory Coast	50	25	75	25,000	na
Kenya	36	54	92	17,000	na
Lesotho	1	3	4	na	...
Liberia	12	3	15	11,500	3,000
Libya	32	...	32	20,000	69,000
Malagasy Republic .	40	5	45	13,800	50,960
Malawi	7	6	13	3,100	6,000
Mali	16	8	24	12,550	71,000
Mauritania	1	...	1	500	na
Mauritius	38	6	44	45,500	na
Morocco	214	...	214	120,000	426,000
Mozambique	35	...	35	12,400	40,000
Niger	9	7	16	3,000	21,000
Nigeria	83	100	183	36,800	500,000[c] 875,000[d]
Rhodesia	22	1	23	8,800	na
Rwanda	8	85	93	na	na
Senegal	87	2	89	50,415	na
Sierra Leone	13	25	38	7,260	20,000
Somali Republic	24	1	25	19,000	26,000
South Africa	2,953	551	3,501	522,000	1,000,000
Sudan	...	75	75	70,000	194,000
Swaziland	11	2	13	600	1,000
Tanzania	39	16	55	25,000	2,075[e]
Togo	2	...	2	2,000	5,700
Tunisia	108	na	108	61,000	112,224
Uganda	14	8	22	11,200	40,000
Upper Volta	...	8	8	10,000	40,000
Zambia	26	35	61	13,570	na

Source: USIA, *Communications Data Book for Africa, 1966,* pp. 69–71.
[a] 1959.
[b] Projection sites.
[c] Indoor.
[d] Outdoor.
[e] Zanzibar only.

NOTES

INTRODUCTION

1. For an example, see Leonard Doob, *Communication in Africa.*

CHAPTER 1

1. William A. Payne, "American Press Coverage of Africa," *Africa Report* 11:1, Jan. 1966, p. 45.
2. Ibid., p. 45.
3. Rosalynde Ainslie, *The Press in Africa*, p. 142.
4. G. A. Almond and J. S. Coleman, *Politics of Developing Areas*, p. 345.
5. Ibid., p. 345.
6. Robert Gardiner, "International Economic Development: The Significance of Aid to Africa" (a talk given to International Press Institute assembly at Nairobi, Kenya, June 3, 1968).
7. St. Clair Drake, "Social Change and Social Problems," in Walter Goldschmidt (ed.), *The United States and Africa*, p. 238.
8. Paul Bohannon, *Africa and Africans*, p. 213.
9. Leonard Doob, *Communication in Africa*, p. 24.
10. Ibrahim Abu-Lughod, "The Mass Media and Egyptian Village Life," *Social Forces* 42:1, Sept. 1963, p. 97.
11. *U.S. Army Area Handbook for Morocco*, p. 267.
12. Victor C. Ferkiss, *Africa's Search for Identity*, p. 114.
13. Thomas Hodgkin, *Nationalism in Colonial Africa*, p. 67.
14. Bernard Taper, "A Lover of Cities," *The New Yorker*, Feb. 1, 1967, p. 39.
15. U.S. Information Agency, "Media Preferences of Better Educated Nigerians and Radio Listening Habits of the General Population," Dec. 1964, p. 14.
16. See UNESCO, *Rural Mimeo Newspapers* (Reports and Papers on Mass Communications No. 46); and UNESCO, *Radio Broadcasting Serves Rural Development* (Reports and Papers on Mass Communication No. 48).
17. "Further Strictures in the North-East," *Africa Report*, Nov. 1966, p. 26.
18. U.S. Information Agency, *Communications Data Book for Africa*, p. 1.
19. UNESCO, *Mass Media in the Developing Countries* (Reports and Papers on Mass Communication No. 33), p. 16.
20. USIA, *Communications*, p. 1.

CHAPTER 2

1. U.S. Information Agency, "Mass Media Habits in West Africa," p. iii.
2. Rosalynde Ainslie, *The Press in Africa*, p. 154.
3. Lord Hailey, *An African Survey*, p. 1246.
4. UNESCO, *World Communications*, p. 28.
5. Robert Hartland, "Press and Radio in Post Independence Africa," in U.S. National Commission for UNESCO, *Africa and the United States: Images and Realities* (Eighth Annual Conference, Boston, Mass., Oct. 22–26, 1961), p. 194.
6. Tom Hopkinson, "Newspapers Must Wait in Priority Queue," *IPI Report* 16:2, June 1967, p. 18.
7. Griffith J. Davis, "Sector Analysis—Communications Media" (AID paper, June 1962), p. 3.
8. U.S. Information Agency, "Radio Listening in Four West African Cities," p. 11.
9. USIA, "Mass Media Habits," p. 1.
10. Ibid.

11. U.S. Information Agency, "Basic Attitudes and General Communication Habits in Four West African Capitals," p. 12.

12. U.S. Information Agency, "Media Use Among Africans in Nairobi, Kenya," p. 4.

13. Victor C. Ferkiss, *Africa's Search for Identity,* p. 163.

14. "World Daily Newspapers and Circulations, 1968–69," *Britannica Book of the Year 1970* (Chicago: Encyclopaedia Britannica, 1970), p. 650.

15. William John Hanna (ed.) *Independent Black Africa,* p. 244.

16. Hartland, "Press and Radio," p. 198.

17. U.S. Information Agency, *Kenya: A Communications Fact Book* (Dec. 12, 1961), p. 15.

18. "La Presse en Afrique Noire," *Vente et Publicite* (Paris), July–Aug. 1954, p. 116.

19. USIA, "Mass Media Habits," p. 39.

20. U.S. Information Agency, "Overseas Television Growth in 1965," p. 8.

21. U.S. Information Agency, *Communications Data Book for Africa,* p. 62.

22. U.S. Information Agency, "Overseas Television," p. 21.

23. Hartland, "Press and Radio," p. 200.

24. USIA, *Communications,* p. 79.

25. W. Phillips Davison, *International Political Communication,* p. 152.

26. Russell Warren Howe, "Reporting from Africa: A Correspondent's View," *Journalism Quarterly* 43:2, Summer 1966, p. 317.

27. Interview with Hilary Ng'weno by author in Nairobi, Feb. 1965.

28. Leonard Doob, *Communication in Africa,* p. 286.

29. U.S. Information Agency, "Radio Listening in Four West African Cities," p. 16.

CHAPTER 3

1. Richard Hall, "The Press in Black Africa; How Free Is It?" *Optima* 18:1, Mar. 1968, p. 13.

2. "Toils of the Press," *IPI Report* 14:6, Oct. 1965, p. 11.

3. Walter Emery, *National and International Systems of Broadcasting* (East Lansing: Michigan State University Press, 1969), p. 673.

4. UNESCO, *World Communications,* p. 17.

5. Ibid., p. 16.

6. U.S. Information Agency, *Communications Data Book for Africa,* p. 82.

7. Interview by author with Nigerian Ministry of Information officials in Lagos, Mar. 1968.

8. Interview by author with Dr. Imam, head of MENA, in Cairo, Feb. 1, 1965.

9. Rosalynde Ainslie, *The Press in Africa,* p. 207.

10. Interview with Swinton by Robert Bishop in New York, Dec. 27, 1966.

11. Ainslie, *The Press,* p. 19.

12. "Toils of the Press," p. 11.

13. Ainslie, *The Press,* p. 20.

14. Frank Barton, *African Assignment,* p. 41.

15. Tom Hopkinson, "The Press in Africa," in Colin Legum, *Africa: A Handbook to the Continent,* p. 437.

16. "Uganda Editor Jailed, Cleared, Jailed Again," *IPI Report* 17:11, Mar. 1969, p. 2.

17. Hopkinson, "The Press," p. 437.

CHAPTER 4

1. Russell Warren Howe, "Reporting from Africa: A Correspondent's View," *Journalism Quarterly* 43:2, Summer 1966, p. 316.

2. Ralph E. Kliesch, "The Press Corps Abroad Revisited: A Fourth World Survey of Foreign Correspondents" (a paper read at Association for Education in Journalism Convention, Berkeley, Aug. 1969), p. 8.

3. Interview by author with Kenneth Whiting, Associated Press bureau chief in Johannesburg, Apr. 1968.

4. William A. Payne, "American Press Coverage of Africa," *Africa Report* 11:1, Jan. 1966, p. 46.

5. Ibid., p. 47.

6. Ibid.

7. James Wallington, "UPI and African News" (unpublished research paper, Michigan State University, 1963), p. 2.

8. William Attwood, *The Reds and the Blacks,* p. 327.

9. Rosalynde Ainslie, *The Press in Africa,* p. 191.

10. Ibid.

11. Peter Enahoro, "Reporting Africa" (a background paper for the 17th General Assembly of the International Press Institute at Nairobi, June 5, 1968), p. 2.

12. Hilary Ng'weno and Pierre de Vos, "Paradrop Stanleyville," *IPI Report,* Jan. 1965, p. 7.

13. John Strohmeyer, "What Passes for American News in Africa," *Harper's* 231:1386, Nov. 1965, p. 104.

14. Virginia Thompson and Richard Adloff, *French West Africa,* p. 551.

15. Information on AFP operations was obtained from AFP executives in Nairobi, June 1968.

16. Enahoro, "Reporting," p. 3.

17. Mark Hopkins, *Mass Media in the Soviet Union* (New York: Pegasus, 1970), p. 256.

18. U.S. Information Agency, *Communication Data Book for Africa,* p. 79.

19. George Clay, Philippe Decraene, and Colin Legum, "Reporting Africa," *IPI Report,* Aug. 1962, p. 5.

20. Interview with Stan Swinton by Robert Bishop in New York, Dec. 27, 1966.

21. Wilbur Schramm, *Mass Media and National Development,* p. 58.

22. Ibid., p. 23.

23. William A. Hachten, "The Flow of News and Underdevelopment: A Pilot Study of the African Press" (a paper delivered to the Association for Education in Journalism, Iowa City, Aug. 30, 1966), p. 13.

24. Ibid., p. 14.

25. Daniel Lerner, "Toward A Communication Theory of Modernization," in Lucian Pye (ed.), *Communications and Political Development,* p. 333.

26. Held at Tunis, Tunisia, Apr. 1–6, 1963.

27. "OAU Conference Calls for Pan-African News Agency," a Reuters item in the *Egyptian Mail* (Cairo), Jan. 30, 1965, p. 1.

28. Ainslie, *The Press,* p. 210.

29. Ibid.

30. *IPI Report* 15:8, Dec. 1966, p. 2.

31. "News in Brief," *Africa Report* 13:2, Feb. 1968, p. 25.

32. "Pan-African Agency Aim," *IPI Report,* Jan. 1968, p. 4.

33. Enahoro, "Reporting," p. 1.

34. Strohmeyer, "What Passes," p. 104.

CHAPTER 5

1. Edwin S. Munger, "Africa in 240 Minutes," *Africa Report* 12:7, Oct. 1967, p. 67.

2. Clyde Sanger, "The Foreign Correspondent in Independent Africa: Problems and Prospects," *Africa Report* 11:1, Jan. 1966, p. 42.

3. Peter Enahoro, "Reporting Africa" (a background paper for the 17th General Assembly of the International Press Institute at Nairobi, June 5, 1968), p. 1.

4. Blaine Littell, *South of the Moon* (New York: Harper and Row, 1966), p. 6.

5. Ralph E. Kliesch, "The Press Corps Abroad Revisited: A Fourth World Survey of Foreign Correspondents" (a paper read at the Association for Education in Journalism Convention, Berkeley, Aug. 1969), p. 8.

6. John Wilhelm, "The Re-Appearing Foreign Correspondent," *Journalism Quarterly* 40:2, Spring 1963, p. 151.

7. Ibid.

8. Russell Warren Howe, "Reporting from Africa: A Correspondent's View," *Journalism Quarterly* 43:2, Summer 1966, p. 318.

9. William A. Payne, "American Press Coverage of Africa," *Africa Report* 11:1, Jan. 1966, p. 45.

10. Peter Webb, "Session on Reporting Africa" (a talk at the International Press Institute assembly in Nairobi, June 5, 1968), p. 2.

11. Interview by author with Webb in Nairobi, Feb. 23, 1965.

12. Ibid.

13. Webb, "Session," p. 3.

14. Tom Mboya, "This is What the Press Must Do," *IPI Report*, June 1962, p. 5.

15. "Two African Views of the U.S. Press," *Africa Report*, May 1961, p. 16.

16. Ibid.

17. Kenneth Kaunda in an address to the International Press Institute assembly in Nairobi, June 4, 1968.

18. Payne, "American Press," p. 46.

19. Sanger, "The Foreign Correspondent," p. 44, and interview by author with Sanger in Nairobi, Feb. 1965.

20. Vernon McKay, *Africa in World Politics*, p. 267.

21. Fred Yu and John Luter, "The Foreign Correspondent and His Work," *Columbia Journalism Review* 31:1, Spring 1964, p. 9.

22. Laurence Fellows, "Session on Reporting Africa" (a talk at the International Press Institute assembly at Nairobi, June 5, 1968), p. 1.

23. *IPI Report*, Jan. 1965, p. 6.

24. Rosalynde Ainslie, *The Press in Africa*, p. 63.

25. Hilary Ng'weno and Pierre de Vos, "Paradrop Stanleyville," *IPI Report*, Jan. 1965, p. 7.

26. William Attwood, *The Reds and the Blacks*, p. 218.

27. Russell Warren Howe, "The United States Press and Africa" (a speech on Oct. 25, 1961, to the Seventh Plenary Session of the U.S. Commission on the United Nations), p. 5.

28. Ibid.

29. *IPI Report*, July/Aug. 1967, p. 24.

30. Ibid., Apr. 1967, p. 11.

31. Ibid., Mar. 1967, p. 11.

32. Ibid., Jan. 1967, p. 13.

33. Ibid., May 1966, p. 12.

34. Ibid., Apr. 1966, p. 11.

35. Yu and Luter, "The Foreign Correspondent," p. 6.

36. Enahoro, "Reporting," p. 6.

37. Letter from Fellows to Knut S. Royce at the University of Iowa, Feb. 5, 1966.

38. Based on author's interview with Garrison in Lagos, Apr. 1965, and Lloyd Garrison, "Biafra Revisited," *Times Talk* XII, Sept. 1968, p. 8.

39. "Three Reporters Rescued from Katanga Mob," *Editor & Publisher*, Jan. 5, 1963, p. 12.

40. *Associated Press Log*, June 17–23, 1965.

41. Ibid., Oct. 27–Nov. 2, 1965.

42. McKay, *Africa*, p. 268.

43. Philip W. Quigg, "The Changing American View of Africa," *Africa Report* 14:1, Jan. 1969, p. 8.

CHAPTER 6

1. Rosalynde Ainslie, *The Press in Africa*, p. 140.

2. Theodore Draper, "World Politics: A New Era? *Encounter* 31:2, Aug. 1968, p. 11.

3. W. Phillips Davison, *International Political Communication*, p. 2.

4. Ibid., p. 10.

5. U.S. Information Agency, "Communist Propaganda Activities in Africa," p. 25.

6. J. C. Clews, *Communist Propaganda Techniques*, p. 277.

7. Ibid., p. 280.

8. John K. Cooley, *East Wind Over Africa*, p. 197.

9. Ibid.
10. Ibid.
11. "Peking's New Diplomatic Setbacks in Africa," *Communist Affairs,* Jan.–Feb. 1966, p. 24.
12. USIA, "Communist Propaganda," p. 25.
13. Cooley, *East Wind,* p. 195.
14. "Communist Radio Propaganda to Africa," *Communist Affairs,* May–June 1964, p. 29.
15. Cooley, *East Wind,* p. 196.
16. USIA, "Communist Propaganda," p. 25.
17. "Propaganda," *Britannica Book of the Year 1968* (Chicago: Encyclopaedia Britannica, 1968), p. 647.
18. Cooley, *East Wind,* p. 196.
19. Ibid., p. 200.
20. USIA, "Communist Propaganda," p. 18.
21. Robert and Elizabeth Bass, "Eastern Europe," in Zbigniew Brzezinski (ed.), *Africa and the Communist World,* p. 111.
22. Richard Lowenthal, "China," in Brzezinski, *Africa,* p. 158.
23. Ignatius Peng Yao, "The New China News Agency: How It Serves the Party," *Journalism Quarterly* 40:1, Winter 1963, p. 85.
24. Cooley, *East Wind,* p. 195.
25. "The Casual Correspondent," *Newsweek,* Aug. 9, 1965, p. 45.
26. Yao, "The New China," p. 84.
27. Theodore Kruglak, *The Two Faces of TASS* (New York: McGraw-Hill, 1963), p. 5.
28. Ibid., p. 134.
29. UPI news dispatch from Dar es Salaam, Dec. 10, 1966.
30. Fritz Schatten, *Communism in Africa,* p. 233.
31. "African Journalists Discuss Political Role," *Africa Report,* July 1961, p. 10.
32. *Special Warfare Area Handbook for Ghana,* p. 296.
33. Cooley, *East Wind,* p. 149.
34. *Hearings Before a Subcommittee on Appropriations, House of Representatives, 87th Congress, Second Session,* p. 150.
35. Cooley, *East Wind,* p. 116.
36. "The Drama of the Press of Algeria," *IPI Report,* July 1961, p. 4.
37. "Press Reshuffle to Cut Deficit," *IPI Report,* Dec. 1964, p. 7.
38. For the following description of the USIA's rapid buildup in Africa the author has relied heavily on an unpublished master's thesis by Daniel Ruskin, "USIA Comes to Africa: A Case Study of U.S. Overseas Information, 1960–1965" (University of Wisconsin, June 1967).
39. Davison, *International,* p. 258.
40. Wilson P. Dizard, *The Strategy of Truth* (Washington: Public Affairs Press, 1961), p. 122.
41. Interview by Daniel Ruskin with Michael G. Guiffrida, press officer, USIA (Africa), in Washington, Jan. 24, 1967.
42. *U.S. House of Representatives Appropriations Hearings, Fiscal Year 1965,* p. 33.
43. Interview by Ruskin with John Russell, chief of African programs, USIA Motion Picture and Television Service, Washington, D.C., Jan. 26, 1967.
44. *U.S. House of Representatives, USIA Appropriations Hearings, Fiscal Year 1966,* p. 77.
45. New York *Times,* Nov. 25, 1965, p. 77.
46. *"Time* Essay: The Distant Message of the Transistor," *Time,* Nov. 24, 1967, p. 45.
47. U.S. Information Agency, *Communications Data Book for Africa,* p. 48.
48. U.S. Information Agency, "Communications Fact Book for Ghana (1961)," p. 16.
49. Ainslie, *The Press,* p. 62.
50. Vernon McKay, "South African Propaganda: Methods and Media," *Africa Report,* Feb. 1966, p. 41.
51. Francis Pollack, "America's Press on Safari," *Nation,* Nov. 7, 1966, p. 479.
52. Ibid.

53. Ibid.

54. McKay, "South African," p. 45.

55. "S.A. Finds Big Propaganda Tool in TV," *The Star* (Johannesburg), Apr. 24, 1968, p. 6.

56. Information obtained by author from South African Broadcasting Corporation, Johannesburg, Apr. 1968.

57. McKay, "South African," p. 44.

58. Ibid., p. 46.

CHAPTER 7

1. E. J. Moulton, "Satellite over Africa," *Africa Report* 12:5, May 1967, p. 13.

2. "News in Brief," *Africa Report* 14:1, Jan. 1969, p. 27.

3. Moulton, "Satellite," p. 14.

4. Thomas J. Hamilton, "Russia Plans Competitor for Comsat," *International Herald-Tribune* (Paris) Aug. 15, 1968, p. 1.

5. "*Time* Essay: The Distant Message of the Transistor," *Time*, Nov. 24, 1967, p. 45.

6. E. Lloyd Sommerlad, *The Press in Developing Countries*, p. 104.

7. Larry K. Martin, "Mimeographed Village Papers Prove Value in Liberia," *Journalism Quarterly* 41:2, Spring 1964, p. 245.

8. Max Neff Smart, "Newspapers for Africa," *Nieman Reports* 17:1, Mar. 1964, p. 9.

9. Max Neff Smart, "Newspapers in Developing Nations—Antidote to Illiteracy," *The Quill* 55:5, May 1966, p. 18.

10. UNESCO, *Rural Mimeo Newspapers* by Robert de T. Lawrence (Reports and Papers on Mass Communications No. 46), p. 7.

11. Mary Ellen Hughes, "The Rural Mimeo Newspaper Experiment in Liberia" (unpublished master's thesis in journalism, University of Wisconsin, 1969).

12. UNESCO, *Developing Information Media in Africa* (Reports and Papers on Mass Communication No. 37), p. 34.

13. D. Klaus von Bismarck and E. J. B. Rose, *Probleme der Publizistik in Afrika*, p. 68.

14. Interview with Michael Curtis by author in Nairobi, Feb. 1965.

15. Some of the material on training appeared originally in William A. Hachten, "The Training of African Journalists," *Gazette* 14:2, 1968, p. 101.

16. Ronald A. Watts, "African Journalism Institute," *Gazette* 14:2, 1968, p. 153.

17. Ladislav Mareda, "The International Organization of Journalists Looks After the Professional Training of Journalists from Developing Countries," *Gazette* 14:2, 1968, p. 158.

18. Mareda, "International," p. 162.

CHAPTER 8

1. James S. Coleman, *Nigeria*, p. 186.

2. St. Clair Drake in George H. T. Kimble, *Tropical Africa*, Vol. 2: *Society and Polity*, p. 144.

3. F. A. O. Schwarz, Jr., *Nigeria: The Tribes, the Nation or the Race—The Politics of Independence* (Cambridge: MIT Press, 1965), p. 162.

4. In this section the author relied heavily on an unpublished master's thesis in journalism done under his supervision at the University of Wisconsin in 1967. The title is "Nationalism and the Press in British West Africa," and the author is E. Lloyd Murphy.

5. Christopher Fyfe, *A History of Sierra Leone* (London: Oxford University Press, 1952), p. 59.

6. Ibid., p. 89.

7. Herbert Passin and K. A. B. Jones-Quartey (eds.), *Africa: The Dynamics of Change*, p. 148.

8. Ibid.

9. Increase Coker, "Notes on the History of the Press in Nigeria" (unpublished paper, Lagos, 1965).

10. Thomas Hodgkin, *African Political Parties*, p. 46.

11. Dennis Austin, *Politics in Ghana*, p. 119.

12. Gabriel Almond and James S. Coleman, *Politics of Developing Areas*, p. 351.

13. Ibid.

14. K. A. B. Jones-Quartey, *A Life of Azikiwe*, p. 158.

15. Hodgkin, *African*, p. 32.

16. James S. Coleman, "African Political Systems," in Walter Goldschmidt (ed.), *The United States and Africa*, p. 51.

17. U.S. Information Agency, *Communications Data Book for Africa. World Radio TV Handbook, 1969* lists 1,260,000 radios and 53,000 television sets for Nigeria.

18. Richard Hall, 'The Press in Black Africa; How Free Is It?" *Optima* 18:1, Mar. 1968, p. 15.

19. Interview by author with *Pilot* editorial personnel in Apr. 1965 and Mar. 1968.

20. Interview by author with Increase Coker at Lagos in Mar. 1965.

21. Information based on visit to *Daily Sketch* in Ibadan, Apr. 1965.

22. Information obtained from Federal Ministry of Information in Lagos, Mar. 1968.

23. These were speculations by officials in the Federal Ministry of Information in Lagos, Mar. 1968.

24. "Dateline Africa," *West Africa*, Nov. 13, 1965, p. 1283.

25. *IPI Report* 14:10, Feb. 1966, p. 3.

26. Based on author's monitoring of broadcasts and his visits to NBC in 1965 and 1968.

27. Interview by author with Segun Smith, news director of NTS, Mar. 1965.

28. Interview by author with S. Ayo-Vaughn, head of news at WNBS in Ibadan, Apr. 1965.

29. Interview by author with Alhagi Dodo Mustapha, acting general manager of BCNN in Kaduna, Mar. 1965.

30. Interview by author with Lloyd Garrison of New York *Times* in Lagos, Apr. 1965.

31. *IPI Report* 12:8, Dec. 1963, p. 9.

32. Adolphus Paterson, "The African Press: A Case Study," *The Journalist's World* 3:4, 1965–66, p. 27.

33. "Shock and Dismay at Takeover of the Ashanti Pioneer," *IPI Report* 11:7, Nov. 1962, p. 1.

34. *Special Warfare Area Handbook for Ghana*, p. 307.

35. Ibid., p. 291.

36. Ibid., p. 293.

37. "Television," *West Africa*, June 3, 1965, p. 3.

38. *Handbook for Ghana*, p. 299.

39. U.S. Information Agency, "Communications Fact Book for Ghana" (1961), p. 35.

40. *Handbook for Ghana*, p. 299.

41. Lloyd Garrison, "Ghana Facing Tighter Rule," New York *Times*, Feb. 9, 1966, p. 129.

42. Henry Bretton, *The Rise and Fall of Kwame Nkrumah* (New York: Praeger, 1966), p. 129.

43. *IPI Report* 15:5, Sept. 1966, p. 3.

44. Adolphus Paterson, "After Ghana's Coup—A Hunger for News," *IPI Report* 15:1, May 1966, p. 11.

45. "Ghana's New 'Pioneer' Makes Vow," *IPI Report* 15:9, Jan. 1967, p. 3.

46. "Soldiers and Editors," *West Africa*, Jan. 27, 1968, No. 2643, p. 1.

47. Interview by author with John Dumoga in Accra, Mar. 1968.

48. "News in Brief," *Africa Report*, Mar. 1968, p. 32, and Apr. 1968, p. 3.

49. Interview by author with Henry Ofori in Accra, Mar. 1968.

50. Information obtained at Ghana Broadcasting Corporation in Accra, Mar. 1968.

51. USIA, "Fact Book," p. 33.

CHAPTER 9

1. Gabriel Almond and James S. Coleman, *Politics of Developing Areas,* p. 352.
2. Rosalynde Ainslie, *The Press in Africa,* p. 130.
3. Committee on Inter-African Relations, *Report on the Press in West Africa,* p. 19.
4. Virginia Thompson, "The Ivory Coast," in Gwendolen Carter (ed.), *African One-Party States,* p. 272.
5. Thomas Hodgkin, *African Political Parties,* p. 32.
6. Committee on Inter-African Relations, *Report,* p. 19.
7. Thompson, "Ivory Coast," p. 272.
8. Ainslie, *The Press,* p. 132.
9. Committee on Inter-African Relations, *Report,* p. 19.
10. Almond and Coleman, *Politics,* p. 352.
11. "On the Threshold of Take-Off," *Newsweek,* Aug. 9, 1965, p. 46.
12. Victor DuBois, "Houphouët-Boigny: Francophone Africa's Man of the Year," *Africa Report* 10:11, Dec. 1965, p. 8.
13. Claire Sterling, "Houphouët-Boigny Wins a Bet," *The Reporter,* June 16, 1966, p. 27.
14. *U.S. Army Area Handbook for the Ivory Coast,* p. 277.
15. Interview by author with Dona-Fologo in Abidjan, Apr. 1965.
16. Ainslie, *The Press,* p. 139.
17. Interview by author with Laspeyres in Abidjan, Apr. 1965.
18. U.S. Information Agency, "Basic Attitudes and General Communication Habits in Four West African Capitals," p. iii. In Abidjan, some 1,003 respondents were asked: "To know what is going on elsewhere in the world, how do you personally get your information?" The responses were: from the radio, 68%; friends or relatives, 50%; daily newspapers, 52%; magazines, 23%; newsreels, 26%; books, 13%; other, 2%.

The same persons were asked: "From which do you get the best information?" The responses were: from radio, 59%; friends or relatives, 31%; daily newspapers, 28%; newsreels, 3%; books, 1%; magazines, 3%; other, 2%.

When asked, "How often do you listen to the radio?" the Abidjan listeners gave this response: 50% said every day; 15% said several times a week; 3% said once a week; and 1% said once or twice a month.

For Abidjan residents, these questions were asked: "Do you read, even though only seldom, a daily newspaper?" (If "yes"): "How often?" Answers were: Every day, 27%; several times a week, 10%; once or twice a week, 7%; a few times a month, 2%; very seldom, 9%; never, 45%.
19. U.S. Information Agency, "The Ivory Coast: A Communications Fact Book" (1963), p. 12.
20. *Area Handbook,* p. 277.
21. Interview by author with De Bergevin at Dakar, May 1965.
22. Interview by author with AFP bureau chief in Dakar, 1965.
23. Interview by author with Adotevi in Dakar, May 1965.
24. Information on broadcasting obtained from officials at Radio Senegal in Dakar, May 1965.
25. A first report on the UNESCO-Senegal television project is contained in *Television and the Social Education of Women* by Pierre Fougeyrollas (UNESCO Reports and Papers on Mass Communication No. 50).

CHAPTER 10

1. Felice Carter, "The Press in Kenya," *Gazette* 14:2, 1968, p. 85.
2. See Tom Mboya, "This Is What the Press Must Do," *IPI Report,* June 1962, p. 5, for an African leader's preindependence assessment of the European press.
3. Nick Russel, "Tabloid and Broadsheet Face Same Odds," *IPI Report* 17:2, June 1968, p. 15.
4. Carter, "The Press," p. 86.
5. Ibid., p. 85.
6. George H. T. Kimble, *Tropical Africa,* p. 147.

7. President Kenyatta recounted his journalistic experiences when addressing the International Press Institute assembly in Nairobi in June 1968. He commented, "I was the first African to reach the dizzy heights of editor."

8. "An African Press Survey: East and Central Africa," *New Commonwealth,* Aug. 19, 1954, p. 171.

9. "Lost Opportunity on Kenya's Vernacular Press," *IPI Report,* Jan. 1953, p. 5.

10. Norman Miller, "Kenya: Nationalism and the Press—1951–1961" (1963), quoted in Joseph G. Healey, "Press Freedom in Kenya" (Freedom of Information Center Report No. 191, Columbia, Missouri, Dec. 1967), p. 2.

11. Healey, "Press Freedom," p. 2.

12. Lord William Malcolm Hailey, *An African Survey,* p. 1238.

13. Gabriel Almond and James S. Coleman, *Politics of Developing Areas,* p. 346.

14. Interviews by author with Ministry of Information and Broadcasting officials in Nairobi, June 1968.

15. Benjamin Nimer, "Television, Language, and National Cohesion in Kenya and Uganda" (a paper delivered at the African Studies Association meeting in Bloomington, Oct. 1966), p. 10.

16. Ibid., p. 3.

17. This information was supplied by Voice of Kenya officials in Nairobi, June 1968. However, a USIS source said the total number of television receivers in use was closer to 12,000 of which only 1,000 were owned by black Kenyans.

18. Interview by author with Peter Gichathi, Permanent Secretary, Ministry of Information, in Nairobi, June 1968.

19. Richard Hall, "The Press in Black Africa; How Free Is It?" *Optima* 18:1, Mar. 1968, p. 33.

20. Russel, "Tabloid and Broadsheets," p. 15.

21. Ibid., p. 16.

22. Ibid.

23. Interview by author with Dr. Jerry Kallas, former USIA research officer in East Africa, in Nairobi, June 1968.

24. Interview by author with Francis Khamisi in Nairobi, June 1968.

25. Russel, "Tabloid and Broadsheet," p. 16.

26. Interview by author with George Githii in Nairobi, June 1968.

27. This view was expressed by several editors interviewed by the author in Nairobi in 1965 and in 1968.

28. Russel, "Tabloid and Broadsheet," p. 15.

29. Carter, "The Press," p. 87.

30. *The Reporter,* Feb. 12, 1965, p. 10.

31. Interview by author with Henry Reuter in Nairobi, Feb. 1965.

32. Carter, "The Press," p. 87.

33. Healey, "Press Freedom," p. 6.

34. Laurence Fellows, "Kenya Threatens to Purge Press Unless It Stops 'Exaggerating' the Plight of Indians," New York *Times,* Jan. 15, 1969, p. 8.

35. *IPI Report* 18:5, Sept. 1969, p. 2.

36. Wilbur Schramm and E. Lloyd Sommerlad, "Northern Rhodesia: Training in Mass Communications" (Paris: UNESCO, Aug. 1964), p. 2.

37. Clyde Sanger, *Central African Emergency,* p. 328.

38. Hall, "The Press in Black Africa," p. 13.

39. Rosalynde Ainslie, *The Press in Africa,* p. 96.

40. Ibid.

41. Sanger, *Central African,* p. 330.

42. U.S. Information Service sources in Lusaka claimed the *Times*'s circulation was only 34,000 in 1968, whereas Derek Taylor, a *Times* editor, told the author it was 40,000 to 48,000.

43. These views were expressed by Derek Taylor, political editor of the *Times,* in an interview in Lusaka, May 1968.

44. Robert I. Rotberg, "Tribalism and Politics in Zambia," *Africa Report* 12:9, Dec. 1967, p. 33.

45. "Top Loser in Zambia in Lonrho," *Rand Daily Mail* (Johannesburg), Apr. 23, 1968, p. 13.

46. "New Rules in Zambia," *The Times* (London), Aug. 20, 1968, p. 3.

47. Richard Hall, *Zambia* (New York: Praeger, 1965), p. 129.

48. By P. J. Fraenkel.
49. Interview by author with Alick Nkata, director of broadcasting, in Lusaka, May 1968.
50. During the author's visit to Zambia in May 1968, Radio Zambia failed to report a major wildcat strike involving 2,200 miners at Kabwe, despite the fact that the newspapers carried the story.
51. Schramm and Sommerlad, "Northern Rhodesia," p. 3.

CHAPTER 11

1. Leo Marquard, *The Story of South Africa* (London: Faber and Faber, 1954, 1963), p. 257.
2. *State of South Africa Year Book 1968* (Johannesburg, 1968), p. 68.
3. Data obtained from U.S. Information Agency sources, Feb. 1967.
4. Trevor Brown, "No News for 170 Years?" (a paper delivered at the Association for Education in Journalism meeting at Berkeley, Aug. 1969), p. 2.
5. Rosalynde Ainslie, *The Press in Africa*, p. 41.
6. Helen Kitchen, *The Press in Africa*, p. 43.
7. Ainslie, *The Press*, p. 48.
8. Ibid., p. 47.
9. Ibid., p. 49.
10. Lord William Malcolm Hailey, *An African Survey*, p. 1234.
11. Sampson wrote *Drum*, and Hopkinson, *In the Fiery Continent*.
12. Newspaper circulations were supplied by U.S. Information Service in Johannesburg, Apr. 1968.
13. Ainslie, *The Press*, p. 74.
14. "The Argus Printing and Publishing Company Limited" (77th Annual Report for the Year ending 31 Dec. 1967), p. 6.
15. Thomas Karis, "South Africa," in Gwendolen Carter, *Five African States*, p. 512.
16. "Anti-Apartheid Paper in Johannesburg is Honored," New York *Times*, Feb. 25, 1966, p. 3.
17. Interview by author with Joel Mervis in Johannesburg, Apr. 1968.
18. Mervis interview.
19. Allen Drury, *A Very Strange Society* (London: Michael Joseph, 1968), p. 113.
20. Rene de Villiers, "The Press and the People" (an address to the South African Institute for Race Relations, Johannesburg, Nov. 1967), p. 8.
21. Interview with Hennie Kotze in Johannesburg, Apr. 1968.
22. Kotze interview.
23. Interview with Charles Still in Johannesburg, Apr. 1968.
24. Interview with Howard Laurence in Cape Town, Apr. 1968.
25. "South Africa's Press Council and the Government," *IPI Report* 12:8, Dec. 1963, p. 7.
26. Ainslie, *The Press*, p. 86.
27. Ibid.
28. "South Africa: Tougher Laws?" *IPI Report* 16:5, Sept. 1967, p. 3.
29. For the following discussion of South African law, the author has quoted liberally from material supplied by Raymond Louw, editor of the *Rand Daily Mail*.
30. These views were expressed by several editors interviewed by the author in South Africa in Apr. 1968.
31. *IPI Report* 12:5, Sept. 1963, p. 15.
32. Ibid. 12:6, Oct. 1963, p. 11.
33. Ibid. 12:7, Nov. 1963, p. 11.
34. Ibid. 13:11, Mar. 1965, p. 12.
35. Ibid. 13:10, Feb. 1965, p. 8.
36. Ibid. 8:6, Oct. 1969, p. 7.
37. "Hertzog Says News Agency Biased," *IPI Report* 15:6, Oct./Nov. 1966, p. 11.
38. *IPI Report* 13:9, Jan. 1965, p. 10.
39. Ibid. 15:2, June 1966, p. 11.
40. Ibid. 15:8, Dec. 1966, p. 15.

41. Paul Blanshard, "Censorship and Apartheid," *The Reporter* 38:4, Feb. 22, 1968, p. 38.

42. *The Star* (Johannesburg), Apr. 18, 1968, p. 8.

43. Blanshard, "Censorship," p. 39.

44. This and other data on radio were obtained from interviews with SABC officials in Johannesburg, Apr. 1968.

45. South African Broadcasting Corporation, *Annual Report 1967*, p. 52.

46. Arnold Beichman, "South Africa: Future Tense," *Columbia University Forum* 11:3, Fall 1965, p. 30.

47. Beichman, "South Africa," p. 30.

BIBLIOGRAPHY

BOOKS

Advertising and Press Annual of Africa, 1968. Cape Town: National Publishing Co., 1968.

African Newspapers in Selected American Libraries. A union list. 3rd ed. Washington, D.C.: Serial Division, Reference Department, Library of Congress, 1965.

Ainslie, Rosalynde. *The Press in Africa: Communications Past and Present.* Rev. ed. New York: Walker & Co., 1968.

Almond, Gabriel, A., and Coleman, James S., eds. *Politics of Developing Areas.* Princeton: Princeton University Press, 1960.

Attwood, William. *The Reds and the Blacks.* New York: Harper & Row, 1967.

Austin, Dennis. *Politics in Ghana: 1946–60.* New York: Oxford University Press, 1964.

Barton, Frank. *African Assignment: The Story of IPI's Six-Year Training Programme in Tropical Africa.* Zurich: International Press Institute, 1969.

———. *The Press in Africa.* Nairobi: East African Publishing House, 1966.

Bebey, Francis. *La Radiodiffussion en Afrique Noire.* Paris: Editions St. Paul, 1963.

Behn, Hans Ulrich. *Die Presse in Westafrika.* Hamburg: German Institute of African Studies, 1968.

Bismarck, D. Klaus von, and Rose, E. J. B. *Probleme der Publizistik in Afrika.* Assen: Van Gorcum & Co., 1962.

Blair, T. L. V. *Africa: A Market Profile.* London: Business Publications, 1965.

Brzezinski, Zbigniew K., ed. *Africa and the Communist World.* Stanford, Calif.: Stanford University Press, 1963.

Carter, Gwendolen Margaret, ed. *African One-Party States.* Ithaca, N.Y.: Cornell University Press, 1962.

———. *Five African States: Responses to Diversity.* Ithaca, N.Y.: Cornell University Press, 1963.

Clews, John C. *Communist Propaganda Techniques.* London: Methuen, 1964.

Coleman, James. *Nigeria: Background to Nationalism.* Berkeley: University of California Press, 1963.

Committee on Inter-African Relations. *Report on the Press in West Africa.* Ibadan: University College, 1960.

Cooley, John K. *East Wind Over Africa: Red China's African Offensive.* New York: Walker & Co., 1965.

Davison, W. Phillips. *International Political Communication.* New York: Frederick A. Praeger, 1965.

Dizard, Wilson P. *Television: A World View.* Syracuse, N.Y.: Syracuse University Press, 1966.

Doob, Leonard W. *Communication in Africa: A Search for Boundaries.* New Haven, Conn.: Yale University Press, 1961.

Ferkiss, Victor C. *Africa's Search for Identity.* New York: George Braziller, 1966.

Feuereisen, Fritz, and Schmacke, Ernst, eds. *Die Presse in Afrika; Ein Handbuch fur Wirtschaft und Werbung.* Munich: Pulloch, 1968.

Fraenkel, P. J. *Wayaleshi: Radio in Central Africa.* London: Weidenfeld and Nicholson, 1959.

Gale, W. D. *The Rhodesian Press.* Salisbury: Rhodesian Printing and Publishing Co., 1962.

Goldschmidt, Walter, ed. *The United States and Africa.* New York: Frederick A. Praeger, 1963.

Gras, Jacqueline. *Situation de la Presse dans les États de l'Union Africaine et Malgache, en Guinée, au Mali, au Togo.* Paris: La Documentation Française, 1963.

Hailey, Lord William Malcolm. *An African Survey.* Rev. ed. London: Oxford University Press, 1956.

Hodgkin, Thomas. *African Political Parties.* London: Penguin Books, 1961.

———. *Nationalism in Colonial Africa.* New York: New York University Press, 1957.

Hopkinson, Tom. *In the Fiery Continent.* New York: Doubleday & Co., 1962.

———. *Two Years in Africa.* Zurich: International Press Institute, 1965.

Hughes, John. *The New Face of Africa South of the Sahara.* New York: Longmans, Green, 1961.

Huth, Arno G. *Communications Media in Tropical Africa.* Washington, D.C.: International Cooperation Administration, 1961.

Jones-Quartey, K. A. B. *A Life of Azikiwe.* Baltimore: Penguin Books, 1965.

Kimble, George H. T. *Tropical Africa.* Vol. 2: *Society and Polity.* New York: Anchor Books, 1960.

Kitchen, Helen. *The Press in Africa.* Washington, D.C.: Ruth Sloan Associates, 1956.

Legum, Colin. *Africa: A Handbook to the Continent.* Rev. & enl. ed. New York: Frederick A. Praeger, 1966.

Lerner, Daniel. *The Passing of Traditional Society.* Glencoe, Ill.: Free Press, 1958.

Lessing, Pieter. *Africa's Red Harvest.* New York: John Day, 1962.

McFadden, Tom J. *Daily Journalism in the Arab States.* Columbus: Ohio State University Press, 1953.

MacKay, Ian K. *Broadcasting in Nigeria.* Ibadan: Ibadan University Press, 1964.

McKay, Vernon. *Africa in World Politics.* New York: Harper & Row, 1963.

Mackenzie, W. J. M., and Robinson, Kenneth, eds. *Five Elections in Africa.* New York: Oxford University Press, 1960.

Muddathir, Ahmed. *Die Arabische Presse in den Maghreb-Staaten.* Hamburg: Deutsches Institut fur Afrika-Forschung, 1966.

Nugent, John Peer. *Call Africa 999.* New York: Coward-McCann, 1965.

Passin, Herbert, and Jones-Quartey, K. A. B. *Africa: The Dynamics of Change.* Ibadan: Ibadan University Press, 1963.

Powdermaker, Hortense. *Copper Town: Changing Africa.* New York: Harper & Row, 1962.

Prakke, H. J. *Publizist und Publikum in Afrika.* Cologne: Verlag Deutscher Wirtschaftdienst GMBH, 1962.
Pye, Lucian, ed. *Communications and Political Development.* Princeton: Princeton University Press, 1963.
Sampson, Anthony. *Drum: The Newspaper That Won the Heart of Africa.* New York: Houghton Mifflin, 1957.
Sanger, Clyde. *Central African Emergency.* London: William Heinemann, 1960.
Schatten, Fritz. *Communism in Africa.* New York: Frederick A. Praeger, 1966.
Schramm, Wilbur. *Mass Media and National Development.* Stanford, Calif.: Stanford University Press, 1964.
Sommerlad, E. Lloyd. *The Press in Developing Countries.* Sydney: Sydney University Press, 1966.
South African Broadcasting Corporation. *Annual Report 1967.*
Special Warfare Area Handbook for Ghana. Washington, D.C.: Foreign Areas Studies Division, The American University, 1962.
Thompson, Virginia, and Adloff, Richard. *The Emerging States of French Equatorial Africa.* Stanford, Calif.: Stanford University Press, 1960.
———. *French West Africa.* Stanford, Calif.: Stanford University Press, 1957.
UNESCO. *World Communications: Press, Radio, Television, Film.* New York: UNESCO, 1964.
United Nations, Statistical Office. *Statistical Yearbook Annuaire Statistique 1967.* New York: UN Publishing Service, 1968.
U.S. Army Area Handbook for the Ivory Coast. Washington, D.C.: Foreign Areas Studies Division, The American University, 1962.
U.S. Army Area Handbook for Morocco. Washington, D.C.: Foreign Areas Studies Division, The American University, 1965.
U.S. Army Area Handbook for Nigeria. Washington, D.C.: Foreign Areas Studies Division, The American University, 1964.
U.S. Army Area Handbook for Senegal. Washington, D.C.: Foreign Areas Division, The American University, 1963.
U.S. Information Agency. *Communications Data Book for Africa.* Washington, D.C.: Government Printing Office, 1966.
U.S. Information Agency. *Revised Annotated Listing of the African Press.* Washington, D.C.: Government Printing Office, 1964.
Van der Linden, Fred. *Le Probleme de l'Information en Afrique.* Brussels: Academie Royale des Sciences d'Outre-Mer, 1964.
Voss, H. *Rundfunk und Fernsehen in Afrika.* Cologne: Verlag Deutscher Wirtschaftsdienst, 1962.
World Radio TV Handbook 1969. 23rd ed. Hallerup, Denmark: World Radio-Television Handbook Co., 1968.

ARTICLES

Abu-Lughod, Ibrahim. "The Mass Media and Egyptian Village Life." *Social Forces* 42 (September 1963): 97.
"An African Press Survey: East and Central Africa." *New Commonwealth* 28 (August 19, 1954): 169.
"An African Press Survey: Southern Africa." *New Commonwealth* 28 (August 5, 1954): 115.

"An African Press Survey: West Africa." *New Commonwealth* 28 (July 22, 1954): 62.

Ainslie, Rosalynde. "Efforts to Establish a Popular Press in Independent Africa." *The Democratic Journalist* 14 (September 1966): 121, 126.

Aloba, Abiodun. "Journalism in Africa: Nigeria." *Gazette* (Leiden) 5 (2, 1959).

————. "Journalism in Africa: Tabloid Revolution." *Gazette* (Leiden) 5 (3, 1960).

————. "Journalism in Africa: Yesterday and Today." *Gazette* (Leiden) 5 (4, 1960).

Alsbrook, James E. "Reaction of the World's Press to the Overthrow of Nkrumah." *Journalism Quarterly* 44 (Summer 1967): 307.

Barton, Frank. "Success Goes with Speed in a Hurrying Continent." *IPI Report* 17 (June 1968): 7.

Bienen, Henry. "Kenya and Uganda: When Does Dissent Become Sedition?" *Africa Report* 14 (March–April 1969): 10.

Blanshard, Paul. "Censorship and Apartheid." *The Reporter* 38 (February 22, 1968): 33.

Bogart, Leo. "The Overseas Newsman: A 1967 Profile Study." *Journalism Quarterly* 45(Summer 1968): 293.

Carter, Felice. "The Press in Kenya." *Gazette* 14 (2, 1968): 85.

Ching, James C. "Mass Communications in the Republic of the Congo (Leopoldville)." *Journalism Quarterly* 41 (Spring 1964): 237.

Coker, Increase. "Government Sponsors the Competition." *IPI Report* 17 (June 1968): 16.

Coltart, J. M. "The Influence of Newspapers and Television in Africa." *African Affairs* (July 1963): 202.

Condon, John C. "Nation Building and Image Building in the Tanzanian Press." *Journal of Modern African Studies* 5 (3, 1967): 335.

————. "Some Guidelines for Mass Communications Research in East Africa." *Gazette* 14 (2, 1960): 141.

Crawford, Robert W. "Cultural Change and Communications in Morocco." *Human Organization* 24 (Spring 1965): 73.

Director of Documentation, Ministry of Information. "Broadcasting in the Ivory Coast." *Gazette* 9 (4, 1963): 316.

Doob, Leonard W. "An Experimental Approach to the Press in Underdeveloped Areas." *Gazette* 3 (1/2, 1957): 17.

————. "Informational Services in Central Africa." *Public Opinion Quarterly* 17 (Spring 1953): 7.

Dorkenoo, M. S. "How Ghana Censors the Press." *IPI Report* (October 1962): 3.

Dumoga, John W. K. "Getting the News Is Only Half the Battle." *IPI Report* 17 (June 1968): 13.

Enahoro, Peter. "The Test: Can Press Protect the People?" *IPI Report* 14 (July–August 1965): 15.

"Gandar Trial: Ex-Prisoner Describes Torture by Warder." *IPI Report* 18 (May–June 1969): 14.

Garrison, Lloyd. "Biafra Revisited: Tears, Air Raids, Censorship, Despair." *Times Talk* 12 (September 1968): 8.

"Ghana: A Year's Black Record." *IPI Report* (November 1962): 11.

Hachten, William A. "Four Types of Newspapers." *Nieman Reports* 22 (September 1968): 22.

————. "The Press in a One-Party State: The Ivory Coast Under Houphouët." *Journalism Quarterly* 44 (Spring 1967): 107.

————. "The Press in a One-Party State: Kenya Since Independence." *Journalism Quarterly* 42 (Spring 1965): 262.

————. "Training of African Journalists." *Gazette* (Leiden) 14 (2, 1968): 101.

Hall, Richard. " 'Economizing Truth'—Africa's Dilemma." *IPI Report* 16 (October 1967): 5.

————. "The Press in Black Africa; How Free Is It?" *Optima* 18 (March 1968): 13.

Head, Sydney W. "Can a Journalist Be a 'Professional' in a Developing Country?" *Journalism Quarterly* 40 (Autumn 1963): 594.

Hopkinson, Tom. "Fears for the Press in Africa." *Nieman Reports* (September 1963): 24.

————. "A New Age of Newspapers in Africa." *Gazette* 14 (2, 1968): 79.

————. "Newspapers Must Wait in Priority Queue." *IPI Report* 16 (June 1967): 18.

Howe, Russell Warren. "Reporting from Africa: A Correspondent's View." *Journalism Quarterly* 43 (Summer 1966): 314.

Jaja, Emmanuel Adagogo. "Problems of the Editor of an African Daily." *Africa Report* 11 (January 1966): 40.

Kempton, Murray. "The Washrooms of Power: Those Anonymous Propaganda Peddlers." *The New Republic* (August 3, 1963): 9.

Kiba, Simon. "When Television Comes to Africa." *Atlas* 7 (January 1964): 21.

"Lost Opportunity on Kenya's Vernacular Press." *IPI Report* 1 (January 1953): 5.

McClurg, James. "The Impact of TV on African Development: Part One." *Corona* (February 1961): 54.

————. "The Impact of TV on African Development: Part Two." *Corona* (March 1961): 97.

McKay, Vernon. "South African Propaganda: Methods and Media." *Africa Report* 11 (February 1966): 41.

————. "South African Propaganda on the International Court's Decision." *African Forum* 2 (Fall 1966): 51.

Makosso, Gabriel. "Congo's Voice." *IPI Report* 17 (September 1968): 10.

Mareda, Ladislav. "The International Organization of Journalists Looks After the Professional Training of Journalists from Developing Countries." *Gazette* 14 (2, 1968): 160.

Martin, Larry K. "Mimeographed Village Papers Prove Value in Liberia." *Journalism Quarterly* 41 (Spring 1964): 245.

Mboya, Tom. "This Is What the Press Must Do." *IPI Report* (June 1962): 5.

Meisler, Stanley. "Look—Reads." *Africa Report* 14 (May–June 1969): 80.

Moulton, E. J. "Satellite over Africa." *Africa Report* 12 (May 1967): 13.

Mukupo, Titus. "What Role for the Government in the Development of an African Press." *Africa Report* 11 (January 1966): 39.

Munger, Edwin S. "Africa in 240 Minutes: A Review of ABC-TV's Africa." *Africa Report* 12 (October 1967): 67.

Mybergh, Tertius. "The South African Press: Hope in an Unhappy Land." *Nieman Reports* (March 1966): 3.

Mytton, Graham L. "Tanzania: The Problems of Mass Media Development." *Gazette* 14 (2, 1968): 89.

Nelson, Daniel. "Newspapers in Uganda." *Transition* 7 (February–March 1968): 29.

"Newspapers and Periodicals on Africa in Microfilm." *African Studies Bulletin* 12 (September 1969): 193.

Ng'weno, Hilary, and de Vos, Pierre. "Paradrop Stanleyville." *IPI Report* (January 1965): 6.

Nixon, Raymond B. "Freedom in the World's Press: A Fresh Appraisal with New Data." *Journalism Quarterly* 42 (Winter 1965): 3, 118.

Nord, Bruce A. "Press Freedom and Political Structure." *Journalism Quarterly* 43 (Autumn 1966): 531.

Omu, Fred I. A. "The Dilemma of Press Freedom in Colonial Africa: The West African Example." *Journal of African History* 9 (2, 1968): 279.

Orlik, Peter B. "Under Damocles' Sword—The South African Press." *Journalism Quarterly* 46 (Summer 1969): 343.

Oton, Esuakama U. "Development of Journalism in Nigeria." *Journalism Quarterly* 35 (Winter 1958): 72.

——. "The Training of Journalists in Nigeria." *Journalism Quarterly* 43 (Spring 1966): 107.

Paterson, Adolphus. "The African Press: A Case Study." *The Journalist's World* 3 (4, 1965–66): 26.

——. "After Ghana's Coup—A Hunger For News," *IPI Report* 15 (1966): 11.

Payne, William A. "American Press Coverage of Africa." *Africa Report* 11 (January 1966): 44.

Pollock, Francis. "America's Press on Safari." *The Nation* (November 7, 1966): 479.

Post, Kenneth W. J. "Nigerian Pamphleteers and the Congo." *Journal of Modern African Studies* (2,3; 1964): 405.

"La Presse au Maroc." *Maghreb* (17, September–October 1966): 30.

"La Presse en Afrique au Sud du Sahara." *Afrique* (19, December 1962): 35.

"Presse und Funk in Ostafrika." *Afrika Spectrum* (Hamburg), Heft 2 (1966).

"Reluctant Witness Tells of Trap for Newsman." *IPI Report* 17 (February 1969): 5.

"Reporting Africa: Where Images Matter, Bans Are Risk." *IPI Report* (July–August 1968): 15.

Rose, E. J. B. "Training Is the Key to a Free African Press." *Optima* 12 (1962): 155.

——. "Training Is Most Urgent Need For African Press." *IPI Report* 10 (January 1962).

Russel, Nick. "Tabloid and Broadsheet Face Same Odds." *IPI Report* 17 (June 1968): 15.

Sanger, Clyde. "The Foreign Correspondent in Independent Africa: Problems and Prospects." *Africa Report* 11 (January 1966): 42.

——. "Some Reflections on Leaving East Africa." *Africa Report* 10 (October 1965): 29.

"Shock and Dismay at Takeover of 'Ashanti Pioneer.'" *IPI Report* 11 (November 1962): 1.

Singleton, Derrick. "Broadcasting in East Africa." *The Listener* (August 3, 1961): 167.

Smart, Max Neff. "Newspapers for Africa." *Nieman Reports* 17 (March 1964): 9.

———. "Newspapers in Developing Nations—Antidote to Illiteracy." *The Quill* 55 (May 1966): 17.

Smythe, Hugh H. "Problems of Public Opinion Research in Africa." *Gazette* 10 (2, 1964): 144.

Sommerlad, E. Lloyd. "Problems in Developing a Free Enterprise Press in East Africa." *Gazette* 14 (2, 1968): 74.

"South Africa: IPI Member Faces Trial." *IPI Report* 17 (December 1968): 6.

Strohmeyer, John. "Stepping Out of a Primitive Past." *ASNE Bulletin 1964* (October 1, 1965): 10.

———. "What Passes for American News in Africa." *Harper's* (November 1965): 98.

Tedros, G. "Television in Africa." *Telecommunication Journal* 28 (9, 1961): 595.

"Television in Africa." *West Africa* (2474, October 31, 1964): 1229.

Voss, Harold. "Rundfunk und Fernsehen in Westafrika." *Afrika—Informationdienst* (Bonn) 2 (22, 1959).

"Whither African Television." *West Africa* (2473, October 24, 1964): 1187.

Wilhelm, John. "The Re-Appearing Foreign Correspondent." *Journalism Quarterly* 40 (Spring 1963): 147.

Williams, Colin. "News from Britain Still Leads the Field." *IPI Report* 17 (June 1968): 18.

Yu, Frederick T. C., and Luter, John. "The Foreign Correspondent and His Work." *Columbia Journalism Review* 3 (Spring 1964): 5.

MISCELLANEOUS

Brown, Trevor. "The South African Press: No News for 170 Years?" Paper presented to the Association for Education in Journalism, Berkeley, August 1969.

Ekwelie, Sylvanus. "The Content of Broadcasting in Nigeria." Unpublished master's thesis, University of Wisconsin, 1968.

Enahoro, Peter. "Africa—The Press in a One-Party State." Talk delivered at IPI General Assembly, London, May 25–27, 1965.

———. "Reporting Africa." Background paper for IPI Assembly, Nairobi, June 5, 1968.

Fellows, Laurence. "Session on Reporting Africa." Talk delivered at IPI General Assembly, Nairobi, June 5, 1968.

Hachten, William A. "The Flow of News and Underdevelopment: A Pilot Study of the African Press." Paper presented to the Association for Education in Journalism, Iowa City, August 30, 1966.

———. "Zambia: Mass Communications on the 'Line of Rail.'" Paper presented to the Association for Education in Journalism, Berkeley, August 1969.

Healey, Joseph G. "Media Growth in Kenya." Unpublished master's thesis, University of Missouri, 1968.

———. "Press Freedom in Kenya." Freedom of Information Center Report, No. 191, Columbia, Missouri, December 1967.

Hopkinson, Tom. "IPI in Africa—Report on the Past Year." Paper presented to IPI General Assembly, London, May 25–27, 1965.

Howe, Russell Warren. "The United States Press and Africa." Speech delivered at Seventh Plenary Session of U.S. Commission on U.N. October 25, 1961.

Huff, Lonnie R. "The Press and Nationalism in Kenya, British East Africa." Unpublished master's thesis, University of Wisconsin, 1968.

Hughes, Mary Ellen. "The Rural Mimeo Newspaper Experiment in Liberia." Unpublished master's thesis, University of Wisconsin, 1969.

Kliesch, Ralph E. "The Press Corps Abroad Revisited: A Fourth World Survey of Foreign Correspondents." Paper presented to the Association for Education in Journalism, Berkeley, August 1969.

Kucera, Geoffrey Z. "Broadcasting in Africa: A Study of Belgium, British and French Colonial Policies." Unpublished PhD dissertation, University of Michigan, 1968.

Mlenga, Kelvin G. "What Sort of Press Freedom." Address delivered at Zambia Association for National Affairs, February 18, 1965.

Murphy, E. Lloyd. "Nationalism and the Press in British West Africa." Unpublished master's thesis, University of Wisconsin, 1967.

Ng'weno, Hilary. "Africa—The Press in a One-Party State." Talk delivered at IPI General Assembly, London, May 25–27, 1965.

Nimer, Benjamin. "Television, Language, and National Cohesion in Kenya and Uganda." Paper presented to African Studies Association Meeting, Bloomington, Indiana, October 1966.

Royce, Knut S. "American Correspondents in the Sub-Sahara: Some of Their Problems." Unpublished master's thesis, University of Iowa, 1966.

Ruskin, Daniel. "USIA Comes to Africa: A Case Study of U.S. Overseas Information, 1960–1965." Unpublished master's thesis, University of Wisconsin, 1967.

Schaar, Stuart H. "The Mass Media in Morocco." AUFS Reports, North Africa Series 14, No. 2, Morocco, 1968.

Schramm, Wilbur, and Sommerlad, E. Lloyd. "East Africa: Mass Media Training Needs." UNESCO, Paris, August 1964.

———. Northern Rhodesia: Training in Mass Communications." UNESCO, Paris, August 1964.

Starkey, Posie L. "Arab Daily Journalism: The Press in Saudi Arabia, Tunisia and the United Arab Republic." Unpublished master's thesis, University of Wisconsin, 1968.

Turpeau, Anne B. "The Government and the Newspaper Press of Nigeria." Unpublished master's thesis, Howard University, 1962.

UNESCO. *Developing Information Media in Africa*. Reports and Papers on Mass Communication No. 37.

———. *Mass Media in the Developing Countries*. Reports and Papers on Mass Communication No. 33.

———. "Meeting of Experts on Development of News Agencies in Africa." Tunis, April 1–6, 1963.

———. "Meeting on the Introduction and Development of Television in Africa." Lagos, Nigeria, September 21–29, 1964.

———. *Professional Training for Mass Communication*. Reports and Papers on Mass Communication No. 45.

————. *Rural Mimeo Newspapers.* Prepared by Robert de T. Lawrence. Reports and Papers on Mass Communication No. 46, 1966.

————. *Space Communication and the Mass Media.* Reports and Papers on Mass Communication No. 41.

U.S. Information Agency. "Basic Attitudes and General Communication Habits in Four West African Capitals." Pubn. PMS-51 (July 1961).

————. "Communist Propaganda Activities in Africa January 1963–June 1964." Pubn. R-186-1964.

————. "Mass Media Habits in West Africa." Pubn. R-64-66 (March 1966).

————. "Media Preferences of Better Educated Nigerians and Radio Listening Habits of the General Population." (December 1964.)

————. "Media Use Among Africans in Nairobi, Kenya." Pubn. R-91-63 (May 1963).

————. "Overseas Television Growth in 1965." Pubn. R-111-66 (June 1966).

————. "Radio Listening in Four West African Cities." Pubn. PMS-43 (December 1960).

————. "Worldwide Distribution of Radio Receiver Sets 1965." Pubn. R-95-66 (May 1966).

de Villiers, Rene. "The Press and the People." Address delivered to South African Institute of Race Relations, Johannesburg, November 1967.

Wallington, James. "UPI and African News." Unpublished paper, Michigan State University, 1963.

Webb, Peter. "Session on Reporting Africa." Talk delivered at IPI General Assembly, Nairobi, June 5, 1968.

Wright, George F. "Comparision of the Function of the Press of Ghana and Nigeria." Unpublished thesis, Columbia University, 1966.

INDEX